Christianity and Modern Politics

Christianity and Modern Politics

Edited by
Louisa S. Hulett

Walter de Gruyter · Berlin · New York
1993

∞ Printed on acid-free paper which falls
within the guidelines of the
ANSI to ensure permanence and durability.

Library of Congress Cataloging-in-Publication Data

Christianity and modern politics / edited by Louisa S. Hulett.
p.   cm.
Includes bibliographical references
ISBN 3-11-013462-4 (cloth). — ISBN 3-11-013461-6 (pbk.)
1. Christianity and politics. I. Hulett, Louisa Sue.
BR115.P7C3816   1993
261.7'0973—dc20
92-36923
CIP

Die Deutsche Bibliothek — Cataloging-in-Publication Data

Christianity and modern politics / ed. by Louisa S. Hulett. —
Berlin ; New York : de Gruyter, 1993
ISBN 3-11-013461-6 brosch.
ISBN 3-11-013462-4 Gewebe
NE: Hulett, Louisa S. [Hrsg.]

© Copyright 1993 by Walter de Gruyter & Co., D-1000 Berlin 30.

Typesetting: Satzpunkt, Braunschweig
Printing: Kanters B. V., Alblasserdam.
Binding: Dieter Mikolai, Berlin.
Printed in The Netherlands.

Preface

Many people have helped me prepare this anthology. My Knox College colleagues, Lane Sunderland and MaryAnne Borrelli and my spiritual mentor, Evelyn Campbell, Dean of Students at Augustana College (Illinois), read several chapters and offered advice on analysis and selections. My family and friends entertained me for periodic respites from the travail of writing and being denied therapy time on the tennis courts. My students, especially those who suffered through my courses on Christianity and Politics and International Relations, asked hard questions and provided prodigious research service. The Knox administration and the Lilly Foundation sent needed funds my way. Students in the Intervarsity Christian Fellowship gave invaluable inspiration and direction, as did my patient editors, Hasko v. Bassi and Richard Koffler. For comments and other courtesies, I thank Michael Cromartie, James Guth, Ted Jelen, Corwin Smidt, and the research staff of the Institute for the Study of American Evangelicals at Wheaton College (Illinois) and the Knox College Library. Penultimately, I owe a debt of gratitude to the authors and publishers who allowed their marvelous works to be edited by a friendly, but nonetheless "outside" hand. In the process of editing, all carefully crafted footnotes were eliminated in the interest of conserving space. Readers are advised to review the articles in their entirety to remedy this egregious omission. This leaves, then, a final debt to the unacknowledged authors referred to in the deleted footnotes.

Contents

Introduction

The purpose of this anthology is to create a set of readings that crosses fields, disciplines, and centuries to cover a number of diverse topics of interest to students of religion and politics. The topics include the nature of Christianity and politics in America; the origins and purpose of the First Amendment protections of religious liberty; the interface between First Amendment principles and the Supreme Court that reinterpreted these principles in the 20th century; the rise of Christian fundamentalism as it reacted to secular humanism, with its presumed hostility to any religious faith; the ethics of war as they apply to nuclear deterrence theories, pacifism, Just War Doctrine, and the 1991 war in the Gulf; and the debate over the orthodoxy of the theology of liberation.

The authors who tackle these issues are classical and contemporary theologians, some orthodox and some heretical; ancient and modern philosophers and political scientists, some conservative and some liberal; and religious and secular sociologists and lawyers (or professors of law). As a group they provide a wonderful kaleidoscope of viewpoints. Despite, or rather because of, the *ex post facto* choice of selections, most of the contributors fit into the direct debate framework. Traditional Christians and Jews confront liberal secular humanists over the relationship between church and state; strict constructionists, who take a literal interpretation of the First Amendment, confront judicial activists, who believe that 20th century neutralism about religion supercedes outdated 18th century concepts of religion supported by the state; and pacifists and realists battle over the Christian's right to defend self, others, and values.

Before exploring the particulars of these confrontations, we need to ask whether religion in America is robust enough to merit such coverage. Much was said in the 1960s and 1970s about God's presumed demise and the wasting away of remnant worshippers. Much was said about secular humanism, rationalism, and "the good in each of us" as enlightened replacements for transcendence. But belief in God and interest in the phenomenon of religion hang on tenaciously, as predicted by the two major readings in Chapter I. Literature to enlighten us about God and religion abound. *Publisher's Weekly* reports that 2746 books on religion were published in 1988 and 2306 in 1989. Books, like Garry Will's *Under God: Religion and American Politics* (1990), are best sellers. Popular magazines (*Newsweek* in January 1992, for example) offer articles on prayer, religion and elections, and global fundamentalism.

As to the vitality of religion itself, survey data suggest that religion in America is not an obsolete remnant of 18th century thinking. According to Gallup polls conducted from 1950–1964, church membership surged rather than eroded as predicted by secular prophets. While mainline (liberal) churches declined between 1965–1985, conservative churches and new religious groups more than picked up the slack. The Pentecostal Assemblies of God grew in this period by 116%, as did the Mormons who, along with Jehovah's Witnesses, increased by nearly 2 1/2 times. The Church of God outpaced all others increasing its membership by 147%. Southern Baptists and the Church of the Nazarene grew by 34 and 50% respectively.

Gallup polls in the 1980s found 92% of Americans willing to state a religious preference, 62% claiming membership in a church or synagogue, and 44% remaining "unchurched" believers who had not attended religious services except for weddings, funerals or holidays in the six months prior to being surveyed. In 1991, in one of the largest religion surveys ever undertaken, the ICR Survey Research Group found that 9 out of 10 Americans identify with a religious denomination. In data collected through telephone interviews with 113,000 adults, ICR found that 26% of the respondents identified themselves as Roman Catholics, 60% as Protestant, 2% as Jewish, and 1/2% as Muslim. 7.5% professed no religion and 2.3% refused to talk about their faith. According to Gallup polls on religious affiliation, those professing no affiliation rose from 6 to 9% between 1947 and 1988.

Gallup polls in 1989 also sought to find the "amount" of religion the respondents had. The polls found that 55% of Americans considered religion to be a very important part of their lives, 30% reported that it was fairly important, and 43% said they attended services once a week. While commitment, membership, and attendance were reported as higher in the

1940s and 1950s, the Gallup polls indicate a relatively stable American involvement in religion since the 1940s, except for an unusual and temporary dip in the 1960s.

In addition to these statistical indicators that religious belief is alive and well in America, there exists a plethora of Supreme Court cases devoted to the issue of religious liberty. But what an odd lot of cases they are, as modern Americans and jurisprudence stumble forwards and backwards in deciding the extent to which an individual's "inalienable" right to the free exercise of religion supercedes the state's right to legislate for the common good. Legal scholars quote the founders in and out of context, Supreme Court justices race to stand behind and ahead of precedent, and religious petitioners from witches, to mainline Protestants, to secular humanists argue for the free exercise of their brand of religion against the "establishment" of someone else's brand. A common sense understanding of the First Amendment and early American history, which seems to indicate that the founders adopted a laissez-faire support for religion, confronts a second sense that no one wanted the government to enforce or abuse religion or to favor one religion over another.

The inconsistency of the Court, as it bounced between support and non-support for religion, perhaps reflecting an interrupted transition from judicial activism to a stricter constructionism, may best be appreciated by looking at a few specific cases.

In cases addressing the question of a constitutional right to exemptions from laws on the basis of free exercise of religion rights, we often see the Court favor the state over the individual. For example, in *Oregon v. Smith* (1990), the Supreme Court outlawed the peyote (a prohibited drug) ritual of the Native American Church. In balancing government power to regulate drug use versus the free exercise clause, the Court ruled (6–3) in favor of government power. It refused to create a religion-based exemption from a law applicable to all citizens. Specifically, there are no permissible exemptions from drug laws for Peyote-using Indians; or from highway safety laws for anti-modern Amish, who do not want to equip their horse-drawn buggies with "slow-moving vehicle" signs; or from tax laws for churches making profits from sales of religious literature; and so on. According to Justice Scalia, "we have never held that an individual's religious beliefs excuse him from compliance with an otherwise valid law prohibiting conduct that the state is free to regulate." Only laws specifically directed at religion would be unconstitutional. On the other hand, in the peyote case,

Justice O'Connor argues that the First Amendment "ought not to be construed to cover only the extreme and hypothetical situation in which a state directly targets a religious practice." She thus leaves the door open to potential exemptions from laws that infringe on free exercise.

In the meantime, in *Oregon v. Smith*, 6 of 9 justices opted for no exemptions, with Sandra O'Connor, however, suggesting that exemptions were still a case by case matter to be decided according to the extent of the infringement of free exercise. Resisting consistency, or embracing O'Connor's open door policy, the Court opted for free exercise in 1992, when it let stand a Minnesota court's ruling that refused to prosecute two parents whose child died after they prayed for healing rather seek medical attention.

It is in the "no establishment" realm that one truly finds the land of Oz, or rather Humpty Dumpty's world, where a word means whatever one wants it to mean. As the readings in chapters III and IV show, the Supreme Court wanders around the definition of establishment finding new qualifications and entanglements that complicate rather than solve the 200 year old question of what establishment of religion means. Cases involving religious displays on public property provide little help in answering the question clearly.

In one such case in 1989, the Supreme Court justices ruled 5–4 that a Christmas creche on public property, accompanied by the proclamation, "Gloria in Excelsis Deo," violated the First Amendment because it sent "an unmistakable message that it [the state] supports and promotes the Christian praise to God." According to Justice Harry Blackmun, "government may celebrate Christmas in some manner and form, but not in a way that endorses Christian doctrine." Blackmun and five other judges, perhaps in a burst of patriotism, came to a different conclusion about another display that included a sign endorsing liberty as well as a Christmas tree and a menorah. Blackmun held that this more inclusive display "simply recognizes that both Christmas and Hanukkah are part of the same winter-holiday season, which has attained a secular status in our society." Not content with one decision for and one against these displays, the Supreme Court in 1990 refused to hear (i. e., let a lower court ruling stand without comment) a case involving a Nativity scene on government property that was ruled a violation of the separation of church and state because "the unmistakable message conveyed is one of government endorsement of religion."

Justice Anthony Kennedy's plea to revise the establishment clause and related Supreme Court precedents has not been heard, and the resulting confusion plagues school boards as well as city hall. One school board in Illinois, for example, is considering bans on all religious holidays, songs, and programs as a rather draconian remedy for this confusion.

The big question for 1992, in addition to the constitutionality of creches, concerns the tradition of prayers at high school ceremonies. At issue for the Supreme Court, in *Lee v. Weisman*, # 90–1014, is whether a non-denominational blessing at a high school graduation ceremony violates the principle of separation of church and state. Thirty five religious, political, and educational organizations have filed or joined briefs in this case. Included in this unusually high number is a brief from the Bush administration, which asks the court to abandon the *Lemon v. Kurtzman* precedent (see chapter IV), which, in its view, defines establishment in a way that is hostile to religion. Solicitor General Kenneth W. Starr argued before the Court that a commencement exercise is "a celebration;" a prayer in this context is simply an "acknowledgement of God and the role of God in our life as a nation." Justice Antonin Scalia agreed with Starr, and opined that such a prayer differed little from the traditional prayers at the opening of a court or a Congressional session and was merely a reflection of "people, in a country that overwhelmingly believes in God, wanting to invoke God's blessing." Opponents of commencement prayers argued that prayer is prayer and thus unconstitutional in schools because it has the effect of state-sponsored religion.

Waiting in the wings for a decision in this case, are seven or so more cases before the Supreme Court. Two Illinois towns, for example, are appealing to keep their historic city seals which contain religious references or images. (One seal contains an 8th grader's drawing of a church, a water tower, a factory, and a leaf.) Another Illinois town is appealing a federal court ruling against the town's sponsorship of an Italian-language Mass as a part of an Italian festival. A Denver school teacher is appealing a federal court ruling that displaying his Bible on his desk and reading it silently at recess "conveyed an impermissible message that the school endorsed religion."

I do not know if these cases show much beyond the persistence of the controversy surrounding interpretations of the religion clauses of the First Amendment. However, they, and the statistics on religion in America, do show that America is a religious country, if for no other reason than because many people tend to think it is and litigate at will to guarantee their practice of religion. When President George Bush spoke to the National

Religious Broadcasters, in January 1992, he referred to the religious character of America. "Obviously no country can claim a special place in God's heart ... yet we are better as a people because He has a special place in ours."

The eight chapters that follow try to capture the flavor of the controversies from constitutional questions over separation of church and state, to ethical questions of peace and war, to theological/political questions about what constitutes religion in America.

Chapter I

On Christianity, Civil Religion, and Politics

Background: Before studying the classical and modern debates over the nature of the separation of church and state in the U.S., the battle between secular humanists and fundamentalists, and the question of the Christian's obligation to the state and justice versus the obligation to God and Christ's "law of love", we must understand some of the definitions of Christianity, civil religion, and politics. This chapter begins with definitions of power, politics, and government taken from seminal works of classical and modern writers from Aristotle and Machiavelli to John Dewey and Hans Morgenthau.

The chapter ends with two works that define several central features of modern Christianity. Choosing two works to represent Christianity was a daunting task. One could compare treatises from the founding theologians of the Christian church with the great Medieval or Enlightenment philosophers. 18th century Puritans and Deists could be used to engage the reader in the task of comparing early American views on God. A celebrated skeptic could round out the analysis. The list of possible combinations is endless. Given their major 20th century contributions to imaginative theory-building about why to believe in God or in civil religion, works by C. S. Lewis and Robert Bellah were chosen. The first selection showcases Lewis' traditional Protestant (British Anglican) view of Christianity. The second selection offers a secular analysis that speculates about a merger between American Christianity, or the Judeo-Christian tradition in America, and the prevailing sociological and political ideology, which presumably created an American, state-centered "civil religion". The contrasting images in these works provide a sliver of insight into two major forces driving religion in America today, especially as it interacts with political and social behavior.

Authors: C. S. Lewis (1898–1963), a professor of Medieval and Renaissance English Literature at Cambridge University, who embraced Christianity at the age of 33, was a prolific and popular writer of Christian philosophy and fiction. He focuses on humanity's fallen nature, saved only by the intervening grace of God. In the selection below, he provides an interpretation of how one might come to reject the materialistic view "that matter and space just happen to exist," and to believe instead in God and Jesus Christ.

Lewis begins with an exploration of human nature and the "internal voice" that tells humans right from wrong (the Law of Nature or the Moral Law) and greater truth from lesser truth. He asserts that human beings innately know how they ought to behave, regret that they often fail to measure up to high standards of decent behavior and, if willing to acknowledge that God created the universe and put these nagging thoughts into human minds, hear the call to worship. But what kind of God should they worship? Lewis makes the case for Christianity. He then offers a unique proof of Christ's divinity, and explains key elements of Christian doctrine such as repentance and forgiveness of sin, free will, the role of Satan, and the gifts of grace and salvation. (For additional discussion of these doctrines, see the theological exegeses on war and peace in chapter VII, Jerry Falwell's description of Christian fundamentals in chapter VI, and the Vatican's instructions concerning its social (liberation) mission in the last chapter.)

Robert N. Bellah, Professor of Sociology at the University of California at Berkeley, has written extensively on religion and culture in modern America. In the seminal work excerpted below, Bellah describes the existence of an institutionalized, longstanding, and vigorous American civil religion with its own beliefs, symbols, rituals, and adherents. He claims Jean-Jacques Rousseau as the author of the original dogmas of civil religion: "the existence of God, the life to come, the reward of virtue and the punishment of vice, and the exclusion of religious intolerance."

Bellah sees Franklin, Washington, Jefferson, and Lincoln as early American disciples of this nondenominational and utilitarian brand of faith, which mixes together, in one patriotic and spiritual container, references to civic virtues, moral values, historical traditions, and a generic God who blesses a righteous America. The Holy texts of this civil religion, which is neither Christianity nor "religion in general," include the Declaration of Independence, the Constitution and the Gettysburg Address. Washington and Lincoln are the patriarchs. Bellah describes the Civil War as its spiritual testing ground. According to his theory, this war produced the American savior, Lincoln, and the melding of Christian and patriotic themes of sacrifice, rebirth, reconciliation, and manifest destiny.

According to Bellah, since the time of the Civil War, Americans imbibed from both traditional religion and a civil religion that encompassed folk, nationalist, and democratic values. He asserts that they saw no conflict between the two. Americans love God and country, see them linked in the political realm, and believe that America is the promised land – a land chosen by God, endowed with economic riches, exuding democratic principles that are to be a light to the world, and obligated "to carry out God's will on earth." Despite the apparent heavy doses of ethnocentrism and patriotism, Bellah maintains that "the American civil religion is not the worship of the American nation but an understanding of the American experience in the light of ultimate universal reality." In other words, adherents of civil religion believe America, when it honors and reflects spiritual and democratic values and ideals, can "be a society as perfectly in accord with the will of God as men can make it." Where C. S. Lewis speaks of a transcendent God who created and governs the universe, guides human behavior, and calls for a personal spiritual relationship with his creations, Bellah writes of a faith that focuses on "sacred" American historical experiences, martyred national heroes, and God-given human rights and responsibilities.

Key Questions: What is the relationship between human nature, Christianity, politics, and power? How and why have states and democracies come into being? Is the Christian "law of love" relevant to politics? Do all people have the idea that they "ought" to behave in a certain way? Is there a "Law of Human Nature" that tells people right from wrong? Why is C. S. Lewis a Christian? How does American civil religion rely on, yet differ from, Christianity?

On Politics and Power

My notion is that a state comes into existence because no individual is self-sufficing; we all have many needs. ...

So, having all these needs, we call in one another's help to satisfy our various requirements; and when we have collected a number of helpers and associates to live together in one place, we call that settlement a state. So if one man gives another what he has to give in exchange for what he can get, it is because each finds that to do so is for his own advantage.[1]

Observation shows us, first, that every polis (or state) is a species of association, and, secondly, that all associations are instituted for the purpose of attaining some good – for all men do all their acts with a view to achieving something which is, in their view, a good. We may therefore hold [on the basis of what we actually observe] that all associations aim at some good; and we may also hold that the particular association which is the most sovereign of all, and includes all the rest, will pursue this aim most, and will thus be directed to the most sovereign of all goods. This most sovereign and inclusive association is the polis, as it is called, or the political association. ...

Man, when perfected, is the best of animals; but if he be isolated from law and justice he is the worst of all. Injustice is all the graver when it is armed injustice; and man is furnished from birth with arms [such as, for instance, language] which are intended to serve the purposes of moral prudence and virtue, but which may be used in preference for opposite ends. That is why, if he be without virtue, he is a most unholy and savage being, and worse than all others in the indulgence of lust and gluttony. Justice [which is his salvation] belongs to the polis; for justice, which is the determination of what is just, is an ordering of the political association. ...

---

1 Plato, *The Republic,* from W. T. Jones, et al., *Approaches to Ethics,* (New York: McGraw-Hill, 1962), 23.

A *natural impulse* is thus one reason why men desire to live a social life even when they stand in no need of mutual succour; but they are also drawn together by a *common interest*, in proportion as each attains a share in good life [through the union of all in a form of political association]. The good life is the chief end, both for the community as a whole and for each of us individually. But men also come together, and form and maintain political associations, merely for the sake of life. ...

The good in the sphere of politics is justice; and justice consists in what tends to promote the common interests. General opinion makes it consist in some sort of equality.[2]

If man in the state of nature be so free as has been said; if he be absolute lord of his own person and possessions; equal to the greatest subject to no body, why will he part with his freedom? Why will he give up his empire, and subject himself to the dominion and control of any other power? To which 'tis obvious to answer, that though in the state of nature he hath such a right, yet the enjoyment of it is very uncertain and constantly exposed to the invasion of others; for all being kings as much as he, every man his equal, and the greater part no strict observers of equity and justice, the enjoyment of the property he has in this state is very unsafe, very unsecure. This makes him willing to quit this condition which, however free is full of fears and continual dangers; and 'tis not without reason that he seeks out and is willing to join in society with others who are already united, or have a mind to unite for the mutual preservation of their lives, liberties, and estates, which I call by the general name, property.

The great and chief end therefore, of men's uniting into commonwealths, and putting themselves under government, is the preservation of their property; to which in the state of nature there are many things wanting.

First, There wants an established, settled, known law, received and allowed by common consent to be the standard of right and wrong, and the common measure to decide all controversies between them. ...

Secondly, In the state of nature there wants a known and indifferent judge, with authority to determine all differences according to the established law. For everyone in that state being both judge and executioner of the law of nature, men being partial to themselves, passion and revenge is very apt to

---

2 *The Politics of Aristotle* (Books I and III), trans. by Ernest Barker, (London: Oxford University Press, 1969), 1, 7, 111, 129.

carry them too far, and with too much heat in their own cases, as well as negligence and unconcernedness, make them too remiss in other men's.

Thirdly, In the state of nature there often wants power to back and support the sentence when right, and to give it due execution. ... Thus mankind, notwithstanding all the privileges of the state of Nature, being but in an ill condition while they remain in it are quickly driven into society.[3]

All men are bad and ever ready to display their vicious nature, whenever they may find occasion for it. ... Men act right only under compulsion.

Government consists mainly in so keeping your subjects that they shall be neither able nor disposed to injure you. ...

A prince must not mind incurring the charge of cruelty for the purpose of keeping his subjects united and faithful; for, with a very few examples, he will be more merciful than those who, from excess of tenderness, allow disorders to arise, from whence spring bloodshed and rapine; for these as a rule injure the whole community, while the executions carried out by the prince injure only individuals. And of all princes, it is impossible for a new prince to escape the reputation of cruelty, new states being always full of danger. ...

From this arises the question whether it is better to be loved more than feared, or feared more than loved. The reply is, that one ought to be feared and loved, but as it is difficult for the two to go together, it is much safer to be feared than loved.[4]

... True politics can never take a step, without having previously rendered homage to morality; united with this, it is no longer a difficult or complicated art; morality cuts the knot which politics is incapable of untying, whenever they are in opposition to each other. The rights of man ought to be religiously respected, even if sovereigns in maintaining them should have to make the greatest sacrifices. One cannot compromise here between right and utility; politics must bend the knee before morality.[5]

---

3 John Locke, *Two Treatises of Government* (1690) from William Ebenstein, *Great Political Thinkers: Plato to the Present*, (Hinsdale, Il: Dryden Press, 1969); 412–413.
4 Niccolo Machiavelli, *The Prince and Discourses* from Jones, *Approaches to Ethics*, 171–2.
5 Immanuel Kant, *Perpetual Peace* (1795) Appendix I, from Marcus G. Singer and R. R. Ammerman, *Introductory Readings in Philosophy*, (New York: Scribners, 1962), 331.

The key-note of democracy as a way of life may be expressed, it seems to me, as the necessity for the participation of every mature human being in formation of the values that regulate the living of men together: which is necessary from the standpoint of both the general social welfare and the full development of human beings as individuals.

Universal suffrage, recurring elections, responsibility of those who are in political power to the voters, and the other factors of democratic govern-ment are means that have been found expedient for realizing democracy as the truly human way of living. They are not a final end and a final value. They are to be judged on the basis of their contribution to the end. It is a form of idolatry to erect means into the end which they serve. Democratic political forms are simply the best means that human wit has devised up to a special time in history.[6]

Here we shall provisionally use the term to indicate man's deliberate efforts to order, direct, and control his collective affairs and activities; to set up ends for society; and to implement and evaluate those ends. Politics is to collective affairs what the striving for autonomy is in personal matters. In both instances man is seeking, often without success, to cast off uncon-scious and externally imposed patterns of conduct. Just as in the develop-ment of his personality an adolescent will try to emancipate himself from uncriticized governance by his family, so in collective matters a time arises when men begin to reject nondeliberative ways of direction and control and to embrace deliberative ones.

In this sense the term "political" arises when ordering by mere custom and mores breaks down. Men are then compelled to work out standards of action to take the place of habit patterns that no longer govern. ... Political governance ... implies deliberation, aspiration for rationality, and sub-jecting governance by folkways to questioning and criticism. It also entails a dissatisfaction with rule by accident or fortuitous concatenation of social forces, which tends to follow the breakdown of nonpolitical governance.[7]

---

5 Immanuel Kant, *Perpetual Peace* (1795) Appendix I, from Marcus G. Singer and R. R. Ammerman, *Introductory Readings in Philosophy*, (New York: Scribners, 1962), 331.
6 John Dewey, *School and Society* (1937), from Singer and Ammermann, 353–4.
7 Mulford Q. Sibley, *Political Ideas and Ideologies*, (New York: Harper, 1970), 1–2.

When we speak of power, we mean man's control over the minds and actions of other men. By political power we refer to the mutual relations of control among the holders of public authority and between the latter and the people at large.

Political power is a psychological relation between those who exercise it and those over whom it is exercised. It gives the former control over certain actions of the latter through the impact which the former exert on the latter's minds. That impact derives from three sources: the expectation of benefits, the fear of disadvantages, the respect or love for men or institutions. It may be exerted through orders, threats, the authority or charisma of a man or of an office, or a combination of any of these.[8]

Power has to do with whatever decisions men make about the arrangements under which they live, and about the events which make up the history of their times. Events that are beyond human decision do happen; social arrangements do change without benefit of explicit decision. But in so far as such decisions are made, the problem of who is involved in making them is the basic problem of power. In so far as they could be made but are not, the problem becomes who fails to make them?

We cannot today merely assume that in the last resort men must always be governed by their own consent. For among the means of power which now prevail is the power to manage and to manipulate the consent of men. That we do not know the limits of such power, and that we hope it does have limits, does not remove the fact that much power today is successfully employed without the sanction of the reason or the conscience of the obedient.[9]

Political scientist Alfred de Grazia says that politics, or the political, "includes the events that happen around the decision-making centers of government." Charles Hyneman is more specific in claiming that most political scientists have assumed that *legal* government is the subject matter of their discipline. "The central point of attention in American political science ... is that part of the affairs of the state which centers in government, and that kind or part of government which speaks through law ." ...

---

8 Hans Morgenthau, *Politics Among Nations* (New York: Knopf, 1954), 30–31.
9 C. Wright Mills, "The Structure of Power in American Society," in: Pietra S. Nivola and D. H. Rosenbloom, *Classic Readings in American Politics*, (New York: St. Martin's, 1986), 130.

A large number of political scientists would answer that it is a sign of narrow-mindedness, a dangerous trait for a researcher, to use a type of political institution as the basis for a definition of politics. ... Let us quote William Bluhm, a political scientist who provides a rather elaborate definition: "Reduced to its universal elements, then, politics is a social process characterized by activity involving rivalry and cooperation in the exercise of power, and culminating in the making of decisions for a group." The appeal of this definition flows out of its apparent flexibility or wide scope. Politics is found wherever power relationships or conflict situations exist. ...

Consider, for instance, the definition of politics proposed by the German sociologist Max Weber. "Hence, 'politics' for us means striving to share power or striving to influence the distribution of power, either among states or among groups within a state." Power is crucial but apparently only when it is exercised by or around the state or government. ...

Some political scientists have formulated an alternative definition of politics, an in-between position that is neither as restrictive as the government type nor as broad as the power variety. ...

Such in-between definitions are usually functional in nature. That is, they define politics in terms of the functions it supposedly performs for society. Over the centuries, political thinkers have identified numerous functions: maintaining order, resolving conflict, achieving justice, and providing the good life. In each case, politics is viewed as an activity; it probably involves the exercise of power, but more importantly it is an activity that serves a purpose (or purposes). Thus, to Thomas Hobbes, politics' only function is to maintain order among naturally egoistic and competitive human beings. If the function is not adequately performed, it is back to the State of Nature, where there is no morality, no law, and no politics.

Perhaps the most widely known and used alternative of this sort has been provided by David Easton. ... identification of the political system with "the authoritative allocation of values for a society".[10]

Democracy: A system of government in which ultimate political authority is vested in the people. The term is derived from the Greek words "demos" (the people) and "kratos" (authority). Democracy may be direct,

---

10 Alan C. Isaak, *Scope and Methods of Political Science*, (Homewood, Il: Dorsey, 1985); 18–22.

as practiced in ancient Athens and in New England town meetings, or indirect and representative. In the modern pluralistic democratic state, power typically is exercised by groups or institutions in a complex system of interactions that involve compromises and bargaining in the decision process. The Democratic Creed includes the following concepts: (1) individualism, which holds that the primary task of government is to enable each individual to achieve the highest potential of development; (2) liberty, which allows each individual the greatest amount of freedom consistent with order; (3) equality, which maintains that all men are created equal and have equal rights and opportunities; and (4) fraternity, which postulates that individuals will not misuse their freedom but will cooperate in creating a wholesome society. As a political system, democracy starts with the assumption of popular sovereignty, vesting ultimate power in the people. ...

Government: The political and administrative hierarchy of an organized state. Governments exercise legislative, executive, and judicial functions; the nature of the governmental system is determined by the distribution of these powers and by the means and extent of control exercised by the people. Government may take many forms, but to rule effectively it must be sufficiently powerful to command obedience and maintain order. A government's position also depends on its acceptance by the community of nations through diplomatic recognition by other states.[11]

... We remonstrate against the said Bill,

1. Because we hold it for a fundamental and undeniable truth, "that Religion or the duty which we owe to our Creator and the Manner of discharging it, can be directed only by reason and conviction, not by force or violence." The Religion then of every man must be left to the conviction and conscience of every man; and it is the right of every man to exercise it as these may dictate. This right is in its nature an unalienable right. It is unalienable; because the opinions of men, depending only on the evidence contemplated by their own minds, cannot follow the dictates of other men: It is unalienable also; because what is here a right towards men, is a duty towards the Creator. It is the duty of every man to render to the Creator such homage, and such only, as he believes to be acceptable to him. This duty is precedent both in order of time and degree of obligation, to the

---

11 Jack C. Plano and M. Greenberg, *The American Political Dictionary*, (New York: Holt, 1979), 6–7, 9.

claims of Civil Society. Before any man can be considered as a member of Civil Society, he must be considered as a subject of the Governor of the Universe: And if a member of Civil Society, who enters into any subordinate Association, must always do it with a reservation of his duty to the general authority; much more must every man who becomes a member of any particular Civil Society, do it with a saving of his allegiance to the Universal Sovereign. We maintain therefore that in matters of Religion, no man's right is abridged by the institution of Civil Society, and that Religion is wholly exempt from this cognizance. True it is, that no other rule exists, by which any question which may divide a Society, can be ultimately determined, but the will of the majority; but it is also true, that the majority may trespass on the rights of the minority.

2. Because if religion be exempt from the authority of the Society at large, still less can it be subject to that of the Legislative Body. ...

Who does not see that the same authority which can establish Christianity, in exclusion of all other Religions, may establish with the same ease any particular sect of Christians, in exclusion of all other Sects?. ...

Whilst we assert for ourselves a freedom to embrace, to profess and to observe the Religion which we believe to be of divine origin, we cannot deny an equal freedom to those whose minds have not yet yielded to the evidence which has convinced us. If this freedom be abused, it is an offence against god, not against man: To God, therefore, not to men, must an account of it be rendered. As the Bill violates equality by subjecting some to peculiar burdens; so it violates the same principle, by granting to others peculiar exemptions. Are the Quakers and Menonists the only sects who think a compulsive support of their religions unnecessary and unwarrantable? ...

3. Because the establishment proposed by the Bill is not requisite for the support of the Christian Religion. To say that it is, is a contradiction to the Christian Religion itself; for every page of it disavows a dependence on the powers of this world: it is a contradiction to fact; for it is known that this Religion both existed and flourished, not only without the support of human laws, but in spite of every opposition from them; and not only during the period of miraculous aid, but long after it had been left to its own evidence, and the ordinary care of Providence....

4. Because experience witnesseth that ecclesiastical establishments, instead of maintaining the purity and efficacy of Religion, have had a contrary operation. During almost fifteen centuries, has the legal establishment

of Christianity been on trial. What have been its fruits? More or less in all places, pride and indolence in the Clergy; ignorance and servility in the laity; in both, superstition, bigotry, and persecution. ...

5. Because the establishment in question is not necessary for the Support of Civil Government. ...

6. Because, it will destroy that moderation and harmony which the forbearance of our laws to intermeddle with Religion, has produced amongst its several sects. ...[12]

---

12 James Madison, "*Memorial and Remonstrance Against Religious Assessments.*"

C. S. Lewis

Mere Christianity

The Law of Human Nature

Every one has heard people quarelling. ... They say things like this: "How'd you like it if anyone did the same to you?" – "That's my seat, I was there first" – "Leave him alone, he isn't doing you any harm"–"Why should you shove in first?" – "Give me a bit of your orange, I gave you a bit of mine" – "Come on, you promised."

Now what interests me about all these remarks is that the man who makes them is not merely saying that the other man's behaviour does not happen to please him. He is appealing to some kind of standard of behaviour which he expects the other man to know about. And the other man very seldom replies: "To hell with your standard." Nearly always he tries to make out that what he has been doing does not really go against the standard, or that if it does there is some special excuse. He pretends there is some special reason in this particular case why the person who took the seat first should not keep it, or that things were quite different when he was given the bit of orange, or that something has turned up which lets him off keeping his promise. It looks, in fact, very much as if both parties had in mind some kind of Law or Rule of fair play or decent behaviour or morality or whatever you like to call it, about which they really agreed. And they have. If they had not, they might, of course, fight like animals, but they could not *quarrel* in the human sense of the word. Quarrelling means trying to show that the other man is in the wrong. And there would be no sense in trying to do that unless you and he had some sort of agreement as

Harper Collins, © 1952, 1984, 17–60. Used by permission.

to what Right and Wrong are; just as there would be no sense in saying that a footballer had committed a foul unless there was some agreement about the rules of football.

Now this Law or Rule about Right and Wrong used to be called the Law of Nature ... The idea was that, just as all bodies are governed by the law of gravitation and organisms by biological laws, so the creature called man also had *his* law – with this great difference, that a body could not choose whether it obeyed the law of gravitation or not, but a man could choose either to obey the Law of Human Nature or to disobey it.

We may put this in another way. Each man is at every moment subjected to several sets of law but there is only one of these which he is free to disobey ... As an organism, he is subjected to various biological laws which he cannot disobey any more than an animal can. That is, he cannot disobey those laws which he shares with other things; but the law which is peculiar to his human nature, the law he does not share with animals or vegetables or inorganic things, is the one he can disobey if he chooses.

This law was called the Law of Nature because people thought that every one knew it by nature and did not need to be taught it. They did not mean, of course, that you might not find an odd individual here and there who did not know it ... But taking the race as a whole, they thought that the human idea of decent behaviour was obvious to every one ... What was the sense in saying the enemy were in the wrong unless Right is a real thing which the Nazis at bottom knew as well as we did and ought to have practiced? If they had no notion of what we mean by right, then, though we might still have had to fight them, we could no more have blamed them for that than for the colour of their hair.

I know that some people say the idea of a Law of Nature or decent behaviour known to all men is unsound, because different civilisation and different ages have had quite different moralities.

But this is not true. There have been differences between their moralities, but these have never amounted to anything like a total difference. If anyone will take the trouble to compare the moral teaching of, say, the ancient Egyptians, Babylonians, Hindus, Chinese, Greeks and Romans, what will really strike him will be how very like they are to each other and to our own. ... But for our present purpose I need only ask the reader to think what a totally different morality would mean. Think of a country where people were admired for running away in battle, or where a man felt proud of doublecrossing all the people who had been kindest to him .... Men have differed as regards what people you ought to be unselfish to – whether it was only your own family, or your fellow countrymen, or everyone. But they have always agreed that you ought not to put yourself first. Selfishness has never been admired. Men have differed as to whether you should have one wife or four. But they have always agreed that you must not simply have any woman you liked.

But the most remarkable thing is this. Whenever you find a man who says he does not believe in a real Right and Wrong, you will find the same man going back on this a moment later. He may break his promise to you, but if you try breaking one to him he will be complaining "It's not fair" before you can say Jack Robinson. …

It seems, then, we are forced to believe in a real Right and Wrong. People may be sometimes mistaken about them, just as people sometimes get their sums wrong; but they are not a matter of mere taste and opinion any more than the multiplication table. Now if we are agreed about that, I go on to my next point, which is this. None of us are really keeping the Law of Nature. …

I am only trying to call attention to a fact; the fact that this year, or this month, or, more likely, this very day, we have failed to practice ourselves the kind of behaviour we expect from other people. There may be all sorts of excuses for us. That time you were so unfair to the children was when you were very tired. That slightly shady business about the money – the one you have almost forgotten – came when you were very hard up. … I do not succeed in keeping the Law of Nature very well, and the moment anyone tells me I am not keeping it, there starts up in my mind a string of excuses as long as your arm. The question at the moment is not whether they are good excuses. The point is that they are one more proof of how deeply, whether we like it or not, we believe in the Law of Nature. If we do not believe in decent behaviour, why should we be so anxious to make excuses for not having behaved decently? The truth is, we believe in decency so much – we feel the Rule of Law pressing on us so – that we cannot bear to face the fact that we are breaking it, and consequently we try to shift the responsibility. …

These, then, are the two points I wanted to make. First that human beings, all over the earth, have this curious idea that they ought to behave in a certain way, and cannot really get rid of it. Secondly, that they do not in fact behave in that way. They know the Law of Nature; they break it. These two facts are the foundation of all clear thinking about ourselves and the universe we live in.

Some Objections

... I do not deny that we may have a herd instinct: but that is not what I mean by the Moral Law. We all know what it feels like to be prompted by instinct – by mother love, or sexual instinct, or the instinct for food. It means that you feel a strong want or desire to act in a certain way. And, of course, we sometimes do feel just that sort of desire to help another person: and no doubt that desire is due to the herd instinct. But feeling a desire to help is quite different from feeling that you ought to help whether you want to or not. Supposing you hear a cry for help from a man in danger. You will probably feel two desires – one a desire to give help (due to your herd instinct), the other a desire to keep out of danger (due to the instinct for self-preservation). But you will find inside you, in addition to these two impulses, a third thing which tells you that you ought to follow the impulse to help, and suppress the impulse to run away. Now this thing that judges between two instincts, that decides which should be encouraged, cannot itself be either of them. You might as well say the sheet of music which tells you, at a given moment, to play one note on the piano and not another, is itself one of the notes on the keyboard. The Moral Law tells us the tune we have to play: our instincts are merely the keys.

Another way of seeing that the Moral Law is not simply one of our instincts is this. If two instincts are in conflict, and there is nothing in a creature's mind except those two instincts, obviously the stronger of the two must win. But at those moments when we are most conscious of the Moral Law, it usually seems to be telling us to side with the weaker of the two impulses. You probably *want* to be safe much more than you want to help the man who is drowning: but the Moral Law tells you to help him all the same. And surely it often tells us to try to make the right impulse stronger than it naturally is? I mean, we often feel it our duty to stimulate the herd instinct, by waking up our imaginations and arousing our pity and so on, so as to get up enough steam for doing the right thing. But clearly we are not acting *from* instinct when we set about making an instinct stronger than it is. The thing that says to you, "Your herd instinct is asleep. Wake it up," cannot itself *be* the herd instinct. ... Here is a third way of seeing it. If the Moral Law was one of our instincts, we ought to be able to point to some one impulse inside us which was always what we call "good," always in agreement with the rule of right behaviour. But you cannot. There is none of our impulses which the Moral Law may not sometimes tell us to suppress, and none which it may not sometimes tell us to encourage. It is a mistake to think that some of our impulses – say mother love or patriotism – are good, and others, like sex or the fighting instinct, are bad. All we mean is that the occasions on which the fighting instinct or the sexual desire need to be restrained are rather more frequent than those for restraining mother love or patriotism. But there are situations in which it is the duty of a married man to encourage his sexual impulse and of a soldier to encourage the fighting instinct. There are also occasions on which a mother's love for her own children or a man's love for his own country have to be suppressed or they will lead to unfairness towards other people's children or countries. Strictly speaking, there are no such things as good and bad impulses ... The Moral Law is not any one instinct or any set of instincts: it is something which makes a kind of tune (the tune we call goodness or right conduct) by directing the instincts ...

Other people wrote to me saying, "Isn't what you call the Moral Law just a social convention, something that is put into us by education?" I think there is a misunderstanding here. The people who ask that question are usually taking it for granted that if we have learned a thing from parents and teachers, then that thing must be merely a human invention. But, of course, that is not so. ... I fully agree that we learn the Rule of Decent Behaviour from parents and teachers, and friends and books, as we learn everything else. But some of the things we learn are mere conventions which might have been different – we learn to keep to the left of the road, but it might just as well have been the rule to keep to the right – and others of them, like mathematics, are real truths. The question is to which class the Law of Human Nature belongs.

There are two reasons for saying it belongs to the same class as mathematics. The first is. ... that though there are differences between the moral ideas of one time or country and those of another, the differences are not really very great ... You can recognize the same law running through them all: whereas mere conventions, like the rule of the road or the kind of clothes people wear, may differ to any extent. The other reason is this. When you think about these differences between the morality of one people and another, do you think that the morality of one people is ever better or worse than that of another? Have any of the changes been improvements? If not, then of course there could never be any moral progress. Progress means not just changing, but changing for the better. If no set of moral ideas were truer or better than any other, there would be no sense in preferring civilised morality to savage morality, or Christian morality to Nazi morality. In fact, of course, we all do believe that some moralities are better than others. ... The moment you say that one set of moral ideas can be better than another, you are, in fact, measuring them both by a standard, saying that one of them conforms to that standard more nearly than the other. But the standard that measures two things is something different from either. You are, in fact, comparing them both with some Real Morality, admitting that there is such a thing as a real Right, independent of what people think, and that some people's ideas get nearer to that real Right than others. Or put it this way. If your moral ideas can be truer, and those of the Nazis less true, there must be something – some Real Morality – for them to be true about. The reason why your idea of New York can be truer or less true than mine is that New York is a real place, existing quite apart from what either of us thinks. If when each of us said "New York" each meant merely "The town I am imagining in my own head," how could one of us have truer ideas than the other? There would be no question of truth or falsehood at all. In the same way, if the Rule of Decent Behaviour meant simply "whatever each nation happens to approve," there would be no sense in saying that any one nation had ever been more correct in its approval than any other; no sense in saying that the world could ever grow morally better or morally worse.

I conclude then, that though the differences between people's ideas of Decent Behaviour often make you suspect that there is no real natural Law of Behaviour at all, yet the things we are bound to think about these differences really prove just the opposite. But one word before I end. I have met people who exaggerate the differences, because they have not distinguished between differences of belief about facts. For example, one man said to me, "Three hundred years ago people in England were putting witches to death. Was that what you call the Rule of Human Nature or Right Conduct?" But surely the reason we do not execute witches is that we do not believe there are such things. If we did – if we really thought that there were people going about who had sold themselves to the devil and received supernatural powers from him in return and were using these powers to kill their neighbours or drive them mad or bring bad weather, surely we would all agree that if anyone deserved the death penalty, then these filthy quislings did. There is no difference of moral principle here: the difference is simply about matter of fact. It may be a great advance in knowledge not to believe in witches: there is no moral advance in not executing them when you do not think they are there.

The Reality of the Law

The Law of Human Nature tells you what human beings ought to do and do not. In other words, when you are dealing with humans, something else comes in above and beyond the actual facts. You have the facts (how men do behave) and you also have something else (how they ought to behave). In the rest of the universe there need not be anything but the facts. Electrons and molecules behave in a certain way, and certain results follow, and that may be the whole story. But men behave in a certain way and that is not the whole story, for all the time you know that they ought to behave differently....

Some people say that though decent conduct does not mean what pays each particular person at a particular moment, still, it means what pays the human race as a whole; and that consequently there is no mystery about it. Human beings, after all, have some sense; they see that you cannot have real safety or happiness except in a society where every one plays fair, and it is because they see this that they try to behave decently. Now, of course, it is perfectly true that safety and happiness can only come from individuals, classes, and nations being honest and fair and kind to each other. It is one of the most important truths in the world. But as an explanation of why we feel as we do about Right and Wrong it just misses the point. If we ask: "Why ought I to be unselfish?" and you reply "Because it is good for society," we may then ask, "Why should I care what's good for society except when it happens to pay *me* personally?" and then you will have to say, "Because you ought to be unselfish" – which simply brings us back to where we started. You are saying what is true, but you are not getting any further. If a man asked what was the point of playing football, it would not be much good saying "in order to score goals," for trying to score goals is the game itself, not the reason for the game, and you would really only be saying that football was football – which is true, but not worth saying. In the same way, if a man asks what is the point of behaving decently, it is no good replying, "in order to benefit society," for trying to benefit society, in other words being unselfish (for "society" after all only means "other people"), is one of the things decent behaviour consists in; all you are really saying is that decent behavior is decent behaviour. You would have said just as much if you had stopped at the statement, "Men ought to be unselfish." And that is where I do stop. Men ought to be unselfish, ought to be fair. Not that men are unselfish, nor that they like being unselfish, but that they ought to be. The Moral Law, or Law of Human Nature, is not simply a fact about human behaviour in the same way as the Law of Gravitation is, or may be, simply a fact about how heavy objects behave. On the other hand, it is not a mere fancy, for we cannot get rid of the idea, and most of the things we say and think about men would be reduced to nonsense if we did. And it is not simply a statement about how we should like men to behave for our own convenience; for the behaviour we call bad or unfair is not exactly the same as the behaviour we find inconvenient, and may even be the opposite. Consequently, this Rule of Right and Wrong, or Law of Human Nature, or whatever you call it, must somehow or other be a real thing – a thing that is really there, not made up by ourselves. And yet it is not a fact in the ordinary sense, in the same way as our actual behaviour is a fact. It begins to look as if we shall have to admit that there is more than one kind of reality; that, in this particular case, there is something above and beyond the ordinary facts of men's behaviour, and yet quite definitely real – a real law, which none of us made, but which we find pressing on us.

What Lies Behind the Law

Ever since men were able to think, they have been wondering what this universe really is and how it came to be there. And, very roughly, two views have been held. First, there is what is called the materialist view. People who take that view think that matter and space just happen to exist, and always have existed, nobody knows why; and that the matter, behaving in certain fixed ways, has just happened, by a sort of fluke, to produce creatures like ourselves who are able to think. ... The other view is the religious view. According to it, what is behind the universe is more like a mind than it is like anything else we know. That is to say, it is conscious, and has purposes, and prefers one thing to another. And on this view it made the universe, partly for purposes we do not know, but partly, at any rate, in order to produce creatures like itself – I mean, like itself to the extent of having minds. ... You cannot find out which view is the right one by science in the ordinary sense. Science works by experiments. It watches how things behave ... Whether there is anything behind the things science observes – something of a different kind – this is not a scientific question ... Supposing science ever became complete so that it knew every single thing in the whole universe. Is it not plain that the questions, "Why is there a universe?" "Why does it go on as it does?" "Has it any meaning?" would remain just as they were?

Now the position would be quite hopeless but for this. There is one thing, and only one, in the whole universe which we know more about than we could learn from external observation. That one thing is Man. We do not merely observe men, we *are* men. ... Because of that, we know that men find themselves under a moral law, which they did not make, and cannot quite forget even when they try, and which they know they ought to obey. Notice the following point. Anyone studying Man from the outside as we study electricity or cabbages, not knowing our language and consequently not able to get any inside knowledge from us, but merely observing what we did, would never get the slightest evidence that we had this moral law. How could he? For his observations would only show what we did, and the moral law is about what we ought to do. In the same way, if there were anything above or behind the observed facts in the case of stones or the weather, we, by studying them from outside, could never hope to discover it.

The position of the question, then, is like this. We want to know whether the universe simply happens to be what it is for no reason or whether there is a power behind it that makes it what it is. Since that power, if it exists, would be not one of the observed facts but a reality which makes them, no mere observation of the facts can find it. There is only one case in which we can know whether there is anything more, namely our own case, and in that one case we find there is. Or put it the other way round. If there was a controlling power outside the universe, it could not show itself to us as one of the facts inside the universe – no more than the architect of a house could actually be a wall or staircase or fireplace in that house. The only way in which we could expect it to show itself would be inside ourselves as an influence or a command trying to get us to behave in a certain way. And that is just what we do find inside ourselves. Surely this ought to arouse our suspicions? In the only case where you can expect to get an answer, the answer turns out to be Yes; and in the other cases, where you do not get an answer, you see why you do not. Suppose someone asked me, when I see a man in a blue uniform going down the street leaving little paper packets at each house, why I suppose that they contain letters? I should reply, "Because whenever he leaves a similar little packet for me I find it does contain a letter." And if he then objected, "But you've never seen all these letters which you think the other people are getting," I should say ... "I'm explaining the packets I'm not allowed to open by the ones I am allowed to open." It is the same about this question. The only packet I am allowed to open is Man. When I do, especially when I open that particular man called Myself, I find that I do not exist on my own, that I am under a law; that somebody or something wants me to behave in a certain way. I do not, of course, think that if I could get inside a stone or a tree I should find exactly the same thing, just as I do not think all the other people in the street get the same letters as I do. I should expect, for instance, to find that the stone had to obey the law of gravity – that whereas the sender of the letters merely tells me to obey the law of my human nature. He compels the stone to obey the laws of its stony nature. But I should expect to find that there was, so to speak, a sender of letters in both cases, a Power behind the facts, a Director, a Guide.

Do not think I am going faster than I really am. I am not yet within a hundred miles of the God of Christian theology. All I have got to is a Something which is directing the universe, and which appears in me as a law urging me to do right and making me feel responsible and uncomfortable when I do wrong …

Christianity tells people to repent and promises them forgiveness. It therefore has nothing (as far as I know) to say to people who do not know they have done anything to repent of and who do not feel that they need any forgiveness. It is after you have realised that there is a real Moral Law, and a Power behind the law, and that you have broken that law and put yourself wrong with that Power – it is after all this, and not a moment sooner, that Christianity begins to talk. When you know you are sick, you will listen to the doctor. When you have realised that our position is nearly desperate you will begin to understand what the Christians are talking about. They offer an explanation of how we got into our present state of both hating goodness and loving it. They offer an explanation of how God can be this impersonal mind at the back of the Moral Law and yet also a Person. They tell you how the demands of this law, which you and I cannot meet, have been met on our behalf, how God Himself becomes a man to save man from the disapproval of God* …

---

* [Editor's note: Lewis goes on to explain that Christians believe God is "good" and "righteous" and wants his people to follow the law of nature that he gave them. He asserts that Christians believe "a great many things have gone wrong with the world that God made," because of man's free will and the presence of Satan. Lewis then explains why God created free will in the section below.]

God created things which had free will. That means creatures which can go either wrong or right. Some people think they can imagine a creature which was free but had no possibility of going wrong; I cannot. If a thing is free to be good it is also free to be bad. And free will is what has made evil possible. Why, then, did God give them free will? Because free will, though it makes evil possible, is also the only thing that makes possible any love or goodness or joy worth having. A world of automata – of creatures that worked like machines – would hardly be worth creating. The happiness which God designs for His higher creatures is the happiness of being freely, voluntarily united to Him and to each other in an ecstasy of love and delight compared with which the most rapturous love between a man and a woman on this earth is mere milk and water. And for that they must be free.

Of course God knew what would happen if they used their freedom the wrong way: apparently He thought it worth the risk ... The moment you have a self at all, there is a possibility of putting yourself first – wanting to be the centre – wanting to be God, in fact. That was the sin of Satan: and that was the sin he taught the human race ... What Satan put into the heads of our remote ancestors was the idea that they could "be like gods" – could set up on their own as if they had created themselves – be their own masters – invent some sort of happiness for themselves outside God, apart from God. And out of that hopeless attempt has come nearly all that we call human history – money, poverty, ambition, war, prostitution, classes, empires, slavery – the long terrible story of man trying to find something other than God which will make him happy.

The reason why it can never succeed is this. God made us: invented us as a man invents an engine. A car is made to run on gasoline, and it would not run properly on anything else. Now God designed the human machine to run on Himself. He Himself is the fuel our spirits were designed to burn, or the food our spirits were designed to feed on. There is no other. That is why it is just no good asking God to make us happy in our own way without bothering about religion. God cannot give us a happiness and peace apart from Himself, because it is not there. There is no such thing. ...

And what did God do? First of all He left us conscience, the sense of right and wrong: and all through history there have been people trying (some of them very hard) to obey it. None of them ever quite succeeded. Secondly, He sent the human race what I call good dreams: I mean those queer stories scattered all through the heathen religions about a god who dies and comes to life again and, by his death, has somehow given new life to men. Thirdly, He selected one particular people and spent several centuries hammering into their heads the sort of God He was – that there was only one of Him and that He cared about right conduct. Those people were the Jews, and the Old Testament gives an account of the hammering process.

Then comes the real shock. Among these Jews there suddenly turns up a man who goes about talking as if He was God. He claims to forgive sins. He says He has always existed. He says He is coming to judge the world at the end of time.

… One part of the claim tends to slip past us unnoticed: … the claim to forgive sins: any sins. Now unless the speaker is God, this is really so preposterous as to be comic. We can all understand how a man forgives offences against himself. You tread on my toe and I forgive you, you steal my money and I forgive you. But what should we make of a man, himself unrobbed and untrodden on, who announced that he forgave you for treading on other men's toes and stealing other men's money? Yet this is what Jesus did. He told people that their sins were forgiven, and never waited to consult all the other people whom their sins had undoubtedly injured. He unhesitatingly behaved as if He as the party chiefly concerned, the person chiefly offended in all offences. This makes sense only if He really was the God whose laws are broken and whose love is wounded in every sin. In the mouth of any speaker who is not God, these words would imply what I can only regard as a silliness and conceit unrivalled by any other character in history.

Yet … even His enemies, when they read the Gospels, do not usually get the impression of silliness and conceit. Still less do unprejudiced readers. Christ says the He is "humble and meek" and we believe Him; not noticing that, if He were merely a man, humility and meekness are the very last characteristics we could attribute to some of His sayings.

I am trying here to prevent anyone saying the really foolish thing that people often say about Him: "I'm ready to accept Jesus as a great moral teacher, but I don't accept His claim to be God." That is the one thing we must not say. A man who was merely a man and said the sort of things Jesus said would not be a great moral teacher. He would either be a lunatic – on a level with the man who says he is a poached egg – or else he would be the Devil of Hell. You must make your choice. Either this man was, and is, the Son of God: or else a madman or something worse. You can shut Him up for a fool, you can spit at Him and kill Him as a demon; or you can fall at His feet and call Him Lord and God. But let us not come with any patronising nonsense about His being a great human teacher. ...

The Perfect Penitent

We are faced, then, with a frightening alternative. This man we are talking about either was (and is) just what He said or else a lunatic, or something worse. Now it seems to me obvious that He was neither a lunatic nor a fiend: and consequently, however strange or terrifying or unlikely it may seem, I have to accept the view that He was and is God. God has landed on this enemy-occupied world in human form.

And now, what was the purpose of it all? ... The central Christian belief is that Christ's death has somehow put us right with God and given us a fresh start. ...

We are told that Christ was killed for us, that His death has washed out our sins, and that by dying He disabled death itself. That is the formula ...

If you think of a debt, there is plenty of point in a person who has some assets paying it on behalf of someone who has not. Or if you take "paying the penalty," not in the sense of being punished, but in the more general sense of "footing the bill," then, of course, it is a matter of common experience that, when one person has got himself into a hole, the trouble of getting him out usually falls on a kind friend.

Now what was the sort of "hole" man had got himself into? He had tried to set up on his own, to behave as if he belonged to himself. In other words, fallen man is not simply an imperfect creature who needs improvement: he is a rebel who must lay down his arms. Laying down your arms, surrendering, saying you are sorry, realising that you have been on the wrong track and getting ready to start life over again from the ground floor – that is the only way out of a "hole." This process of surrender – this movement full speed astern – is what Christians call repentance. Now repentance is no fun at all. It is something much harder than merely eating humble pie. It means unlearning all the self-conceit and self-will that we have been training ourselves into for thousands of years. It means killing part of yourself, undergoing a kind of death. In fact, it needs a good man to repent. And here comes the catch. Only a bad person needs to repent: only a good person can repent perfectly. The worse you are the more you need it and the less you can do it. The only person who could do it perfectly would be a perfect person – and he would not need it. ...

The same badness which makes us need [repentance], makes us unable to do it. Can we do it if God helps us? Yes, but what do we mean when we talk of God helping us? We mean God putting into us a bit of Himself, so to speak. He lends us a little of His reasoning powers and that is how we think: He puts a little of His love into us and that is how we love one another. When you teach a child writing, you hold its hand while it forms the letters: that is, it forms the letters because you are forming them. We love and reason because God loves and reasons and holds our hand while we do it. Now if we had not fallen, that would be all plain sailing. But unfortunately we now need God's help in order to do something which God, in His own nature, never does at all – to surrender, to suffer, to submit, to die. Nothing in God's nature corresponds to this process at all. So that the one road for which we now need God's leadership most of all is a road God, in His own nature, has never walked. God can share only what He has: this thing, in His own nature, He has not.

But supposing God became a man – suppose our human nature which can suffer and die was amalgamated with God's nature in one person – then that person could help us. He could surrender His will, and suffer and die, because He was man; and He could do it perfectly because He was God. You and I can go through this process only if God does it in us; but God can do it only if He becomes man. Our attempts at this dying will succeed only if we men share in God's dying, just as our thinking can succeed only because it is a drop out of the ocean of His intelligence: but we cannot share God's dying unless God dies; and He cannot die except by being a man. That is the sense in which He pays our debt, and suffers for us what He Himself need not suffer at all. ...

Robert N. Bellah

Civil Religion in America

While some have argued that Christianity is the national faith, and others that church and synagogue celebrate only the generalized religion of "the American Way of Life," few have realized that there actually exists alongside of and rather clearly differentiated from the churches an elaborate and well-institutionalized civil religion in America. ...

Kennedy's inaugural address of 20 January 1961 serves as an example and a clue with which to introduce this complex subject. That address began:

> We observe today not a victory of party but a celebration of freedom – symbolizing an end as well as a beginning – signifying renewal as well as change. For I have sworn before you and Almighty God the same solemn oath our forebears prescribed nearly a century and three quarters ago.
>
> The world is very different now. For man holds in his mortal hands the power to abolish all forms of human poverty and to abolish all forms of human life. And yet the same revolutionary beliefs for which our forebears fought are still at issue around the globe – the belief that the rights of man come not from the generosity of the state but from the hand of God.

And it concluded:

> Finally, whether you are citizens of America or of the world, ask of us the same high standards of strength and sacrifice that we shall ask of you. With a good conscience our only sure reward, with history the final judge of our deeds, let us go forth to lead the land we love, asking His blessing and His help, but knowing that here on earth God's work must truly be our own.

These are the three places in this brief address in which Kennedy mentioned the name of God. If we could understand why he mentioned God, the

Daedalus. Winter 1967 and Summer 1988, 97–118. Used by permission.

way in which he did it, and what he meant to say in those three references, we would understand much about American civil religion. ...

It might be argued that the passages quoted reveal the essentially irrelevant role of religion in the very secular society that is America. The placing of the references in this speech as well as in public life generally indicates that religion has "only a ceremonial significance"; it gets only a sentimental nod which serves largely to placate the more unenlightened members of the community, before a discussion of the really serious business with which religion has nothing whatever to do. A cynical observer might even say that an American president has to mention God or risk losing votes. ...

But we know enough about the function of ceremony and ritual in various societies to make us suspicious of dismissing something as unimportant because it is "only a ritual." What people say on solemn occasions need not be taken at face value, but it is often indicative of deep-seated values and commitments that are not made explicit in the course of everyday life. Following this line of argument, it is worth considering whether the very special placing of the references to God in Kennedy's address may not reveal something rather important and serious about religion in American life.

It might be countered that the very way in which Kennedy made his references reveals the essentially vestigial place of religion today. ... He did not refer to Jesus Christ, or to Moses, or to the Christian church; certainly he did not refer to the Catholic church. In fact, his only reference was to the concept of God, a word which almost all Americans can accept but which means so many different things to so many different people that it is almost an empty sign. Is this not just another indication that in America religion is considered vaguely to be a good thing, but that people care so little about it that it has lost any content whatever? Isn't Eisenhower reported to have said, "Our government makes no sense unless it is founded in a deeply felt religious faith – and I don't care what it is," and isn't that a complete negation of any real religion?

These questions are worth pursuing because they raise the issue of how civil religion relates to the political society, on the one hand, and to private religious organization, on the other. President Kennedy was a ... Catholic Christian. Thus, his general references to God do not mean that he lacked a specific religious commitment. But why, then, did he not include some remark to the effect that Christ is the Lord of the world or some indication of respect for the Catholic church? He did not because these are matters of his own private religious belief and of his relation to his own particular church; they are not matters relevant in any direct way to the conduct of his public office. Others with different religious views and commitments to different churches or denominations are equally qualified participants in the political process. The principle of separation of church and state guarantees the freedom of religious belief and association but at the same time clearly segregates the religious sphere, which is considered to be essentially private, from the political one.

Considering the separation of church and state, how is a president justified in using the word *God* at all? The answer is that the separation of church and state has not denied the political realm a religious dimension. Although matters of personal religious belief, worship, and association are considered to be strictly private affairs, there are, at the same time, certain common elements of religious orientation that the great majority of Americans share. These have played a crucial role in the development of American institutions and still provide a religious dimension for the whole fabric of American life, including the political sphere. This public religious dimension is expressed in a set of beliefs, symbols, and rituals that I am calling the American civil religion. The inauguration of a president is an important ceremonial event in this religion. It reaffirms, among other things, the religious legitimation of the lightest political authority.

Let us look more closely at what Kennedy actually said. First he said, "I have sworn before you and Almighty God the same solemn oath our forebears prescribed nearly a century and three quarters ago." The oath is the oath of office, including the acceptance of the obligation to uphold the Constitution. He swears it before the people (you) and God. Beyond the Constitution, then, the president's obligation extends not only to the people but to God. In American political theory, sovereignty rests, of course, with the people, but implicitly, and often explicitly, the ultimate sovereignty has been attributed to God. This is the meaning of the motto "In God we trust," as well as the inclusion of the phrase "under God" in the pledge to the flag. What difference does it make that sovereignty belongs to God? Though the will of the people as expressed in majority vote is carefully institutionalized as the operative source of political authority, it is deprived of an ultimate significance. The will of the people is not itself the criterion of right and wrong. There is a higher criterion in terms of which this will can be judged; it is possible that the people may be wrong. The president's obligation extends to the higher criterion.

When Kennedy says that "the rights of man come not from the generosity of the state but from the hand of God," he is stressing this point again. It does not matter whether the state is the expression of the will of an autocratic monarch or of the "people"; the rights of man are more basic than any political structure and provide a point of revolutionary leverage from which any state structure may be radically altered. That is the basis for his reassertion of the revolutionary significance of America.

But the religious dimension in political life as recognized by Kennedy not only provides a grounding for the rights of man which makes any form of political absolutism illegitimate; it also provides a transcendent goal for the political process. This is implied in his final words that "here on earth God's work must truly be our own." What he means here is, I think, more clearly spelled out in a previous paragraph:

> Now the trumpet summons us again – not as a call to bear arms, through arms we need – not as a call to battle, though embattled we are – but a call to bear the burden of a long twilight struggle, year in and year out, "rejoicing in hope, patient in tribulation" – a struggle against the common enemies of man: tyranny, poverty, disease and war itself.

The whole address can be understood as only the most recent statement of a theme that lies very deep in the American tradition, namely the obligation, both collective and individual, to carry out God's will on earth. This was the motivating spirit of those who founded America, and it has been present in every generation since. ... That this very activist and noncontemplative conception of the fundamental religious obligation, which has been historically associated with the Protestant position, should be enunciated so clearly in the first major statement of the first Catholic president seems to underline how deeply established it is in the American outlook. Let us now consider the form and history of the civil religious tradition in which Kennedy was speaking.

The Idea of a Civil Religion

The phrase *civil religion* is, of course, Rousseau's. In Chapter 8, Book 4 of *The Social Contract*, he outlines the simple dogmas of the civil religion: the existence of God, the life to come, the reward of virtue and the punishment of vice, and the exclusion of religious intolerance. All other religious opinions are outside the cognizance of the state and may be freely held by citizens. While the phrase *civil religion* was not used, to the best of my knowledge, by the founding fathers, and I am certainly not arguing for the particular influence of Rousseau, it is clear that similar ideas, as part of the cultural climate of the late eighteenth century, were to be found among the Americans. For example, Franklin writes in his autobiography:

> I never was without some religious principles. I never doubted, for instance, the existence of the Deity; that he made the world and govern'd it by his Providence; that the most acceptable service of God was the doing of good to men; that our souls are immortal; and that all crime will be punished, and virtue rewarded either here or hereafter. These I esteemed the essentials of every religion; and, being to be found in all the religions we had in our country, I respected them all, tho' with different degrees of respect, as I found them more or less mix'd with other articles, which, without any tendency to inspire, promote or confirm morality, serv'd principally to divide us, and make us unfriendly to one another.

It is easy to dispose of this sort of position as essentially utilitarian in relation to religion. In Washington's Farewell Address (though the words may be Hamilton's) the utilitarian aspect is quite explicit:

> Of all the dispositions and habits which lead to political prosperity, Religion and Morality are indispensable supports. In vain would that man claim the tribute of Patriotism, who should labour to subvert these great Pillars of human happiness, these firmest props of the duties of men and citizens. The mere politician, equally with the pious man ought to respect and cherish them. A volume could not trace all their connections with private and public felicity. Let it simply be asked where is the security for property, for reputation, for life, if the sense of religious obligation *desert* the oaths, which are instruments of investigation in the Courts of justice? And let us with caution indulge the supposition, that morality can be maintained without religion. Whatever may be conceded to the influence of refined education on minds of peculiar structure, reason and experience both forbid us to expect that National morality can prevail in exclusion of religious principle.

But there is every reason to believe that religion, particularly the idea of God, played a constitutive role in the thought of the early American statesmen.

Kennedy's inaugural pointed to the religious aspect of the Declaration of Independence, and it might be well to look at that document a bit more closely. There are four references to God. The first speaks of the "Laws of Nature and of Nature's God" which entitle any people to be independent. The second is the famous statement that all men "are endowed by their Creator with certain inalienable Rights." Here Jefferson is locating the fundamental legitimacy of the new nation in a conception of "higher law" that is itself based on both classical natural law and biblical religion. The third is an appeal to "the Supreme Judge of the world for the rectitude of our intentions," and the last indicates "a firm reliance on the protection of divine Providence." In these last two references, a biblical God of history who stands in judgment over the world is indicated.

The intimate relation of these religious notions with the self-conception of the new republic is indicated by the frequency of their appearance in early official documents. For example, we find in Washington's first inaugural address of 30 April 1789:

> It would be peculiarly improper to omit in this first official act my fervent supplications to that Almighty Being who rules over the universe, who presides in the councils of nations, and whose providential aids can supply every defect, that His benediction may consecrate to the liberties and happiness of the people of the United States a Government instituted by themselves for these essential purposes, and may enable every instrument employed in its administration to execute with success the functions allotted to his charge.
>
> No people can be bound to acknowledge and adore the Invisible Hand which conducts the affairs of man more than those of the United States. ...
>
> The propitious smiles of Heaven can never be expected on a nation that disregards the eternal rules of order and right which Heaven itself has ordained. ... The preservation of the sacred fire of liberty and the destiny of the republican model of government are justly considered, perhaps, as *deeply*, as *finally*, staked on the experiment intrusted to the hands of the American people.

Nor did these religious sentiments remain merely the personal expression of the president. At the request of both houses of Congress, Washington proclaimed on October 3 of that same first year as president that November 26 should be "a day of public thanksgiving and prayer," the first Thanksgiving Day under the Constitution.

The words and acts of the founding fathers, especially the first few presidents, shaped the form and tone of the civil religion as it has been maintained ever since. Though much is selectively derived from Christianity, this religion is clearly not itself Christianity. For one thing, neither Washington nor Adams nor Jefferson mentions Christ in his inaugural address; nor do any of the subsequent presidents, although not one of them fails to mention God. The God of the civil religion is not only rather "unitarian"; he is also on the austere side, much more related to order, law, and right than to salvation and love. Even though he is somewhat deist in cast, he is by no means simply a watchmaker God. He is actively interested and involved in history, with a special concern for America. Here the analogy has much less to do with natural law than with ancient Israel; the equation of America with Israel in the idea of the "American Israel" is not infrequent. What was implicit in the words of Washington already quoted becomes explicit in Jefferson's second inaugural when he said, "I shall need, too, the favor of that Being in whose hands we are, who led our fathers, as Israel of old, from their native land and planted them in a country flowing with all the necessaries and comforts of life." Europe is Egypt; America, the promised land. God has led his people to establish a new sort of social order that shall be a light unto all the nations. ...

What we have, then, from the earliest years of the republic is a collection of beliefs, symbols, and rituals with respect to sacred things and institutionalized in a collectivity. This religion – there seems no other word for it – while not antithetical to and indeed sharing much in common with Christianity, was neither sectarian nor in any specific sense Christian. At a time when the society was overwhelmingly Christian, it seems unlikely that this lack of Christian reference was meant to spare the feelings of the tiny non-Christian minority. ... Nor was the civil religion simply "religion in general." While generality was undoubtedly seen as virtue by some, as in the quotation from Franklin above, the civil religion was specific enough when it came to the topic of America. Precisely because of this specificity, the civil religion was saved from empty formalism and served as a genuine vehicle of national religious self-understanding.

But the civil religion was not, in the minds of Franklin, Washington, Jefferson, or other leaders, with the exception of a few radicals like Tom Paine, ever felt to be a substitute for Christianity. There was an implicit but quite clear division of function between the civil religion and Christianity. Under the doctrine of religious liberty, an exceptionally wide sphere of personal piety and voluntary social action was left to the churches. But the churches were neither to control the state nor to be controlled by it. The national magistrate, whatever his private religious views, operates under the rubrics of the civil religion as long as he is in his official capacity, as we have already seen in the case of Kennedy. This accommodation was undoubtedly the product of a particular historical moment and of a cultural background dominated by Protestantism of several varieties and by the Enlightenment, but it has survived despite subsequent changes in the cultural and religious climate.

Civil War and Civil Religion

Until the Civil War, the American civil religion focused above all on the event of the Revolution, which was seen as the final act of the Exodus from the old lands across the waters. The Declaration of Independence and the Constitution were the sacred scriptures and Washington the divinely appointed Moses who led his people out of the hands of tyranny. The Civil War, which Sidney Mead calls "the center of American history," was the second great event that involved the national self-understanding so deeply as to require expression in the civil religion. ...

The Civil War raised the deepest questions of national meaning. The man who not only formulated but in his own person embodied its meaning for Americans was Abraham Lincoln. For him the issue was not in the first instance slavery but "whether that nation or any nation so conceived, and so dedicated, can long endure. ..."

But inevitably the issue of slavery as the deeper cause of the conflict had to be faced. In the second inaugural, Lincoln related slavery and the war in an ultimate perspective:

> If we shall suppose that American slavery is one of those offenses which, in the providence of God, must needs come, but which, having continued through His appointed time, He now wills to remove, and that He gives both to the North and South this terrible war as the woe due to those by whom the offense came, shall we discern therein any departure from those divine attributes which the believers in a living God always ascribe to Him? Fondly do we hope, fervently do we pray, that this mighty scourge of war may speedily pass away. Yet, if God wills that it continue until all the wealth piled by the bondsman's two hundred and fifty years of unrequited toil shall be sunk, and until every drop of blood drawn with the lash shall be paid by another drawn with the sword, as was said three thousand years ago, so still it must be said "the judgements of the Lord are true and righteous altogether."

But he closes on a note if not of redemption then of reconciliation – "With malice toward none, with charity for all."

With the Civil War, a new theme of death, sacrifice, and rebirth enters the civil religion. It is symbolized in the life and death of Lincoln. Nowhere is it stated more vividly than in the Gettysburg Address, itself part of the Lincolnian "New Testament" among the civil scriptures. ...

The symbolic equation of Lincoln with Jesus was made relatively early. Herndon, who had been Lincoln's law partner, wrote:

For fifty years God rolled Abraham Lincoln through his fiery furnace. He did it to try Abraham and to purify him for his purposes. This made Mr. Lincoln humble, tender, forbearing, sympathetic to suffering, kind, sensitive, tolerant; broadening, deepening and widening his whole nature; making him the noblest and loveliest character since Jesus Christ. ... I believe that Lincoln was God's chosen one.

With the Christian archetype in the background, Lincoln, "our martyred president," was linked to the war dead, those who "gave the last full measure of devotion." The theme of sacrifice was indelibly written into the civil religion ...

Just as Thanksgiving Day, which incidentally was securely institutionalized as an annual national holiday only under the presidency of Lincoln, serves to integrate the family into the civil religion, so Memorial Day [which grew out of small town ceremonies to honor the Civil War dead], has acted to integrate the local community into the national cult. Together with the less overtly religious Fourth of July and the more minor celebrations of Veterans Day and the birthdays of Washington and Lincoln, these two holidays provide an annual ritual calendar for the civil religion. ...

The Civil Religion Today

... I would argue that the civil religion at its best is a genuine apprehension of universal and transcendent religious reality as seen in or, one could almost say, as revealed through the experience of the American people. Like all religions, it has suffered various deformations and demonic distortions. At its best, it has neither been so general that it has lacked incisive relevance to the American scene nor so particular that it has placed American society above universal human values. I am not at all convinced that the leaders of the churches have consistently represented a higher level of religious insight than the spokesmen of the civil religion. Reinhold Niebuhr has this to say of Lincoln, who never joined a church and who certainly represents civil religion at its best:

> An analysis of the religion of Abraham Lincoln in the context of the traditional religion of his time and place and of its polemical use on the slavery issue, which corrupted religious life in the days before and during the Civil War, must lead to the conclusion that Lincoln's religious convictions were superior in depth and purity to those, not only of the political leaders of his day, but of the religious leaders of the era.

Perhaps the real animus of the religious critics has been not so much against the civil religion in itself but against its pervasive and dominating influence within the sphere of church religion. As S. M. Lipset has recently shown, American religion at least since the early nineteenth century has been predominantly activist, moralistic, and social rather than contemplative, theological, or innerly spiritual. Tocqueville spoke of American church religion as "a political institution which powerfully contributes to the maintenance of a democratic republic among the Americans" by supplying a strong moral consensus amidst continuous political change. ...

It is certainly true that the relation between religion and politics in America has been singularly smooth. This is in large part due to the dominant tradition. As Tocqueville wrote:

> The greatest part of British America was peopled by men who, after having shaken off the authority of the Pope, acknowledged no other religious supremacy: they brought with them into the New World a form of Christianity which I cannot better describe than by styling it a democratic and republican religion.

The churches opposed neither the Revolution nor the establishment of democratic institutions. Even when some of them opposed the full institutionalization of religious liberty, they accepted the final outcome with good grace and without nostalgia for an *ancien régime.* The American civil religion was never anticlerical or militantly secular. On the contrary, it borrowed selectively from the religious tradition in such a way that the average American saw no conflict between the two. In this way, the civil religion was able to build up without any bitter struggle with the church powerful symbols of national solidarity and to mobilize deep levels of personal motivation for the attainment of national goals. ...

The civil religion has not always been invoked in favor of worthy causes. On the domestic scene, an American Legion type of ideology that fuses God, country, and flag has been used to attack nonconformist and liberal ideas and groups of all kinds. ...

With respect to America's role in the world, the dangers of distortion are greater and the built-in safeguards of the tradition weaker. The theme of the American Israel was used, almost from the beginning, as a justification for the shameful treatment of the Indians so characteristic of our history. It can be overtly or implicitly linked to the idea of manifest destiny which has been used to legitimate several adventures in imperialism since the early nineteenth century. Never has the danger been greater than today. The issue is not so much one of imperial expansion, of which we are accused, as of the tendency to assimilate all governments or parties in the world which support our immediate policies or call upon our help by invoking the notion of free institutions and democratic values. Those nations that are for the moment "on our side" become "the free world." A repressive and unstable military dictatorship in South Vietnam becomes "the free people of South Vietnam and their government." It is then part of the role of America as the New Jerusalem and "the last hope of earth" to defend such governments with treasure and eventually with blood. ...

The civil religion has exercised long-term pressure for the humane solution of our greatest domestic problem, the treatment of the Negro-American. It remains to be seen how relevant it can become for our role in the world at large, and whether we can effectually stand for "the revolutionary beliefs for which our forebears fought," in John F. Kennedy's words.

The civil religion is obviously involved in the most pressing moral and political issues of the day. But it is also caught in another kind of crisis, theoretical and theological, of which it is at the moment largely unaware. "God" has clearly been a central symbol in the civil religion from the beginning and remains so today. This symbol is just as central to the civil religion as it is to Judaism or Christianity. ... But today, as even *Time* has recognized, the meaning of the word *God* is by no means so clear or so obvious. There is no formal creed in the civil religion. We have had a Catholic president; it is conceivable that we could have a Jewish one. But could we have an agnostic president? Could a man with conscientious scruples about using the word *God* the way Kennedy and Johnson have used it be elected chief magistrate of our country?

... In conclusion ... the American civil religion is not the worship of the American nation but an understanding of the American experience in the light of ultimate and universal reality. ...

Chapter II

The Free Exercise of Religion

Background: According to the First Amendment, "Congress shall make no law respecting an establishment of religion, or prohibiting the free exercise thereof." The two authors in this chapter debate what "free exercise" means. Michael McConnell favors government accommodation of religion; in other words, he believes that government, as long as it does not prefer one religion over another, may aid or support religion. This non-pre-ferential support includes exemptions from state or national laws that handicap the free exercise of religion. William Marshall, on the other hand, rejects both accommodation and exemptions as unconstitutional assaults on the principle of the separation of church and state. In the process of making their respective cases, McConnell and Marshall provide a historical review of the religious traditions and practices of the 17th and 18th century America. They also offer contrasting interpretations of the impact of Lockean and American Enlightenment philosophies on American political thought, especially as it related to the development of the religion clauses. Finally, the two authors review the still vital doctrines of early American religious leaders like Roger Williams, William Penn, John Leland, and Isaac Backus.

Authors: Michael W. McConnell, Professor of Law at the University of Chicago, has appeared frequently before the Supreme Court to argue church/state cases. He asserts that the free exercise clause mandates ex-emptions from laws and regulations that conflict with religious ob-ligations. In his view, the founders, seeking to protect religious freedom, accepted exemptions as a means of balancing the opposing claims of gov-ernment and God upon an individual. McConnell maintains that James Madison's emphasis on free exercise and the individual's unabridgeable right to follow the dictates of faith contrasts with John Locke's emphasis on legislative supremacy and the secular goals of the state.

McConnell also highlights the key differences between Jefferson, for whom religious liberty means "largely freedom from sectarian religion," and Madison, for whom it means "freedom to practice religion in whatsoever form one chooses." In addition, McConnell argues that an evangelical Protestantism and Madison's affirmative stance toward religion, rather than Jefferson's Deism and enlightenment world view, governed the spiritual and intellectual atmosphere of the revolutionary and post-revolutionary period. Equally governing, according to McConnell, was the consensus that the special protection provided to religion did not apply to secular moral conflicts with the laws of the state because non-believers "do not make judgments stemming from obedience to a higher authority." In his view, then, the founders believed religion merited special constitutional status.

McConnell accepts Madison's argument that the willingness of the American government to grant religion special status and to respect the claims of higher authority was "the surest sign of liberality." McConnell would like to seal this liberality and redress what he see as the "illiberality" of the Supreme Court's efforts, on behalf of extreme separationism, to severely limit religion-based exemptions. He proposes, in an article in FIRST THINGS (May 1990), a modified reformulation of Supreme Court test for free exercise rights.

> A modified test might look like this: 1. A law or policy is unconstitutional if its purpose or likely effect is to increase religious uniformity either by inhibiting the religious practices of the person or group challenging the law (Free Exercise Clause) or by forcing or inducing a contrary religious practice (Establishment Clause); 2. a law or policy is unconstitutional if its enforcement interferes with the independence of a religious body in matters of religious significance to that body; 3. violation of either of these principles will be permitted only if it is the least restrictive means for a) protecting the private rights of others, or b) ensuring that the benefits and burdens of public life are equitably shared.

McConnell argues here for a stricter interpretation of what laws violate the free exercise clause. Rather than exempting religious individuals or groups from laws that infringe on the free exercise of religion, these laws would be declared unconstitutional.

William P. Marshall, Professor of Law at Case Western Reserve School of Law, rejects constitutionally compelled exemptions from laws not intended to involve religion. He believes exemptions would favor religion over non-religion, thus offending the establishment clause and the principle of equal treatment of ideas, and would raise "virtually insoluable" problems in determining when a religious claim is *bona fide* and thus worthy of exemption. In his view, "allowing the courts or government to investigate and label beliefs as 'irreligious' or 'insincere' raises a threat to religious liberty."

Marshall traces the historical and doctrinal underpinnings of the exemption doctrine and relevant Supreme Court cases, lambasts those favoring more stringent free exercise protection, and proposes his own modified doctrine for the Court to follow: the reduction principle or the "free exercise as expression thesis." According to this thesis, claims for exemption would be constitutional "only to the extent that [the] claims would be protected under the speech clause of the First Amendment." This thesis offends those who believe free exercise rights are distinct from the right of free speech and other rights enumerated in the amendments to the constitution.

In making his criticisms and proposal, Marshall refutes McConnell's arguments that Protestant Christianity, rather than Deism, dominated the spiritual and intellectual milieu in 18th century America. He also dismisses McConnell's notion that 20th century American government, in conjunction unofficially or subconsciously with the religious majority (a mythical entity according to Marshall), threatens by design, neglect, or insensitivity the beliefs and practices of minority religious groups. In addition, Marshall doubts that the religious pluralism principle (the principle that diversity of sects and factions acts as a "checks and balances" mechanism to protect against establishment or oppression) sanctions government accommodation of religion. Finally, he rejects McConnell's argument (and McConnell's claim that Madison would agree with him) that religious claims supercede the claims of the state because of the transcendent obligation of believers. In other words, Marshall argues that believer's obligations to God do not oblige governments to exempt them from religiously neutral laws.

Marshall concludes that free exercise protection is alive and well, and needs no addition of a cumbersome and controversial exemption doctrine that legitimizes exemptions from laws that only incidently and/or inadvertently regulate religious behavior. He also insists, in contrast to McConnell, that the First Amendment grants secular and religious beliefs "equal constitutional dignity." In sum, Marshall opposes exemptions because they are impossible to apply consistently, threaten rather than protect religious values and liberties, and favor religious belief systems over all others in violation of the establishment clause.

Key Questions: What was the legacy of Puritanism, Calvinism, Deism, rationalism, and European and American enlightenment for religious practices and freedoms in America in the 17th and 18th century? What did the founders mean by religion, establishment, free exercise, and limited government? What did they determine as the proper relationship between constitutional law and religious freedom? Must the government accommodate free exercise of religion by exempting religious individuals and groups from otherwise neutral laws (laws that do not target religious practices per se) that conflict with their religious values and rituals? Would (and should) such exemptions violate the establishment clause by favoring religious over secular beliefs?

Michael W. McConnell

The Origins and Historical Understanding of Free Exercise of Religion

In the winter of 1812–1813, Daniel Philips entered the confessional ... to confess to God that he had knowingly received stolen goods. ... Under centuries-old church doctrines, he could be confident that his confession would remain between him and God – that the priest would not reveal to anyone what he had to say. After Philips confessed his crime, [his] ... priest appeared before the court but pleaded in these words to be excused from testifying:

> [I]f called upon to testify in quality of a minister of a sacrament, in which my God himself has enjoined on me a perpetual and inviolable secrecy, I must declare to this honorable Court, that I cannot, I must not answer any question that has a bearing upon the restitution in question; and that it would be my duty to prefer instantaneous death or any temporal misfortune, rather than disclose the name of the penitent in question. ...

To this, the district attorney responded:

> [T]he constitution has granted religious "profession and worship" to all denominations, "without discrimination or preferance": but it has not granted exemption from previous legal duties. It has expelled the demon of persecution from our land: but it has not weakened the arm of public justice. Its equal and steady impartiality has soothed all the contending sects into the most harmonious equality, but to none of them has it yielded any of the rights of a well organized government.

Thus was posed an issue that continues to divide and trouble the legal system: does the freedom of religious exercise guaranteed by the constitutions of the states and United States require the government, in the absence

103 Harvard Law Review 1410 (1980). Used by permission.

of a sufficiently compelling need, to grant exemptions from legal duties that conflict with religious obligations? Or does this freedom guarantee only that religious believers will be governed by equal laws, without discrimination or preference?

The New York court in *People v. Philips* ruled that an exemption was constitutionally required. Although the government had a legitimate need and the authority to compel testimony, that need did not outweigh the interference with the relationship between priests and penitents in the Roman Catholic Church. This resolution of the conflict between generally applicable law and religious conscience had deep roots in the practices of the American states both before and after independence. But it was not until the full flowering of the Warren Court that the United States Supreme Court so interpreted the free exercise clause of the first amendment. In the meantime, the Court had upheld enforcement of anti-polygamy laws against Mormons, of child labor laws against a minor who wished to distribute religious tracts in the company of her aunt, of a public university's suspension of students who refused on account of their religious convictions against war to participate in ROTC, and of Sunday closing laws against Orthodox Jews who observed Sabbath on Saturday. ...

In *Sherbert v. Verner* [1963], the first and leading case in the Supreme Court's modern free exercise jurisprudence, the Court held that a Seventh-Day Adventist need not agree to work on Saturday in order to be eligible for unemployment compensation. Although a state has a legitimate need and the authority to limit unemployment benefits to those who make themselves available for work, it may not enforce the limitation when it conflicts with sincere religious practices. The state is "constitutionally compelled to *carve out an exception* – and not to provide benefits – for those whose unavailability is due to their religious convictions," as Justice Harlan disapprovingly put the point in dissent. The *Sherbert* decision thus created the potential for challenges by religious groups and individual believers to a wide range of laws that conflict with the tenets of their faiths, because such laws impose penalties either for engaging in religiously motivated conduct or for refusing to engage in religiously prohibited conduct. For example, in the same year that the Court decided *Sherbert*, it remanded for reconsideration in light of *Sherbert* the contempt conviction of a religious objector who refused jury service. A decade later, the Court exempted members of the Old Order Amish and the Conservative Amish Mennonite churches from compulsory education of children beyond the age of sixteen. Free exercise litigation since *Sherbert* has consisted almost entirely of requests for exemption rather than for general invalidation of restrictive laws.

The Court made no effort in *Sherbert* or subsequent cases to support its holdings through evidence of the historical understanding of "free exercise religion" at the time of the framing and ratification of the first amendment. This evident lack of historical support has made the decisions vulnerable to attack. ...

This Article analyzes the major philosophical, legal, and historical sources that preceded the free exercise clause of the first amendment to determine the probable understanding of those who drafted and ratified it. The focus is on exemptions from generally applicable laws. ...The conclusions of this analysis are (1) that exemptions were seen as a constitutionally permissible means for protecting religious freedom, (2) that constitutionally compelled exemptions were within the contemplation of the framers and ratifiers as a possible interpretation of the free exercise clause, and (3) that exemptions were consonant with the popular American understanding of the interrelation between the claims of a limited government and a sovereign God. While the historical evidence may not be unequivocal (it seldom is), it does, on balance, support *Sherbert*'s interpretation of the free exercise clause. ...

After a brief description of the ... modern free exercise doctrine in Part I, the Article proceeds chronologically. Part II canvasses the preconstitutional history of free exercise of religion in the American colonies and states by analyzing protections found in charters, constitutions, and statutes. This Part also discusses the works of the main philosophical, political, and religious figures of the time and examines actual controversies over free exercise exemptions. Part III discusses the framing of the free exercise clause of the first amendment. ... The conclusion, describes the relation between religion and government that best reflects the original conception of free exercise of religion.

While much of the analysis focuses on the specific doctrinal question of free exercise exemptions, this discussion has implications for the broader controversy involving the proper relationship between law and religious obligation in a liberal republic. ... The characteristic tendency of the modern legal system has been to assimilate the freedom of religion into the more familiar framework of Lockean liberal individualism. This denies the singularity of religion in life and, more particularly, in political life. Under this view the religion clauses of the first amendment become an instrument of secularism to be interpreted in secular terms. An understanding of the historical roots of free exercise exemptions casts doubt on this interpretation. It suggests instead a peculiarly American conception of the relation between religion and government – one that emphasizes the integrity and diversity of religious life rather than the secularism of the state.

A robust principle of liberty of conscience also conflicts with the alternative, nonliberal understanding of the governmental role, known as republicanism, under which the state has a responsibility to promote civic virtue among its citizens. The principle of free exercise of religion effectively removes government from the development and transmission of virtue at its most fundamental level – thus devolving upon voluntary religious societies (including those of atheists or agnostics) the central function thought by "republicans" to be vested in the state. The free exercise principle therefore suggests that modern attempts to understand the Founding as a clash between "liberal" and "republican" elements are radically incomplete. It points instead toward a social order that is neither strictly individualistic nor statist in its understanding of the good.

I. Free Exercise Doctrine Today

The basic framework of the free exercise exemptions doctrine is easily stated. If the plaintiff can show that a law or governmental practice inhibits the exercise of his religious beliefs, the burden shifts to the government to demonstrate that the law or practice is necessary to the accomplishment of some important (or "compelling") secular objective and that it is the least restrictive means of achieving that objective. If the plaintiff meets his burden and the government does not, the plaintiff is entitled to exemption from the law or practice at issue. In order to be protected, the claimant's beliefs must be "sincere," but they need not necessarily be consistent, coherent, clearly articulated, or congruent with those of the claimant's religious denomination. "Only beliefs rooted in religion are protected by the Free Exercise Clause"; secular beliefs, however sincere and conscientious, do not suffice.

Some twenty-five years after *Sherbert*, the legitimacy of this doctrine has increasingly come under attack, and the survival of the principle of free exercise exemptions is very much in doubt. Since 1972, the Court has rejected every claim for a free exercise exemption to come before it, outside the narrow context of unemployment benefits governed strictly by *Sherbert*. What once appeared to be a jurisprudence highly sympathetic to religious claims now appears virtually closed to them. Chief Justice Rehnquist and Justice Stevens have openly declared their opposition to the doctrine. ... Rehnquist has contended that when "a State has enacted a general statute, the purpose and effect of which is to advance the State's secular goals, the Free Exercise Clause does not ... require the State to conform that statute to the dictates of religious conscience of any group." Justice Stevens has stated that there is "virtually no room for a 'constitutionally required exemption' on religious grounds from a valid ... law that is entirely neutral in its general applications. ...

The debate over free exercise exemptions hinges on two different conceptions of the threat government poses to religious liberty. Under the no-exemptions view, the free exercise clause exists solely to prevent the government from singling out religious practice for peculiar disability. ... The remedy is to strike down the offending legislation and to treat religious institutions and practices the same way that comparable nonreligious institutions and practices are treated. Under the exemptions view, on the other hand, the free exercise clause protects religious practices against even the incidental or unintended effects of government action. The evil includes not only active hostility, but also majoritarian presuppositions, ignorance, and indifference. The remedy generally is to leave the government policy in place, but to carve out an exemption when the application of the policy impinges on religious practices without adequate justification.

Under both conceptions, it is unconstitutional for the government to inflict penalties on religious practices as such. For example, zoning ordinances disallowing churches while allowing meeting halls and other uses with comparable effects are unconstitutional, as are "anti-cult" legislation, laws barring clergy from public office, and charitable solicitation regulations crafted to disadvantage a particular religious sect. Under the no-exemptions view, however, religious believers and institutions cannot challenge facially neutral legislation, no matter what effect it may have on their ability or freedom to practice their religious faith. Thus a requirement that all witnesses must testify to facts within their knowledge bearing on a criminal prosecution – the requirement at issue in *Philips* – if applied without exception, could abrogate the confidentiality of the confessional. Similarly, a general prohibition of alcohol consumption could make the

Christian sacrament of communion illegal [and] uniform regulation of meat preparation could put kosher slaughterhouses out of business. ...

Both the exemption and no-exemption views can be expressed in terms of "neutrality" toward religion, but the way in which the two views define "neutrality" differs. Under the no-exemption position, a law or government practice is "neutral" if it makes no reference to religion and has a secular justification unrelated to the suppression of religion. Under the exemption position, a law or governmental practice is not "neutral" if it embodies the majority's view on a contested question of religious significance to the minority, even if that question is of no religious significance to the majority. For example, from the majority's perspective, a requirement that those seeking unemployment benefits be willing to work on Saturday seems secular and neutral. Only from the perspective of a sabbatarian do Saturday work environments have a religious dimension. Both the exemption and no-exemption views thus insist on neutral, "secular" laws and governmental practices, but the no-exemption view makes that judgment exclusively according to the perspective of the government, while the exemption view takes the perspective of the religious claimant, as well as the countervailing interests of the government, into account.

Likewise, these two interpretations agree that laws and governmental practices must be neutral *among* religions, but they differ about how this is to be accomplished. Under the no-exemption position, the best way to ensure equal treatment of all religions is to deny exemptions to all. The proponents of exemption, by contrast, observe that powerful and influential religions will usually receive adequate protection in the political arena. One rarely sees laws that force mainstream Protestants to violate their consciences. Judicially enforceable exemptions under the free exercise clause are therefore needed to ensure that unpopular or unfamiliar faiths will receive the same consideration afforded mainstream or generally respected religions by the representative branches.

Opposition to free exercise exemptions arises from two jurisprudentially distinct positions. The first looks to the constitutionally required separation of powers and is grounded in a philosophy of judicial restraint. This objection holds that courts are not the proper institutions to craft exemptions from generally applicable statutes that have a secular purpose and lack an intent to suppress religious freedom. Exemptions must be made by the legislature or executive officials acting within their delegated authority. ... The second objection, most forcefully articulated on the modern Court by

Justice Stevens, argues that whether made by courts or legislatures, exemptions directed to religion alone are generally unwarranted because determining the "sincerity" of religious claimants is dangerously intrusive, because granting exemptions for religious beliefs discriminates against secular beliefs, and because "special treatment" may give the appearance of aid to and endorsement of religion. While these two positions lead to virtually identical results in free exercise cases, they lead to opposite results in many cases involving the establishment clause, in which legislative exemptions and accommodations are at issue.

As this Article went to press, a five-Justice majority abandoned the free exercise exemptions doctrine except in cases involving a free exercise claim "in conjunction with other constitutional protections." The historical record casts doubt on this interpretation of the free exercise clause.

II. Free Exercise before the Constitution

A. Four Approaches to Church-State Relations in the Colonies

... During the early settlement of the colonies in the seventeenth century, England suffered from chronic religious strife and intolerance. The Church of England was the established church of the realm, and both Roman Catholicism and extreme Protestantism (of which Puritanism was the most prominent element) were suppressed. After the deposition of Charles I in the English Civil War, the Protestant dissenters assumed power, and Parliament took it upon itself to rewrite the prayer book and confession of faith, dissolve the episcopal structure of the Church, and confiscate the property of the bishoprics. Parliament ostensibly guaranteed free exercise of religion to most Protestants but denied religious freedom to "papists, the adherents of prelacy and the advocates of 'blasphemous, licentious or profane' doctrines. ..."

Upon restoration of the monarchy in 1660, Parliament reconstituted the Church of England. ... The Toleration Act of 1688 ended official persecution of Protestant dissenters but left the favored position of Anglicans unchanged. The anti-Catholic elements of the Test Act persisted throughout the eighteenth century.

The English religious policy did not automatically extend to the colonies, where four different approaches to church-state relations developed. The settlers of New England (outside of Rhode Island) were predominantly English Calvinists called "Puritans" or "Congregationalists." They moved to the wilderness of the New World in order to establish a Christian commonwealth where, for the first time in history, society would be directed by the revealed word of God. Both civil and church governance were established in accordance with their "congregational" understanding of church polity, under which each town would constitute a congregation and would select its own minister ... and would maintain a minister and church through compulsory taxes. Authority in the system was decentralized and genuinely democratic, but the results were foreordained. The local churches were invariably of the Congregationalist persuasion. Nonetheless, ministers in the system were accorded a high degree of autonomy from civil control, and indeed frequently lectured colonial authorities on their civic and spiritual derelictions.

Having carved their communities out of the rocky wilderness of a distant land, the Puritans of New England saw no reason to allow ungodly individuals to spoil their vision of a Christian commonwealth. This vision allowed no room for religious pluralism or even for toleration. "Polipiety [a variety of sects] is the greatest impiety in the world," according to a well-known tract by Nathaniel Ward. The great preacher John Cotton declared that "it was Toleration that made the world anti-Christian. ...."

Massachusetts, the most rigorous of the New England Congregationalist establishments, actively persecuted dissenters. Baptists were banished from the colony by statute in 1644, and four Quakers, who insisted on returning after being expelled, were hanged. ... By the 1680's, these violent measures came to an end, although the established church and the hostility to religious diversity continued in New England well into the nineteenth century.

By contrast, in Virginia the Church of England was established by order of the Crown and maintained, in large part, as an instrument of social control by the governing authorities and the local gentry. The government financed and tightly controlled the Church. Although Virginia and New England both maintained religious establishments, the two systems were in a more profound sense opposites. The New England establishments arose from a grassroots movement born of the conviction that religious truth should control all of society, while the Virginia establishment was imposed from above and dedicated to governmental control over religion.

... As in Massachusetts, harsh measures, including banishment, were authorized against Quakers, but there is little evidence that they were put into effect. ... The authorities blocked the Presbyterians' ability to preach at every turn, and the Baptists were "reviled" and "met with violence". ... In the eighteenth century, Virginia was the most intolerant of the colonies.

In time, the Virginia system spread to Maryland and throughout the South, though with less violence toward dissenters. Georgia, the last colony to be settled, represents an interesting variation. The Trustees of the Georgia colony firmly supported the established Church of England. With the assistance of the Anglican-based Society for the Propagation of the Gospel, they financed and supervised ministers, built churches, and encouraged attendance and support for religion. Unlike the Virginians, the Georgia Trustees demonstrated remarkable tolerance toward Protestant dissenters and even toward Jews. ... The third approach to religious liberty might be described as benign neglect. In New York and New Jersey, a policy of de facto religious toleration evolved, largely due to the extraordinary religious diversity of the area. Although the four counties of metropolitan New York had a formally established church, and although there were periodic episodes when the royal governor attempted to enforce conformity to the Anglican Church, for the most part Protestants remained free to live and worship in these colonies as they chose, and Quakers and Jews were generally unmolested.

The fourth approach to religious freedom in seventeenth-century America arouse in those colonies that were established explicitly as havens for religious dissenters. ... Maryland, the first haven for dissenters, was founded by a Catholic proprietor ... to provide a place for English Catholics to escape the persecution they suffered in the mother country. After 1689, however, the proprietor was removed and the Protestant majority in Maryland established the Church of England and initiated a program of discrimination and intolerance toward dissenters, particularly Roman Catholics. In the eighteenth century, Maryland rivaled Virginia for the narrowness and intolerance of its laws. Roger Williams, an extreme Protestant dissenter, founded Rhode Island as a refuge for those who could not endure the Massachusetts establishment. William Penn founded Pennsylvania and Delaware as sanctuaries for Quakers. Although each of these colonies was established for the benefit of a particular religious sect, all extended freedom of religion to groups beyond their own. Finally, Carolina was founded by a group of proprietors, with the assistance of John Locke, who followed Enlightenment principles of toleration. Early in the eighteenth century, North and South Carolina abandoned these principles and instituted a rigid establishment of the Church of England along lines parallel to Virginia's. It was in these colonies – Maryland, Rhode Island, Pennsylvania, Delaware, and Carolina – that the free exercise of religion emerged as an articulated legal principle.

The term "free exercise" first appeared in an American legal document in 1648, when Lord Baltimore required his new Protestant governor and councilors in Maryland to promise not to disturb Christians ("and inparticular no Roman Catholic") in the "free exercise" of their religion. ... The Maryland Assembly passed a statute containing the first "free exercise" clause on the continent: "noe person ... professing to beleive in Jesus Christ, shall from henceforth bee any waies troubled ... for ... his or her religion nor in the free exercise thereof ... nor any way [be] compelled to the beliefe or exercise of any other Religion. ..."

Rhode Island's Charter of 1663 was the first to use the formulation "liberty of conscience." The founder, Roger Williams, was a man of extreme and idiosyncratic religious views who was banished from Puritan Massachusetts. Williams wrote frequently, eloquently, and vituperatively in defense of freedom of conscience. With a few glaring exceptions (Rhode Island barred Jews from citizenship, a provision that was not abandoned until 1842, and barred Catholics from public office), the colony lived up to its royal Charter of 1663 as a "livelie experiment ... with a full libertie in religious concernements." In 1641, the legislature ordered that "none be accounted a delinquent for doctrine, provided that it be not directly repugnant to the government or laws established." This tends to support historian Thomas Curry's statement that "[t]he Rhode Island towns carefully reiterated that liberty of conscience did not exempt one from the civil law." Later, the royal Charter of 1663 protected residents of the colony from being "in any wise molested, punished, disquieted, or called into question, for any differences in opinione in matters of religion, and doe not actually disturb the civill peace of our sayd colony, and stated that they may "freelye and fullye have and enjoye his and theire owne judgments and consciences, in matters of religious concernments ...; they behaving themselves peaceblie and quietlie and not useing this libertie to lycentiousnesse and profanenesse. ..." This provision implies that believers were not required to obey *all* "laws established," but only those directed to maintaining the "civil peace" and preventing licentiousness and profaneness, or the injury of others.

It is tempting to assume that other American colonies observed and eventually imitated the vision of Roger Williams ... for the depth and breadth of the Rhode Island commitment to religious freedom were unparalleled until after the American Revolution. ... In fact, far from being a positive example, Rhode Island was the pariah among the colonies with a reputation for disorder and instability: "During and after the colonial period, Rhode Island, 'the licentious Republic' ... was an example to be shunned." It is unlikely that the Rhode Island provisions had much direct influence on subsequent developments of the free exercise principle.

... In 1664, the proprietors of Carolina issued an "Agreement" with prospective settlers, using words almost identical to the Rhode Island charter ... and two of the Carolina proprietors also obtained the grant of New Jersey, where they promulgated an almost identical provision. The language of the Rhode Island, Carolina, and New Jersey provisions represented the most common form of protection for religious freedom in the early colonies, although the provisions in other colonies were less expansive. The language did not survive in North Carolina, South Carolina, or New Jersey, as it was superseded by later (and more limited) religious freedom provisions. But the substance of these early provisions later reemerged as the most common pattern in the constitutions adopted by the states after the Revolution.

Three features of these early provisions warrant attention. First, the free exercise provisions expressly overrode any "Law, Statute or clause, usage or custom of this realm of England to the contrary." Second, they extended to all "judgments and contiences in matters of religion"; they were not limited to opinion, speech and profession, or acts of worship. Third, they limited the free exercise of religion only as necessary for the prevention of "Lycentiousnesse" or the injury or "outward disturbance of others," rather than by reference to all generally applicable laws. As discussed more fully below, these features are consistent with the idea of free exercise exemptions and indicate the lengthy pedigree of modern exemptions under the free exercise clause of the United States Constitution. ...

In actual practice, the most influential examples of religious pluralism were the middle colonies, where no church was established (except in the four counties of metropolitan New York) and the widest range of religious persuasions lived in relatve harmony. William Penn's colonies were particularly associated with religious freedom and harmony because of Penn's widely read work, *The Great Case of Liberty of Conscience*. ... Pennsylvania and Delaware protected the religious profession of all theists (but confined public office to Christians). This example caught the eye of states-men in other colonies, for Pennsylvania's promise of toleration contributed to the highest level of immigration of any of the colonies, and with immi-gration, prosperity. Madison later contrasted the religious repression of Virginia, which turned away useful settlers, with "[t]he allurements pres-ented by other situations," probably referring to Pennsylvania.

B. Locke and Theories of Religious Toleration

... This section concentrates on the thought of John Locke, both because his discussion of the religion question was most extensive and because his influence on the Americans and the first amendment was most direct. Jefferson carefully read and made notes on Locke's *The Reasonableness of Christianity* and his *Letters on Religious Toleration*. Major portions of Jefferson's Bill for Establishing Religious Freedom derived from passages in Locke's first *Letter Concerning Toleration*. Jefferson's bill, in turn, was one of the major precursors of the religion clauses of the first amendment. Four of the five states used language from Jefferson's bill in their proposals for a religion amendment. ... Locke's ideas also entered the American debate through the writings of Massachusetts Baptist apologist Isaac Backus. Locke's ideas, then, are an indispensable part of the intellectual backdrop for the framing of the free exercise clause. The ways in which American advocates of religious freedom departed from Locke, however, are as significant as the ways in which they followed him. ...

Writing in the aftermath of religious turmoil in England and throughout Europe, he viewed religious rivalry and intolerance as among the most important of political problems. Religious intolerance was inconsistent both with public peace and with good government. Locke's resolution of the problem involved two elements: a modification of the nature and claims of religion and an abandonment of the government's role in upholding truth. ... [He] urged that Christianity be made more rational and tolerant but less engaged in questions of earthly significance. Thus, the dissension among Christian denominations would be softened and would be less likely to create political problems. ...

Locke became an advocate of a sweeping toleration toward religious dissenters, with the exceptions of Catholics (because of their allegiance to a foreign prince), atheists (because they cannot be trusted to carry out their promises and oaths), and those who refuse to support tolerance for others.

"Nobody ... [has] any just title to invade the civil rights and worldly goods of [another], upon pretence of religion. ..."

In Locke's view, religious strife stems from the tendency of both religious and governmental leaders to overstep their bounds and intermeddle in the others' province: "I esteem it above all things necessary to distinguish exactly the business of civil government from that of religion, and to settle the just bounds that lie between the one and the other." The proper division between the realms of government and religion comes down to this: "all the power of civil government relates only to men's civil interests, is confined to the care of the things of this world, and hath nothing to do with the world to come," while "churches have [no] jurisdiction in worldly matters. ..."

To be sure, Locke's ideal of separation was less than complete, for he was willing to countenance governmental encouragement of the state religion. ... "But it is one thing to persuade, another to command; one thing to press with arguments, another with penalties." He also accepted government financial support of state religion and never condemned the English system of supporting the church with taxes. ... While Locke opposed what would be called interference with free exercise, he thus approved of what would be called an establishment under modern constitutional doctrine.

... Two aspects of Locke's teaching are particularly significant: his advocacy of legislative supremacy with respect to conflicts between public power and individual conscience and his rejection of religious exemptions. Although Locke's prescription for religious harmony depends upon the division between the religious and the secular jurisdictions, he anticipated that some matters, such as "[m]oral actions," belong to the jurisdiction both of the ... magistrate and conscience." He recognized that this creates "great danger, lest one of these jurisdictions intrench upon the other." As a practical matter, the possible overlap in jurisdiction did not greatly concern Locke, for "if government be faithfully administered, and the counsels of the magistrate be indeed directed to the public good," it will "seldom happen" that the magistrate enjoins "'any thing by his authority, that appears unlawful to the conscience of a private person.'" In theory, however, such clashes might occur; Locke proposed that under these circumstances the individual should disobey the law and accept punishment from the state. "[T]he private judgment of any person concerning a law enacted in political matters, for the public good, does not take away the obligation of that law, nor deserve a dispensation." ...

Locke's assertion of legislative supremacy and his opposition to special religious exemptions from generally applicable laws are consonant with arguments against free exercise exemptions. Unless there is reason to believe that the understanding of the free exercise clause held by the framers and ratifiers differed markedly from that of their intellectual forebear, Locke, *Sherbert* is historically unsupportable. As the next section demonstrates, however, the movement towards a more expansive notion of religious liberty would gain momentum in the wake of the American Revolution. ...

C. Development of the Expansive Conception of Religious Freedom

I. Disestablishment in the States. – The American Revolution immediately disrupted the relationship between religion and government in those states with an Anglican establishment. The Church of England was discredited during the Revolution by its connection to the Crown and the loyalist sympathies of most of its clergy. ...

The Congregational establishments of Connecticut, Massachusetts, New Hampshire and Vermont were more firmly entrenched and emerged from the Revolution strengthened by their association with the patriot cause. In reference to the Massachusetts Congregationalists, John Adams observed that "[w]e might as soon expect a change in the solar system, as to expect that they would give up their establishment. ..." By 1789 only these states maintained actual legal and financial support for the church. Outside of New England, only Maryland, South Carolina, and Georgia retained constitutional provisions permitting some form of establishment, and in none of these states did actual financial or other material support go into effect.

By 1834, no state in the Union would have an established church, and the tradition of separation between church and state would seem an ingrained and vital part of our constitutional system. But as the delegates gathered at the Constitutional Convention in Philadelphia in 1787 and at the meeting of the First Congress in New York in 1789, some form of establishment still held sway in most of New England, and the resolution of disestablishment controversies elsewhere could not be seen as assured.

2. The Evangelical Impetus Toward Religious Freedom. – The movement for freedom of religion in the 1780's was part of a broad reaction against the dominant but uninspired religious cultures represented by the Congregationalists of New England and the Anglicans of the South. It is a mistake to read the religion clauses under the now prevalent assumption that "the governing intellectual climate of the late eighteenth century was that of deism (or natural law)." America was in the wake of great religious revival. Historian Henry May has commented that the Enlightenment world view "excludes many, probably most, people who lived in America in the eighteenth and nineteenth centuries. To determine the meaning of the religion clauses, it is necessary to see them through the eyes of their proponents, most of whom were members of the most fervent and evangelical denominations in the nation.

One historian's portrait of ... the Virginia Baptists in the 1760's may help recreate the actual intellectual – more precisely, spiritual – climate among the proponents of religious freedom:

> Perhaps because they were at first largely lower class; perhaps because their worship sometimes caused their members to cry, bark like dogs, tremble, jerk, and fall to the ground; perhaps because they openly disdained the established religion and gentry mores; and perhaps because, as one Virginian charged, "they cannot meet a man on the road but they must ram a text of Scripture down his throat," the Baptists were reviled. They were seen as troublesome.

It must have been particularly irksome to the gentry that the Baptists converted slaves in large numbers and included them "as 'brothers' and 'sisters' in their close communities." Even the Presbyterians, now pillars of mainstream Protestantism, were considered dangerously "enthusiastic" (meaning fanatical) by the authorities. ...

The drive for religious freedom was part of this evangelistic movement. It is anachronistic to assume, based on modern patterns, that governmental aid to religion and suppression of heterodoxy were opposed by the more rationalistic and supported by the more intense religious believers of that era. The most intense religious sects opposed establishment on the ground that it injured religion and subjected it to the control of civil authorities. Guaranteed state support was thought to stifle religious enthusiasm and initiative. As Madison noted, the use of compulsory state taxes to support ministers would produce "pride and indolence in the Clergy; ignorance and servility in the laity." Moreover, establishment served as an instrument for state control over religion. This was particularly true in the states of the Anglican establishment, including Virginia, where the governor, legislature, and gentry exercised direct authority over the established church and the power of licensing over preachers of dissenting denominations. ...

The newer, more enthusiastic sects had the most to gain from breaking the monopoly of the old established church. This would allow new, often uneducated and itinerant preachers to conduct worship services and revival meetings and would make the financial support of a preacher dependent on the enthusiasm he generated among his adherents. The greatest support for disestablishment and free exercise therefore came from evangelical Protestant denominations, especially Baptists and Quakers, but also Presbyterians, Lutherans, and others. ...

Madison's *Memorial and Remonstrance Against Religious Assessments,* with its mixed religious and secular arguments against the relatively liberal form of establishment proposed for Virginia in 1785, garnered thousands of supportive signatures. Over twice as many Virginians, however, subscribed to petitions arguing against the assessment in frankly religious terms. ...

Religious rationalists, who are often credited with the leading intellectual role in the movement for religious freedom, were far more likely than the enthusiastic believers to side with the established church (with notable exceptions such as Jefferson). ...

The religious supporters of disestablishment and free exercise in the various states also supported adoption of constitutional protections at the federal level, for essentially the same reasons. They were joined in the latter cause by a heterogeneous coalition called the Antifederalists, who used the absence of a bill of rights as an argument against ratification of the Constitution. This was little more than a marriage of political convenience, for the advocates of religious freedom had little in common with the political principles of most Antifederalists. The Baptists of Virginia must have found it awkward to join forces with Patrick Henry, Virginia's leading Antifederalist, who had so recently championed the movement for religious assessments. Yet in the ratification convention in Virginia it was Henry who took up the issue of religious freedom and the absence of a Bill of Rights, while Madison, the erstwhile supporter of religious freedom, urged ratification of the Constitution without amendment.

The political theory of the advocates of free exercise sharply conflicted with the "republican" ideology that prevailed among most Antifederalists (as well as many Federalists). The central preoccupation of republican political theory was the necessity of public "virtue." In its religious manifestation, this meant that government should support and encourage religion in order to promote public morality. ... The most famous statement of this sort was Washington's farewell address, in which he stated that "[o]f all the dispositions and habits which lead to political prosperity, religion and morality are indispensable supports. ... And let us with caution indulge the supposition that morality can be maintained without religion."

These arguments ran directly contrary to the position of the evangelical advocates of the religion clauses. To be sure, these advocates did not deny that religion is necessary to civil society. Isaak Backus, for example, affirmed that "religion is as necessary for the well-being of human society as salt is to preserve from putrefaction or as light is to direct our way and to guard against enemies, confusion, and misery." But they did deny that governmental support is necessary, or even useful, to religion. ...

The paradox of the religious freedom debates ... is that one side employed essentially secular arguments based on the needs of civil society for the support of religion, while the other side employed essentially religious arguments based on the primacy of duties to God over duties to the state in support of disestablishment and free exercise. It was Baptist preacher John Leland who first stated that "[t]he notion of a Christian commonwealth, should be exploded forever."

Although the secular strain of republicanism was less an object of the evangelicals' polemics, it was no less inconsistent with their understanding of the proper role of the state. Civic republicanism sought to inculcate public virtue through various devices, including sumptuary laws, education, and participatory politics. To the evangelical ... this too was a vain extension of the governmental sphere; virtue is either impossible or incoherent when divorced from duty to God. Their position places the state in the precarious posture of depending upon autonomous institutions to preserve the moral conditions necessary to the survival of republican government.

Thus, the evangelical position ultimately coalesced with the secular liberal position, against ... civic republicanism. This explains why the more fervent evangelicals, including the Baptists, tended to become Jeffersonians, notwithstanding the deism of Jefferson and the piety of his opponents. Religion, the evangelicals believed, is vital to civic harmony. But voluntary religious societies – not the state – are the best and only legitimate institutions for the transmission of religious faith and, with it, virtue. The only support that churches can legitimately expect from the government, apart from equal participation in the benefits of civil society, is protection and noninterference.

3. Advances Beyond Locke in the Popular Understanding of Religious Freedom. – The same evangelical forces converged in support of protections for religious liberty through free exercise provisions in state constitutions.

It is no accident that Locke's vocabulary ("toleration of religion") was rejected in favor of more sweeping terms – not just the "exercise," but the "free exercise" of religion, or "full and equal rights of conscience." When George Mason proposed the term "toleration" for the religious liberty clause of the Virginia Bill of Rights, Madison objected on the ground that the word "toleration" implies an act of legislative grace, which in Locke's understanding it was. Madison proposed, and the Virginia assembly adopted, the broader phrase: "the full and free exercise of [religion]". ...

a) Judicial Review. – One reason that Locke's doctrines may have seemed so limited from an American perspective is that he did not envision an authority within the law that was capable of limiting the sovereign power of the "magistrate" (by which he meant the government, the King, and Parliament). ...

Once the courts are vested with the power to determine the proper boundary between individual conscience and the magistrate's authority, based on the words of a written charter derived from the people, fuller protection for conscience becomes conceivable. An independent judiciary could define religious liberty affirmatively, in terms of what religious liberty requires, and not merely what the legislature concedes. The modern "judicial restraint" position, that legislatures are entitled to make free exercise exemptions but courts are not, is a relic of Lockean legislative supremacy. Once the people empowered the courts to enforce the boundary between individual rights and the magistrate's power, they entrusted the courts with a responsibility that prior to 1789 had been exercised only by the legislature.

b) The Nature and Role of Religion. – To Locke, religious divisions and discord presented a political problem; the solution was to keep the peace by making religion irrelevant to the things of this world – other than a reasonable, uncontroversial advocacy of good morals, which would be fully consistent with the public good, publicly defined. This was not the religious enthusiasts' idea of religion ... [or] religious liberty. To them, the church-state problem was principally a religious problem: the state too frequently used its power to prevent the practice and spread of the gospel. The Baptists languishing in the Culpepper jail and Presbyterians fighting legislative interference with their form of church governance were not fearful of religion. They were fearful of government. To the evangelical spirit of the minority Protestant sects in America, Locke's conception of the separation between the secular and the religious would have seemed absurd. Does not the will of God govern all of life? ... To the preachers who only recently had been among the leading advocates of revolution against the King, Locke's claim that they should be "forbidden meddling with making or executing laws in their preaching" must have seemed quaint, as well as presumptuous. If Locke and Jefferson wished to promote a peaceable, rational religion that minds its own business, is tolerant of others, and does not meddle in affairs of state, their aspirations were diametrically opposed to those whose political efforts produced the first amendment.

These differing conceptions of the purposes of religious freedom have clear implications for the question of free exercise exemptions. From the religious perspective, the scope of free exercise cannot be defined, in the first instance, by asking what matters the public is rightly concerned about. Religion involves itself in many matters of importance to the public. Free exercise must be defined, in the first instance, by what matters God is concerned about, according to the conscientious belief of the individual.

In this respect, Madison's argument in the *Memorial and Remonstrance* echoed evangelical convictions about the roles of religion and civil government. His position that duty to God precedes the claims of civil society strongly resembles the teachings of John Witherspoon, the nation's leading Presbyterian clergyman and President of the College of New Jersey (Princeton) while Madison was a student. ...

The demands of civil society must be judged against the demands of God. That is why the "servants of God" seem "troublesome" and why a society that determines to respect the claims of conscience must recognize exemptions from its laws.

While the argument for exemptions tended to be oblique and by implication, opponents of free exercise automatically assumed that liberty of conscience must entail exemptions, and thus claimed that free exercise was tantamount to anarchy. Proponents of exemptions could have responded by denying any claim to exemptions and confining their opposition to discriminatory treatment. But this was not their approach. Proponents did attempt to minimize the practical consequences of the exemptions position by stoutly declaring their fealty to almost all of the laws. But they cleverly used ambiguous language to leave open the theoretical possibility that conscience would prevail over wrongful legislation. ...

4. *The Views of the Framers.* ... Like Locke, Jefferson favored a mild,

tolerant, and rationalistic brand of religion. ... As Locke advocated a watered-down and de-politicized Christianity ... so Jefferson took the more radical step of composing his own version of the gospels, excluding everything at variance with his understanding of science and natural morality. Jefferson far surpassed Locke in his hostility to orthodox Christianity. Jefferson called Athanasius and Calvin – the pillars of Catholic and Reformed theology – "impious dogmatists" and "mere usurpers of the Christian name, teaching a counter-religion made up of the *deliria* of crazy imaginations." He denied the divinity of Christ and the authority of scripture, condemned the Protestant doctrine that forgiveness of sins is achieved through repentance as opposed to good works, and ridiculed Presbyterians, among others, for "fanaticism" in matters of religion. He was equally contemptuous of Judaism, whose theology he called "degrading and injurious" and whose ethics he called "repulsive."

Jefferson advocated religious freedom, in large part, as a means of combatting religious enthusiasm and advancing the day when all would become adherents of Unitarianism, his idea of rational and sensible religion. ...

In many respects, Jefferson advocated a fuller freedom of religion than Locke ... Jefferson opposed any form of state-established church, even the broad multiple establishment proposed for Virginia. Unlike Locke, Jefferson would extend toleration to atheists and Catholics, though he appeared to agree that toleration should be denied those who would not tolerate others. Unlike Locke, Jefferson would deny all power to the government to provide financial support for religious teaching, arguing that "to compel a man to furnish contributions of money for the propagation of opinions which he disbelieves and abhors, is sinful and tyrannical". ...

Jefferson's understanding of the scope and rationale of free exercise rights, however, was more limited than Locke's. Like Locke, he based his advocacy of freedom of religion on the judgment that religion, properly confined, can do no harm: "The legitimate powers of government extend to such acts only as are injurious to others. But it does me no injury for my neighbour to say there are twenty gods or no god." On this rationale, Jefferson espoused a strict distinction between belief, which should be protected from governmental control, and conduct, which should not. As he wrote in his famous "wall of separation" letter to the Danbury Baptist Association, "legislative powers of government reach actions only, and not opinions ... [M]an ... has no natural right in opposition to his social duties." It was in reliance on Jefferson that the Supreme Court later held that there can be no free exercise right to exemption from a generally applicable law when such laws are directed at actions and not opinions.

Jefferson's advocacy of a belief-action distinction placed him at least a century behind the argument for full freedom of religious exercise in America. William Penn wrote in 1670 that "by *Liberty of Conscience*, we understand not only a meer *Liberty of the Mind*, in believing or disbelieving ... *but the exercise of ourselves in a visible way of worship*." ... St. George Tucker, no radical, wrote in 1803 that "[l]iberty of conscience in matters of religion consists in the absolute and unrestrained exercise of our religious opinions, *and duties,* in that mode which our own reason and conviction dictate." Thus, while Jefferson was one of the most advanced advocates of disestablishment, his position on free exercise was extraordinarily restrictive for his day.

Although often linked with Jefferson's "Enlightenment-deist-rationalist" stance toward religious freedom, Madison's views on the religion-state question should be distinguished from those of his fellow Virginian, and hence from Locke. To begin with, Madison possessed a far more sympathetic attitude toward religion than did Jefferson. ... None of Madison's writings displayed the disdain Jefferson expressed for the more intense manifestations of religious spirit. Indeed, the sight of "5 or 6 well meaning men" – Baptist preachers imprisoned in Culpepper, Virginia "for publishing their religious Sentiments which in the main are very orthodox" – sparked his concern for religious freedom. ... In all Jefferson's writings about liberty of conscience, he never once showed concern for those who wish to practice an active faith; to Jefferson, unlike Madison, liberty of conscience meant largely freedom from sectarian religion, rather than freedom to practice religion in whatever form one chooses.

Consistent with this more affirmative stance toward religion, Madison advocated a jurisdictional division between religion and government based on the demands of religion rather than solely on the interests of society. In his *Memorial and Remonstrance*, he wrote:

> The Religion then of every man must be left to the conviction and conscience of every man; and it is the right of every man to exercise it as these may dictate. ... It is the duty of every man to render to the Creator such homage, and such only, as he believes to be acceptable to him.

Moreover, Madison claimed that this duty to the Creator is "precedent both in order to time and degree of obligation to the claims of Civil

Society," and "therefore that in matters of Religion, no man's right is abridged by the institution of Civil Society."

This striking passage illuminates the radical foundations of Madison's writings. ... While it does not prove that Madison supported exemptions, it suggests an approach toward religious liberty consonant with them. If the scope of religious liberty is defined by religious duty (man must render to God "such homage ... as he believes to be acceptable to him"), and if the claims of civil society are subordinate to the claims of religious freedom, it would seem to follow that the dictates of religious faith must take precedence over the laws of the state, even if they are secular and generally applicable. This is the central point on which Madison differs from Locke, Jefferson, and other Enlightenment advocates of religious freedom. ...

No other political figure played so large a role in the enactment of the religion clauses as Jefferson and Madison. To a large extent, Jefferson reflected the rationalist premises of Locke, and it is these premises that the modern courts and commentators have relied upon in arguing for a no-exemption interpretation of the free exercise clause. The evidence indicates, however, that Madison, with his more generous vision of religious liberty, more faithfully reflected the popular understanding of the free exercise provision that was to emerge both in state constitutions and the Bill of Rights.

D. Legal Protections After Independence

... Eleven of the thirteen states (plus Vermont) adopted new constitutions between 1776 and 1780. Of those eleven, six (plus Vermont) included an explicit bill of rights; three more states adopted a bill of rights between 1781 and 1790. With the exception of Connecticut, every state, with or without an establishment, had a constitutional provision protecting religious freedom by 1789, although two states confined their protections to Christians and five other states confined their protections to theists. There was no discernible difference between the free exercise provisions adopted by the states with an establishment and those without. ...

These state constitutions provide the most direct evidence of the original understanding, for it is reasonable to infer that those who drafted and adopted the first amendment assumed the term "free exercise of religion" meant what it had meant in their states. The wording of the state provisions thus casts light on the meaning of the first amendment. ...

1. Scope of the Liberty. – Each of the state constitutions first defined the scope of the free exercise right in terms of the conscience of the individual believer and the actions that flow from that conscience. None of the provisions confined the protection to beliefs and opinions, as did Jefferson, nor to expression of beliefs and opinions, as some recent scholars have suggested. The language appears to have been drafted precisely to refute those interpretations. Maryland, for example, prohibited punishment of any person "on account of his religious persuasion *or* profession, *or* for his religious practice." Opinion, expression of opinion, and practice were all expressly protected. The key word "exercise," found in six of the constitutions, was defined in dictionaries of the day to mean "action." Two other constitutions used terms as broad or broader. ... The free exercise provisions defined the free exercise right affirmatively, based on the scope of duties to God perceived by the believer. The New Hampshire formulation defined the believer's right by "the dictates of *his own* conscience, and reason"; it extended to all "matters of religious concernment," according to Rhode Island. These could, and often would, include matters of concern to the public. This is consistent with the proposition, reflected in Madison's *Memorial and Remonstrance*, that the right of free exercise precedes and is superior to the social contract.

Although the free exercise right plainly extends to some forms of conduct, the scope of protected conduct in these clauses is less clear. ... Four states – Virginia, Georgia, Maryland, and Rhode Island – protected all actions stemming from religious conviction, subject to certain limitations. The Virginia Bill of Rights, the model for three of the state proposals for the first amendment and presumably the greatest influence on Madison, is especially clear on this point. It provides that "all men are equally entitled to the free exercise of religion, according to the dictates of conscience" and defines "religion" as "the duty which we owe to our creator. ..."

By contrast, eight states ... plus the Northwest Ordinance, confined their protection of conduct to acts of "worship." The word "worship" usually signifies the rituals or ceremonial acts of religion, such as the administration of sacraments or singing of hymns, and thus would indicate a more restrictive scope for the free exercise provisions.

The limitation to "worship" was not carried over into the federal free exercise clause. ... No direct evidence suggests whether the adoption of the broader formulation was deliberate, but this seems consistent with the general theological currents of Protestant America, which were "low church" and anti-ritualistic. One of the main elements of the Great Awakening was the insistence that duties to God extend beyond the four walls of the church and the partaking of the sacraments. From the evangelical Protestant perspective, "worship" would not have been sharply distinguished from "the duty we owe to our Creator." The ready availability of narrow models in the ... Northwest Ordinance and the constitution of final drafter Fisher Ames' home state of Massachusetts makes it likely that the choice of broader language was deliberate. The federal free exercise clause seems in every respect to have followed the most expansive models among the states.

Even in the states that apparently limited free exercise to acts of "worship," it is not clear that the limitation had any actual effect. In none of the state free exercise cases in the early years of the Republic did the lawyers argue or the courts hold that religiously motivated conduct was unprotected because it was not "worship". ...

It would be difficult on this evidence to conclude that the framers of the free exercise clause intended it to be confined to acts of "worship." That would require the assumption that Fisher Ames and the First Congress accidentally failed to use familiar language that would have precisely expressed their meaning and adopted instead new language that went beyond their intentions. Either the broader meaning was intended, or no thought was given to the matter at all.

2. *Limits on the Liberty*. ... Nine of the states limited the free exercise right to actions that were "peaceable" or that would not disturb the "peace" or "safety" of the state. Four of these also expressly disallowed acts of licentiousness or immorality. ...

These provisos are the most revealing and important feature of the state constitutions. They further confirm that the free exercise right was not understood to be confined to beliefs. Beliefs without more do not have the capacity to disturb the public peace and safety. ... Moreover, the state provisions make sense only if free exercise envisions religiously compelled exemptions from at least some generally applicable laws. Since even according to the Lockean no-exemptions view, religious persons cannot be prohibited from engaging in otherwise legal activities, the provisos would only have effect if religiously motivated conduct violated the general laws in some way. The "peace and safety" clauses identify a narrower subcategory of the general laws; the free exercise provisions would exempt religiously motivated conduct from these laws up to the point that such conduct breached public peace or safety. ...

The wording of the state constitutions also provides some guidance regarding when the government's interest is sufficiently strong to override an admitted free exercise claim. The modern Supreme Court has stated only that the government's interest must be "compelling," "of the highest order," "overriding," or unusually important. ...

The most common feature of the state provisions was the government's right to protect public peace and safety. ... Where the rights of others are not involved, however, the free exercise right prevails. The state constitutional provisions give no warrant to paternalistic legislation touching on religious concerns. They protect the "public" peace and safety but respect the right of the believer to weigh spiritual costs without governmental interference. Thus, some modern free exercise controversies, such as the refusal by Jehovah's Witnesses to receive blood transfusions or the enforcement of minimum wage laws in a religious community, should be easy to resolve and require no subjective judicial judgments about the importance of public policy. Moreover, the early free exercise clauses seem to allow religious institutions to define their own doctrine, membership, organization, and internal requirements without state interference. ...

Obvious connections exist between the scope of the free exercise right defined by these provisions and the wider liberal political theory of which they are an expression. The central conception of liberalism, as summarized in the Declaration of Independence, is that government is instituted by the people in order to secure their rights to life, liberty, and the pursuit of happiness. Governmental powers are limited to those needed to secure these legitimate ends. ... Except as needed for mutual protection and a limited class of common interests, government must leave the definition of the good life to private institutions, of which family and church are the most conspicuous. Even in the absence of a free exercise clause, liberal theory would find the assertion of governmental power over religion illegitimate, except to the extent necessary for the protection of others.

To eighteenth-century evangelicals, this issue was posed in theological terms but the answer was much the same. God instituted government for the punishment of wrongdoing, which they interpreted to mean injury to others. While the evangelicals could not accede to the Lockean proposition that the reach of governmental authority is defined by the judgments of civil authorities, they found the liberal theory of government a way to reconcile their insistence on the primacy of conscience with their equal insistence on the divinely ordained authority of government. ...

The "peace and safety" limitations of the state constitutions are therefore neither simple restatements of governmental supremacy in a clash with religious precepts, nor mere expedient exceptions to what would otherwise be unlimited rights of religiously motivated conduct. Both the affirmative free exercise protections and the peace and safety limitations follow logically from the liberal and evangelical theories of government, which reached similar conclusions from different premises about the origin and scope of legitimate government.

E. Actual Free Exercise Controversies

An examination of actual free exercise controversies in the preconstitutional period bears out these conclusions. To be sure, the issue of exemptions did not often arise. The American colonies were peopled almost entirely by adherents of various strains of Protestant Christianity. The Protestant moral code and mode of worship was, for the most part, harmonious with the mores of the larger society. Even denominations like the Quakers, whose theology and religious practice differed sharply from the others, entertained similar beliefs about the public decorum. Moreover, the governments of that era were far less intrusive than the governments of today. Thus, the occasions when religious conscience came into conflict with generally applicable secular legislation were few.

Nonetheless, the issue of exemptions did arise, primarily centered around three issues: oath requirements, military conscription, and religious assessments. The resolution of these conflicts suggests that exemptions were seen as a natural and legitimate response to the tension between law and religious convictions. ...

Rather than make oaths, military service, and tithes voluntary for everyone, which would undercut important public programs and objectives, and rather than coerce the consciences of otherwise loyal and law-abiding citizens who were bound by religious duty not to comply, the colonies and states wrote special exemptions into their laws. Lest the exemptions be extended too broadly, they confined the exemptions to denominations or categories known or proven to be "conscientiously" opposed. This aspect of the historical practice parallels in its purposes the requirement of "sincerity" under current law, although the tendency to recognize only those beliefs that are a formal part of the religious dogma of the claimant's denomination has been superseded by a more individualistic view of religious conscience.

An obvious objection to all these examples would be that they were initiated by the legislature. ... If, however, as seems to be the case, the exemptions were granted because legislatures believed the free exercise principle required them, it is reasonable to suppose that framers of constitutional free exercise provisions understood that similar applications of the principle would be made by the courts, once courts were entrusted with the responsibility of enforcing the mandates of free exercise.

III. The Federal Free Exercise Clause

The original Constitution ... contained no provision protecting the general freedom of religion. It was not, however, entirely silent about religion. Two provisions of the Constitution reflect a spirit and purpose similar to that of the free exercise clause: the prohibition on religious tests for office in article VI, and the allowance of affirmations in lieu of oaths in articles I, II, and VI. Both provisions were designed to prevent restrictions hostile to particular religions and thus to make the government of the United States more religiously inclusive. Neither provision, however, used the device of a religion-specific exemption.

The framer's decision to ban religious tests was a dramatic departure from the prevailing practice in the states, eleven of which then banned non-Christians and at least four of which banned non-Protestants from office. While innovative in practice, however, the provision was unexceptional in theory ... Religious tests for office are classic examples of laws that single out particular religious beliefs for peculiar disability, and they would be unconstitutional under any intelligible construction of the religion clauses. ...

The significance of the "oath or affirmation" provisions is more subtle. Oaths of office were serious matters. ... The 1787 Constitution requires that *state* as well as federal officers be "bound by Oath or Affirmation, to support this Constitution" – one of the few provisions of the Constitution directed at state officers. Yet the framers of the Constitution realized that several small religious sects, including the influential Quakers, refused to swear oaths. ... Lest members of these sects be excluded from office, it was necessary to provide alternatives.

As has already been noted, this problem had arisen in most of the states in connection with the oaths required of witnesses in court, as well as with oaths of office. The usual solution was to create an exemption only for those with the religious objection and to require all others to take the oath. The framers of the federal Constitution, however, did not follow this model; they allowed any person, whether "conscientiously scrupulous" or not, to promise by affirmation instead of oath. ...

The new Constitution made no other provision for religious differences. ... The prevailing view among Federalists, supporters of the Constitution, was that additional guarantees of individual liberty were unnecessary. Explicit guarantees might even be counterproductive, since the express mention of some liberties might be taken to disparage the existence of other rights, which were adequately secured through the careful enumeration and delimitation of federal powers.

Other participants in the debate were less trustful of the novel and distant federal government. Patrick Henry complained that a too-powerful federal government could override religious freedoms that had been hard won at the state level. "Philadelphiensis," a Pennsylvania pamphleteer, objected to the transfer of control over military service to the federal government for fear that the Quakers would lose the exemptions from compulsory service they had won at the state level. ... John Leland, opposed ratification on the ground that religious freedom was "not sufficiently secured." "[I]f Oppression dose not ensue," he wrote, "it will be owing to the Mildness of administration & not to any Constitutional defence." In the Rhode Island town meetings of 1788–89, citizens spoke out against the lack of protection for liberty of conscience "and other fundamental liberties," and the state refused to ratify the Constitution until after the Bill of Rights had been proposed. Others, perhaps more numerous, supported ratification but demanded amendments incorporating a bill of rights. These advocates were sufficiently persuasive (or sufficiently numerous) to extract the promise of a Bill of Rights as the price for ratification of the rest of the Constitution.

Perhaps the most significant political battleground for future development of a strong protection for religious freedom was in Virginia, where James Madison, recently returned from the Constitutional Convention, was seeking a seat in the first House of Representatives. Like other proponents of the Constitution of 1787, Madison initially lacked enthusiasm for adding a Bill of Rights, though he came to recognize the need for one to assuage the demands of the Antifederalist opposition. ... On advice of his political adviser. ... Madison contacted Baptist leaders and proclaimed his support for "the most satisfactory provisions for all essential rights, particularly the rights of Conscience in the fullest latitude." He then championed a constitutional provision for religious liberty as a campaign issue. The Baptist leaders responded by giving him their electoral support, which contributed to his narrow margin of victory. ...

There were two strands to the Federalist argument against a free exercise amendment. First, under the Constitution, the new federal government was not given any powers to pass laws affecting religion. As Madison told the Virginia ratifying convention, "There is not a shadow of right in the general government to intermeddle with religion. Its least interference with it would be a most flagrant usurpation." Proponents of a free exercise amendment understandably rejected this argument. The federal government would exercise plenary regulatory authority in the territories, the District of Columbia, and the military. Its powers of taxation, spending, immigration and naturalization, international trade, and relations with Indian tribes and foreign governments could, with little imagination, be expected to affect the exercise of religion. The potential of the necessary and proper clause ... was viewed, according to Madison as the most threatening of all. Thus, a federal government bent on religious oppression could accomplish such oppression under pretext of one of the enumerated powers. Moreover, the argument that the lack of enumerated power could serve as a sufficient assurance of religious liberty offered no comfort to those who understood free exercise of religion to entail exemption from otherwise legitimate general legislation. ...

The second strand of the Federalist argument was more persuasive. The Federalists argued that the structure of government, combined with the multiplicity of religious sects, would provide an effective guarantee against religious oppression. Madison ... typified this position:

> Religion is not guarded; there is no bill of rights declaring that religion should be secure. ... Happily for the states, they enjoy the utmost freedom of religion. This freedom arises from that multiplicity of sects which pervades America, and which is the best and only security for religious liberty in any society; for where there is such a variety of sects, there cannot be a majority of any one sect to oppress and persecute the rest.

This argument exactly parallels Madison's famous defense of the Constitutional structure in *Federalist* No. 51. There he says that the "security for civil rights must be the same as that for religious rights. It consists in the one case in the multiplicity of interests, and in the other in the multiplicity of sects." The best cure for factional oppression is a large republic with many conflicting factions and a representative government with check and balances.

If the principal danger to religious liberty was the deliberate oppression of religious minorities by the majority, then the Madisonian vision offered a more powerful answer to those demanding a free exercise clause. In a nation of many different religious groups, each jealous of the others, it would be difficult if not impossible for any group to impose its beliefs on the others. Yet Madison's argument did not carry the day. Perhaps the reason is that his argument did not satisfy the concerns of those ... who feared not deliberate oppression, but the unintended effects of legislation passed without regard to the religious scruples of small minorities. The multiplicity of sects provides no protection against ignorance or indifference. ...

Federalist assurances thus failed to assuage the concerns of America's religious sects, including many of Madison's own constituents. Only a bill of rights would do.

Framing and Ratifying the Free Exercise Clause

1. Debates in the First Congress. – Madison admitted that the lack of a provision protecting the rights of conscience had "alarmed many respectable Citizens," and he pledged to work for "the most satisfactory provisions for all essential rights, particularly the rights of Conscience in the fullest latitude." ... Lawmakers in other states responded to the same popular pressure. Seven states drafted proposals for amendments, and five of them (plus the minority report in Pennsylvania) urged protection for religious freedom. ...

The recorded debates in the House over these proposals cast little light on the meaning of the free exercise clause. Indeed, the main controversy during these debates centered on establishment. The key changes in free exercise language ... took place after the recorded debate. Thus, we must rely primarily on the successive drafts of the clause during its passage through the First Congress.

Madison undertook an initial draft of the Bill of Rights, to be proposed to the House of Representatives. His draft free exercise clause did not follow the language of the state proposals. ... "The civil rights of none shall be abridged on account of religious belief or worship, [n]or shall any national religion be established, nor shall the full and equal rights of conscience be in any manner, nor on any pretext, infringed." Three aspects of the Madison proposal are suggestive. First, the formulation "full and equal rights of conscience" implies that the liberty has both a substantive and an equality component: the rights must be both "full" and "equal." Hence, the liberty of conscience is entitled not only to equal protection, but also to some absolute measure of protection apart from mere governmental neutrality.

Second, the formulation that the rights in question shall not "in any manner nor on any pretext" be infringed suggests protection from infringements in any form, even those not expressly directed at religious practice. This proposal recognized that infringements on rights of conscience could result from Congress' exercise of its enumerated powers even when the legislation made no direct reference to religion. For the most part these infringements would be indirect – secular laws that invaded religious freedom as applied, rather than acts directed toward religious practice or belief as such.

Third, Madison favored the formulation "rights of conscience" over the formulation "free exercise of religion," which was found both in his own state's laws and in three of the five state proposals. ...

Rather than debating Madison's proposal, the Select Committee proposed a shorter version: "no religion shall be established by law, nor shall the equal rights of conscience be infringed." ... If this change was more than stylistic, which seems doubtful, it might suggest a move toward a no-exemptions view of free exercise, since it emphasizes equal treatment rather than full substantive protection.

The Select Committee language ran into trouble in the House, largely because of concerns that its establishment provision might interfere with the ability of the states to support religion – an issue especially important to those states with established churches. ... The House adopted a formulation proposed by Fisher Ames of Massachusetts: "Congress shall make no law establishing religion, or to prevent the free exercise thereof, or to infringe the rights of conscience." This version omitted the modifiers "full" and "equal" from the phrase "rights of conscience." This suggests that the deletion of "full" by the Committee was no more than stylistic and that the word "equal" was deleted so as not to create a negative inference.

More strikingly, the Ames version introduced a new term into the debate: "free exercise of religion." "Free exercise" had been part of most of the state proposals but had not appeared in the Madison, Select Committee, or New Hampshire proposals previously debated in the House, all of which had used the alternative formulation "rights of conscience." In many contexts, the phrases "rights of conscience" and "free exercise of religion" seem to have been used interchangeably. But here, Ames, a notoriously careful draftsman and meticulous lawyer, thought it necessary to use both terms. ... the House passed and sent to the Senate a proposed amendment slightly different from the Ames proposal: "Congress shall make no law establishing Religion, or prohibiting the free exercise thereof, nor shall the rights of conscience be infringed." ...

In the Senate, the debate was not recorded, but ... the versions adopted, in order, were as follows:

(1) "Congress shall make no law establishing one religious sect or society in preference to others, nor shall the rights of conscience be infringed."

(2) "Congress shall make no law establishing religion, or prohibiting the free exercise thereof."

(3) "Congress shall make no law establishing articles of faith or a mode of worship, or prohibiting the free exercise of religion. ..."

Note that each of these versions used either the phrase "rights of conscience" or the phrase "free exercise of religion." No version used the phrases in conjunction, as had the Ames proposal.

The third version passed the Senate and was transmitted to the House, which rejected it, presumably because of its narrow provision on establishment. A Conference Committee, on which Madison served, proposed the version of the religion clauses that was ultimately ratified. The free exercise clause itself was unchanged from the final Senate bill.

... In addition to the provision already discussed, which applied only to the federal government, Madison proposed an amendment that would have been applicable to the states. It read: "[N]o State shall infringe the equal rights of conscience, nor the freedom of speech or of the press, nor of the right of trial by jury in criminal cases." Madison said that he conceived this to be "the most valuable amendment in the whole list. If there were any reason to restrain the Government of the United States from infringing upon these essential rights, it was equally necessary that they should be secured against the State Governments." Significantly, Madison did not propose that the establishment clause be made applicable to the states; this reflects the prevailing view at the time that states should be permitted to set their own course with respect to establishment, but that liberty of conscience was an unalienable right. ... Later the Senate rejected the proposal, presumably in deference to states' rights. This left the provisions of the Bill of Rights solely as limitations against the federal government, as they were to remain until the Supreme Court held that they had been selectively "incorporated" pursuant to the fourteenth amendment. ...

2. *Ratification.* – The ratification debates in the state legislatures were unilluminating. Most states ratified the proposed amendments quickly, with little debate or controversy. Three states – Georgia, Massachusetts, and Connecticut – failed to ratify, but the refusal seems to have been unrelated to questions of religious freedom. Only in Virginia is there record of opposition to the religion clauses as proposed by Congress. In Virginia, the Senate delayed ratification of the first amendment, partly on the ground that it "does not prohibit the rights of conscience from being violated or infringed". ...

3. *Two Issues of Interpretation.* ...

a) *The Meaning of "Prohibiting."* – The prior drafts considered by the House used the verbs "infringing" or "preventing" to describe the forbidden effect on the rights of conscience. Moreover, in parallel clauses of the first amendment, the framers used the verb "abridging" to protect the freedoms of speech, assembly, and petition. The Supreme Court later relied on this choice of words to support a restrictive reading of the free exercise clause. In *Lyng v. Northwest Indian Cemetery Protective Association,* the Court reasoned: "The crucial word in the constitutional text is 'prohibit'"; therefore, the free exercise clause does not require the government "to bring forward a compelling justification" for actions "which may make it more difficult to practice certain religions but which have no tendency to coerce individuals into acting contrary to their religious beliefs." This textual argument is further developed in the Department of Justice study of the origins of the free exercise clause: "'[P]rohibiting' and 'abridging' are denotatively and connotatively distinct. 'Prohibiting' means to forbid or prevent, while 'abridging' means to reduce or limit. Thus, 'prohibiting' connotes a finality, certitude, or damning not present in 'abridging,' which connotes limitations falling short of the finality of prohibition or pre-vention". ...

The report concludes that laws that discourage or inhibit religious exer-cise by denying government benefits (even those enacted in "purposeful discrimination" against a religion) do not violate the free exercise clause. Only laws that make a religious practice unlawful or impossible are forbid-den.

While contemporaneous definitions of "prohibit" indicate that it was a stronger and narrower term than "abridge" or "infringe," the distinction is probably overdrawn in the context of the free exercise debate in 1789. ...

No one in the debate, in or out of Congress, expressed the view that infringements that are not final, certain, or "damning" should be allowed. Madison had promised to support "the most satisfactory provisions for all essential rights, particularly the rights of Conscience in the fullest latitude," and Daniel Carroll, a Roman Catholic from Maryland, had stated that the "rights of conscience ... will little bear the gentlest touch of governmental hand" and that "many sects have concurred in opinion that they are not well secured under the present constitution." If the final version had been understood to allow infringements short of outright prohibition, one of these gentlemen would surely have spoken up. But both seemed satisfied with the bill's language, as did their constituents. ...

The argument had been made (by no less a figure than John Marshall) that Congress had greater power over the press than over the establishment of religion, because the term "abridging" was less encompassing than the term "respecting." Madison, in response, stated that "the liberty of con-science and the freedom of the press were *equally* and *completely* exempted from all authority whatever of the United States." He went on to argue:

> [I]f Congress may regulate the freedom of the press, provided they do not abridge it, because it is said only "they shall make no law respecting it," the analogy of reasoning is conclusive that Congress may *regulate* and even *abridge* the free exercise of religion, provided they do not *prohibit* it; because it is said only "they shall not prohibit it," and is *not* said "they shall make no law *respecting*, or no law *abridging* it."

Madison found this interpretation of the free exercise clause so absurd that to state it was to refute it. Despite its plausibility as a textual matter, the narrow interpretation of "prohibiting" should therefore be rejected, and the term should be read as meaning approximately the same as "infringing" or "abridging."

b) The Substitution of "Free Exercise of Religion" for the "Rights of Conscience". ... The Senate first voted to protect "rights of conscience" and then settled upon protecting the "free exercise of religion" alone, a formulation that ultimately carried the day. It is possible that these changes in language were without substantive meaning, for in many of the debates in the preconstitutional period, the concepts of "liberty of conscience" and "free exercise of religion" were used interchangeably. There are, nonetheless, three principal differences between the terms that may have significance for interpretation.

The least ambiguous difference is that the term "free exercise" makes clear that the clause protects religiously motivated conduct as well as belief. This point merits emphasis, because in 1879 the Supreme Court, relying on Jefferson, explicitly rejected this reading. Only in 1940 did the Court begin to include religiously motivated conduct within the ambit of the free exercise clause, and even then, only to a limited degree. The belief-action distinction is often used to suggest that protection for religiously motivated conduct is far weaker than that accorded to free speech or other, seemingly "absolute" freedoms. The choice of the words "free exercise of religion" in lieu of "rights of conscience" is therefore of utmost importance. As defined by dictionaries at the time of the framing, the word "exercise" strongly connoted action. ...

By using the term "free exercise," the first amendment extended the broader freedom of action to all believers. As noted, the freedom of religion was almost universally understood (with Jefferson being the prominent exception) to include conduct as well as belief. Accordingly, free exercise is more likely than mere liberty of conscience to generate conflicts with, and claims for exemption from, general laws and social mores.

A second important difference between the terms "conscience" and "religion" is that "conscience" emphasizes individual judgment, while "religion" also encompasses the corporate or institutional aspects of religious belief. In the great battle cry of the Protestant Reformation – "God alone is Lord of the conscience" – the individual conscience was used in contradistinction to the teaching of the institutional church. "Religion," by contrast, connotes a community of believers. ... Religion binds believers together; conscience refers to the inner faculty of judgment. Thus, the "free exercise of religion" suggests that the government may not interfere with the activities of religious bodies, even when the interference has no direct relation to a claim of conscience. ...

The third, and most controversial, difference between the "free exercise of religion" and the "rights of conscience" is that the latter might seem to extend to claims of conscience based on something other than religion – to belief systems based on science, history, economics, political ideology, or secular moral philosophy. By deleting references to "conscience," the final version of the first amendment singles out religion for special treatment. And so the Supreme Court has held: "A way of life, however virtuous and admirable, may not be interposed as a barrier to reasonable state regulation ... if it is based on purely secular considerations; to have the protection of the Religion Clauses, the claims must be rooted in religious belief."

This distinction between religion and other belief systems has come under substantial attack in academic circles. Religion is understood to be a product of individual choice, and protected as such. It said to be arbitrary (and even unconstitutional) to differentiate between belief systems, all of which are the product of individual judgment, on the ground that some are "religious" and some are not.

David A. J. Richards has presented the most sustained and thoughtful exposition of this position. ... He views religious freedom as an aspect of the "equal respect" that must be shown "for the capacity to exercise our twin moral powers of rationality and reasonableness". ... A definition of "conscience" sufficiently broad to encompass all that "neutrality requires" would "include[ ] everything and anything, including purely scientific beliefs about the causal structure of the world integrated into some larger rational and reasonable conception of one's ends". ... Richards thus contends that "the motivation for universal toleration must encompass all belief systems, religious and nonreligious, expressive of our moral powers of rationality and reasonableness."

Under this view, religious claims have no higher status than non-religious claims – and maybe even lower status, to the extent that modern moral philosophy elevates "rationality and reasonableness" over the characteristic religious claims of revelation, tradition, and spirit-filled inspiration. And if the distinction between religious and nonreligious conscience is arbitrary, then it amounts to an indefensible preference – an establishment of religion – to accommodate religious and not nonreligious claims of comparable magnitude.

The question is therefore whether the principle of free exercise, as enacted by the framers and ratifiers of the first amendment, was a specific instantiation of a wider liberty of conscience encompassing individual moral judgments rooted in nonreligious as well as religious sources, or whether religious conscience is different in some fundamental respect from other forms of individual judgment, in which case the free exercise clause would provide no warrant for protecting a broader class of claims. The question is significant for the practical reason that if the exercise of religion extends to "everything and anything," the interference with ordinary operations of government would be so extreme that the free exercise clause would fall of its own weight. To protect everything is to protect nothing.

The historical materials uniformly equate "religion" with belief in God or in gods, though this can be extended without distortion to transcendent extrapersonal authorities not envisioned in traditionally theistic terms. By contrast, Noah Webster's *Dictionary of the English Language,* the first comprehensive American dictionary (published in 1807), defined "conscience" as: "natural knowledge, or the faculty that decides on the right or wrong of actions in regard to one's self". ... And Samuel Johnson's great *Dictionary of the English Language* gave as the first definition: "The knowledge or faculty by which we judge of the goodness or wickedness of ourselves." In none of these definitions was there specific reference to religion, although about half of the literary examples Johnson gave in the four volume edition had a religious context.

On the other hand, outside of dictionaries, the vast preponderance of references to "liberty of conscience" in America were either expressly or impliedly limited to religious conscience. A few examples suffice to make the point. ... St. George Tucker's 1803 commentary on American constitutional law divided "[t]he right of personal opinion" into two subcategories: "liberty of conscience in all matters relative to religion" and "liberty of speech and of discussion in all speculative matters, whether religious, philosophical, or political." Madison himself used the terms "free exercise of religion" and "liberty of conscience" interchangeably when explaining the meaning of the first amendment. The laws of at least ten of the states expressly linked "liberty of conscience" to religion. ... John Leland's *The Rights of Conscience Inalienable* focused on attacking religious establishments and state-supported religion. There was no recorded controversy in preconstitutional America in which the right of "conscience" was invoked on behalf of beliefs of a political, social, philosophical, economic, or secular moral origin.

In any event, the final version of the amendment adopted by Congress and ratified by the states omitted any reference to "rights of conscience" and protected the "free exercise of religion" instead. There are two possible explanations for this. The reference to conscience could have been dropped because it was redundant, or it could have been dropped because the framers chose to confine the protections of the free exercise clause to religion.

The "redundancy" explanation can be supported by the absence of any recorded speech or discussion of differences between the terms. The drafters alternated between the two formulations without apparent pattern. ... Still, the theory that the phrase "free exercise of religion" was deliberately used in order to exclude nonreligious conscience seems more likely, since the different drafts called attention to the question. If no distinction was intended, it would have been more natural to stick with a single formulation and to concentrate on the wording of the contested establishment clause. This theory also derives support from Samuel Huntington's comment that he hoped "the amendment would be made in such a way as to secure the rights of conscience, and a free exercise of the rights of religion, but not to patronize those who professed no religion at all". ...

In any event, it does not matter which explanation ... is correct, for under either explanation, nonreligious "conscience" is not included within the free exercise clause. If "the rights of conscience" were dropped because they were redundant, "conscience" must have been used in its narrow, religious, sense. If the omission was a substantive change, then the framers deliberately confined the clause to religious claims. Neither explanation supports the view that free exercise exemptions must be extended to secular moral conflicts

The textual insistence on the special status of "religion" is, moreover, rooted in the prevailing understandings, both religious and philosophical, of the difference between religious faith and other forms of human judgment. Not until the second third of the nineteenth century did the notion that the opinions of individuals have precedence over the decisions of civil society gain currency. ... In 1789, most would have agreed with Locke that "the private judgment of any person concerning a law enacted in political matters, for the public good, does not take away the obligation of that law, nor deserve a dispensation."

Religious convictions were of a different order. Conflicts arising from religious convictions were conceived not as a clash between the judgment of the individual and of the state, but as a conflict between earthly and spiritual sovereigns. ...

Not only were the spiritual and earthly authorities envisioned as independent, but in the nature of things the spiritual authorities had a superior claim. "[O]bedience is due in the first place to God, and afterwards to the laws," according to Locke ... The key passage in Madison's *Memorial and Remonstrance* reads as follows:

> Before any man can be considered as a member of Civil Society, he must be considered as a subject of the Governor of the Universe: And if a member of Civil Society, who enters into any subordinate Association, must always do it with a reservation of his duty to the general authority; much more must every man who becomes a member of any particular Civil Society, do it with a saving of his allegiance to the Universal Sovereign.

Far from being based on the "respect for the person as an independent source of value," the free exercise of religion is set apart from mere exercise of human judgment by the fact that the "source of value" is prior and superior to both the individual and the civil society. The freedom of religion is unalienable because it is a duty to God and not a privilege of the individual. The free exercise clause accords a special, protected status to religious conscience not because religious judgments are better, truer, or more likely to be moral than nonreligious judgments, but because the obligations entailed by religion transcend the individual and are outside the individual's control.

It is important to remember that the framers and ratifiers of the first amendment found it conceivable that a God – that is, a universal and transcendent authority beyond human judgment – might exist. If God might exist, then it is not arbitrary to hold that His will is superior to the judgments of individuals or of civil society. Much of the criticism of a special deference to sincere religious convictions arises from the assumption that such convictions are *necessarily* mere subcategories of personal moral judgments. This amounts to a denial of the possibility of a God (or at least of a God whose will is made manifest to humans). But while this skeptical position is tenable as a theoretical or philosophical proposition, it is a peculiar belief to project upon the framers and ratifiers of the first amendment, for whom belief in the existence of God was natural and nearly universal. It is an anachronism, therefore, to view the free exercise clause as a product of modern secular individualism. From the perspective of the advocates of religious freedom in 1789, the protection of private judgment (secular "conscience") fundamentally differs from the protection of free exercise of religion.

... From the religious point of view, the difference between religious and secular forms of conscience is that the former represent an obligation to an authority higher than the individual, while the latter are manifestations of mere individual will or judgment. From the Enlightenment point of view, the difference is that the government has no basis for evaluating the truth of religious claims, while it inevitably must evaluate claims based on rational inquiry and knowledge. The religious view emphasizes the importance of the individual; the Enlightenment, the incapacity of the government. Madison combined these points in his *Memorial and Remonstrance.* Both perspectives lead to the same conclusion: it is sensible to restrict the power of government to influence or coerce religious conscience, even when government has the power to influence or coerce judgments based on science, history, political ideology, economics, moral philosophy, or other secular sources. ...

For the most part, the prohibition on an establishment of religion should suffice to protect unbelievers from discrimination, ill-treatment, or coercion (from test oaths, for example). There should be no doubt that government action that abridges the unbeliever's right not to engage in or support a religious practice is unconstitutional. By 1789, it was generally agreed that compelled homage is of no value to God or to man. In Madison's words, "[i]t is the duty of every man to render to the Creator such homage, and such only, as he believes to be acceptable to him."

As a practical matter, the question whether the free exercise clause protects atheists arises only with reference to claims for exemption. If it is true that the right to exemption from generally applicable laws on ground of conflict with religious doctrine is confined to those who have duties arising from their religious beliefs, then it has no application to unbelievers. Unbelievers undoubtedly make judgments of right and wrong that sometimes conflict with generally applicable law. But if these do not stem from obedience to a transcendent authority prior to and beyond the authority of civil government, they do not receive exemption under the free exercise clause. To subject an atheist to civil disabilities would be a violation of free exercise; but to require an atheist who objects to war on secular grounds to go to war would not, since his conduct is not (and by definition could not be) motivated by his religious belief.

4. The Militia Exemption Clause. ... Three states (North Carolina, Virginia, and Rhode Island) had proposed that "any person religiously scrupulous of bearing arms ought to be exempted, upon payment of an equivalent to employ another to bear arms in his stead." Madison's draft bill of rights contained a similar proposal, appended to what is now the second amendment, although Madison left the requirement of a substitute to legislative discretion. The Select Committee proposed and the House of Representatives debated a more generous exemption: "no person religiously scrupulous shall be compelled to bear arms." The proposal was quite controversial; it passed the House by a mere 24–22 vote and was rejected by the Senate ...

The most eloquent defender of the proposal, Elias Boudinot of New Jersey, Presbyterian and later President of the American Bible Society, hoped "that in establishing this Government, we may show the world that proper care is taken that the Government may not interfere with the religious sentiments of any person." He argued that it would be both pointless and unjust to compel "men who are conscientious in this respect ... to bear arms, when, according to their religious principles, they would rather die than use them."

One may wonder why, if this is so, objectors were not protected under the free exercise clause without need for a separate provision. There are at least three possible answers. First, the militias are arms of the state governments except when in actual service; thus, the free exercise clause probably did not apply to them. Second, it does not necessarily follow from the fact of free exercise exemptions that the particular case of military service will be held protected. ... Third. ... if Congress struck out the militia exemption clause, this would create an inference that there is an intention in the general government to compel all its citizens to bear arms. Indeed, some scholars have cited Congress' rejection of the militia exemption clause as conclusive evidence that there is no constitutional right to conscientious objection from military service.

The significance of Boudinot's position for present purposes is that he, with a majority of the House, considered exemption from a generally applicable legal duty to be "necessary" to protect religious freedom. Whether or not the particular application of this principle to bearing arms would be accepted by the Senate (it was not) or the courts (it was not), it strongly suggests that the general idea of free exercise exemptions was part of the legal culture. ...

The most cogent argument against the militia exemption clause came from Egbert Benson of New York. Benson argued that "[n]o man can claim this indulgence of right. It may be a religious persuasion, but it is no natural right, and therefore ought to be left to the discretion of the Government." Benson did not oppose religious exemptions in principle, however. On the contrary, he had "reason to believe but the Legislature will always possess humanity enough to indulge this class of citizens in a matter they are so desirous of; but they ought to be left to their discretion". ...

Benson's position was ambiguous on the key question of interest here. Did he believe there is no natural right to exemption from militia service because there is no natural right to exemption from any generally applicable law? Or did he believe there is no natural right to exemption from militia service because the government's interest is potentially compelling, and the degree of necessity for universal military service must be left to legislative discretion? The latter seems slightly more probable. ...

Summary of the Evidence

While the historical evidence is limited and on some points mixed, the record shows that exemptions on account of religious scruple should have been familiar to the framers and ratifiers of the free exercise clause. There is no substantial evidence that such exemptions were considered constitutionally questionable, whether as a form of establishment or as an invasion of liberty of conscience. Even opponents of exemptions did not make that claim. The modern argument against religious exemptions, based on the establishment clause, is thus historically unsupportable. Likewise unsupportable are suggestions that free exercise of religion is limited to opinions or to profession of religious opinions, as opposed to conduct.

It is more difficult to claim, on this evidence, that the framers and ratifiers specifically understood or expected that the free exercise clause would vest the courts with authority to create exceptions from generally applicable laws on account of religious conscience. Exemptions were not common enough to compel the inference that the term "free exercise of religion" necessarily included an enforceable right to exemption, and there was little direct discussion of the issue. Without overstating the force of the evidence, however, it is possible to say that the modern doctrine of free exercise exemptions is more consistent with the original understanding than is a position that leads only to the facial neutrality of legislation.

Indeed, the evidence suggests that the theoretical underpinning of the free exercise clause, best reflected in Madison's writings, is that the claims of the "universal sovereign" precede the claims of civil society, both in time and in authority, and that when the people vested power in the government over civil affairs, they necessarily reserved their unalienable right to the free exercise of religion, in accordance with the dictates of conscience. Under this understanding, the right of free exercise is defined not by the nature and scope of the laws, but by the nature and scope of religious duty. A religious duty does not cease to be a religious duty merely because the legislature has passed a generally applicable law making compliance difficult or impossible.

The language of the free exercise and liberty of conscience clauses of the state constitutions ... strongly supports this hypothesis. These constitutions curtailed free exercise rights when they would conflict with the peace and safety of society. These "peace and safety" provisos would not be necessary if the concept of free exercise had been understood as nothing more than a requirement of nondiscrimination against religion. Moreover, in the actual free exercise controversies ... prior to passage of the first amendment, the rights of conscience were invoked in favor of exemptions from such generally applicable laws as oath requirements, military conscription, and ministerial support. Many of the framers, including Madison, a majority of the House of Representatives in the First Congress, and the members of the Continental Congress of 1775, believed that a failure to exempt Quakers and others from conscription would violate freedom of conscience. These experiences, while not so frequent or notorious to warrant firm conclusions, nonetheless suggest that exemptions were part of the legal landscape. ...

The history subsequent to adoption of the first amendment ... tends to point against exemptions. One lower court squarely adopted the exemptions interpretation, and the supreme courts of Pennsylvania and South Carolina rejected it. None of these decisions was handed down within twenty years of the first amendment, and they are therefore weak indicators of the original understanding. The Pennsylvania holding is entitled to especially little weight since it was connected to a rejection of constitutional judicial review in general. Indeed, the contrast between the rationale of ... the Pennsylvania court and the rationales offered by Madison for religious liberty tends, if anything, to reinforce the conclusion that Madison's position requires exemptions.

IV. Conclusion: The New American Philosophy

The free exercise clause may well be the most philosophically interesting and distinctive feature of the Constitution. Viewed in its true historical light, as the product of religious pluralism and intense religious sectarianism in the American states and colonies, which limited influence from the rationalistic Enlightenment, the free exercise clause represents a new and unprecedented conception of government and its relation to claims of higher truth and authority. ...

The Enlightenment writers on the subject tended to concentrate on the danger of religious rivalry. Sectarian intolerance and struggle for hegemony was a major cause of unrest, violence, rebellion, and persecution. There were two promising ways to ameliorate and, if possible, eliminate such violence. ... One solution was to suppress religious differences by establishing a national church and supporting it with public funds. ...It would have two advantages: by unifying religion, it would reduce religious factionalism, and by guaranteeing financial support to the clergy, it would cause them to become indolent and subservient. The difficulty with this solution was that it would enrage dissenters from the established church ... and might well exacerbate religious unrest. For this reason, the mature Locke proposed the second approach: to extend toleration to all (except Catholics and atheists), on condition that each religion adopt toleration as one of the tenets of its faith. Toleration, it was hoped, would calm the fevers of religious dissension. To the Enlightenment skeptic, convinced of the absurdity of the more intense varieties of religious expression and likewise convinced of the power of reason, this approach seemed to offer the additional advantage that reason, and with it rational religion, would prevail over the sectarians. ...

As with the establishment solution, however, the toleration solution seemed less than realistic from the American side of the Atlantic. Too many Americans had come to these shores precisely because they could not practice their faith in the controlled environs of Europe. Too many sectarians were spreading their views, and religious factionalism was already too deeply ingrained. Dissenters were a vexatious minority in Britain; in America they were (in the aggregate) a large majority, divided into many sects. And experience had shown that Americans were attracted – not repulsed – by the "irrational" surges of enthusiastic religion that peaked in the Great Awakening.

Madison, for one, grasped that the United States was not amenable to the Enlightenment solutions. In a letter to Jefferson, he stated that "[h]owever erroneous or ridiculous these grounds of dissention and faction may appear to the enlightened Statesman or the benevolent philosopher, the bulk of mankind, who are neither Statesman nor philosophers, will continue to view them in a different light." Religious sectarianism will not go away ... The Madisonian contribution, familiar to us from *The Federalist* Nos. 10 and 51, is to understand factions, including religious factions, as a source of peace and stability. If there are enough factions, they will check and balance one another and frustrate attempts to monopolize or oppress, no matter how intolerant or fanatical any particular sect may be.

This point of view is consistent with an aggressive interpretation of the free exercise clause, which protects the interests of religious minorities in conflict with the wider society and thereby encourages the proliferation of religious factions. To increase the number of religious sects and the vigor of the small ones will not, as Locke appeared to believe, exacerbate the problem of religious turmoil. More likely, it will make religious oppression all the more impossible. ... Rather than try to foster an ecumenical spirit, the state allows each sect to promote its own cause with zeal. The Madisonian perspective points toward pluralism, rather than assimilation, ecumenism, or secularism, as the organizing principle of church-state relations. Under this view, the Supreme Court errs if it attempts to calm or suppress religious fervor by confining it to the margins of public life. It should welcome religious participation in all its diversity and dissension ... Most of all, the Court should extend its protection to religious groups that, because of their inability to win accommodation in the political process, are in danger of forced assimilation into our secularized Protestant culture. The happy result of the Madisonian solution is to achieve *both* the unrestrained practice of religion in accordance with conscience (the desire of the religious "sects") *and* the control of religious warfare and oppression (the goal of the Enlightenment).

So understood, the free exercise clause also makes an important statement about the limited nature of governmental authority. While the government is powerless and incompetent to determine what particular conception of the divine is authoritative, the free exercise clause stands as a recognition that such divine authority may exist and, if it exists, has a rightful claim on the allegiance of believers who happen to be American citizens. The occasions for free exercise exemptions may be rare now, as in our early

history; but the importance of the principle outstrips its practical consequences. If government admits that God (whomever that may be) is sovereign, then it also admits that its claims on the loyalty and obedience of the
citizens is partial and instrumental. Even the mighty democratic will of the
people is, in principle, subordinate to the commands of God, as ... understood in the individual conscience. In such a nation, with such a commitment, totalitarian tyranny is a philosophical impossibility.

... Locke and Jefferson may well have been animated, in Justice
Frankfurter's words, by the "freedom from conformity to religious dogma." But that is not what the Baptists, Quakers, Lutherans, and Presbyterians who provided the political muscle for religious freedom in America had
in mind. To them, the freedom to follow religious dogma was one of this
nation's foremost blessings, and the willingness of the nation to respect the
claims of a higher authority than "those whose business it is to make laws"
was one of the surest signs of its liberality.

William P. Marshall

The Case against the Constitutionally Compelled Free Exercise Exemption

Free exercise jurisprudence is unique in constitutional law. Because direct regulation of religious activity almost never occurs, the litigation surrounding free exercise addresses only incidental and inadvertent regulation of religious conduct. For this reason, the issue in a free exercise challenge typically is not whether a law is constitutional; the law under attack is usually constitutionally unassailable outside of its incidental effect on religious practice. Rather, the issue is whether certain individuals should be exempted from otherwise valid, neutral laws of general applicability solely because of their religious conviction. The jurisprudence of free exercise, in short, is the jurisprudence of the constitutionally compelled exemption.

There are a number of tensions underlying the notion of the constitutionally compelled exemption, and underlying the constitutional treatment of religion and religious belief, that make free exercise jurisprudence a particularly difficult subject for coherent analysis. First, because special exemptions of any kind raise concerns of undue favoritism, they are normally suspect as violating fundamental constitutional principles of equal treatment. Thus, as the Court noted just last week, the conclusion that the Constitution may require the creation of an exemption directly contradicts the constitutional norm.

Second, the difficulties inherent in exemptions are exacerbated when an exemption favors religion. Beyond general equality notions, the advancement of religion triggers a separate and specific constitutional provision, the establishment clause. Thus, as has been commonly noted, the free exercise

40 *Case Western Reserve Law Review* 357 (1989–90). Used by permission.

claim for constitutionally compelled exemptions leads to a first amendment jurisprudence that simultaneously calls for special deference to religion under the free exercise clause and a prohibition of special deference under the establishment clause.

Third, the claim for constitutionally compelled free exercise exemptions raises virtually insoluble problems in determining when a religious claim is *bona fide*. Such an inquiry necessarily requires investigation into the religiosity and sincerity of the religious belief at stake; however, defining religion and ascertaining sincerity have proved to be highly elusive undertakings. Furthermore, any inquiry into definition or sincerity is itself risky. Allowing the courts or the government to investigate and label beliefs as "irreligious" or "insincere" raises a threat to religious liberty. Moreover, the importance of the sincerity and definition inquiries to free exercise claims for exemption cannot be overstated. In effect, sincerity and religiosity are the only criteria for determining what constitutes a legitimate religious claim. Because religious beliefs are so diverse, as one observer has written, "everything is [potentially] covered by the free exercise clause."

Finally, as has been noted in recent academic literature, religious matters do not easily lend themselves to existing constitutional analysis. Constitutional analysis is individual-rights-oriented; religion is often communal. Rights-oriented thinking presupposes that the individual has numerous equally viable avenues through which to exercise her freedom of choice; religion in a legal framework often raises a square-peg/round-hole problem.

A number of years ago I proposed. ... that free exercise claims advanced by those seeking relief from laws of general applicability should be resolved under the speech clause. In essence, free exercise claimants would be entitled to relief only to the extent their claims would be protected under the speech clause. ... If free exercise is treated as expression, the result will obviously be that the religious and non-religious groups will be accorded the same level of protection. In short, under this theory a religious claimant will be entitled to no greater protection than a non-religious claimant, the presence of a free exercise interest notwithstanding.

The second component of the thesis, admittedly more controversial, concerns the scope of religious activities entitled to constitutional protection. It argues that the boundaries of protected free exercise activity should be defined by the boundaries of free speech. Although, according to the current jurisprudence, a claim under the free exercise clause will often also

implicate the speech clause, many claims currently recognized as implicating free exercise protection do not easily fit within a speech analysis. For
example, the religious objection to working in an armaments factory,
recognized as implicating rights of free exercise in *Thomas v. Review
Board*, does not, at least under existing speech theory, present a colorable
speech claim. Under the theory posited here, the religious claim will not be
constitutionally protected unless protection is also extended to parallel
objections based on non-religious grounds, such as those of moral philosophy. In short, whether an activity implicates the first amendment ought not
turn on whether the activity is religious or secular. ...

I. Free Exercise as Expression: Doctrinal Underpinnings

A. Religiously Motivated Activity as Expression

In *Widmar v. Vincent*, the Court reviewed the claim of members of a
religious organization who alleged that they were unconstitutionally denied the right to pray together on a state-university campus. The Court
held that the appropriate vehicle for review of his constitutional claim was
the free speech clause. Prayer, in short, was speech. The *Widmar* Court's
reliance on the speech clause was not surprising. It was simply illustrative of
a long line of cases which had reviewed under the speech clause the claims
of religious organizations to engage in religiously directed practice. ...

What is surprising, however, is the extent to which the free speech
inquiry has dominated the free exercise inquiry. The two freedoms were
intertwined in the Jehovah's Witnesses cases of the 1930's and 1940's. In
those cases, the Court reviewed the constitutionality of state restrictions on
religiously motivated activities such as solicitation, proselytizing, distribution of religious literature, and preaching. In almost all of the cases in which
the Jehovah's Witnesses prevailed, the Court found the governing provision to be the speech clause. Although the free exercise clause was occasion-
ally mentioned, in no case did the Court recognize a free exercise claim
where a speech claim would have failed. The message of these cases was
clear: No activity was so essentially religious that it warranted protection
only under the free exercise clause.

B. Protection for Rights of Conscience Under the Speech Clause

The speech clause's dominion over claims involving religious exercise is not limited to expressive activities. It also includes more passive activities like the rights of conscience. In a series of cases, the Court has upheld on speech clause grounds the rights of persons, whether religiously motivated or not, to refrain from certain state-compelled activities because the participation in those activities conflicted with their consciences.

West Virginia State Board of Education v. Barnette and more recently, *Wooley v. Maynard* are examples of cases in which the Supreme Court has recognized that a right to forego an activity because of religious principle is protected under the speech clause. *Barnette* invalidated a compulsory flag-salute requirement that was repugnant to Jehovah's Witnesses. Although the objection was based on religion, the Court, viewing the issue as involving freedom of conscience, found the conscientious objection to have arisen under the speech clause irrespective of its religious basis. ... Thus these cases and others establish that the free exercise clause is not the exclusive guardian for rights of conscience and that significant protection for rights of conscience exists under the speech clause.

C. The Current Free Exercise Jurisprudence

The Supreme Court's current free exercise approach does not, in theory, reject the constitutionally compelled exemption. Beginning in 1963, with *Sherbert v. Verner,* the Court adopted a separate free exercise inquiry which allowed for the creation of constitutionally compelled exemptions for religious exercise in certain circumstances. From 1963 until quite recently, the Court has been consistent in articulating the test it ostensibly applies in its free exercise decisions. According to the Court, government infringement on free exercise rights will be upheld as constitutional only when supported by a compelling state interest. Essentially, this test parallels the strict scrutiny inquiry the Court uses in reviewing purported infringements of the most fundamental constitutional rights. Nevertheless, despite the Court's professed allegiance to a fixed constitutional standard, free exercise jurisprudence has never been consistent in result. Rather, the only consistency that has emerged is the Court's extraordinary reluctance to vindicate free exercise claims outside those protected under the speech clause. It has done so in only five cases, and those five cases are extremely limited in scope. One, *Wisconsin v. Yoder*, which held that the Amish were entitled to constitutional exemption from compulsory-education laws, is so tied to its facts that it is without strong precedential value. The Court emphasized the uniqueness of the Amish and conceded that "few other religious groups or sects" would be entitled to similar exemption.

The other cases include the seminal *Sherbert* decision and the trilogy of *Thomas v. Review Board, Hobbie v. Unemployment Appeals Commission*, and *Frazee v. Illinois Department of Employment Security*, three cases which are essentially *Sherbert* re-visited. In all four cases, the Court addressed the same issue: whether a state could deny unemployment benefits to an applicant whose failure to be available for work was due to religious conviction. In each case the Court concluded that the free exercise clause prohibited the state from withholding benefits. A claimant could not be forced to choose between adhering to his beliefs and forfeiting state benefits on the one hand, and accepting work that violated his religious convictions on the other.

The unemployment-benefits cases have not, however, been accorded strong precedential force. In subsequent cases, the Court has denied claims for religious exemption from the minimum wage, overtime, and record-keeping provisions of the Fair Labor Standards Act, tax payment requirements of the Social Security Act, and the government's use of social security number registration requirements in food stamp and welfare programs. In these cases, the governmental interests, primarily ease of administration and fear of fraudulent claims, were "relatively weak." In addition, the Court has been quick to reject free exercise claims that have arisen in prison and military contexts on the grounds that these institutions should be accorded unusual judicial deference. Finally, the Court has unanimously rejected the free exercise claims for special exemption from tax laws that have been brought before it. The denial of religious claims in all of these circumstances has led a number of commentators to question whether the Court actually applies strict scrutiny or a substantially less stringent mode of review in free exercise cases.

... There is no question that free exercise protection exists at best in diluted form. Indeed, its most recent free exercise pronouncement, the Court in *Employment Division, Department of Human Resources v. Smith (Smith II)*, imposed the most far-reaching limitation on *Sherbert* yet. In *Smith II* the Court was faced with the free exercise claims of two Oregon state employees who had engaged in religiously motivated peyote smoking.

Characterizing the peyote smoking as work-related misconduct, the state had fired the employees from their position as drug and alcohol abuse counselors. The Supreme Court rejected their free exercise challenges. The *Smith II* opinion is immediately notable for its limited reading of free exercise precedent. Distinguishing *Sherbert* and *Yoder*, the Court virtually denied even the existence of the constitutionally compelled free exercise exemption. The Court stated that it had "never held that an individual's religious beliefs excuse him from compliance with an otherwise valid law prohibiting conduct the state is free to regulate" and that its previous decisions "have consistently held that the right of free exercise does not relieve an individual of the obligation to comply with a 'valid and neutral law of general applicability ...'" A serious question thus remains after *Smith II* as to whether the free exercise exemption will survive in any form.

Even in its narrowest reading, the limitation *Smith II* places on free exercise exemption is dramatic. The Court held that even if it

> were inclined to breathe into *Sherbert* some life beyond the unemployment compensation field, we would not apply it to require exemptions from a generally applicable criminal law.
> ... To make an individual's obligation to obey such a law contingent upon the law's coincidence with his religious beliefs, except where the State's interest in "compelling" – permitting him, by virtue of his beliefs, "to become a law unto himself" – contradicts both constitutional tradition and common sense.

Smith II thus holds that rights of free exercise do not extend to criminally proscribed activity ...

In summary, the current free exercise jurisprudence disfavors exemptions. The combination of 1) the extraordinarily limited circumstances in which free exercise claims have been upheld; 2) the less-than-compelling instances in which claims have been denied; 3) the *Bowen/Lyng* refusal to extend such protection to matters affecting the government's internal operations; 4) the *Smith II* refusal to extend free exercise protection to otherwise illegal activities; and 5) the significant protection religious activity has been accorded outside of the speech clause, lead to one salient conclusion: The explicit adoption of the position that free exercise claims for exemption should be denied would not produce a dramatic alteration of the current jurisprudence.

II. The Arguments in Favor of Constitutionally Compelled Exemptions for Religious Exercise

Commentators generally do not dispute the conclusions set forth in the previous section. They agree that, prior to *Sherbert*, the protection of free exercise rights was afforded solely by the speech clause and that the results under the Court's current approach differ little, if at all, from the results that would be achieved under a free exercise as expression methodology. They also agree that the creation of free exercise exemptions necessitates inquiry into the sincerity and definition of religious belief and that such investigation itself may be harmful to religious-liberty interests. Finally, commentators generally concede that a theory that seeks exemption for religious exercise in effect advocates preferred treatment for religion and religious belief. Indeed, the central argument of those favoring free exercise exemptions is that the Court's failure to provide special protection to free exercise rights apart from that provided by the speech clause is exactly what is wrong with the current jurisprudence. ...

A. Text

The first argument raised by those seeking more stringent free exercise protection is textual. The first amendment explicitly provides for the protection of rights of free exercise. Some commentators contend that, in order to make this provision meaningful, the free exercise clause must be given its independence from the speech clause, in part through constitutionally compelled exemptions. Accordingly, denying claims for free exercise and redressing such claims only under the speech clause must be misguided, since it would turn the free exercise clause into a textual redundancy.

This textual argument, however, is deficient on a number of grounds. For one, it is descriptively inaccurate. The free exercise position advocated here pertains only to claims for special exemption from laws of general applicability. The free exercise clause may have independent vitality in restricting judicial involvement in intra-church property and employment disputes. More clearly, the clause retains an independent vitality with respect to laws that directly attempt to infringe upon religious freedom. While there have been thankfully few instances of direct persecutions for the free exercise clause to redress, the fact that protection from direct prosecution has been largely unneeded does not make the clause a redundancy.

Nor is the clause a redundancy because even persecutory laws could arguably be invalidated under another constitutional provision, the equal-protection clause. ...

Moreover, it is hardly novel to assert that mention in the text of the first amendment does not require constitutionally favored treatment other than protection against direct persecution. The press clause, also located in the first amendment, has been held not to confer a favored status on the media. Rather, the press clause has been interpreted only to protect the media from "invidious discrimination."

Finally, the argument that a textual passage must be given concrete meaning is misleading when that argument is used to advance a specific interpretation of that text. Separate arguments must be given in support of the substance behind the purported textual interpretation. In the free exercise context, proponents of more stringent free exercise exemptions must present arguments that demonstrate why the free exercise clause should be interpreted to require constitutionally compelled exemptions from neutral laws of general applicability. That the text of the first amendment explicitly mentions free exercise does not by itself establish this position.

Historical inquiry also does not support the claim for the constitutionally compelled claim for free exercise exemption. For one, the relevant historical evidence, like that underlying other issues concerning the religion clauses of the first amendment, is unclear. As Dean Choper has stated, "there is no clear record as to the Framers' intent, and such history as there is reflects several varying purposes." Moreover, any historical evidence must be tempered by the understanding that the first amendment was not intended to apply to the states. Federalism concerns, as well as issues of substantive religious liberty, surrounded the adoption of the religion clauses.

Some observations, however, are interesting, if not dispositive. For example, there is a significant question as to whether even the concept of a religious exemption is consistent with the framers' intellectual framework. The framers obviously were aware that the beliefs of religious adherents could stand in opposition to the religious mandates of the state. The foisting of religious values upon religious dissidents by state enforcement of an established church's precepts was one of the central religion clause concerns. The framers were also aware of another infringement on religious freedom caused by state laws: A number of states imposed disabilities on persons refusing to take oaths, although oath-taking was offensive to the religious tenets of some sects. However, outside of these conflicts with state religious laws or test requirements, it is difficult to find examples where religious objections to the *secular* law of the state were recognized. In fact, outside of religious laws or tests, one can convincingly argue that the framers did *not* envision potential religious exemptions as applying to neutral laws of general applicability. A number of reasons support this contention.

One is that the governing intellectual climate of the late eighteenth century was that of deism, or natural law, which assumed that religious tenets and the laws of temporal authority coincided. The first Supreme Court decisions on free exercise, decided roughly 100 years after the passage of Bill of Rights, are classic, if somewhat vitriolic, examples of this approach to religion and the law of the state. In *Reynolds v. United States* and *Davis v. Beason,* for example, the Supreme Court rejected the contention that the Mormon practice of polygamy was religious. In the words of the Court, "to recall their advocacy [of polygamy] a tenet of religion is to offend the common sense of mankind." Accordingly, the Court rejected the Mormon protests against restrictions on polygamy as not failing within the definition of religious exercise protected by the first amendment. The Court stated that "[i]t was never intended or supposed that the amendment could be invoked as a protection against legislation for the punishment of acts inimical to the peace, good order and morals of society." As *Reynolds* and *Davis* suggest, there is little room in a natural-law framework for the creation of a constitutionally compelled religious exemption for activities outside the social norm.

Deism and natural law were not, however, the only philosophies that might have influenced the first amendment; evangelical influence existed as well. Nevertheless, there are additional reasons which suggest that even those not sharing a deistic philosophy would have had difficulty anticipating religious objection to religiously neutral state provisions.

First of all, there were few religiously neutral state provisions with which the religious practices could have been in conflict. The regulatory state did not exist. There were no unemployment compensation benefits programs that might have disadvantaged sabbatarians and no compulsory school programs that might have compromised the Amish or their historical predecessors. For a conflict to occur, then, it would have had to arise within the state's criminal law.

This conflict, in turn, was unlikely for a second reason. Although there were varieties of religious beliefs at the end of the eighteenth century, there was not a great disparity in the types of religious practices. Rather, the culture of the United States in the late eighteenth century was fairly homogeneous, being composed almost entirely of Christian sects whose practices were unlikely to violate non-religious societal norms. Thus, there existed neither the practices nor the laws that would make a conflict between religious exercise and religiously neutral laws likely.

Finally, there is no suggestion, in any event, that the framers conceived of a constitutionally mandated exemption. Article VI, for example, bans the religious test. It does not create an exemption. Those arguing for a textual interpretation in favor of the constitutionally compelled exemption must also demonstrate that the unique remedy of exemption is consistent with the framers' constitutional purposes. The historical evidence, however, is lacking. History, therefore, is no guide to the purported right to constitutionally compelled free exercise exemptions from religiously neutral laws of general applicability.

B. Equality

A second contention made by supporters of a free exercise exemption is that the creation of such an exemption adds to, rather than subtracts from, equality concerns. This argument contends that the application of neutral regulations creates its own inequality. For example, a Seventh-Day Adventist, who is not entitled to receive unemployment compensation because she is unavailable to work on Saturdays, is at a disadvantage with those whose religious beliefs do not forbid Saturday employment and who, if they are religiously forbidden from working on Sundays, may already be protected by legislative exemption. Creating an exemption for the sabbatarian therefore equalizes her rights with those of other religious adherents. Creation of this exemption also ensures that a religious majority, while never likely to place disabilities on the exercise of its own beliefs, might "inadvertently" inhibit the religious rights of minority groups. Professor Tushnet has questioned the accuracy of this argument. As he points out, there probably is no mythical majority intentionally protecting its own religious beliefs and "inadvertently" placing disabilities on the beliefs of others: "In a pluralistic society with crosscutting group memberships, the overall distribution of benefits and burdens is likely to be reasonably fair."

Yet, even aside from Tushnet's criticism, inequality among religions is not the governing equality concern. Even if a special exemption for religious adherents equalizes the effects of otherwise neutral laws on all religious believers, it does not equalize the effects of those laws on individuals presenting parallel secular objections. Again, those advocating a free exercise exemption for religious groups must convincingly argue that religious exercise is special.

C. Pluralism

Some commentators also rely heavily on notions of pluralism to support expanded free exercise protection. The value in pluralism has been succinctly stated by Justice Brennan: It is beneficial to have diverse sub-groups within society because "each group contributes to the diversity of association, viewpoint, and enterprise essential to a vigorous, pluralistic society." ...

The problem with the pluralism theory is not that it is misguided. Indeed, its aims and structure are highly attractive. Its deficiency is that it is not an argument for special protection for religious exercise. The values inherent in pluralism are also advanced by the protection of non-religious groups.

First secular mediating groups such as ethnic associations and socio-political organizations also serve as buffers between the individual and the state. Religious groups are, after all, not the sole mediating institutions in society. Second, religion does not lay claim to a monopoly in the inculcation of civic virtue. As Professor Tushnet has explained, "[r]eligion may now be one of several methods of inculcating civic virtue." Finally, cultural diversity is not solely the product of religious multiplicity. Other types of heterogeneity – ethnic, lingual, and regional – enrich the culture as well.

The pluralist argument thus fails to establish why only religious groups, and not secular groups that share the same characteristics, merit special treatment. In short, the pluralist argument is either one for broad associational rights that include, but extend beyond, religious affiliations to other types of societal subgroups, or it is an argument for the development of a constitutional theory that assimilates community rights into its individual-rights methodology. The pluralist argument does not, however, support special exemption for religion.

D. The Special Nature of Religion

Religion, some commentators contend, is not simply another belief system. Unlike other types of beliefs, religion seeks a truth and a morality that stem from divine authority. Accordingly, the obligations religion places on its adherents transcend those imposed by temporal sources. In the words of Professor McConnell, "religious claims – if true – are prior to and of greater dignity than the claims of the state [and the individual]."

As Professor Garvey explains, the belief in a transcendent authority has significant ramifications for its adherents. If the law of the state and the religious tenet differ, the religious adherent is in the unwelcome position of being subject to conflicting duties. ...

These concerns are indisputably serious; however, none are unique to religion. Conflicting duties occur anytime one's beliefs conflict with those of the state, whether those beliefs are religious or not. Some beliefs, like those underlying an individual's objection to the draft, may be moral or political. ...

The conclusion that there is a special suffering associated with the violation of a religious tenet is also overbroad at best. Not all religious beliefs are held with equal fervor by the religious adherent, nor are religious beliefs necessarily more deeply felt than secular beliefs. A person who has a secular, moral objection to killing in war and a religious objection to working on the Sabbath might well suffer a greater psychic harm in being forced to kill than in being forced to work. ...

Professor Garvey ultimately concludes that what separates religion from non-religion is that the former "is a lot like insanity." According to Garvey, this conclusion has two aspects. The first is cognitive. Garvey asserts that the process of understanding reality through religious beliefs is dissimilar to developing that understanding through practical reasoning – the cognitive process by which reality is generally understood in the society. The second aspect is volitional. The religious believer is compelled by his belief to engage in certain activities. He therefore lacks the will in the same way an insane person lacks the will to conform his practices to societal expectations. For this reason, Garvey suggests, exempting the religious adherent is appropriate.

There are two deficiencies in Garvey's thesis. First, it is not at all clear that religion is the only belief system that bases its understanding of the world upon a cognition other than that achieved through practical reasoning.

Most other types of beliefs and moral values have non-rational components. ...

Second, it is unclear that, even if lack of volition underlies religious belief,
the appropriate response is to defer to this non-volitional understanding by
creating special exemptions. There is, after all, a presumption of free will
that underlies the principle of individual freedom expressed throughout the
Constitution, and there is a principle of voluntariness which specifically
underlies American religion and the religion clauses. The analogy to insanity alone does not support the free exercise exemption.

Nevertheless, although no one factor conclusively establishes a special
status for religion and religious belief for constitutional law purposes, it
may be, as Garvey suggests, that the aggregation of a number of factors
leads to the conclusion that religion is entitled to special protection. As will
be shown in the next section, however, the constitutional difficulties created by special protection for religion militate against the conclusion that
special treatment for religion is constitutionally compelled.

III. The Arguments Against the Constitutionally Compelled
Free Exercise Exemption

A. Avoiding The Sincerity and Definition Inquiry

Creating constitutionally compelled exemptions under the free exercise
clause necessitates inquiry into the sincerity and religiosity of the religious
claim. The inquiry poses its own threat to religious values. On the other
hand, abandoning the free exercise exemption obviates the need for defining religion in free exercise cases and wholly avoids judicial inquiries into
sincerity, except in cases involving legislatively created exemptions. Avoiding religious inquiry thus promotes religious liberty.

The problems inherent in defining religion and the harms definition
creates for free exercise purposes are, of course, apparent. As Professor
Stanley Ingber has argued:

> The danger in defining religion lies in the possibility of violating the very
> purpose of the religion clauses by proposing a definition that excludes
> non-traditional religious beliefs from the ambit of the first amendment.
> To define religion is to limit it ... [A]ny attempt to fulfill this mandate
> risks a delineation of a religious orthodoxy.

This exclusion of non-traditional beliefs is one of the most serious threats to religious values. As Justice Stevens has argued, evaluating the merits of religious claims creates "[t]he risk that government approval of some and disapproval of others will be perceived as favoring one religion over another is an important risk the Establishment Clause was designed to preclude." Steven's position is supported by two of the Court's most famous pronouncements on the illegitimacy of legal determination of orthodoxy. In *Watson v. Jones*, the Court stated that "[t]he law knows no heresy, and is committed to the support of no dogma, the establishment of no sect." In *West Virginia State Board of Education v. Barnette*, it declared, "[i]f there is any fixed star in our constitutional constellation it is that no official, high or petty, can prescribe what shall be orthodox in politics, nationalism, religion, or other matters of opinion."

Similar problems exist with sincerity. If protection of religious practice means anything, it means that the government cannot reject as false particular religious creeds. Yet how can one judge the sincerity of an individual's belief without judging the reasonableness of the belief? As Justice Jackson argued in *United States v. Ballard*, the problem is essentially insoluble.

Moreover, there is difficulty even in the act of inquiring into an individual's religious beliefs, since such an inquiry raises the troublesome spectre of state inquisition into religious motivation and governmental attempts to impeach professed religious convictions. According to Chief Justice Warren: "[A] state-conducted inquiry into the sincerity of the individual's religious beliefs [is] a practice which a State might believe would itself run afoul of the spirit of constitutionally protected religious guarantees."

It is, thus, not an overstatement to suggest that avoiding the sincerity and religiosity inquiries might alone support abandoning the free exercise exemption. When one combines the possibility that any activity could potentially be characterized as religious with the conclusion that there are no appropriate ways to distinguish legitimate from illegitimate religious assertions, the case against expanding free exercise protection becomes more compelling ...

B. Elimination of Favoritism for Religious Belief and Exercise

The second argument against the free exercise claim for exemption is that it seeks a favoritism for religion that itself raises serious constitutional concerns. The concern with such favoritism is most evident when the exemption sought is from regulatory measures that directly affect the dissemination of ideas. The exemption of religious proponents vests them with a distinct competitive advantage over their secular counterparts. For example, assume a rule that restricts all solicitations at a state fair to fixed-booth locations. If a religious organization, because of the religious belief of its members, is exempted from the rule and accordingly is allowed to engage in unrestricted face-to-face solicitation, it will be better able to raise money, expound its philosophy, and seek converts than will the non-religious groups that remain restricted to fixed locations. Thus, given a religious and a secular organization of similar size and budget, the exempted religious group will be better placed than its secular counterpart to raise funds and exert its influence – a significant advantage given the Supreme Court's canon that "money is speech." The special exemption, in effect, grants to those advancing religious views more power than their secular counterparts.

This favoritism toward religious organizations, of course, violates the central principle in speech jurisprudence that every idea has equal dignity in the competition for acceptance in the marketplace of ideas. Providing greater protection for religious speakers suggests, in direct opposition to this principle, that there exists a constitutional hierarchy in which religious ideas occupy a higher position than secular ideas. This preferred status undercuts the "equal liberty of expression guaranteed by the first amendment". ....

Favoritism for religious speech over non-religious speech is also antithetical to establishment clause policies. Singling out religion for special treatment raises establishment concerns in any case, but as the recent *Texas Monthly* case attests, the difficulty is exacerbated when the special treatment concerns speech. Part of the underlying theory of freedom of speech is that it creates the discourse necessary for self-government. The establishment clause, however, imposes a unique limitation on direct religious influence over government that does not apply to non-religious sources. Although religion undoubtedly should play a part in the political process, it is untenable to assert that religion ought to have special advantage in the public debate. Giving a competitive advantage to religious speech in the marketplace of ideas and in the discourse that leads to self governance turns the establishment clause on its head.

Perhaps because of the speech and establishment clause problems, the consensus is that when speech and religion overlap, special protection for free exercise claims need not be maintained. The primary concern is what is to be protected. Yet, to find the scope of free exercise broader than the scope of free speech ultimately leads to the same kinds of concerns.

The *Thomas* case, for example, involved a person who objected to working in an armaments factory. Because the person's objection was based on religious belief, the Court found it constitutionally protected. The Court was equally clear, however, that if the claim were based on secular moral grounds, it would be denied. But why should the objection on religious grounds to working in an armaments factory be entitled to constitutional protection, while an objection to the same work based on moral grounds be denied? A similar problem exists in *Yoder*. Why should the Amish be exempted from Wisconsin compulsory school education while other groups that desire to have their children free of public school influence not be entitled to the exclusion?

If only the religion claim is protected, religious beliefs are accorded a more favorable position in the constitutional hierarchy than are secular beliefs. However, as we have already seen, such a hierarchy is constitutionally suspect, since it denies religious and secular beliefs equal constitutional dignity.

Moreover, as with expressive religious activity, favored treatment raises concerns of political effect. ... Indeed, the infusion of religious beliefs into the political process is an important, necessary, and perhaps even unavoidable part of democratic decision-making. Similarly, as has been noted in civic-republicanism theory, religion and religious belief promote the values in the citizenry that are necessary for responsible public decision-making. Religious belief, in short, cannot and should not be segregated from its political effect.

If this is so, however, then freeing religious exercise from neutral strictures gives religious beliefs an unfair advantage over competing value systems in the political marketplace. If religious beliefs are subsidized in a way secular beliefs are not (as in *Thomas*) or if they are insulated from the societal forces that routinely challenge any belief system (as in *Yoder* or as was requested by the plaintiffs in *Mozert v. Hawkins County Board of*

Education, the public school textbooks case), they become reinforced with an artificial vitality. This favoring of religious ideas runs counter to both establishment clause concerns with religious domination of the political process and speech clause concerns with the need for equality in the marketplace of ideas.

Finally, the creation of constitutionally compelled protection for religious beliefs is also problematic because it judicially legitimizes the religious belief in comparison to the non-religious. The moral authority of the Court is placed, in effect, behind the religious belief. ...

C. Legislative Exemptions for Religion – A Cautionary Note

... The first issue centers on establishment. The arguments against constitutionally compelled free exercise exemptions depend, in part, on anti-establishment policies. These arguments do not, however, call for the invalidation of legislatively created exemptions under the establishment clause. In certain cases, establishment clause concerns might inform free exercise analysis and, conversely, free exercise concerns may inform establishment analysis without either provision being violated. Professor McConnell is correct when he asserts that there is room between the two clauses for permissible government action. Moreover, the establishment inquiry asks a very different question than does free exercise; specifically, establishment asks whether the challenged government action connotes the *endorsement* of religion. Legislative exemptions from certain types of regulation do not imply this endorsement as readily as do affirmative grants or subsidies.

This is not to suggest that legislative exemptions should be immune from establishment clause review. The Court has indicated, for example, that an "unyielding weighting" of a state provision in favor of religion may raise establishment concerns. Statutory exemptions from regulations directly affecting this dissemination of ideas or otherwise allowing religious groups to disproportionately extend their "worldly influence" may also be particularly suspect under establishment analysis. These establishment limitations on legislative exemptions exist, however, irrespective of the specific arguments advanced in this Article.

The conclusion that free exercise is not independent from speech has more serious implications for review of legislative exemptions under the speech clause. If religious activity is speech, favorable treatment for religious activity would presumably violate the content-neutrality requirements of the speech clause. For example, if the hiring and firing of employees is considered symbolic speech, the Title VII exemption from liability of religious employers in certain hiring and firing decisions could be construed as a content-based regulation. The Title VII exemption might, therefore, be unconstitutional under the speech clause, despite being constitutional under the establishment clause.

On the other hand, this concern may be overstated. There is no absolute prohibition against statutorily exempting certain speech from government restriction on expression. ...

IV. Failure to Take Religion Seriously

... Critics contend that the current jurisprudence and the approach advocated here are, in essence, antagonistic to religion. If the results in the cases have been criticized as not taking free exercise seriously, then the jurisprudence as a whole has been accused of not taking religion seriously. Purportedly it has failed to incorporate a religious, as opposed to a secular, understanding of religion into its methodology.

There are three manifestations of this criticism. One is that contemporary constitutional theory rejects religion because it sees religion as irrational. A second is that it rejects religion because constitutional theory is individual-rights oriented, while religion is communal. A third is that constitutional theory has failed to accept religion on the latter's own terms because constitutional theory is based upon notions of freedom of choice, while religion is based upon notions of absolutism and obligations to a transcendent authority, notions which deny the right to choose any competing value systems.

... The argument that constitutional theory rejects religion because of the latter's supposed irrationality is simply a red herring. A great deal of irrational activity has been protected under the constitution, including that so-called model of rationality, the speech clause. ...

What is true, as Professors Gedicks and Hendrix claim, is that the languages of law and religion are incongruent. Law's language of "objectivity, rationality, and empiricism" is not compatible with religion's language of "faith, belief, and divine judgment." However, the inability to capture the essence of religion in a logical medium is not hostility to religion; rather, it is the inevitable result of placing any non-rational belief system, religious or secular, into a rational process.

The contention that free exercise jurisprudence demonstrates the inability of constitutional law to come to grips with non-individualistic values is perhaps partially correct, but, in any event, essentially misses the point. Constitutional theory has had difficulty providing a framework within which communal rights can be protected. However, free exercise is not the only area in which this has occurred and, indeed, it is not accurate to place free exercise rights solely in the communal-rights camp. Religious exercise is often individualistic, and non-religious value systems and beliefs are often communal. More importantly, the non-individualist criticism strays far from the attack on the rejection of the free exercise exemption. Even if the jurisprudence unduly minimizes communal rights, the question remains why religious, and only religious, groups or individuals should be entitled to exemption.

The critics are correct, however, when they contend that constitutional law does not recognize religious claims, or at least the claims of some religions, to transcendent authority. Constitutional law does not recognize that to some religious adherents, religious beliefs are not products of individual choice, but are absolute truths imposed by an external authority. Liberal constitutional theory, in short, treats religion as simply another belief system. ...

The mistake, however, is to view this treatment as pejorative. Constitutional theory protects freedom of choice by assuming that there are a number of belief systems that an individual may adopt and that the individual is free to choose among the competing systems. Liberal constitutional theory recognizes the possibility that any one of the belief systems may be true, but because its underlying theory is based on possibility rather than authority, it cannot treat any particular system as the Truth. ...

Liberal constitutional theory treats religious belief as a function of individual choice, while some religion treats religious beliefs as "externally imposed upon the faithful." That liberal constitutional theory resolves this tension in favor of itself, by assuming that an individual's beliefs are the product of choice and not of externally imposed authority, is not indicative of hostility. An approach which treats religious beliefs as equal to non-religious beliefs cannot be characterized as hostile to religion; there is no antagonism in equal treatment.

Moreover, the hostility argument loses its force because it cannot seriously be contended that either the Court's current approach or a speech methodology is non-protective of religious values. The constitutional standard applied in speech cases is, after all, the Court's most stringent. The reluctance to inquire into sincerity and religiosity is also based on concerns protective of religious values. ...

Religious issues must be decided according to the methodology of constitutional theory because, after all, it is the constitutional issues involving religion that are being decided. Logically, for a constitutional theory based on freedom of choice to advance absolutism would be to deny itself. All liberal theory can do is recognize the varieties of beliefs and protect the rights of anyone who chooses to pursue a particular mode of belief, including an absolutist one.

The foregoing, of course, is no surprise to the critics. Indeed, it is their central contention. They would argue, however, that if liberal constitutional theory subordinates a religious understanding to, or exorcises it from, its treatment of religious cases, the methodology must be abandoned in favor of one more sympathetic to religious values. ...

The claims of hostility to religion miss the mark because they ignore the fact that the rejection of the absolutist understanding of religion in favor of individual choice is itself deeply rooted in religious principle. Critics of the constitutional methodology have argued that the liberal state should defer to religion because religion seeks a Truth that is transcendent and because the possibility exists that a religious belief system reflects a transcendent truth. This position suggests that it would be consistent with the liberal understanding to grant deference to belief systems that are possibly True. Yet, if there is true knowledge, there must also be false knowledge, and if the state should defer to the possibility of higher Truth, this goal may best be served by supporting notions of individual freedom rather than claims of externally imposed duties. Even though it is theologically controversial, one must not dismiss the argument that even if it does not reflect the religious absolutist's understanding of religion, liberal constitutional theory reflects a profoundly religious understanding of the search for Truth; specifically that the search must be a product of man's freedom rather than of his obligation. Therefore, it is not anti-religious secularism to contend that the Constitution protects only *freedom* of religion and that the protection of religion itself, like the protection of any belief system, religious or secular, true or false, is only derivative. ...

Chapter III

God and Government:
The Establishment Clause

Background: In this chapter the two authors debate the meaning of the First Amendment clause, "Congress shall make no law respecting an establishment of religion." Accommodationists, like Gary Glenn, believe the government may aid or support religion in a "non-preferential" way. Separationists, like Leonard Levy, hold a stricter, no special accommodation view of the separation of church and state. This debate, conducted for over 200 years, analyzed in countless articles and books, and carried on in an ever expanding number of court cases in the 20th century, captures the soul of America and American law. Is the U. S. a religious country as several Supreme Court justices have declared? May local school boards allow prayer or moments of silence in the classroom? May convocation speakers invoke the name of God? May nativity scenes, menorahs, and the crescent emblem of Islam grace the public square? All these questions indicate that Americans still do not agree on what "establishment of religion" means.

According to accommodationists, the founders intended to prevent only the establishment of *One National State Church* like the Church of England. They also remind us that, in various acts of Congress since 1791, the government actively supported religion since the people and officials viewed it as a worthy civic and moral endeavor. Federal and state governments supported Bible readings and religious instruction in schools, prisons, the territories, and Indian reservations. The Federal government made provisions for military and legislative chaplains, exempted religious property from taxation, paid for Christmas vacations for federal workers, and underlined links between government and God with official opening prayers in Congress and the Supreme Court. These and a host of other examples indicate to accommodationists that the establishment clause was not intended to prevent *any* and *all* government aid to religion, but rather to prevent establishment of a national religion. In their view, not all aid constituted an establishment of religion.

Separationists disagree and point to the founders' concern that Congress should have no power to legislate religion, either to abuse or assist it. In their view, the free exercise clause prevents abuse and the establishment clause forbids government aid to religion. What do we do with these flat contradictions about the establishment clause? In this round of wrestling with the divided opinion on the founders' original intentions regarding the nature of Congressional power, state versus federal rights, and the protection needed for and from religion, one might be forgiven for recalling Mark Twain's advice: "to have constitutional rights and the common sense not to use them." But to whom are the two authors in this chapter offering advice? To the courts and Congress – not to establish religion, or not to allow concern for avoiding establishment interfere with the free exercise of religion? Or, is it to the public – not to abuse separation of church and state by eliciting government support for religion, or not to accept a sacrifice of free exercise rights in the face of governmental insensitivity to religion?

Authors: Gary Glenn, Professor of Political Science at Northern Illinois University, has written extensively on the debate between the Federalists and Anti-Federalists over the degree to which the unamended constitution threatened or guaranteed religious liberty. In his view, while the Federalists insisted that no threat existed, Anti-Federalists feared the "implied" and "necessary" powers delegated to the federal government. They also feared, according to Glenn, that the only reference to religion in the Constitution, the prohibition of religious tests for public office holding, denigrated religion, opened the door to atheists to govern, and undervalued the moral restraint and civic virtue fostered by religion. Given these fears and a dedication to preserve state's rights, the Anti-Federalists fought to adopt a Bill of Rights to curb the powers of the central government, ensure the free exercise of religion, combat the anti-religious bias of the Deist founders, and permit government encouragement of religion.

Glenn refers to Anti-Federalist arguments to refute Levy who relies on Federalist arguments alone to explain the meaning of the religion clauses. Glenn points out that these clauses emerged only after the Anti-Federalists (and others who favored government support for religion) forced the Federalists (and others opposed to such support) to compromise on the wording of the religion clauses. Glenn notes, for example, the successful

Anti-Federalist rejection of Madison's proposal of a "full and equal rights of conscience" clause to provide legal equality between religious belief and unbelief. Levy disputes the relevance of this presumed defeat for Madison, and argues that the Federalist's victory in inserting "respecting an establishment of religion" showed that the framers intended to prohibit government support of religion. Glenn suggests that "respecting" could just as well mean that the First Amendment prohibits Congress from interfering with on-going state establishments of religion.

In sum, Glenn confronts the strict separationism of Levy (and Jefferson and Madison) by emphasizing the countervailing and popular arguments of the Anti-Federalists and religious dissenters who worried about unprotected liberties, including religious ones, in the unamended constitution. He concludes that these drafters of the First Amendment did not intend for the religion clauses to protect non-religion or require the government to be neutral between religion and non-religion; nor did it imply that all support for religion constituted establishment.

Leonard Levy, former Professor of History at the Claremont Graduate School and current editor of the *Encyclopedia of the American Constitution*, is a prolific writer/editor of over 20 books and numerous articles on the religion clauses of the First Amendment. He concludes, after a review of the drafting of the First Amendment, that Congress rejected the accommodationist or narrow interpretation that the framers intended only to prevent the establishment of a national church or national preference for one religious sect over another.

Levy finds nothing in the debate over the First Amendment to indicate that anyone wanted to give the federal government any power to legislate religion. The Federalists at first rejected the very concept of a Bill of Rights because the Congress was, by design, "bereft of any authority over the subject of religion" or other personal liberties. In addition, according to Levy, since the Anti-Federalists demanded amendments to more expressly limit the power of Congress, it seems unlikely that they intended to give Congress power – previously nonexistent in the federal constitution – to aid religious groups. Thus in direct contrast to Glenn and McConnell, Levy argues that Madison, Jefferson, and most other framers and the Baptists and most dissenters all sought to prohibit not only government meddling in religion, but also "aid to either one or many sects or religions."

As proof of this assessment, Levy notes Senate and House rejections of non-preferential language. For example, House members deleted the word "national" from Madison's original proposal that read, "nor shall any national religion be established." On the other hand, as Glenn points out, the drafters also rejected separationist language. They changed the wording of the clause from "no law touching religion" (surely a most inclusive prohibition) to "no law establishing religion" (a more ambiguous prohibition, perhaps referring only to the prohibition of a national church.) After this review, we may find Levy most apt when he comments that "if anything is really clear about this problem of 'meaning' and 'intent,' however, it is that nothing is clear."

After a lengthy review of the ratification process, the colonial experience with multiple establishments (state sponsorship of more than one church or sect), and the decline of these state churches after the American Revolution, Levy is ready to explain what establishment means. First, he reminds us of the differences between what establishment meant in Europe (an established national church) and colonial America. He then concludes that, since establishment in America increasingly meant non-preferential government sponsorship of religion, when the drafters of the First Amendment voted to prohibit establishment, they intended to prohibit what had been the American multiple establishment experience. In other words, the federal government could not aid or sponsor religion, even in a non-preferential way. He does not accept the possibility that, since the colonies and the states had already rejected the European single establishment model in favor of their multiple systems, the states may have intended merely to reject the European model at the American federal level.

Questions: Does the First Amendment prohibit all state and Congressional legislation respecting religion? Or, may governments provide non-discriminatory support for religion? Were the drafters of the First Amendment unanimous in their view of Congressional power, the role of religion, and the institution(s) most able to secure religious freedom? Who opposed the First Amendment and why did they oppose it?

Gary D. Glenn

Forgotten Purposes of the First Amendment Religion Clauses

The present judicial understanding of the religion clauses constitutes a policy paradox. On the one hand, it reads the establishment clause as excluding from public support religious prayers, readings, education, traditions, practices, and symbols. On the other hand, it reads the free exercise clause as requiring exemption on religious grounds from otherwise valid laws. In other words, what the free exercise clause sometimes requires is sometimes indistinguishable from what the establishment clause sometimes prohibits.

One goal of this study is to discover whether the foregoing policy paradox is inherent in the religion clauses as originally intended but only recently discovered, or whether it is a relatively recent creation of the Court.

A second goal is to clarify another puzzle related to the broader conventional view which understands the Bill of Rights to derive from criticisms of those who opposed the unamended Constitution (the anti-Federalists). If that is correct, why does the conventional view interpret the original meaning of the religion clauses on the basis of the thought of Madison and Jefferson who supported the original Constitution? ...

I

This study assumes that if the Bill of Rights were adopted primarily at the behest of anti-Federalists, then the meaning of the religion clauses must be sought, at least initially, in what they had to say about religion during the

49 *Review of Politics* (Summer 1987), 340–365. Used by permission.

ratification debates. ... One has to pay attention also to the First Congress debates themselves. But these debates look different when read in light of the essentially anti-Federalist demands which produced them.

The ratification debates do not reveal exactly what one would have expected on the basis of the standard historiography. One does find the expected anti-Federalist demands for a bill of rights in general explicitly restricting the new government's power respecting certain individual and state liberties among which is religion. But with respect to religion, the argument in this form is both relatively infrequent and also shared by Jefferson who supported the Constitution. ... Anti-Federalists more commonly complained that the unamended Constitution was manifestly non-religious, allegedly dangerous to religion, and hence the new government would be at least dereligionized and perhaps antireligion.

This anti-Federalist fear might seem strange. It becomes more plausible by considering the following. First, where the Articles of Confederation acknowledge the importance of "the Great Governor of the World" in the nation's political life, and most state Constitutions contained explicit acknowledgements of God and man's dependence on him, and many contained provisions providing for public worship and support of religion, none of these existed in the new Constitution. Second, anti-Federalists knew that the Constitution had been produced by a convention in which enlightenment skepticism and indifference to traditional theistic or revealed religion predominated at least in many of its leading members. Third, they knew that advanced enlightenment hostility toward traditional, revealed, theistic religion was being articulated in the ratification debates by a few *supporters* of the new Constitution. In language reminiscent of the *philosophes*, these supporters publicly praised the Constitution's dispensing with religion. Fourth, they perceived the Constitution as aiming at encouraging citizens to turn away from "politics and religion, to the pursuit of wealth."

These arguments became focused in anti-Federalist concern about the meaning of the fact that the only mention of religion in the proposed Constitution was the "non-religious test" clause. ... There was not one neatly defined anti-Federalist position but rather a cluster of arguments. All related to a central fear that this clause was actually or potentially harmful to religion itself and to religion's beneficial and perhaps indispensable influence on public life and public order. The unity even of this central fear should not be overstated for "religion" was sometimes Protestantism, sometimes Christianity, and sometimes revealed religion as such. Much of the time it is not clear which of these meanings is intended. The most general anti-Federalist meaning is "belief of the existence of a Deity and of a state of future rewards and punishments." ...

Article VI, paragraph 3, of the Constitution requires that all officers of the new government and of the states take an oath or affirmation to support the Constitution. Some anti-Federalists argued that there was no security for such an oath or affirmation unless the oath taker was known to have "principles of virtue," that "professed atheists" or "infidels" could not be known to have such principles, and hence their oath or affirmation could not be trusted. Since the "no religious test" clause permitted such people to govern, it subverted that security upon which free constitutional government was said to depend.

Anti-Federalists also said that papists could not to be trusted to keep the oath. Papists "acknowledge a foreign hand, who can relieve them from the obligation of an oath." In one formulation, this fear was combined with the common anti-Federalist fear of the treaty power to suggest that the Roman Catholic religion could thereby be established in the United States "which would prevent people from worshiping God according to their own consciences." This seemingly fantastic fear was not entirely unfounded. The statement that "the government of the United States of America is not, in any sense founded on the Christian religion" was put into a 1797 treaty between the United States and Tripoli. If the "no religious test" clause was a red flag to those who feared for the fate of Christian religion under the proposed Constitution, the treaty language would seem to somewhat confirm those fears.

Sometimes anti-Federalists tied their objection to the "no religious test" clause to their concern about its effect on the oath requirement. But sometimes they simply objected to the "no religious test" clause itself. Luther Martin argued "a belief of the existence of a Deity, and of a state of future rewards and punishments would be some security for the good conduct our rulers." ... "Aristocrotis" thought religion an indispensable restraint on rulers. "David" thought professed atheists should be excluded from governing. Henry Abbott thought religious liberties unsafe if "pagans, Deists, and Mahometans" governed. ... David Caldwell thought it "an invitation for Jews and pagans of every kind to come among us [which] at some future period ... might endanger the character of the United States."

Anti-Federalists also defended the necessity of the moral restraint fostered by religion to make the people governable. "Civil government can't be well supported without the assistance of religion." "The turbulent passions of mankind" can best be controlled "by forming the opinion of the people at large in favour of virtue and religion." This requires "affording public protection to religion." But the "no religious test" clause does not clearly afford such protection. It even seems to permit official indifference and/or hostility. This argument's focus is the political utility of religion and the consequences to government if religion is not publicly protected and if the people are freed from the moral restraints of religion. ...

Another anti-Federal objection concerned permitting avowed non-Christians to govern. This objection argued the indispensability of Christianity for instilling the requisite moral virtue in the people. "A person could not be a good man without being a good Christian." Christianity was said to "make good members of society on account of its morality." "Aristocrotis" argued that the deism of the "leading members" of the Convention had a special tendency to encourage moral laxity. ...

The foregoing evidence shows that anti-Federalists objected to the "no religious test" clause because of concerns about fidelity to oaths to support the Constitution taken by professed atheists and papists; about the fate of "religion" (sometimes understood as Protestantism, sometimes as Christianity, sometimes as revealed, theistic religion generally) under a government in which non-Protestants, non-Christians, and even "avowed atheists" were permitted to govern; and also concerns related to the fate of the new government if it was indifferent or hostile to that religiously grounded moral virtue which anti-Federalists thought was useful or indispensable to that government's preservation. ...

The prevalent historiography believes anti-Federalists were primarily concerned about "religious liberty" in one of three senses: they wanted assurance either that the new government would not legislate concerning individual's religious beliefs and practices, or establish religion, or interfere with the states' right to legislate about these things. ... Nowhere does the prevalent historiography acknowledge anti-Federalist fears that the unamended Constitution was tilted against religion. Nowhere does it appear they thought "public protection for religion" was ... necessary to preserve free government. Nowhere is the relevance of their defense of religious tests acknowledged. The prevalent historiography even has difficulty taking seriously anti-Federalist insistence on explicit guarantees of religious liberty. Leonard Levy puts his view quite strongly.

> Indeed, it is a fact, not an interpretation that the unamended Constitution vests no power over religion. ... It is a fact that the Framers of the Constitution insisted that no limitations on the government's power over religion were necessary, because the government possessed only delegated authority, plus the authority necessary to execute delegated powers; under no circumstances, argued the Framers, could the government legislate on the subject of religion.

Elsewhere the same study says that "The United States had no power [under the unamended Constitution] to legislate on the subject of religion" [and that this] was "a point on which the entire nation agreed."

The evidence of the foregoing pages demonstrates that the entire nation did not agree. Indeed the "no religious test" clause was itself construed as an exemption from a power which Congress otherwise had over religion. The reasoning was that if Congress did not have power to legislate concerning religion, why was the exception necessary? This reasoning was reported to Madison by Randolph who wanted to know how to respond to it. Randolph did not profess to accept this reasoning but that a prominent member of the Convention and a supporter of the Constitution did not know how to respond suggests that the issue was not "a point on which the entire nation agreed." The shrewd anti-Federalist "Aristocrotis" saw the same possibility that Congress could claim power to legislate concerning religion and tied it to the quite common anti-Federalist argument that the Constitution granted the new government unlimited power.

On the basis of the foregoing evidence, it can be said that the prevalent historiography has missed or forgotten the most common anti-Federalist argument about the unamended Constitution's treatment of religion.

II

If the First Amendment religion clauses were intended to assuage anti-Federalist concerns, then they should have been partly intended to address this perceived danger to religion and government as well as to religious liberty. To see the extent to which this is true, we must examine the First Congress debates. However, we are now prepared to find a rather different emphasis and purpose than conventional scholarship suggests. Instead of looking only for "strict separationism" or its antecedents, we also look for some redressing of the alleged antireligious tilt.

What became the Bill of Rights was introduced in the House of Representatives by Madison 8 June 1789. Madison chose to take the initiative in doing so to preempt even more radical amendments from the anti-Federalists, some of whom hoped for a second convention or, failing that, for substantial "states' rights" amendments. Storing argues that Madison's successful strategy means the anti-Federalists demanded a Bill of Rights but the Federalists decided which ones we got. But Storing's generally correct thesis is insufficiently precise respecting the religion clauses because the Federalists had to substantially compromise with those who feared that the Constitution would harm religion. ...

Madison proposed two religion amendments. One read "No State shall violate the equal rights of conscience." Madison said that this was "the most valuable amendment on the whole list." It was also the only amendment not requested by any of the state conventions. Hence Madison's claim in his speech introducing the amendments that his aim was to quiet the fears of opponents of the Constitution by acceding to their reasonable demands was not true of his amendment. Its eventual rejection by the Senate is the clearest evidence that what the Bill of Rights ultimately said about religion was not entirely what Madison wanted.

His other amendment read: "The Civil Rights of none shall be abridged on account of religious belief or worship, nor shall any national religion be established nor shall the full and equal rights of conscience be in any manner, or on any pretext abridged." This amendment became the religion clauses of the First Amendment. But it was drastically altered. How one describes these alterations depends on one's point of view. For Madison, it narrowed his preferred meaning of religious liberty. For his opponents it redressed the original Constitution's tilt against religion and inserted into the Constitution some positive grounds for public support and protection for religion.

Madison had anticipated this result. During the ratification debates Jefferson had written to Madison insisting that explicit guarantees of various freedoms, including "freedom of religion," should be added to the Constitution by amendment. Madison responded that he did not oppose such explicit guarantees but feared

> ... that a positive declaration of some of the most essential rights could not be obtained in the requisite latitude. I am sure that the rights of Conscience in particular, if submitted to public definition would be narrowed much more than they are likely ever to be by an assumed power. One of the objections [to ratification] in New England was that the Constitution by prohibiting religious tests opened a door for Jews, Turks, and infidels.

Clearly Madison wanted "rights of conscience" defined as including these latter but he feared this would not be achievable if pressed publicly. He preferred to secure his broader definition by the new government's assuming the power to do so. ... It could be claimed as an inference from the "no religious test" clause, the "necessary and proper" clause, and the Constitution's otherwise silence about religion. This power could perhaps even be extended to the states through the supremacy clause. These possibilities were seen and opposed by anti-Federalists in the ratification debates.

Some Federalists had argued against the necessity of a bill of rights in general on the grounds that they were unnecessary. The new government was limited in its powers. Hence there was no need to guard against the abuse of powers not delegated. ...

Madison only ambiguously accepted [this] argument at this time. He wrote to Jefferson 17 October 1788 that he "has always been in favor of a bill of rights; provided it be so framed as not to imply powers not meant to be included in the enumeration ... [but] I have not viewed it in an important light 1. because I conceive that in a certain degree ... the rights in question are reserved by the manner in which the federal powers are granted. ...

Against Patrick Henry's complaint that the Constitution omitted explicit guarantees of freedom of religion, he argued that "there is not a shadow of right in the general government to intermeddle with religion." However, on the other hand, "it is better that this security [for religious freedom] should be depended upon from the general legislature, than from one particular state. ... the United States abound in such a variety of sects, that it is a strong security against religious persecution ..." It is difficult to see how Congress is a better security for religious freedom than the individual state legislatures, unless Congress has some power to secure religious freedom. It was clearly not crazy for anti-Federalists to fear that Congress had some unspecified power over religion notwithstanding some Federalists' (and Madison's quite ambiguous) denial of such power.

As late as October 1788, Madison preferred to avoid a confrontation over a "public definition" concerning "rights of conscience" precisely because he feared he could not get it defined inclusively enough. But his fear makes no sense if "the entire nation agreed: [that] the United States had no power to legislate on the subject of religion." If that was true, then "Jews, turks and infidels" were already protected, from the new government, by its lack of power to legislate concerning religion. In any case, by early 1789 it had become clear he could not avoid the issue. To get elected to the First Congress, he was driven to pledge (to the Virginia Baptists) that he would seek and support such an amendment.

Madison's explicit wish to include "Jews, turks, and infidels" in "rights of conscience" shows he understood this language to extend beyond ... Christianity, and even to atheism. In this he agreed with Jefferson, for whom "rights of conscience" included those who believe in "twenty gods or no god." On the other hand religion, the free exercise of which Madison defended in the *Memorial and Remonstrance,* is narrower: "the duty which we owe to our Creator and the manner of discharging it." Religion thus understood presupposes belief in a Creator toward whom individuals have duties, thereby including Jews and "turks" but excluding nonbelievers ("infidels" or "atheists"). Accordingly, freedom of religion is not necessarily identical to "rights of conscience." The latter language could be construed, as Madison and Jefferson did, as reflecting governmental indifference to religion as against nonreligion and hence an openness to hostility toward religion to which anti-Federalists had objected in the ratification debates. We might then expect to find anti-Federalist objections to "rights of conscience" language in the debate over Madison's proposed religion amendments.

The House Debate

On 15 August 1789 the House took up Madison's amendment aimed at Congress. But it had been changed by the select committee to which it had been referred on 28 July. The committee version read "no religion shall be established by law, nor shall the equal rights of conscience be infringed."

The committee language was immediately attacked by anti-Federalists. Sylvester thought it "liable to a construction different from what had been made by the committee," namely, "to have a tendency to abolish religion altogether." The extant reports do not elaborate this objection further. But considering the anti-Federalist concerns already noted, it could mean either of two things. "Established" could be construed as prohibiting *any* government support, even "public protection," for religion and in that way rather directly harming the interests of religion. Or "equal rights of conscience" could be construed as giving constitutional protection to those opposed to religion and in that way endangering religion's interests and/or political influence. Huntington agreed that "the words might be taken in such a latitude as to be extremely hurtful to the cause of religion." He hoped that "the amendment would be made in such a way as to secure the rights of conscience, and a free exercise of the rights of religion, but not to patronize those who professed no religion at all." Huntington's argument shows that he grasped the potential difference between rights of conscience and freedom of religion, namely that the former could be construed to include the right of unbelief. ...

The Sylvester-Huntington position reflects, to a limited but clear extent, the core of the primary anti-Federalist objection to the Constitution's treatment of religion during the ratification debates. The proposed amendments might meet that objection, but they might only recapitulate and even exacerbate it if they failed to remove the implication that religion was a matter of governmental indifference. ... Anti-Federalists wanted not only freedom from federal government interference with religious opinion and practice but also they opposed this constitutional indifference toward religion. They thought neither government nor religion nor religious liberty was secure unless the new government was somehow permitted to encourage and support religion. It was dangerous enough that the Constitution permitted non- or antireligious representatives. It would be even more dangerous if the new government were further *constitutionally* prohibited from giving "public protection" to religion.

The discussion surrounding the Sylvester-Huntington objections resulted in replacing the committee language by the language proposed by the New Hampshire ratifying convention: "Congress shall make no laws touching religion, or infringing the rights of conscience."

This language omitted "equal" from "rights of conscience" but the House debates do not directly explain what that meant. ... The New Hampshire Constitution's version of "rights of conscience" differs from that of Madison and Jefferson in that while "every individual" has such rights, the right is only to worship God. Because unbelief was not included in "rights of conscience," New Hampshire's Constitution decidedly favored religion against nonreligion.

Since we know that Madison wanted atheists included in "rights of conscience," and absent any other interpretation, it would seem he inserted "equal" before "rights of conscience" to exploit the ambiguity of "rights of conscience" and thereby give grounds for construing constitutional equality for nonbelievers ("infidels") and hence between religion and nonreligion. Removing "equal" thus appears to be a defeat for Madison and a partial victory for those anti-Federalists who wished to prevent "dereligionizing" of the new government further than the unamended Constitution could already be construed to have done.

However, the New Hampshire wording was a defeat for those anti-Federalists who wished to permit some sort of Congressional support for religion. "No laws touching religion" seems even less open to such support than either the Madison or the committee language. In particular it seems inconsistent with the Northwest Ordinance which explicitly authorized schools for teaching "religion, morality, and knowledge." ...

The New Hampshire wording ... was changed to: "Congress shall make no law establishing religion, or to prevent the free exercise thereof, or to infringe the rights of conscience." Levy speculates that "The House believed that the draft clause based on Livermore's motion might not satisfy the demands of those who wanted something said specifically against establishments of religion." This is a strange explanation since prohibiting *any* laws touching religion, *a fortiori* prohibits any laws about religious establishments. The Livermore language is even stronger than an explicit prohibition which leaves arguable what precisely constitutes establishment.

Levy's suggestion seems less likely than that the House, on reflection, realized it wanted the government to be able to make laws "touching," but not "establishing," religion. "No law establishing" was, in the context, more open to governmental support for religion than "no law touching." And if Congress could not touch religion, then Huntington's original complaint would recur, that is courts might not even enforce contracts involving religious congregations.

... Another possible explanation is the inconsistency between the New Hampshire wording and the Northwest Ordinance. The assumption that Congress did not want to make unconstitutional the newly repassed Northwest Ordinance would explain why the 20 August language only forbade Congress to *prevent* free exercise. The pointed permission for Congress to *support* or *promote* or *protect* free exercise could provide constitutional grounds justifying the Ordinance. This construction would mean that such support was not "establishing religion."

The 20 August wording also retained the New Hampshire version of rights of conscience," that is, excluding "equal." This is the first time "free exercise" and "rights of conscience" appear together. Since the revision came from the Federalist Fisher Ames, and was purportedly written by

Madison who preferred not to submit it in his own name, in the context this looks like the Madisonian-Federalist response to eliminating "equal" from "rights of conscience." Having failed to insinuate nonbelievers ("infidels") into "rights of conscience," the next strategy was to give grounds for construing them into the two phrases taken together. One could argue that, since both free exercise of religion and rights of conscience were guaranteed, and since nonreligion is clearly not religion, what else could be meant by rights of conscience except the equal right of nonbelievers? This seems the most plausible interpretation suggested by the strategic situation and by what we know [of Madison]. ...

The Senate Debate

The Senate debate apparently focused on whether "religion" referred only to particular sects (churches) or more generally to belief in God or a Creator. If it meant the former, then "no law establishing religion" would protect pluralism among citizens and sects which believed in a Creator but would leave open the question of government's relation to nonreligion. If it meant the latter, it required governmental indifference or neutrality toward belief in a Creator (what we would now call secularism although that word did not yet exist) and hence equality between religion as such and nonreligion.

The Senate critics of the House amendment tried to clarify what "religion" meant. They first tried to define it in terms of sects while retaining the rights of conscience language. ... When that failed, they tried to defeat the whole amendment. When that failed, they tried their first definition again but that failed. Supporters of the amendment then moved its adoption, and that failed. Then the rights of conscience language was stricken and the amendment passed reading: "Congress shall make no law establishing religion, or prohibiting the free exercise thereof."

It seems implausible that the Senate controversy was merely over a redundancy, since mere sloppiness in drafting does not explain the fact that the amendment was adopted only after three failed attempts to pass it with "rights of conscience" included. Three failures suggests a substantive disagreement. Nor is it plausible that the controversy was merely about a state's right to have legally established religion since "Congress shall make no law," which clearly reserved to states the right to establish religion, was never challenged and all sides seem to have agreed that there should be no national establishment of religion.

A more plausible explanation is that "rights of conscience" language even without "equal" is still somewhat open to being construed as establishing constitutional equality between religious belief and nonbelief and providing grounds to argue that Congress had no right to support or protect religion. "Free exercise of religion" by itself cannot be so construed since nonreligion (especially atheism) is rather obviously not religion within any of the anti-Federalist meanings, that of Madison's *Memorial and Remonstrance*, or of the amendments proposed by the state ratifying conventions. Hence, forbidding Congress from prohibiting free exercise of religion would not forbid Congress from prohibiting nonreligion and *a fortiori* would permit Congress to protect, prefer or encourage religion as such as against nonreligion. It would appear the Sylvester-Huntington view was ultimately reflected in the Senate language.

The Senate reconsidered this amendment September 9 and changed "religion" to "articles of faith or a mode of worship." ...

The interpretation presented here contradicts Levy's view that the First Congress debates concerned Madison's attempted "reassurance that the [federal] government would not legislate on religious matters." No language adopted at any time clearly prohibited all such federal legislation. The closest such language was "Congress shall make no laws touching religion or infringing the rights of conscience," which still arguably permitted federal legislation to *protect* or *support* the rights of conscience. But this language was rejected in favor of "Congress shall make no law establishing religion, or to prevent the free exercise thereof, or to infringe the rights of conscience." Since the "rights of conscience" exists in both, the change was from "no laws touching religion" to "no law establishing religion, or to prevent the free exercise thereof." For Levy's view to be correct the first clause must be equivalent to the last two.

... Both in the context and in principle, "no law establishing religion, or to prevent the free exercise thereof" seems more permissive of some federal legislation about religion than "no law touching religion." For Congress was only forbidden to *prevent* free exercise. It was not forbidden to *protect* free exercise. But one could say, with Levy, that Congress was simply prohibited from legislating on religious matters and hence could permit free exercise *only* by remaining silent. But then what about circumstances *requiring* legislation to permit free exercise, such as those "religiously scrupulous of bearing arms." ... If Congress is required to remain silent in such cases, then free exercise would not be protected. More generally, when governmental support is *necessary* in order to permit free exercise, to say that such support is prohibited is to say that what is *necessary* is *prohibited*. This Orwellian reasoning is necessary to defend the view that the religion clauses were adopted to reassure that the federal government was prohibited from legislating on religious matters and that it is to be neutral about (*i.e*, neither favor nor hinder) religion. When proponents of this interpretation have seen this Orwellian quality they have sometimes sensibly but inconsistently said that what is *necessary* is *permitted*.

Madison's "No State" amendment is additional evidence that the debates concerned more than "reassurance that the government would not legislate on religious matters." Had it been adopted would it not obviously have permitted the federal government to "legislate on religious matters"? Or would that government have been powerless in the face of state infringements on rights of conscience? ...

Moreover, if "Madison sought to accommodate ... those who wanted reassurance that the government would not legislate on religious matters," why would he obviously provoke them by his "No state" amendment? This amendment manifestly gave the federal government power to define rights of conscience and to enforce such rights against state actions. Proposing this amendment suggests he was not trying to conciliate those who opposed such power. Rather he was attempting to win the battle to define "rights of conscience" in "the requisite latitude." Prior to the First Congress debates, Madison's opponents understood (and feared) that the un-amended Constitution might already be construed to give such power. ...

This evidence suggests the issue concerned more than "reassurance that the government would not legislate on religious matters." Instead Congress wrestled with several interrelated issues about how to draw amendments concerning religion. What exactly is "religion," the freedom of which we mean to guarantee? Should it include freedom not to believe in a Creator? If so, should this freedom be equal to the freedom to believe in a Creator? Would religious freedom be sufficiently protected by prohibiting any federal legislation about religion? If not, what language would enable that government to "protect" or foster or encourage or support free exercise of religion without enabling it to "establish" religion or interfere with free exercise? Should the federal government be allowed to establish a national religion? Or to disestablish state religious establishments? Or to interfere with state laws which interfere with religious freedom or rights of conscience? ...

Conference Committee

... The wording under consideration in conference was substantially different from that originally proposed by Madison 8 June. His first proposal had sought to protect against the federal government, both the civil rights of persons with different religions and the equal rights of conscience of religious believers and nonbelievers. But Madison had lost the best language (equal rights of conscience) protecting nonbelievers against acts of Congress. ... Madison's second proposal had sought to protect against the states, the equal rights of conscience of both believers and nonbelievers. This proposal, rejected by the Senate 7 September, was not in the conference agenda.

The conference added "respecting" to the establishment wording, so it now read "Congress shall make no law respecting an establishment. ..." A common view reads this as meaning that, not only may Congress not establish religion but it may not provide any support for religion short of formal establishment. This plausible reading seems compatible with Madison and the Federalists' known views. But an equally plausible reading, compatible with known anti-Federalist views, is that Congress is not only prohibited from disestablishing state religious establishments and from establishing a national religion, but also from interfering with state religious establishments short of disestablishing them. It may not interfere with state laws which define freedom of religion or rights of conscience. It may not tell the states what constitutes "an establishment of religion." Thus "respecting" can plausibly be read as intensifying the prohibition on congressional interference with any state laws concerning religion. It need not be read as intensifying the prohibition on Congressional support for religion. No decisive or even plausible evidence exists that either set of meanings prevailed in conference. ...

The conference also preferred "religion" to the Senate's "articles of faith or a mode of worship." A common view reads this as evidence that "separation of sect and state in the narrow sense was rejected in favor of a broader concept of separation of religion and government. This reading requires governmental neutrality between religion and nonreligion because Congress is prohibited from *establishing* religion (in the sense of any one or some or all sects) and from *any support* for religion as such in preference to nonreligion. This plausible reading has some difficulties which have never been resolved by its advocates. To accept it we have to explain (1) why the Senate accepted this meaning when the Senate debate suggests the Senate majority opposed it on 3 and 9 September, and (2) why the conference chose to indicate this not by using the more familiar "rights of conscience" language but the utterly novel "respecting an establishment" language. ...

Absent answers to these questions, an alternative interpretation is that the Senate conferees compromised rather than acquiesced. After all "religion" was the traditional word used by the six state ratifying conventions ... whereas the Senate language was neither traditional nor recommended by any of the conventions. Hence, the conference might well have thought the conventional term to be more straightforward, more likely to calm fears, and less open to suspicions of deviousness. ...

Madison's 8 June language included both "religion" and "equal rights of conscience" and the latter aimed at constitutional equality between religious belief and unbelief. The Ames (putatively Madison) version of 20 August had the same intention. But only "religion" not "rights of conscience" survived to the conference stage. Thus the House conferees would apparently have to restore the latter language to restore Madison's original intention. Since they failed to do so, the "neutrality between religion and nonreligion" interpretation is seriously undermined. Nor did the addition of "respecting" unambiguously mean such neutrality.

This alleged neutrality is further undermined by the consideration that, if "religion" included nonreligion, then "religion" would be indistinguishable from its opposite and consequently lose all meaning. ... "Religion" as Madison, anti-Federalists, and three state ratifying conventions defined it clearly excluded nonreligion. But then the establishment clause prohibits only no law respecting an establishment of *religion.* It does not similarly prohibit laws respecting *nonreligion.* It neither prohibits Congress establishing, nor requires Congress to establish, nonreligion (or secularism as we now say). Since what it neither *prohibited* nor *required* is *permitted,* the establishment clause permits Congress to do anything it wishes about nonreligion – permit, encourage, grant legal equality, discourage, or whatever. Similarly "religion," the free exercise of which is protected, does not include non-religion. ...

If the foregoing interpretation is sound, then the conference language did not require constitutional protection for nonreligion. Madison won ... protection for Jews and "turks" and did not lose entirely even on "infidels" because he got constitutional *openness to* Congress's being neutral between religion and nonreligion. But he failed to get a constitutional *requirement* that Congress be so neutral.

This interpretation contradicts a now common view which, at least in principle if not always in practice, regards any governmental preference for religion as such as prohibited by the establishment clause. This view reads this clause as requiring governmental secularism (*i.e.,* indifference to or neutrality between religion and nonreligion) as distinguished from governmental religious pluralism (*i.e,* governmental support or protection for religion as such, in preference to nonreligion, but neutrality among religious sects). The evidence suggests that the framers of the First Amendment leaned toward the latter but did not foreclose a choice between them.

This interpretation explains why the Supreme Court has become enmeshed in seemingly endless line drawing ... in attempting to distinguish permissible from impermissible support. The reason is that the First Amendment, as developed by the First Congress, left the question of the degrees and kinds of support somewhat constitutionally open, to be decided by the political process of the multiplicity of sects and nonbelievers represented in Congress. It prohibited establishment but not all support was thought to be establishment. Hence any drawing of lines on the basis of the Constitution's intended meaning (short of what is unarguably establishment) is constitutionally arbitrary.

Levy's view that "the entire nation agreed ... the United States [under the unamended Constitution] had no power to legislate on the subject of religion" can even be shown to be contrary to Madison's understanding at least in 1788. In both the *Federalist Papers* and in the Virginia ratifying convention, Madison argued that the best and sufficient security for religious liberty with respect to the federal government was the multiplicity of sects which existed in society and which would be represented in the national legislature. "A religious sect, may degenerate into a political faction in a part of the Confederacy; but the variety of sects dispersed over the entire face of it, must secure the national Councils against any danger from that source." This argument makes no sense unless Madison supposed that the unamended Constitution gave Congress power to legislate concerning religion.

But perhaps Madison's argument does not imply the Congress had a constitutional power to legislate concerning religion but rather that the multiplicity of sects was the best political security against an unconstitutional assertion of such power. Yet Madison here treats religion exactly like any other legitimate object of legislative power. "A religious sect" could give rise to the same sort of political problems as "a rage for paper money, for an abolition of debts, for an equal division of property, or for any other improper or wicked project." For the Madison of 1788, the unamended Constitution appeared to no more deny majorities power to act regarding religion than regarding money, debts, and property. The problem was the same in each case, namely to prevent the illegitimate use of constitutional power ("majority faction") not its legitimate use ("majority rule"). Madison's solution in each case was multiplicity of interests, in particular, multiplicity of religious sects.

... A prevalent view regards Madison and Jefferson (*i.e*, their alleged strict separationism") as authoritative sources for the constitutional meaning of the [religion] clauses. This view ... is decisively misleading concerning the constitutional relation between religion and nonreligion. One incident suggests how far the final First Amendment language, as understood by the First Congress, was from Madison's later "strict separationism." The day after the House approved the final wording of the First Amendment it passed a resolution requesting President Washington to "recommend to the people of the United States, a day of public Thanksgiving and prayer to be observed, by acknowledging, with grateful hearts, the many signal favors of Almighty God, especially by affording them an opportunity peaceably to establish a Constitution of government for their safety and happiness." The Senate ... concurred. Later as president, Madison argued that such a proclamation violated the religion clauses and this is cited by advocates of "strict separationism" as authoritative evidence of their original meeting. The House-Senate Resolve suggests that Congress's understanding is contrary to the later Madison's. It requires explaining why the later Madison's understanding is more authoritative in this regard than that of the Congress which passed the language. ...

Conclusion

Separationism has remembered Madison's and Jefferson's 1785 theory of religious liberty (partly shared by Patrick Henry and Virginia Baptists) but has forgotten the partly different demands of those anti-Federalists concerned about the consequences potentially contained in the "no religious test" clause. Thus separationism misleadingly oversimplifies the concerns and intentions which went into and emerged from the First Congress debates and erroneously sees the final wording as exclusively embodying separationism.

Both paradoxes identified in the beginning can now be resolved. The meaning of the religion clauses is now derived from Federalists because contemporary interpretation has mostly forgotten a large part of anti-Federalists' demands. Similarly, the irreconcilability in principle of the establishment and free exercise clauses was not in the original meaning but is a consequence of the Court's departure from that meaning. That departure stems from attributing to the religion clauses Madison's and Jefferson's desire that government be neutral not only among religions but between religion and nonreligion. On the basis of that interpretation, but only on that basis, is there a paradox. On the alternative interpretation, that government is to some extent permitted to support religion, to prefer it to nonreligion, and is required to support free exercise of religion, no paradox need exist. The Court's paradox stems from its first imputing to the establishment clause neutrality between religion and nonreligion and then having to disover (or invent) ways around it to accommodate free exercise. The attempt to constitutionally close the question left open by Congress, that is, how much and what sorts of governmental support are permitted (short of what is unarguably establishment), is the root of this paradox.

Leonard W. Levy

The Original Meaning of the Establishment Clause of the First Amendment

The First Amendment begins with the clause against an establishment of religion: "Congress shall make no law respecting an establishment of religion." There are two basic interpretations of what the framers meant by this clause.

The U. S. Supreme Court advanced the broad interpretation most authoritatively in *Everson* v. *Board of Education* in 1947. Justice Hugo Black, speaking for the majority, declared:

> The "establishment of religion" clause of the First Amendment means at least this: Neither a state nor the Federal Government can set up a church. Neither can pass laws which aid one religion, aid all religions, or prefer one religion over another. Neither can force nor influence a person to go to or to remain away from church against his will or force him to profess a belief or disbelief in any religion. No person can be punished for entertaining or professing religious beliefs or disbeliefs, for church attendance or non-attendance. No tax in any amount, large or small, can be levied to support any religious activities or institutions, whatever they may be called, or whatever form they may adopt to teach or practice religion. Neither a state nor the Federal Government can, openly or secretly, participate in the affairs of any religious organizations or groups and vice versa. In the words of Jefferson, the clause against establishment of religion by laws was intended to erect "a wall of separation between Church and State."

The dissenting justices in the *Everson* case, while disagreeing with the majority on the question of whether the "wall of separation" had been breached by the practice at issue, concurred with the majority on the

From James E. Wood, Jr. *Religion and the State*. Waco, TX: Baylor Univ. Press, 1985, 43–77. Used by permission.

historical question of the intention of the framers. Wiley Rutledge's opinion, endorsed by all the dissenting justices, declared: "The Amendment's purpose was not to strike merely at the establishment of a single sect, creed or religion, outlawing only a formal relation such as had prevailed in England and some of the colonies. Necessarily it was to uproot all such relationships, but the object was broader than separating church and state in this narrow sense. It was to create a complete and permanent separation of the spheres of religious activity and civil authority by comprehensively forbidding every form of public aid or support for religion." Thus, the heart of this broad interpretation is that the First Amendment prohibits even government aid impartially and equitably administered to all religious groups.

The second or narrow interpretation of the Establishment Clause holds that it was intended to prevent government recognition of a single state church that would have preferences of any sort over other churches. According to this interpretation, the members of the First Congress understood "establishment of religion" as "a formal, legal union of a single church or religion with government, giving the one church or religion an exclusive position of power and favor over all other churches." Advocates of this view reject Rutledge's contention that every form of public aid or support for religion is prohibited; they also reject Justice Black's opinion that government cannot aid all religions. In their view, the wall of separation was intended merely to keep the government from abridging religious liberty by discriminatory practices against religion generally or against any particular sects or denominations. The wall was not intended, however, to create a sharp division between government and religion or to enjoin the government from fostering religion in general.

These two interpretations of the Establishment Clause are patently *irreconcilable*, yet almost every writer who has explored the evidence has concluded that the interpretation of his choice is historically "right" or "wrong." ... A preponderance of the evidence indicates that the Supreme Court's interpretation is historically the more accurate one.

The Background

The Constitutional Convention of 1789 gave only slight attention to the subject of a Bill of Rights and even less to the subject of religion. In contrast to the Declaration of Independence and to many acts of the Continental Congress, the Constitution contained no references to God. ... Its only reference to religion was in reference to qualifications for federal office-holders. ... "No religious test shall ever be required as a qualification to any office or public trust under the United States."

... In the absence of the clause, Congress might have had the power to require subscription to the articles of faith of some particular church, or to Protestantism, or to Christianity generally. The scope of the protection, however, was not defined by anyone at the time; that is, the implied ban against an establishment of religion is no aid in explaining the meaning of such an establishment.

No other references to the subject of religion occurred at the Constitutional Convention. When George Mason of Virginia expressed a wish that the new Constitution "had been prefaced with a Bill of Rights," he offered no suggestions as to the contents of such a bill. Nor did Elbridge Gerry [who] moved for a committee to prepare a Bill of Rights. This motion aroused opposition on the ground that the state bills of rights "being in force are sufficient." Mason rejoined, "The Laws of the U.S. are to be paramount to State Bills of Rights," but without further debate the motion that a Bill of Rights be prepared was defeated 10 to 0, the delegates voting as state units. Thus, on its face, the record of the Constitutional Convention is no guide to discerning the understanding of the framers as to establishments of religion.

The failure of the Convention, however, to provide for a Bill of Rights should not be misunderstood. The members of the Convention did not oppose personal liberties; in the main, they simply regarded a Bill of Rights as superfluous. The new national government possessed only limited powers; no power had been granted to legislate on any of the subjects that would be the concern of a Bill of Rights. Because no such power existed, none could be exercised or abused and, therefore, all provisions against that possibility were unnecessary. ...

The framers of the Constitution have left abundant evidence of their belief that Congress was bereft of any authority over the subject of religion. Congress was powerless, therefore, even in the absence of the First Amendment, to enact laws that benefited one religion or church in particular or all of them equally and impartially. Although it is important to try to understand the Establishment Clause of the First Amendment, this effort must be viewed within the larger framework of the Constitution.

The Ratification Controversy

... Opponents of ratification feared most of all that the centralizing tendencies of a consolidated national government would extinguish the rights of states and individuals. They objected most particularly to the failure of the instrument to provide for a Bill of Rights, and the Constitution probably would not have received the requisite number of state votes for ratification had not James Madison and other Federalist leaders pledged themselves to seek amendments constituting a Bill of Rights as soon as the new government went into operation. Indeed, six of the thirteen original states accompanied their instruments of ratification with recommendations for amendments that would secure specific personal liberties.

In the light of these facts, it is astonishing to discover that the debate on a Bill of Rights was conducted on a level of abstraction so vague as to convey the impression that Americans during 1787–88 had only the most nebulous conception of the meanings of the particular rights they sought to insure. The insistent demands for the "rights of conscience" or "trial by jury" or "liberty of the press" by the principal advocates of a Bill of Rights were unaccompanied by a reasoned analysis of what these rights meant, how far they extended, and in what circumstances they might be limited. ...

This generalization applies to the subject of establishments of religion. An awareness of the need for precision and analysis in discussing the subject might be expected, considering the variety of historical experiences with establishments before and after independence and considering the diversity of relevant state constitutions and statutory provisions. At the very least, one would expect frequent expressions of fear and concern on the subject. Amazingly, however, it received rare and then only brief mention. ...

The debates of the state ratifying conventions offer no help either. ...

Massachusetts, which maintained an establishment of religion at the time of ratification, was the first state to ratify with amendments, but the only rights mentioned were those of the criminally accused. Isaac Backus, agent for the New England Baptists ... described the Constitution as a door "opened for the establishment of righteous government, and for securing of equal liberty." Backus, and Baptists generally, passionately opposed the Massachusetts church-state system, by which the state mandated support for all Protestant churches. Clearly, he had not the slightest suspicion that the federal government could do likewise. No person in the state convention believed that the new government would have any power in religious matters.

Maryland ratified without amendments, although fifteen had been recommended, including a proposal "that there be no national religion established by law; but that all persons be equally entitled to protection in their religious liberty." Maryland's constitution permitted an establishment of religion, though none existed. All fifteen defeated amendments were designed chiefly to protect state governments from infringement by the national government. They failed not because the Federalist-dominated convention of Maryland disagreed with them, but because it wished to ratify unconditionally for the purpose of demonstrating confidence in the new system of government. The same may be said of Pennsylvania and all the other states that ratified without recommending amendments.

In South Carolina, Rev. Francis Cummins made the only reference to an establishment of religion when he condemned "religious establishments; or the states giving preference to any religious denomination." The convention's recommendations for amendments, however, mentioned nothing about a Bill of Rights. At the time, South Carolina proclaimed the "Christian Protestant ... religion to be the established religion of this state."...

In Virginia, where the most crucial struggle against establishments of religion had ended in victory just three years before the state ratifying convention met, only two speakers during the course of the lengthy debates alluded to an establishment. Edmund Randolph, defending the Constitution against Patrick Henry's allegation that it endangered religious liberty, pointed out that Congress had no power over religion and that the exclusion of religious tests for federal officeholders meant "they are not bound to support one mode of worship, or to adhere to one particular sect."

... *James Madison*, also addressing himself to Henry's general and unsupported accusation, argued at this time that a "*multiplicity of sects*" *would secure freedom of religion, but that a Bill of Rights would not.* He pointed out that the Virginia Declaration of Rights (which guaranteed "the free exercise of religion, according to the dictates of conscience") would not have exempted people "from paying to the support of one particular sect, if such sect were exclusively established by law." If a majority were of one sect, liberty would be poorly protected by a Bill of Rights. "Fortunately for this commonwealth," he added, "a majority of the people are decidedly against any exclusive establishment. I believe it to be so in the other states. There is not a shadow of right in the general government to intermeddle with religion. Its least interference with it would be a most flagrant usurpation. ... A particular state might concur in one religious project. But the United States abound[s] in such a variety of sects, that it is a strong security against religious persecution.". ...

Nonetheless, Madison and his party could not muster sufficient votes to secure Virginia's ratification of the Constitution without accepting a recommendation for amendments, which were first submitted by Patrick Henry. ... Among the recommended amendments was a provision that "no particular religious sect or society ought to be favored or established, by law, in preference to others."

In New York, Thomas Tredwell, an antiratificationist, in his speech favoring a Bill of Rights, made the only reported reference to an establishment: "I could have wished also that sufficient caution had been used to secure to us our religious liberties, and to have prevented the general government from tyrannizing over our consciences by a religious establishment." The New York debates were fully reported until the closing days of the Convention, when John Lansing, an antiratificationist leader, introduced a Bill of Rights to be prefixed to the Constitution. ... The Convention members left no explanation of what they understood by their recommendation "that no Religious Sect or Society ought to be favored or established by Law in preference of others." This wording matched that used in the state constitution of 1777, which abolished establishments of religion in New York.

North Carolina, which had abolished its establishment in 1776, recommended an amendment like that of Virginia and New York. The subject first arose in the Convention when Henry Abbot, a delegate expressing concern about the possibility of the general government's infringing religious liberty. ... [also] expressed a belief that the exclusion of religious tests was "dangerous," because Congressmen "might all be pagans."

James Iredell responded to Abbot's fears by pointing out that the exclusion of a religious test indicated an intent to establish religious liberty.

Congress was powerless to enact "the establishment of any religion whatsoever. ... If any future Congress should pass an act concerning the religion of the country, it would be an act which they are not authorized to pass, by the Constitution, and which the people would not obey." ...

Conclusions

1. No state or person favored an establishment of religion by Congress. On those few occasions when a Convention delegate or a contemporary writer mentioned an establishment of religion, he spoke either against its desirability and/or against the likelihood that there would be one.

2. The evidence does not permit a generalization as to what was meant by an establishment of religion. To be sure, most of the few references to an establishment expressly or in context referred to the preference of one church or sect or religion above others. Clearly, however, this fact taken by itself proves little. Madison, for example, was simply saying to those who believed that religious liberty was endangered by the proposed national government, "Not even your least fears shall come to pass." As for the recommendations for amendments by Virginia, New York, North Carolina, and Rhode Island, they are not clarifying. ... They do indicate the preference of one sect over others was something so feared that to assuage that fear by specifically making it groundless became a political necessity.

3. The members of the Constitutional Convention and Americans throughout the states shared a widespread understanding that the new central government would have no power whatever to legislate on the subject of religion either to aid one sect exclusively or to aid all equally. Many contemporaries, especially in New England, believed that governments could and should foster religion, or at least Protestant Christianity. All agreed, however, that the matter pertained to the realm of state government and that the federal government possessed no authority to meddle in religious matters.

Drafting and Ratification of the Establishment Clause

In the first Congress, Madison championed a Bill of Rights. Only after considerable prodding, however, did he succeed in getting a House preoccupied with what it considered the more important subject of getting the government organized to turn its attention to this matter. Madison's determination represented a change of heart. Originally he opposed a Bill of Rights on several grounds. He thought it unnecessary because the Constitution gave the national government no power to interfere in matters touching personal freedoms; he believed that liberty would be best protected not by "paper barriers," but by competition and a multiplicity of interests in society and sects in religion. In addition, he feared that a Bill of Rights might even endanger liberty by implying that the federal government possessed powers not specifically denied it.

A number of factors combined to change his mind. He realized that acceding to the demand for a Bill of Rights would deflate the movement for a new Convention and assist in the ratification of the Constitution. Moreover, Jefferson, as well as the Virginia Baptists, whose support he needed to be elected to the Congress, insisted on the need for a Bill of Rights. Jefferson, then American minister to France, sent back to Madison a steady stream of commentary on the need for a Bill of Rights, including a statement to ensure that "religious faith shall go unpunished." Jefferson has left ample evidence of his understanding of the proper relationship between church and state, especially in his Bill for Establishing Religious Freedom. Considered by Jefferson himself as one of the three crowning achievements of his life, the Act forbade Virginia's government to meddle in religion in any way. ...

The First Amendment as passed perfectly satisfied Jefferson's desire for the protection of religious liberty on the national level, as was demonstrated by his famous statement to the Danbury (Connecticut) Baptist Association in 1802: "I contemplate with sovereign reverence the act of the whole American people which declared that their legislature should 'make no law respecting an establishment of religion, or prohibiting the free exercise thereof,' thus building a wall of separation between church and state."

Virginia's Baptists, too, insisted vehemently that religion be supported only by voluntary, not by tax, contributions. They reasoned that if "the State provide a Support for Preachers of the gospel, and they receive it in Consideration of their Services, they must certainly when they Preach act as officers of the State." ... When John Leland ... represented Baptists' fears to Madison personally, he ... promised to work for a Bill of Rights including a protection for religious liberty. ... That the amendment in its final form "completely satisfied" both Jefferson and the Baptists lends strong support to the argument that the parties most interested in its passage saw it as prohibiting the government from interfering in religious matters in order to aid either one or many sects or religions.

On 8 June 1789, at the first session of the first Congress, Madison proposed ... a series of amendments to the Constitution. ... The section on religion read: "The civil rights of none shall be abridged on account of religious belief or worship, nor shall any national religion be established, nor shall the full and equal rights of conscience be in any manner, or on any pretext, infringed."

Proponents of the narrow interpretation of the Establishment Clause see in the word "national" proof of their contention that Madison intended nothing more than a prohibition against the preference for one church or religion over others. This argument presumes a drastic change of opinion on Madison's part for which no evidence exists. He had been one of the principal leaders in the fight against a general assessment in Virginia in 1785. Although that plan proposed tax support not for one religion exclusively but for all Christian religions, Madison, in his famous *Memorial and Remonstrance*, referred to it repeatedly as an "establishment of religion." ...

His subsequent actions show that he became even more scrupulous on church-state separation. As president, he vetoed a land-grant bill intended to remedy the peculiar situation of a Baptist church that had, through a surveying error, been built on public land. Congress sought to rectify the error by permitting the church to have the land rather than buy it or be dispossessed. ... He also vetoed a bill that would have incorporated a church in the District of Columbia.

In his "Detached Memoranda," written in 1817 after he had retired from the presidency, Madison expressed his disapproval of presidential proclamations of days of thanksgiving and of tax-supported chaplains for Congress and the armed services. Significantly, he described these as "establishments" or "the establishment of a national religion." ... The evidence points to the conclusion that in 1789, as in 1817, he used the phrase "national establishment" to signify not a preference for a single religion, but national action on behalf of one or all religions. Indeed, the fact that he followed his statement limiting the national government in religion with one that read, "No state shall violate the equal rights of conscience," adds further weight to this interpretation.

Without debate, Madison's recommendations for amendments were referred for consideration to a select committee of the House ... including

Madison. ... From the proposal on religion, the committee deleted the clause on "civil rights" and the word "national." The proposed amendment then read: "No religion shall be established by law, nor shall the equal rights of conscience be infringed." ... No explanation of changes was included. ...

The House began and ended its debate on the amendment on 15 August. The only account of the debate, in the *Annals of Congress,* is probably more of a condensed and paraphrased version than it is a verbatim report. ...

Amendment to the Constitution

Article 1. Between paragraphs two and three insert "no religion shall be established by law, nor shall the equal rights of conscience be infringed."

Mr. Sylvester had some doubts of the propriety of the mode of expression used in this paragraph. He apprehended that it was liable to a construction different from what had been made by the committee. He feared it might be thought to have a tendency to abolish religion altogether. ...

Mr. Gerry said it would read better if it was, that no religious doctrine shall be established by law.

Mr. Sherman thought the amendment altogether unnecessary, inasmuch as Congress had no authority whatever delegated to them by the constitution to make religious establishments. ...

Mr. Carroll. – As the rights of conscience are, in their nature, of peculiar delicacy, and will little bear the gentlest touch of governmental hand; and as many sects have concurred in opinion that they are not well secured under the present constitution, he said he was much in favor of adopting the words. He thought it would tend more towards conciliating the minds of the people to the Government than almost any other amendment he had heard proposed. ...

Mr. Madison said, he apprehended the meaning of the words to be, that Congress should not establish a religion, and enforce the legal observation of it by law, nor compel men to worship God in any manner contrary to their conscience. Whether the words are necessary or not, he did not mean to say, but they had been required by some of the State Conventions, who seemed to entertain an opinion that under the clause of the constitution, which gave power to Congress to make all laws necessary and proper to carry into execution the constitution, and the laws made under it, enabled them to make laws of such a nature as might infringe the rights of conscience, and establish a national religion; to prevent these effects he presumed the amendment was intended, and he thought it as well expressed as the nature of the language would admit.

Mr. Huntington said that he feared, with the gentleman first up on this subject, that the words might be taken in such latitude as to be extremely hurtful to the cause of religion. He understood the amendment to mean what had been expressed by the gentleman from Virginia; but others might find it convenient to put another construction upon it. The ministers of their congregations to the Eastward were maintained by the contributions of those who belonged to their society; the expense of building meeting-houses was contributed in the same manner. These things were regulated by by-laws. If an action was brought before a Federal Court on any of these cases, the person who had neglected to perform his engagements could not be compelled to do it; for a support of ministers, or building places of worship might be construed into a religious establishment.

By the charter of Rhode Island, no religion could be established by law; he could give a history of the effects of such a regulation; indeed the people were now enjoying the blessed fruits of it. [Intended as irony.] He hoped, therefore, the amendment would be made in such a way as to secure the rights of conscience, and a free exercise of the rights of religion, but not to patronize those who professed no religion at all.

Mr. Madison thought, if the word national was inserted before religion, it would satisfy the minds of honorable gentlemen. He believed that the people feared one sect might obtain a pre-eminence, or two combine together, and establish a religion to which they would compel others to conform. He thought if the word national was introduced, it would point the amendment directly to the object it was intended to prevent.

Mr. Livermore was not satisfied with that amendment; but he did not wish them to dwell long on the subject. He thought it would be better if it was altered, and made to read in this manner, that Congress shall make no laws touching religion, or infringing the rights of conscience. ...

Present-day proponents of both the narrow and the broad interpretations of the Establishment Clause are quick to see in this House debate conclusive proof for their respective points of view. In fact, however, it proves nothing conclusively. It was apathetic and unclear: ambiguity, brevity, and imprecision in thought and expression characterized the comments of the few members who spoke. That the House understood the debate, cared deeply about its outcome, or shared a common understanding of the finished amendment is doubtful.

Not even Madison himself ... seems to have troubled to do more than was necessary to get something adopted in order to satisfy popular clamor and deflate Antifederalist charges. ... The difficulty, however, lies in the fact that neither Sherman, Madison, nor anyone else took the trouble to define what "religious establishments" were. ... Livermore's motion for a change of wording apparently expressed what Madison meant by ... "national" and satisfied the Committee of the Whole. The proposed amendment, adopted by a vote of thirty-one to twenty, then read: "Congress shall make no laws touching religion, or infringing the rights of conscience." A few days later, however, on 20 August, when the House took up the report of the Committee of the Whole ... an additional change was made. ... Apparently there was a feeling that the draft of the clause based on Livermore's motion might not satisfy the demand of those who wanted something said specifically against establishments of religion. The amendment as submitted to the Senate reflected a stylistic change: "Congress shall make no law establishing religion, or prohibiting the free exercise thereof, nor shall the rights of conscience be infringed."

The Senate ... debate was conducted in secrecy and no record of it exists except for the bare account ... in the *Senate Journal.* According to the record of 3 September, three motions of special interest here were defeated on that day. These motions were clearly intended to restrict the ban in the proposed amendment to establishments preferring one sect above others. The first motion would have made the clause in the amendment read: "Congress shall make no law establishing one religious sect or society in preference to others." After the failure of a motion to kill the amendment, a motion was made to change it to read: "Congress shall not make any law infringing the rights of conscience, or establishing any religious sect or society." The last defeated motion restated the same thought differently: "Congress shall make no law establishing any particular denomination of religion in preference to another."

The failure of these three motions, each of which clearly expressed a narrow intent, would seem to show that the Senate intended something broader than merely a ban on preference to one sect. If anything is really clear about this problem of "meaning" and "intent," however, it is that nothing is clear. When the Senate returned to the clause six days later, the House amendment was changed to read: "Congress shall make no law establishing articles of faith or a mode of worship, or prohibiting the free exercise of religion." Like the three previously defeated motions, this has the unmistakable meaning of limiting the ban to acts that prefer one sect over others or which ..., establish a single state church. ...

In voting on the Senate's proposed amendments, the House ... rejected the Senate's article on religion. To resolve the disagreement between the two branches, the House proposed a joint conference committee. ... The House members of the conference committee flatly refused to accept the Senate's version of the amendment on religion, indicating that the House would not be satisfied with merely a ban on preference of one sect or religion over others. ... On 24 September, Ellsworth reported to the Senate that the House would accept the Senate's version of the other amendments provided that the amendment on religion "shall read as follows: 'Congress shall make no law respecting an establishment of religion, or prohibiting the free exercise thereof.'" ... The Senate by a two-thirds vote accepted the condition laid down by the House. Congress had passed the Establishment Clause.

Conclusions

The outstanding fact that emerges from this review of the drafting of the amendment is that Congress very carefully considered and rejected the phraseology spelling out the narrow interpretation. Through its rejection of the Senate's version of the amendment ... the House showed its intent *not* to frame an amendment that banned only Congressional support to one sect, church, denomination, or religion. ... The amendment was an expression of the fact that the framers of the Constitution had not intended to empower Congress to act in the field of religion. The "great object" of the Bill of Rights, as Madison explicitly said when introducing his draft of amendments to the House, was to "limit and qualify the powers of Government" for the purpose of making certain that the powers granted could not be exercised in forbidden fields, such as religion.

The history of the drafting of the Establishment Clause does not provide any understanding of what was meant by "an establishment of religion." To argue, however ... that the amendment permits Congressional aid and support to religion in general or to all churches without discrimination leads to the impossible conclusion that the First Amendment added to Congress' power. ... Every bit of evidence goes to prove that the First Amendment, like the others, was intended to restrict Congress to its enumerated powers. Since the Constitutional Convention gave Congress no power to legislate on matters concerning religion, Congress had no such power even in the absence of the First Amendment. It is, therefore, unreasonable to believe that an express prohibition of power – "Congress shall make no law respecting an establishment of religion" – creates the power, previously nonexistent, of supporting religion by aid to one or all religious groups. The Bill of Rights, as Madison said, was not framed "to imply powers not meant to be included in the enumeration."

Ratification of the First Amendment

By mid-June of 1790, nine states had summarily approved the Bill of Rights. Georgia, Connecticut, Massachusetts, and Virginia had not yet taken action; indeed, the first three states did not ratify the Bill of Rights until 1939. ...

Of these states, Georgia took the position that amendments were unnecessary until experience under the Constitution demonstrated the need for them. Connecticut's lower house voted to ratify ... but the state senate, apparently in the belief that a Bill of Rights was superfluous, adamantly refused to do so. ... The same sentiment was prevalent in Massachusetts. There Federalist apathy to the Bill of Rights was grounded on satisfaction with the Constitution as it was, unamended, while Antifederalists were more interested in amendments that would weaken the national government and strengthen the states than in efforts to protect personal liberties. ... In Virginia ... ratification was held up for nearly two years while the amendment was attacked as inadequate. ... Senators who opposed it explained their vote publicly in these words: "The 3d amendment [now First Amendment] recommended by Congress does not prohibit the rights of conscience from being violated or infringed: and although it goes to restrain Congress from passing laws establishing any national religion, they might, notwithstanding, levy taxes to any amount, for the support of religion or its preachers; and any particular denomination of christians might be so favored and supported by the General Government, as to give it a decided advantage over others, and in process of time render it as powerful and dangerous as if it was established as the national religion of the country."

Taken out of context and used uncritically, this statement by the eight Virginia state senators has been offered as proof that the Establishment Clause carried only the narrowest intent, that the Virginia legislators so understood it, and that the state ultimately approved it only in that narrow sense. Because the eight senators who favored a broader ban were ultimately defeated, the conclusion is drawn that the amendment did not purport to ban government aid to religion generally or to all sects without discrimination. Examination of the intricate party maneuverings and complex motives in the Virginia ratification dispute, however, sheds a different light on the senator's statement.

Virginia's Antifederalists, led by Patrick Henry ... opposed the ratification of the Constitution for a variety of reasons. Chief among these was the belief that it established too strong a central government at the expense of the states. ... It is true enough that they were also in the forefront of the movement for amendments that would protect personal liberties, but there is considerable reason to suspect that many deplored the absence of a Bill of Rights primarily for the purpose of defeating the Constitution itself. Antifederalists in the first session of Congress sought to secure amendments that would aggrandize state powers, but they failed in this effort. Then, in order to force Congress to reconsider the whole subject of amendments, Virginia's Antifederalists attempted to defeat the proposed Bill of Rights. Virginia's Federalists, however, eagerly supported the Bill of Rights in order to prevent additional amendments that might hamstring national government.

On 30 November 1789, Virginia's lower house, dominated by the Federalists, "and without debate of any consequence," quickly passed all the amendments proposed by Congress. ... The senate, by a vote of eight to seven, did decide to postpone final action on what are now the First, Sixth, Ninth and Tenth Amendments until the next session of the legislature, thereby allowing time for the electorate to express itself. It was on this occasion that the eight senators ... made their statement on the alleged inadequacy of the First Amendment, bidding for electoral support against an allegedly weak Bill of Rights by presenting themselves as champions of religious liberty and advocates of separation between government and religion.

Madison remained unworried by this tactic. ... Madison knew that the First Amendment had the support of the Baptists, the one group most insistent upon the voluntary support of religion. Second, he knew that the eight senators did not come before the electorate with clean hands. Like Henry, who laid out their strategy for them, they had consistently voted against religious liberty and in favor of taxes for religion. ... By contrast, the seven senators who favored ratification ... had stood with Jefferson and Madison ... against a state establishment of religion and for religious liberty. Finally, Madison reasoned that the statement by the eight senators was an inept piece of propaganda. ... The eight senators alleged that "any particular denomination of Christians might be so favored and supported by the general government, as to give it a decided advantage over others," – a construction of the First Amendment that not even proponents of the narrow interpretation would accept – and the same senators also asserted that the amendment "does not prohibit the rights of conscience from being violated or infringed" – whereas anyone might read for himself the Amendment's positive statement that Congress shall not abridge the free exercise of religion.

... On 15 December 1791, after a session of inaction on the Bill of Rights, the state senate finally ratified it without a record(ed) vote. In the context of Antifederalist maneuverings, there is every reason to believe that Virginia supported the First Amendment with the understanding that it had been misrepresented by the eight senators. There is no reason to believe that Virginia ratified with the understanding that the Amendment permitted government aid to religion.

What conclusions can one come to, then, in connection with ratification of the First Amendment by the states? In Virginia, the ... evidence does not support the narrow interpretation of the Establishment Clause. In nine other states there was perfunctory ratification, with no record of the debates, and in the remaining three states there was inaction. In the absence of other evidence, therefore, it is impossible to determine solely on the basis of ratification just what the general understanding of the Establishment Clause actually was.

Meaning of the Clause

... James O'Neill, one of the first advocates of the narrow interpretation, without examining establishments of religion in colonial America or the establishments that existed after the Revolution ... concluded in capital letters that an establishment of religion has always and everywhere meant "A SINGLE CHURCH OR RELIGION ENJOYING FORMAL, LEGAL, OFFICIAL, MONOPOLISTIC PRIVELEGE THROUGH A UNION WITH THE GOVERNMENT OF THE STATE."

Other scholars who insist that the First Amendment only banned a single privileged state church also fail to deal with the history of colonial and revolutionary periods, which provide repeated examples demonstrating that establishment of religion in America commonly meant something different than it did in Europe. Indeed, at the time of the framing of the Bill of Rights all state establishments that still existed in America were *multiple* establishments of *several* churches, something unknown in European experience.

The Colonial Experience

On the eve of the Revolution, establishments of religion in the European sense existed only in the Southern colonies of Virginia, Maryland, North Carolina, and Georgia, where the Church of England or Episcopalian Church was the state church. All persons, regardless of belief or affiliation, were taxed for its support as the official church of these colonies. Taxes were spent to build and maintain church buildings and pay salaries of Episcopalian clergy. ...

The record in Rhode Island, Pennsylvania, Delaware, and New Jersey is equally clear; these four colonies never experienced any establishment of religion. ...

New York's colonial history of church-state relationships provides the first example of an establishment of religion radically different from the European type, an establishment of religion in general – or at least of Protestantism in general – and without preference to one church over others. When the English conquered New Netherlands in 1664, renaming it New York in honor of its new proprietor, the Duke of York (James II), they found that the Dutch Reformed Church (Calvinist) was exclusively established as the state church. After the colony passed to English control, however, this church lost its government support. In 1665. ... Any church of the Protestant religion could become an established church. In a sense, of course, this was an exclusive establishment of one religion, Protestantism; but the system involved a multiple establishment of several different Protestant churches, in sharp contrast to European precedents, which provided for the establishment of one church only.

Under the "Duke's Laws," every township was obliged publicly to support some Protestant church and a minister. The denomination of the church did not matter. ...

Following the Glorious Revolution of 1688, the English government expected and instructed its governors of New York to implement an establishment of Anglicanism there. In 1693, Governor Benjamin Fletcher managed to have a recalcitrant legislature, composed almost entirely of non-Anglicans, pass "An Act for Settling a Ministry & raising a Maintenance for them". ... The law called only for "a good and sufficient Protestant Minister" and nowhere mentioned the Church of England. The royal governors, together with most Anglicans, asserted that the Act had established their church; but many non-Anglican New Yorkers disagreed. ...

For much of the remainder of the colonial period, Anglicans managed to pry a minister's salary out of the reluctant inhabitants, but not without constant complaints. ...

Although New York Anglicans claimed an exclusive establishment of their church, a large number of the colony's population understood the establishment set up by the Act of 1693 not simply as a state preference for one religion or sect over others, but as allowing public support for many different churches to be determined by popular vote. Thus, in 1775, Alexander Hamilton, New York's leading citizen, was able to define "an established religion" as "a religion which the civil authority engaged, not only to protect, but to support."

Massachusetts, the major and archetypal New England colony, proclaimed no establishment of the Congregational church by name after 1692. That year the general court provided for an establishment of religion on a town basis by simply requiring every town to maintain an "able, learned and orthodox" minister, to be chosen by the voters of the town and supported by a tax levied on all taxpayers. By law, several different denominations could benefit from the establishment. In fact, Congregationalists, since they constituted the overwhelming majority in nearly every town, reaped the benefits of the establishment of religion. ...

The growing number of dissenters, however, forced Congregationalists to retreat and make concessions. ... In 1728, Massachusetts exempted Quakers and Baptists from taxes for the payment of ministerial salaries. ...

Frequent abuses occurred under the system of tax exemption, which also prevailed in Connecticut. ... Many Quakers and Baptists were unconscionably forced to pay for the support of Congregational churches, and even Episcopalians who lived too far from a church of their own denomination to attend its services were taxed for support of Congregational ones. These abuses of both the letter and spirit of the law, however, do not alter the basic fact that after 1728 the establishments of religion in both colonies meant government support of two churches, Congregationalist and Episcopalian, without specified preference to either.

These injustices arose out of the overwhelming numerical superiority of Congregationalists. Although Congregationalists in fact made up the establishment in New England, prominent spokesmen among them understood that they did not constitute an exclusive establishment. ...

The situation did not substantially differ in New Hampshire. ... Some towns maintained dual establishments, others maintained multiple establishments, with free exercise for dissenters. ... Clearly New Englanders understood that an individual town could decide which denomination would be established within its precincts.

Early State Constitutions

In the wake of the American Revolution and its attendant atmosphere of liberty, those exclusive establishments of religion inherited from the colonial period collapsed. States that had never had establishments renewed their barriers against them, except for Rhode Island, which did not adopt a new state constitution. ...

The six states that continued to provide for public support of religion were careful to make concessions to the spirit of the times by extending their establishments to embrace many different groups. ...

Establishment in Massachusetts meant government support of religion and of several different churches in an equitable manner. As in colonial days, the Congregationalists were the chief beneficiaries of the establishment, primarily because they were by far the most numerous and because they resorted to various tricks to fleece non-Congregationalists out of their share of religious taxes. The fact remains, however, that Baptist, Episcopalian, Methodist, Unitarian, and even Universalist churches were publicly supported under the establishment after 1780. The establishment in Massachusetts lasted until 1833.

In New Hampshire, the state constitution of 1784 ... created a statewide multiple establishment with the guarantee that no sect or denomination should be subordinated to another. As in Massachusetts, which was the model for New Hampshire, all Protestant churches benefited. The multiple establishment ended in 1819. ...

In Maryland, where the Church of England had been exclusively established, the constitution of 1776 provided that no person could be compelled "to maintain any particular place of worship, or any particular ministry," thus disestablishing the Episcopalian Church. The same constitution, however, provided for a new establishment of religion: "Yet the Legislature may, in their discretion, lay a general and *equal tax*, for the support of the Christian religion; leaving to each individual the power of appointing the payment over of the money, collected from him, to the support of any particular place or worship or minister." "Christian" rather than "Protestant" was used in Maryland because of the presence of a large

Catholic population, thus insuring nonpreferential support of all churches existing in the state. ... In 1810, the power to enact a multiple establishment was taken from the legislature by a constitutional amendment providing that "an *equal* and *general* tax or any other tax ... for the support of *any religion*" was not lawful.

Georgia's constitution of 1777 tersely effected the disestablishment of the Church of England while permitting a multiple establishment of all churches without exception: "All persons whatever shall have the free exercise of their religion; ... and shall not, unless by consent, support any teacher or teachers except those of their own profession." ... According to the 1785 law, all Christian sects and denominations were to receive tax support in proportion to the amount of property owned by their respective church members. ... In the state constitution adopted in 1798, however, Georgia separated church and state by a guarantee against any religious taxes and by placing the support of religion on a purely voluntary basis.

South Carolina's constitution of 1778 was the sixth state constitution providing for a multiple establishment of religion. Article 28 most elaborately spelled out the details for the maintenance of the "Christian Protestant religion" as "the established religion of this State." ... In 1790 South Carolina, reflecting the influence of the federal Bill of Rights, adopted a new constitution with no provisions whatever for public support of religion. ...

In 1776, North Carolina banned state support for religion and disestablished the Church of England. By contrast, Virginia's constitution of 1776 was noncommittal on the subject of an establishment. At the close of 1776, the Church of England was for all practical purposes disestablished in Virginia by a statute that forever exempted all nonmembers from taxes for its support. ... The statute ... however, expressly reserved for future decision the question whether religion ought to be placed on a private, voluntary basis or be supported on a non-preferential basis by a new "general" assessment.

In 1779, a bill for support on a nonpreferential basis was introduced; at the same time, however, Jefferson's Bill for Establishing Religious Freedom was introduced, providing, in part, "that no man shall be compelled to frequent or support any religious worship, place, or ministry whatsoever." The principle underlying this provision was Jefferson's belief that religion was a personal matter between the individual and God and not rightfully a subject under the jurisdiction of the civil government. By contrast, the

"General Assessment Bill" was predicated on the supposition, that the state must encourage religion. This bill stipulated that the Christian religion should be "the established religion," that societies of Christians organized for the purpose of religious worship should in law be regarded as churches of the established religion, each to have its own "name or denomination" and each to share the tax proceeds. ... Every person was to designate the church of his membership, and that church alone would receive his taxes; money collected from persons not designating membership was to be divided proportionately among all churches of his county.

Confronted by two diametrically opposed bills, the Virginia legislature deadlocked, and neither bill could muster a majority. In 1784, Patrick Henry reintroduced the general assessment plan ... in which the stated purpose was to require "a moderate tax or contribution annually for the support of the Christian religion, or of some Christian church, denomination or communion of Christians, or for some form of Christian worship." A resolution in favor of the bill was passed against the opposition of a minority led by Madison.

Only the notes of Madison's speech against the measure remain. These show that he argued that religion is a matter of private rather than civil concern, and that taxes in support of religion violated religious liberty. The true question, he declared, was not "Is religion necessary?" but rather "Are religious establishments necessary for religion?," to which he argued in the negative. ... He brought his case to the people by writing his famous "Memorial and Remonstrance Against Religious Assessments." This widely distributed pamphlet acted as a catalyst for the opposition to the assessment bill and resulted in the election of a legislature with an overwhelming majority against it. The new legislature let the bill die unnoticed, and by a vote of sixty-seven to twenty enacted instead Jefferson's bill for religious freedom with its provision against government support of religion.

Conclusions

The struggle in Virginia ... is usually featured in accounts of the history of separation of church and state in America. Historians focus their attention on the Virginia story because the sources are uniquely ample, the struggle was important and dramatic, and the opinions of Madison, the principal framer of the Bill of Rights, not to mention those of Jefferson, were fully elicited. As a result, the details of no other state controversy over church-state relationships are so familiar. If, however, one is concerned with attempting to understand what was meant by "an establishment of religion" at the time of the framing of the Bill of Rights, the histories of the other states are equally important. ... Five states actually had constitutional provisions authorizing general assessments for religion, and a sixth (Connecticut) provided for the same by statute. Had the assessment bill in Virginia been enacted, it would simply have increased the number of states maintaining multiple establishments from six to seven.

Clearly the provisions of these six states show that to understand the American meaning of "an establishment of religion" one cannot arbitrarily adopt a definition based on European experience. In every European precedent of an establishment, the religion established was that of a single church. ... Establishments in America, however, both in the colonial and early state periods, were not limited in nature or in meaning to state support of one church. *An establishment of religion in America at the time of the framing of the Bill of Rights meant government aid and sponsorship of religion, principally by impartial tax support of the ... churches.*

In no state or colony ... was there ever an establishment of religion that included every religion ... Neither Judaism, nor Buddhism, nor Islam, nor any but a Christian religion was ever established in America. In half of the six multiple establishments existing in 1789, Protestantism was the established religion; in the other half, Christianity was. No member of the First Congress came from a state that supported an exclusive establishment of religion; no such example could have been found in colonial America. Of those states that provided public support for religion, half of them had provided for such at least theoretically since the early eighteenth century; the remainder did so from the time of the American Revolution. Their experience told the legislators in 1789 that an establishment of religion meant not simply state preference for one religion but nonpreferential support for any or all.

Chapter IV

Religion Clauses and
Supreme Court Cases

Background: From 1787 to 1940, when the First Amendment applied to the national government and not the states, Bible readings and singing of religious songs in public schools did not violate the constitutions of the majority of American states. But did these practices violate the "fundamental rights" of those who did not want to pray or sing? Did a school board's sanction of the prayers constitute an establishment of religion? In 1963 the Supreme Court ruled it did. According to the Court, the First Amendment now applied to the states, due to the principle of incorporation – applying most of the provisions of the Bill of Rights to the states through the intervention of the 14th Amendment. The 14th Amendment prohibits states from abridging the privileges or immunities of citizens or depriving them of due process and equal protection of the laws.

The Supreme Court took the first step toward incorporation in 1925 when it ruled, in *Pierce v. the Society of Sisters,* that states could not require children to attend public, as opposed to private, schools because this "unreasonably interferes with the liberty of parents and guardians to direct the upbringing and education of children under their control." The Court thus found a constitutional right of parents to send their children to private (including parochial/religious) schools. The second and determining step that made incorporation official also occurred in 1925. In *Gitlow v. New York,* the Supreme Court assumed for the sake of argument that freedom of speech and the press "are among the fundamental personal rights and 'liberties' protected by the due process clause of the 14th Amendment from impairment by the states." From this point on, the Court began ruling that most of the freedoms and prohibitions against federal action enumerated in the Bill of Rights applied to the states.

The incorporation of the free exercise clause came in 1940 in *Cantwell v. Connecticut*. The Supreme Court held that states could not prohibit the right of a Jehovah's Witness to witness (or, in this case, to assault a neighborhood made up almost entirely of Catholics with anti-Catholic propaganda shouted out by bull-horn and strong lungs.) According to the Court, "the First Amendment declares that Congress shall make no law respecting an establishment of religion or prohibiting the free exercise thereof. The 14th Amendment has rendered the legislation of the states as incompetent as Congress to enact such laws."

Three years later the Court ruled against a state law that required saluting the American flag in public schools. It affirmed the right of Jehovah's Witness children to abstain from this practice which violated their religious scruples against worshipping a "graven image." (*West Virginia State Board of Education v. Barnette*, 1943). Justice Murphy expressed the majority opinion, "Official compulsion to affirm what is contrary to one's religious beliefs is the antithesis of freedom of worship." Justice Jackson concurred. "The very purpose of a Bill of Rights was to withdraw certain subjects from the vicissitudes of political controversy, to place them beyond the reach of majorities and officials and to establish them as legal principles to be applied by the courts. One's right to life, liberty, and property, to free speech, a free press, freedom of worship ... may not be submitted to vote; they depend upon the outcome of no elections."

The Court incorporated the establishment clause four years later in *Everson v. the Board of Education*, 1947. In so doing, it also expanded, revised, or clarified (the choice of verb varies depending on one's separationist or accommodationist credentials) the definition of 'establishment' to include the prohibition against "aid to all religion." In this chapter, the authors explore the constitutionality of this definition as the Court applied it in cases after 1947. The cases discussed below involve individuals and groups making claims against state and federal governments for free exercise protection versus individuals, groups, and governmental agencies balancing "no establishment of religion" considerations and legislative exigencies against these claims.

Authors: George S. Goldberg is an attorney and a member of the Bar of the Supreme Court. In a refreshingly irreverent book on the Supreme Court, he takes a non-preferentialist view of the religion clauses, and assumes the First Amendment forbids the establishment of a national church and national interference with religious practices. In his view, the designers of the 14th Amendment did not intend to subject the states to similar prohibitions. In a scathing conservative critique of the activist Court's assault on the free exercise of religion, Goldberg focuses on cases dealing with impartial government aid to children attending parochial/sectarian schools, released time to allow school children to receive religious instruction either on or off campus, and the end of prayer in school. He is especially critical of the decisions in *Everson* and *Lemon v. Kurtzman*, which rejected non-preferential aid to religion because aid presumably entailed de facto establishment of religion. He assails these cases for contributing to what he calls "the federal takeover of religion" by a largely separationist court that sacrifices free exercise on the altar of no establishment.

Goldberg concludes that the greatest threat to religion is not the presumably inevitable tension between the establishment and free exercise clauses, when one must be sacrificed for the other, so much as it is the Supreme Court's ahistorical and contradictory philosophy that considers any governmental aid to religion, no matter how evenhanded, prohibited by the establishment clause. Relying on this philosophy produces tensions because under its Catch-22 logic, according to Goldberg, "what the free exercise clause requires ... the establishment clause forbids." Goldberg's call for tearing down the Court-built wall between church and state is echoed in Michael McConnell's rejection of strict separationism. (See his comments in Chapter II.)

In McConnell's article in this chapter, he criticizes the misleading and overemphasized Jeffersonian metaphor: the "wall of separation between church and state." In his view, while the wall of separation protects both church and state, the recent application of the concept by the Supreme Court threatens to overwhelm "the wider and more important ideal of religious freedom." McConnell condemns, for example, its application in recent cases that prevented public remedial teachers from going into parochial schools, prohibited students from airing religious doctrines on high school campuses, and denied Native Americans exemption from federal regulation of their sacred wilderness areas. He blames the separationist Supreme Court doctrine for putting "religious freedom and diversity on a collision course with the welfare-regulated state," and undermining governmental accommodation of "the religious needs of religious minorities." Both McConnell and Goldberg advocate a constitutional doctrine that "preserves separation without stifling religious choice," i.e., a mixture of government neutrality toward, and accommodation of, religion – with the accent on accommodation.

Reverend Dean M. Kelley, Director for Religious Liberty at the liberal-leaning National Council of Churches, disagrees with McConnell's assessment and accent. He notes that strict separation "has not retained much currency in the court's opinions since 1970." Kelley worries more about the Court's deference to "the needs of the state" (statism) than about its supposed separationist tendencies or establishment phobia, and concludes that "neither religious clause should be subordinated to the other." In his view, this subordination can be avoided if one accepts Chief Justice Warren Burger's concept of "benevolent neutrality which will permit religious exercise to exist without sponsorship and without interference."

Given this obligation to neutrality, Kelley objects to McConnell's advocacy of public funding, without restrictions, for church-related service agencies. In his view, such a linkage between church and state threatens separation, is "inherently unstable, and will tend to move in one direction or the other" – secularization or religionization of public services. In other words, Kelley fears that if the government funds church-run agencies (hospitals and drug rehabilitation centers, for example) without imposing regulations and guidelines, then churches might use these agencies as platforms to prosletyze. On the other hand, no one wants to see churches prohibited from participation. Hence the call for neutrality: churches may help, but not preach when they do.

Leo Pfeffer, former general counsel for the American Jewish Congress, has appeared numerous times before the Supreme Court to support a strict separation of church and state. He takes issue with the claims of Goldberg and McConnell that *Everson* and *Lemon v. Kurtzman*, cases in which the Supreme Court ruled non-preferential aid to religion unconstitutional, violate the original intent of the founders. Pfeffer would remind Goldberg and McConnell that the Court, not legal scholars, define what is or is not unconstitutional. Therefore "the Establishment Clause means just what the Supreme Court or a majority thereof at any particular time wants it to mean, neither more nor less."

Pfeffer also argues that separation of church and state (embodied in the establishment clause) and the free exercise of religion are not opposing principles, but rather unitary or interdependent concepts: "separation guarantees freedom and freedom requires separation." Pfeffer thus challenges the dualistic (non-preferentialist or accommodationist) approach, which objects to an absolute separation of church and state and sees two independent mandates in the first amendment: one against establishment and one against impairment of free exercise of religion, with the latter being primary.

According to Pfeffer, history and Supreme Court decisions not only fail to support dualism, but show that the Court, which seeks to avoid declaring one religion clause subordinate to another, nonetheless often implicitly favors the establishment clause. He uses the following cases and issues to support his assertions: tax exemption for church property, which he sees as doomed; aid to parochial schools, which the Court ruled violative of the establishment clause; and religious tests for public office, which violate one or both of the religion clauses, as well as the 14th Amendment. Based on his analysis of these and other cases, Pfeffer concludes that disestablishment of religion is not merely a means to achieve the free exercise of religion, but that both clauses together guarantee separation and freedom.

The position of Paul J. Weber, Professor of Political Science at the University of Louisville, falls somewhere between the extremes represented by Goldberg and Pfeffer. Like the first four authors, Weber also tackles the problem of defining separation of church and state in both its historical and current contexts. He discovers five meanings, with only one meeting the legal requirements that the definition be just, realistic, and reflective of the framer's intent.

He believes that most of the founders opted for a definition of separation as a "structural separation" – wherein government offices, organizations, and laws were independent of religion. This option differs from "absolute separation" which holds that "no aid of any kind should flow from government to religion." Weber sees this absolutist version as ahistorical, unrealistic, and contrary to the laws and customs of the land. A more extreme and equally objectionable version is "transvaluing separation," advocates of which hope to secularize American political culture completely.

In stark contrast, "supportive separationists" (accommodationists) "favor aid and support religion, holding only that government may not support one religion over another." Weber believes this definition is ahistorical and unlikely to win favor anytime soon. Finally there is "equal separation" or "strict neutrality" – a hybrid type which will provide "protection for religion without providing privileges." Weber finds this type reminiscent of Madison and thus most appealing. His defense of neutrality and equal protection for non-religious groups and individuals, which denies a special status for religious rights, brings him closer to Pfeffer's strict separationist position than to the accommodationist position.

Key Questions: What led the U.S. Supreme Court to apply the religion clauses of the First Amendment to state action via the 14th Amendment (incorporation theory)? Does the principle of the strict separation of church and state mandate that the no establishment clause supercedes the free exercise of religion clause? Has the judicial activism of the mid 20th century Supreme Court, which embraced a broadened view of establishment, enhanced or undermined religious liberty and freedom of conscience in the U.S? Do prayers in public schools, tax exemptions for religious institutions, or state aid to religious schools constitute an establishment of religion? Do the religion clauses prohibit government action that either confers a benefit or imposes a burden on religion? Or, do they allow non-preferential accommodation with respect to religious institutions and practices?

George Goldberg

Church, State and the Constitution

It never occurred to anyone that in prohibiting the federal government from interfering in church-state relations, the First Amendment would have any effect at all on state activities in that area. In the words of Chief Justice John Marshall, perhaps the greatest jurist in American history:

> Had the people of the several states, or any of them, required changes in their constitutions, had they required additional safeguards to liberty from the apprehended encroachments of their particular governments, the remedy was in their own hands, and would have been applied by themselves. The unwieldy and cumbrous machinery of procuring a recommendation from two-thirds of Congress and the assent of three-fourths of their sister states, could never have occurred to any human being as a mode of doing that which might be effected by the state itself.

In its own proper sphere, where its own affairs were concerned, it was naturally assumed that the federal government would maintain friendly relations with the various faiths represented by its members. Thus the first Congress, which proposed the Bill of Rights, appointed chaplains at the outset of its first session. It also appointed chaplains for the armed forces and resolved that George Washington's inaugural should culminate in a divine service at St. Paul's chapel. ... Indeed, on the very day that it approved the First Amendment, the Congress called upon President Washington to proclaim a day of "public thanksgiving and prayer." Sessions of the U.S. Supreme Court were, as they still are, commenced with a prayer that "God save the United States and this honorable Court."

The federal government was forbidden to interfere with the people's religious life. It was not required to abandon its own.

Regnery Gateway, 1987, 12–137. Used by permission.

As for religious toleration, the results could not have been better. By mid-century, all the state establishments had been dismantled. Americans were by far the freest people in the world in their religious lives. Pockets of intolerance continued to exist here and there, to be sure. But precisely because church-state relations were a local concern, progress could be achieved without confrontations on the national level; and in extreme cases members of a persecuted minority could seek a more congenial community without having to abandon their country. ...

After the Civil War three amendments to the Constitution were passed which expressly limited the powers of the states. ... The [Fourteenth] Amendment ... required each state to treat all persons within its jurisdiction on an equal basis. It provided that:

> No State shall make or enforce any law which shall abridge the privileges or immunities of citizens of the United States; nor shall any State deprive any person of life, liberty or property, without due process of law; nor deny to any person within its jurisdiction the equal protection of the laws.

As we shall see, it was this Amendment which the Supreme Court ultimately used to extend the religion clauses of the First Amendment to the states. Surprisingly, it was not the "privileges and immunities" clause or even the "equal protection" clause that the Court fastened upon, but the "due process" clause. But that was much later. At the time, religion was not mentioned or thought of in connection with any of the Civil War Amendments. ...

[In 1875] the Blaine Amendment would have extended the religious clauses of the First Amendment to the states and, for good measure, have added a prohibition of aid to parochial schools.

The House passed the Blaine Amendment and sent it to the Senate where it was proposed by Senator Frelinghuysen. ... [who] noted that the First Amendment was "an inhibition on Congress, and not on the States." He continued:

> The [Blaine Amendment] very properly extends the prohibition of the first amendment of the Constitution to the States. Thus the [Blaine Amendment] prohibits the States, for the first time, from the establishment of religion, from prohibiting its free exercise, and from making any religious test a qualification to office.

Senator Eaton of Connecticut found the Blaine Amendment offensive. "I am opposed," he said, "to any State prohibiting the free exercise of any religion; and I do not require the Senate or the Congress of the United

States to assist me in taking care of the State of Connecticut in that regard." Senator Whyte agreed: "The first amendment to the Constitution prevents the establishment of religion by congressional enactment; it prohibits the interference of Congress with the free exercise thereof, and leaves the whole power for the propagation of it with the States exclusively."

Both proponents and opponents of the Blaine Amendment agreed that nothing in the Constitution prohibited the states from establishing a religion or from interfering with the free exercise thereof. Certainly no one imagined that the Fourteenth Amendment had extended the religion clauses of the First Amendment to the states. As many members of the Congress which considered the Blaine Amendment had sat in the Congress which voted for the Fourteenth Amendment seven years earlier, it is unlikely they overlooked its possible significance.

The Blaine Amendment did not receive the necessary votes in the Senate. For the next half century it was reintroduced in Congress after Congress. It never passed. It was not abandoned, however, until the Supreme Court, by judicial fiat, made it superfluous.

Judicial Nonsense

World War II was raging ... but [Arch] Everson and his friends were distracted from the war effort by their concern that, under a state statute authorizing school boards to defray the transportation costs of all school children within their jurisdictions, Catholic parochial school children would have their fares paid. ...

Everson argued that, to the extent its benefits flowed to parochial school children, the statute constituted an establishment of religion. There was no suggestion, that any one religion was being preferred over any other. The fare reimbursement plan was apparently available to all school children, public, parochial, and private secular alike. Claims under the establishment clause normally charge some governmental authority with playing favorites among religions – many scholars believe that that is precisely the meaning of establishment as used in the First Amendment. But Everson opposed any public benefit to religion *no matter how nondiscriminatory.*

That was a very extreme interpretation of the establishment clause. Indeed, to deny the benefits of a publicly financed program to specified groups solely on the basis of their religious orientation would seem to be just what the religion clauses of the First Amendment were designed to *prevent*. But before that issue could even be addressed in the Everson case, the Court had to extend the establishment clause to the states, which in 1947, when the Everson case reached the Supreme Court, had never been done.

Perhaps, applying the Court's test for extending provisions of the Bill of Rights to the states, the right to the free exercise of one's religion is "a fundamental principle of liberty and justice which inheres in the very idea of free government and is the inalienable right of a citizen of such a government." That is, apart from the history of the Fourteenth Amendment, which showed that it had not been intended to extend the free exercise clause to the states, many people might readily agree that no government, federal, state, or local, should be allowed to interfere with how a person worships. ...

There are thus good reasons for treating the establishment clause differently from those provisions of the Bill of Rights, including the free exercise clause, ... which had been made applicable to the states via the due process clause of the Fourteenth Amendment. At least, whether it should be treated the same or differently was the threshold issue before the Court. But the opinion for the majority was written by Justice Hugo Black, who for years had been pressing the Court to incorporate into the due process clause of the Fourteenth Amendment the entire Bill of Rights and thereby make every clause in it fully applicable to the states. It was therefore no surprise that, after referring to the cases which had incorporated other provisions of the Bill of Rights, Black simply declared, "There is every reason to give the same application and broad interpretation to the 'establishment of religion' clause."

But extending the reach of the establishment clause to the states was only half of the job. Now Black had to extend the meaning of the establishment clause beyond its traditional import of playing favorites among religions. He went on:

> The 'establishment of religion' clause of the First Amendment means at least this: Neither a state nor the Federal Government can set up a church. Neither can pass laws which aid one religion, *aid all religions,* or prefer one religion over another.

The italicized phrase, slipped by Black into the middle of an otherwise unexceptional definition of establishment, may qualify as the most momentous three-word phrase in judicial history. It is on the basis of these three little words, unsupported by judicial precedent or history, that the Court has sought to destroy the financial underpinning of religious education in America while excising all reference to God from the public schools.

After all that, one would naturally expect the Court to strike down the New Jersey fare reimbursement plan as unconstitutional. But Black ... did precisely the opposite. It was to be another example of the time-tested judicial technique of assuming a new, far-reaching power while declining to exercise it, so as to neutralize opposition to the assumption of power. ...

His four concurring brethren liked the result and the four dissenters not only wanted to extend the establishment clause to the states but wanted to use it in this case to void the New Jersey statute. No Justice was in a position to protest Black's coup.

Indeed, Justice Rutledge, writing for the dissenting minority of four Justices, stated the strict separationist position: ... as establishment and free exercise are but two sides of the same coin, anything protected as free exercise cannot, by reason of the establishment clause, receive any public support.

The danger of the Court's overextension of the free exercise clause was now becoming apparent. ... For while it may be possible to accept a very wide interpretation of free exercise as an expansion of freedom, if government support of or even association with any subject subsumed under the rubric free exercise is to be ruled out under the establishment clause, then every extension of the free exercise clause may paradoxically result in a narrowing rather than a broadening of personal freedom. ...

Almost the only justification for extending the establishment clause to the states is that the Court had finally been persuaded by Justice Black that the entire Bill of Rights had to be so extended, and that to make any exception to total incorporation was to muddy the constitutional waters. But in fact the Court was not at all ready for total incorporation, despite appearances to the contrary in the Everson case, for only a few months later it again held that the Fifth Amendment privilege against self-incrimination, which some people might think closer to the core meaning of freedom than the right to make Catholic kids pay their own bus fares, was not applicable to the states. Indeed, Justice Frankfurter, whose dissenting opinion in Everson had *assumed* the incorporation of the establishment clause into the Fourteenth Amendment, now wrote an opinion in which he ridiculed the very idea of incorporation.

For seventy years after the adoption of the Fourteenth Amendment,

Frankfurter wrote, forty-three Justices, including "those whose services in the cause of human rights and the spirit of freedom are the most conspicuous in our history," passed on its scope and "only one, who may respectfully be called an eccentric exception, ever indicated the belief that the Fourteenth Amendment was a shorthand summary of the [Bill of Rights] and that due process incorporated [it] as restrictions upon the powers of the states." ...

Black's incorporation doctrine, one of the most influential doctrines in American constitutional history, has been subjected to a great deal of scholarly criticism, almost all of it negative. One scholar ... found that there was no more judicial than historical support for Black's position, which he characterized "as nothing more than a bald attempt to amend the Constitution by judicial fiat."

The attempt was eminently successful. The result of Black's amendment was that the establishment clause became ever more voracious until it threatened to swallow up the free exercise clause, thereby turning the original design on its head – from which undignified position, said Catholic theologian John Courtney Murray, "it cannot but gurgle judicial nonsense."

The Court had completed the federal takeover of religion in America. We shall now see what it did with its new power. ...

Released Time

[In 1940] the Champaign Council on Religious Education was formed to provide religious instruction in the public schools of Champaign, Illinois. ... The Council was made up of Protestant, Catholic, and Jewish parents who wished to use school time to afford their children the religious instruction they were apparently unwilling to receive after school or on weekends. In keeping with the "released time" concept then in use by some two million children in communities across the United States, the Champaign parents asked their Board of Education to permit teachers hired and paid by the Council to give a half hour per week of religious instruction to those children whose parents formally requested such instruction. The children would be released from their regular classes for this period to go to separate classrooms for instruction in the religion of their expressed preference, while children whose parents did not request religious instruction would continue with their secular studies. The Board agreed.

Terry [McCollum] loved the religious class and was strongly affected by it. ... "The children made posters of the Resurrection," Vashti [McCollum] remembered some years later, and Terry "sat and gazed at his worshipfully. This bothered me." Vashti was sufficiently bothered by the success of the religion classes that when Terry entered the fifth grade she adamantly refused to renew his permission to attend them.

The school now waged a campaign against ten-year-old Terry which made a mockery of its later claim that the released time program was voluntary. One day, for example, while the religion classes were in operation, Terry was made to sit alone in a small anteroom outside the teachers' toilet, where teachers coming and going made manifest their disapproval. ...

Vashti sued.

Precedent was squarely against her. When Mrs. McCollum brought her suit, in 1944, the Court had not yet extended the establishment clause to the states. It had recently, in the Cantwell case in 1940, incorporated the free exercise clause into the Fourteenth Amendment, but it had never held that nonbelievers were protected under that clause. At the outset, then, she had to avoid a summary dismissal on the ground that there was no constitutional provision under which relief could be granted.

Then there was the twenty-year-old Oregon case in which the Court had held that parents had a constitutional right to send their children to private schools. ... If the Constitution required that a child be released from public school entirely to attend a church school, how could it be argued that the same Constitution forbade his release for a half hour of religious instruction a week?

Perhaps the most adverse precedent was the second Witness flag salute case, which the Court had just decided. It was McCollum's strongest argument that the released time program in the Champaign schools was not really voluntary, despite the school board's insistence that it was, for there were subtle pressures, and some not so subtle, on every student to participate. Thus the state was using public funds and its compulsory education law to compel children to worship, surely a violation of the establishment clause and perhaps of the free exercise clause also.

But the argument of subtle or even overt pressure seemed untenable in light of the Witness flag salute cases. While the Court had just overruled its prior decision and now held that Witness Children could not be compelled against their religious scruples to salute the American flag, it had not held or even suggested that therefore, to avoid possible pressure on the Witness children to violate their consciences, nobody could salute the flag. Yet the pressures on children daily to salute the flag, especially in wartime, might be expected to be far fiercer than the pressures to participate once a week in a program of religious instruction. ...

The Supreme Court held the Champaign released time program unconstitutional by a vote of eight to one. Justice Black, who exactly one year before had written the opinion in the Everson case which extended the establishment clause to the states, again dealt with the essential issues and inconvenient precedents by ignoring them all, even the Oregon case which had established the right of parents to take their children out of the public schools altogether for education in parochial schools. Black wrote:

> Pupils compelled by law to go to school for secular education are released in part from their legal duty upon the condition that they attend the religious classes. [This] falls squarely under the ban of the First Amendment (made applicable to the States by the Fourteenth) as we interpreted it in Everson.

Justice Frankfurter, who had been passionately opposed to allowing Witness children to abstain from saluting the flag while everyone else pledged allegiance, now wrote with equal passion that Terry McCollum must not only be allowed to abstain from attending religious instruction, but that, because he wished to abstain, everyone else must be required to abstain lest Terry be pressured into participating. Ironically, Justice Frankfurter was most concerned with the divisive effects of allowing any form of religious activity in the public schools, for there now ensued a battle royal over the meaning and scope of the Court's decision. In school districts across the country parents and teachers and school administrators wondered whether all forms of religious instruction were now illegal, and if they were, whether the ban extended to school prayers, Bible readings, Christmas and Hanukkah pageants, annual performances of Handel's *Messiah* or *Judas Maccabeus*, and perhaps even the singing at assemblies of "God Bless America." ...

It was all unnecessary. Had the Court adhered to its fundamental principle of judicial restraint ... under which cases are decided on the narrowest available grounds, it could easily have avoided rendering so far-reaching a decision. For it should have been clear that the Champaign program, as administered, was not voluntary. Pressures from fellow students are one thing. ... But official pressures are a very different thing, from which students are entitled to be protected. The open attempts by the teachers in Terry's school to compel him to take religious instruction despite his parents' known opposition rendered the program coercive as to him and, as such, patently unconstitutional.

But that did not make the concept of released time inherently improper, any more than the possibility of being beaten into a confession by the police renders all confessions invalid. ... The possibility that a particular program of ostensibly voluntary religious instruction might not be truly voluntary need not invalidate all programs of religious instruction. It should be possible for a court in a particular case to determine whether a program claimed to be voluntary truly respected every student's freedom of choice and to strike down only those programs where coercive pressures were brought to bear by the authorities. ...

But in the McCollum case, the Court did not even consider such distinctions, preferring to issue a blanket condemnation of an activity which had been going on for many years – the released time movement antedated the First World War – and which many people seemed to like. ...

The End of School Prayer

One of the admitted problems with school prayers is the danger of offending one or another religious group if a prayer offensive to it is chosen. If the authority of Jesus Christ is invoked the prayer must offend every Jewish child (and parent), but if His authority is not invoked Christian children (and parents) may be upset. ...

The New York Board of Regents, charged to foster the well-being of one of the most religiously diverse student populations in the country, endeavored to solve this problem by composing a truly nondenominational prayer. This is what it produced:

> Almighty God, we acknowledge our dependence upon Thee, and we beg Thy blessings upon us, our parents, our teachers and our Country.

This little prayer was disparaged as "more doctrinally flavorless than grace before a community chest luncheon" ... and "such a pathetically vacuous assertion of piety as hardly to rise to the dignity of a religious exercise."

Nevertheless, when the school board of New Hyde Park ... adopted the Regents' Prayer, suit was immediately filed by "members of the Jewish faith, of the Society for Ethical Culture, of the Unitarian Church, and one non-believer." They claimed ... that "The saying of the prayer and the manner and setting in which it is said are contrary to the religion and religious practices of those petitioners, and their children, who are believers, and to the beliefs concerning such matters held by the petitioner, and his children, who are non-believers."

For its part, the Board of Regents conceded that its prayer, though recited in conjunction with the Pledge of Allegiance, was a religious exercise. It claimed, however, and the trial judge found, that unlike the situation in McCollum there was no element whatsoever of coercion. The Board had directed that no child was to be compelled or even encouraged to say the prayer, and there was no evidence that the New Hyde Park school had violated this order.

Thus the issue was squarely presented for the first time: Is any religious exercise in a public school, no matter how brief and voluntary, prohibited by the United States Constitution?

Judge Bernard S. Meyer, the trial judge, ... concluded "that neither the sense of the nation, the debates, nor the individual views of the framers proscribe prayer as the ceremonial opening of a school day." ... He referred to the Supreme Court decisions in the Oregon case (children must be released from public school to attend private schools even if they are run by a church), Everson ... McCollum ... and Zorach (the New York released time case – religious classes during school hours but off school grounds are valid), and concluded that "The Zorach decision constitutes a retreat from both Everson and McCollum. The Zorach case holds that the Constitution does not require separation in every and all respects and, as we have seen, constitutional history confirms a tradition of prayer in the schools."

As for the issue of coercion, Judge Meyer reviewed the safeguards prescribed by the Board of Regents and found them essentially adequate. ... But he emphasized that he was speaking about official coercion – "overt acts of the teachers or other school authorities" – and not possible embarrassment or peer pressure. "To recognize 'subtle pressures' as compulsion under the [First] Amendment is to stray far afield from the oppressions the Amendment was designed to prevent; to raise the psychology of dissent, which produces pressure on every dissenter, to the level of governmental force; and to subordinate the spiritual needs of believers to the psychological needs of nonbelievers." Had the Supreme Court adopted such a sensible position in the McCollum case, a generation of judicial conflict could have been avoided.

Judge Meyer found the Regents' Prayer constitutional. His decision was unanimously affirmed by the five-man Appellate Division. ... New York's highest court, in an opinion written by the Chief Judge, held:

> Not only is this prayer not a violation of the First Amendment ... but a holding that it is such a violation would be in defiance of all American history, and such a holding would destroy a part of the essential foundation of the American governmental structure.

A concurring judge went even further:

> It is not mere neutrality to prevent voluntary prayer to a Creator; it is an interference by the courts, contrary to the plain language of the Constitution, on the side of those who oppose religion. ...

[These rulings did not dissuade six] Supreme Court Justices from declaring the prayer an unconstitutional establishment of religion.

The land was filled with roars of incredulity and outrage. It seemed amazing to persons unversed in legal legerdemain that in 1962 it should be discovered for the first time that the First Amendment (adopted 1791), even as supposedly extended by the Fourteenth Amendment (adopted 1868), forbade something which had been going on without interruption since the colonization of the American continent. ...

[In 1963] The Supreme Court heard oral argument in ... a similar case involving a family named Schempp. ... [According to a] Pennsylvania statute: "Any child shall be excused from such Bible reading upon the written request of his parent or guardian." Thus the Schempp children needed only a note from their parents, Unitarians who disapproved of parts of the Bible, to be excused from hearing it read. But the Schempps argued that they should not be put in the position of having to single out their children for special treatment and perhaps reprisals. As they did not want their children to hear readings from the Bible, nobody should be permitted to hear them.

The Court held eight to one that the reciting of Biblical passages in a public school was an unconstitutional establishment of religion. One hundred and fourteen pages of opinions made one thing clear: the Supreme Court was as determined as Madalyn Murray to stamp out every last vestige of religion in all public schools in the country. "The result of the decision," Bishop Pike said, "is not neutrality but an imposition upon the public school system of a particular perspective on reality, namely, secularism by default, which is as much an 'ism' as any other." The Wall Street Journal was blunter: "Atheism," it editorialized, was now "the one belief to which the State's power will extend its protection." ...

Judicial Chaos

Shortly after the Supreme Court approved New York's statute providing for the loan of textbooks to all students in the state, including those attending parochial schools, Rhode Island passed a statute providing salary supplements for teachers in all private elementary schools ... and Pennsylvania sought to provide direct subsidies of teacher's salaries and secular textbooks in all elementary and secondary schools. ... At the time these statutes were passed, 25 percent of elementary school pupils in Rhode Island, and 20 percent of elementary and secondary school pupils in Pennsylvania, attended private schools, nearly all of them parochial schools of the Catholic Church.

The Supreme Court heard oral argument in cases attacking both of these statutes just ten months after its decision in Walz [allowing tax exemptions for church property]. It was widely hoped that Chief Justice Burger would render another "eminently sensible" opinion. The opinion he did render in Lemon v. Kurtzman, in which an eight-Justice majority struck down both statutes as unconstitutional establishments of religion, could not have been more disappointing. Indeed, the tripartite test which Burger now laid down for these cases became the tests which would drive everyone, including Burger, crazy for years to come. Burger wrote:

> First, the statute must have a secular legislative purpose; second, its principal or primary effect must be one that neither advances nor inhibits religion; finally, the statute must not foster an excessive government entanglement with religion. ...

It is immediately obvious that tax exemption of churches fails at least the first two tests. As failure of *any* of Burger's tests was supposed to render a statute unconstitutional, the tax exemptions were evidently doubly invalid. But the Court had held them valid by an overwhelming majority. Thus the Chief Justice wrote two opinions a year apart, the first of which approved the most massive possible aid to religious institutions through total tax exemptions, and the second of which condemned programs of much less significance pursuant to tests which would have utterly invalidated the first.

Read in the light of his opinion in Walz, Burger's opinion in Lemon v. Kurtzman seems to have been written by the Mad Hatter. First the Chief Justice found that both of the statutes under review had legitimate secular purposes (to aid all education) and that a sincere attempt had been made ... to avoid assisting religious activities (by expressly limiting aid to secular subjects and by prescribing auditing and reporting procedures to implement such limitations). Under the first two tests now laid down by Burger, then, the Rhode Island and Pennsylvania school aid statutes were far less offensive, from a constitutional point of view, than the church tax exemption upheld in Walz. Nevertheless, indeed *as a consequence* of the legislature's efforts to avoid improper subvention of religious institutions, "the cumulative impact of the entire relationship arising under the statutes ... involves excessive entanglement between government and religion."

... Justice White, the lone dissenter, perceived the Catch-22 aspects of the Court's decision:

> The State cannot finance secular instruction if it permits religion to be taught in the same classroom; but if it exacts a promise that religion not be so taught – a promise the schools and its teachers are quite willing and on this record able to give – and enforces it, it is then entangled in the "no entanglement" aspect of the Court's Establishment Clause jurisprudence. ...

The Golden Rule

There is little question but that to the Founding Fathers "religion" did essentially have one meaning: the beliefs and practices associated with the worship of God, whether the Christian God, the Jewish God, nature's God, or Divine Providence. With that broad definition, and with the concomitant understanding, which the Founding Fathers also shared, that the only thing prohibited by the establishment clause of the First Amendment was *compulsion* of worship or the *preferential* treatment of one religion over competing religions, there would be little trouble today over interpretation and application of the establishment clause, and little "tension" between it and the free exercise clause.

But the Supreme Court greatly expanded both the definition of "religion" and the scope of the prohibitions of the establishment clause, with the result that an impasse ... was created. As phrased by the Court, "tension inevitably exists between the Free Exercise and the Establishment clauses." But there was nothing inevitable about it.

There are good reasons for expanding the definition of "religion" to include virtually anything anybody deems sacred. The alternative puts the courts in the business of defining and assessing professed religious beliefs, a business for which they are neither equipped nor suited. ...

Actually, if establishment continued to be defined as compulsion or preferential treatment, religion could be defined as broadly as might be desired. The "tension" only appears when the definition of religion is broadened for free exercise purposes *and* it is held that any governmental aid of religion, no matter how evenhanded, is prohibited by the establishment clause. *Then* it is inevitable that there will be tension between what the free exercise clause *requires* and what the establishment clause *forbids* ...

The preference of the courts for the establishment clause over the free exercise clause has given rise to much comment. It has been observed that free exercise is the goal of *both* of the religion clauses, the prohibition of establishment merely constituting a necessary means by which to realize it. According to this interpretation, whenever tension appears between the clauses, free exercise should prevail. ...

The trouble is not an "inevitable" conflict between the clauses, obliging us to choose between them, but the "absolute non-establishment theory." ... The rigid prohibition of every form of governmental aid of religious endeavor and expression, never intended by the Founding Fathers, of course results in tension with any sensible definition of free exercise. Indeed, the very tension referred to by the courts should suggest to them that something may be amiss in their treatment of the religion clauses.

That brings us to the central questions: (1) What is an establishment of religion? and (2) What is the free exercise thereof? ...

The free exercise clause is perhaps the simpler one to understand. ... In essence it means that, consistent with public morals and an orderly society, every person should be allowed, and wherever possible helped, to worship whatever it is he deems sacred in whatever manner he deems appropriate. The qualifying phrase, "consistent with public morals and an orderly society," should be and usually has been interpreted to require a showing of significant public harm to justify inhibiting a religious practice. Thus an

Indian tribe was permitted to use an hallucinatory drug in its rituals despite its general proscription as a "controlled substance," Old Order Amish were permitted to remove their children from school at fourteen despite a state statute requiring school attendance until sixteen, and Jehovah's Witness children were permitted to abstain from pledging allegiance to the flag, which their religion held was a graven image, but no exemptions from the general laws were granted to polygamists or to Amish employers who did not wish to pay social security taxes for their employees. ...

Establishment clause cases are inherently more difficult; ...

Why? Because of Justice Black's formulation of the establishment clause forty years ago:

> The "establishment of religion" clause of the First Amendment means at least this: Neither a state nor the Federal Government can set up a church. Neither can pass laws which aid one religion, *aid all religions*, or prefer one religion to another.

The answer to Justice Black is that he was wrong, and that forty years of adherence by the Supreme Court to a wrong theory is enough. As stated by a leading American legal scholar:

> The historical record shows beyond peradventure that the core idea of "an establishment of religion" comprises the idea of *preference*; and that any act of public authority favorable to religion in general cannot, without manifest falsification of history, be brought under the ban of that phrase."

There remains but one church-state issue to consider: religious activities in public schools – prayers, Bible recitations, hymn singing, Christmas and Hanukkah pageants. ... The arguments in favor of school religious exercises boil down to a belief that spiritual values must be inculcated in our children and that the home and the church are unequal to the job. The principal argument against them is that religion in our pluralistic society is essentially divisive and must be kept out of the public schools. ...

I think the proponents of school prayers expect too much from them and the opponents fear them too much. Both sides exaggerate the significance of what inevitably must be a rather formal exercise necessarily drained of deep meaning by the requirement of sectarian neutrality. ...

But the issue must be discussed against the background of the First Amendment. ... The idea that secular or "humanistic" ideals are entitled to the same constitutional consideration as religious principles, or that agnosticism and even atheism must be given equal constitutional billing with traditional religion, is simply false. ...

Michael W. McConnell

Why 'Separation' is not the Key to
Church-State Relations

Ask most educated Americans what the Constitution has to say about religion and they will respond: it requires a "separation between church and state." Never mind that these words appear nowhere in the Constitution, nor even in the First Amendment ("Congress shall make no law respecting an establishment of religion or prohibiting the free exercise thereof"), nor in the debates over its framing, nor in the documents that were its source and inspiration. The guiding metaphor, the "wall of separation between church and state," first appeared in a letter written by Thomas Jefferson 14 years after the First Amendment was drafted. Now it has overshadowed the actual language of the First Amendment.

Metaphors are not necessarily bad things, and this one captures an important element of religious freedom. If the institutions of religion and government were merged, the result would surely be, in the Supreme Court's words, "to destroy government and to degrade religion." Neither the government controlled by a church nor a church controlled by the government will be what a government or a church ought to be.

In recent church state controversies, however, the ideal of separation has come in conflict with the wider and more important ideal of religious freedom. A few examples, taken from recent Supreme Court cases, illustrate this point.

When Congress decided in 1965 to fund special remedial educational programs for needy youngsters, it recognized that many inner-city children attend private religious schools, either out of religious convictions or

106 *Christian Century* (January 18, 1989), 43–47. Used by permission of Christian Century Foundation.

because such schools are the only affordable alternative to deficient public schools. Wanting to reach all eligible children, Congress required that remedial programs for those attending private schools be "comparable" in quality to public school programs. It turned out that the least expensive and most effective way to accomplish this was to send remedial teachers onto the premises of private schools. ...

For 19 years the program operated on this basis in cities like New York without a single complaint that the remedial teachers had stepped over the line into religious matters. An extensive factual record, developed in the lower court, confirmed this situation.

In 1985 the Supreme Court ordered the program to stop. Allowing public remedial teachers to go onto the premise of parochial schools, it said, was an "excessive entanglement between church and state." The court opined (contrary to all the evidence) that the "pervasively sectarian" atmosphere of the parochial schools might cause remedial teachers, either "subtly or overtly," to begin to "indoctrinate the students in particular religious tenets at public expense." The most striking feature of this opinion is its almost mystical fear of religious influence. Few believers would be so bold as to claim that the mere atmosphere of their institutions is so spiritually charged that professionally trained secular teachers start to preach the gospel as part of remedial English and math. ...

For the needy children and their families – not to mention for the legislation's social objectives – the ruling was a disaster. The schools were forced to adopt substitute programs that were at once more costly and less effective. By one official estimate, 5,000 fewer needy children could be served in New York City alone because of the money spent transporting them to other locations.

This case also demonstrates how separation can conflict with religious freedom. Poor parents, no less than rich, have the constitutional right to educate their children in their religious faith. This is a right more prized by members of minority faiths who fear that the public schools will undermine their religious identity – and by families like the Roman Catholic and Orthodox Jewish ones that were the largest participants in the program in New York City. ... Parents were put to a cruel choice: either give up their plans for a religious education or forfeit their child's right to the kind of remedial education program Congress provides for all other children. When the First Amendment is interpreted to penalize religious choice in this way, there is a problem with the interpretation.

At public high schools across the country, students are permitted to form clubs and organizations, to speak and distribute leaflets or petitions, and to exercise free-speech rights not dissimilar to those we all have under the First Amendment. Sometimes their speech is rude or offensive; sometimes they support causes, like gay rights or the legalization of marijuana, that many in the community do not approve of. But so long as they do not disrupt the disciplines of the school, and their speech is strictly student-initiated and noncurricular, their rights are scrupulously protected.

Unless the students want to talk about religion.

Court after court has held that "while students have First Amendment rights to political speech in public schools," First Amendment considerations "limit their right to air religious doctrines." "Students' free speech and associational rights ... are severely circumscribed by the Establishment Clause in the public school setting." Loosely translated, this means that the First Amendment does not protect, but restricts, free speech in public schools if it is religious in nature.

This requires public officials to engage in continuous, discriminating, intrusive censorship of student expression. Students have the right to air extremist political "doctrine," secular philosophical "doctrine," even, presumably, the "doctrine" that God is dead and that religion is the opiate of the people. This is elementary free speech. But – as one court recently held – if a student hands another student a piece of paper stating that "if any man is in Christ he is a new creature," that act violates the principle of separation of church and state.

The Department of Agriculture's Forest Service owns large tracts of wilderness in California held sacred by certain Native American tribes. Their members have come from time immemorial to worship in the solitude of these places. But now the Forest Service proposes to build a logging road through the area, a step that, as the district court noted, "would virtually destroy the ... Indians' ability to practice their religion."

The words of the First Amendment would seem to apply: Congress shall make no law "prohibiting the free exercise [of religion]." But the metaphor of separation so dominates our legal thought that one instead turns to the question: how does the government avoid "entanglement" without religion? The government cannot own or maintain a church. Can it own or preserve an outdoor worship area? Should the government be permitted to promote the religious interests of a religious group by subordinating the secular interests of other citizens in access to logging areas?

The Native Americans in this case were asking the Forest Service to become deeply entangled with religion by adapting its policies to their religious beliefs. Once again separationism stood in conflict with religious freedom. Sad to say, once again separationism won and religious freedom lost.

Even some who call themselves "separationists" agree that some or all of these decisions are unfortunate, recognizing that the theory of separation must be leavened with concern for religious freedom as well. Unfortunately, the theory in its most rigid form (call it "strict separation") has tended to impede development of more attractive interpretations of the First Amendment. The result in the courts has been a doctrinal muddle. The courts frequently stop short of insisting on strict separation, but they have failed to offer a principled or predictable alternative. ...

The Supreme Court, in a famous decision in 1971 (*Lemon v. Kurtzman*), announced a three-part test for an unconstitutional establishment of religion. Government action violates the Constitution if it: (1) has no "secular purpose"; (2) has a "primary effect" that "advances religion"; or (3) entails an "excessive entanglement between church and state." While the first two tests might be interpreted to require neutrality toward religion, the "entanglement" test is pure separationism. Whether neutral or not, government action is unconstitutional if the spheres of religion and government are involved with each other. The public sphere must be strictly secular.

This test has had two unfortunate results. First, it has put religious freedom and diversity on a collision course with the welfare-regulatory state. If the public sphere must be secular, then an expanding public sphere implies a shrinking sphere for religion and religious diversity. In the early days of the Republic, Jefferson could speak with some accuracy of a "wall of separation between church and state" because the limited sphere of government so rarely intersected the sphere of religion. The best protection for religion was to leave it alone. Since then, and especially in the 20th century, the scope of governmental activity has broadened to encompass areas, like education and social welfare, which in Jefferson's day were private and mostly religious. These areas of overlap between a socially involved religious sector and a socially involved state tend to be the areas of church-state conflict today.

Social welfare activities typically involve interaction between government funding agencies and a variety of private service providers, both religious and nonreligious. Private groups can often deliver assistance to the needy more quickly, cheaply and humanely than can government bureaucracies, with greater sensitivity to the diverse interests, backgrounds and beliefs of the client population. Emergency shelters and feeding programs, for example, rely heavily on church and synagogue facilities and religious volunteers: the government supplies all or a part of the operating costs of food, blankets and the like. The same is true for international disaster relief, orphanages, family planning, refugee resettlement, adoption services and hospitals. In all these areas and more, religious and other private organizations perform a large part of the services, and federal, state and local governments provide a large part of the funding.

To the strict separationist, these religious-governmental interactions are, at best, tolerable deviations from the separationist ideal. In principle, strict separationists are committed to a long-term policy of secularizing government-supported social welfare activities. ...

The result, of course, is less diversity in the mixed government-private philanthropic sector. Instead of having a variety of options, poor people dependent on government funding will be confined to a homogenously secular set of alternatives. Their range of choice will shrink; the overall level of pluralism and diversity in society will decline; the financial pressure of government subsidies will tempt religiously affiliated organizations to abandon their religious witness in order to serve more of the needy. Under conditions of the modern welfare-regulatory state, separationism is a powerful engine of secularization.

The second unfortunate consequence of the *Lemon* test is that it calls into question attempts to accommodate the religious needs of religious minorities. If the government takes affirmative action to facilitate the free exercise of religion, does this action have a "secular purpose"? Accommodating free-exercise rights necessarily "advances religion," and not infrequently will generate "entanglements with religion" as well. Thus, in recent years the Supreme Court has invalidated a Connecticut law (passed to replace the prior Sunday closing law) allowing workers to select their sabbath day as their day off from work, struck down a Massachusetts statute allowing churches and schools to object to the issuance of liquor licences in their near vicinity, and abolished an Alabama law allowing students in public schools a moment of silence.

None of these accommodations would induce or encourage anyone to adopt a religious practice against his or her will. Each of them seeks to protect the freedom to follow a religious practice in circumstances in which social or governmental action might threaten or inhibit it. But each runs afoul of the Supreme Court's *Lemon* test.

Indeed, the separationist logic of the *Lemon* test has come into direct conflict with the free-exercise clause, which has been given poor second place in the Supreme Court's First Amendment cases. Since 1972, the year after *Lemon*, the Supreme Court has rejected *every* claim by an individual to a free-exercise exemption, with the sole exception of claims for unemployment compensation which are controlled by clear precedent dating back to 1963. Orthodox Jews have been expelled from the military for wearing yarmulkes; a religious community in which all members worked for the church and believed that acceptance of wages would be an affront to God has been forced to yield to the minimum wage; religious colleges have been denied tax exemptions for enforcing what they regard to be religiously compelled moral regulations; Amish farmers who refuse Social Security benefits have been forced to pay Social Security taxes; and Muslim prisoners have been denied the right to challenge prison regulations that conflict with their worship schedule.

Part of the explanation for these decisions is an exaggerated deference by conservative justices to assertions of governmental interests. But these justices would be in a minority if they were not joined by others who vote against free-exercise claims on separationist grounds. Justice John Paul Stevens, probably the most thoroughgoing separationist on the Supreme Court, has stated frankly that in his view, there is "virtually no room" for a free-exercise challenge to a facially neutral governmental practice. Free-exercise claims, he says, conflict with the "overriding interest in keeping the government ... out of the business of evaluating the relative merits of differing religious claims." Note the way in which the ideal of separation ("keeping the government out of the business") has come to overshadow even the free-exercise clause itself.

The results of these and other Supreme Court decisions call to mind the warning issued by Justice Arthur Goldberg (no Moral Majoritarian, he) some 25 years ago in the *School Prayer Cases*. He commented that rigid interpretations of the establishment clause can lead to

> results which partake not simply of that noninterference and noninvolvement with the religious which the Constitution commands, but of a brooding and pervasive devotion to the secular and a passive, or even active, hostility to the religious.

Given these results, why is separationism still the dominant position of many civil libertarians, including most Jewish and mainline Protestant leaders in the field of church-state thought? One reason, I suspect, is a reflexive hostility to fundamentalists and socially conservative Catholics whose religious way of life is most likely to come into conflict with the dominant strains of our liberal secular culture. ...

More substantial is the fear that if separationism is abandoned, advocates of a "Christian nation" or some other version of religious uniformity will come to the fore. At least we know that separationism will fend off the worst evils of church-state combination. If the "wall of separation" is lowered, we are told, our schools may be returned to the days of prayers prescribed by state legislatures; evolution may be banished from the classroom and replaced by "creation science"; and religious minorities may be at the mercy of intolerant majorities. ...

We need a definition of constitutional religious liberty that preserves the protections of separation without stifling religious choice. I would propose to replace "separation" with the ideals of neutrality and accommodation.

While separationism focuses on government involvement with religion, neutrality focuses instead on the effect of government action on individuals. Government action is "neutral" if it neither induces nor discourages religious belief or action – in other words, if it offers neither incentive nor disincentive to practice a faith. When the federal government provides the same remedial education to children whether they choose religious or secular education, it is being neutral. No parent will be induced to send a child to parochial school because of the program, since he or she can get the same program at public school. Separation, by contrast, is *not* neutral – the child can obtain remedial help only by forgoing religious education. Separation thus introduces a powerful incentive to abandon a religious practice.

Similarly, when public schools treat all student speech the same way, they neither advance nor inhibit religion. They no more endorse religion when they allow the Fellowship of Christian Athletes to meet than they endorse a political candidate when they allow political clubs to meet. ...

The real reason to be troubled by official spoken prayers in the public schools, for example, is not that they breach the "wall of separation" but that they encourage (and, given peer pressure, probably coerce) adoption of a bureaucratically dictated religious practice. Under the neutrality-accommodation approach, the Supreme Court's school prayer decisions can be seen as protecting the independence and vitality of religious life (something most Americans support) rather than as succumbing to secularism (something most Americans oppose).

Some may be concerned that a policy of neutrality sometimes allows religious organizations to benefit from government programs, and thus from the expenditure of tax dollars. But this does not mean that religion is being favored by the state. If religious organizations – be they homeless shelters, international aid agencies, day-care centers, colleges or hospitals – are performing services the government wishes to support, there is no reason why they should not be eligible to participate on equal terms with nonreligious organizations. A truly neutral government will direct its support according to neutral, secular criteria, neither favoring nor disfavoring organizations with a religious affiliation.

Accommodation is a special kind of neutrality. Sometimes a facially neutral governmental practice will affect some beliefs or institutions more severely than others. In order to ensure that the *effect* of government action is neutral toward religion, it is sometimes necessary for the government to tailor its programs to religious needs. Congress prohibits employment discrimination based on sex, for example, but quite properly exempts the Roman Catholic position on employing male priests. The government keeps its doors open on Jewish high holy days, but it grants leaves of absence to Jewish workers. Fortunately, despite some false starts and great confusion arising from the *Lemon* tests, the Supreme Court has recently recognized that religious accommodations can be permissible under the establishment clause.

Accommodations to religion should be upheld so long as they merely facilitate a religious choice freely made by the individual, do not invade the religious freedom of others, and do not discriminate among different religions. The government should not be permitted to create incentives for religious practice or belief (like giving favored status to religious organizations, as compared to other nonprofits), to facilitate the religious practices of some at the expense of others (like offering vocal prayers in public schools), or to accommodate one religion but not others with similar needs or problems (like limiting draft exemptions to members of traditional "peace churches"). Within these guidelines, religious accommoodations are fully in keeping with the First Amendment – albeit in conflict with strict separation.

Some say that accommodations of religion are not neutral because they require special treatment of religion. This represents a deep misunderstanding of the purpose of the First Amendment. The Constitution requires neutrality toward religion; it does not require neutrality towards religious choice. On the contrary, the Constitution extends the highest protection to what the framers believed to be the inalienable right to exercise religion according to the dictates of individual conscience. Nor does the Constitution seek to create a secular public sphere. Religious pluralism and diversity – not secularism – are the animating principles of the First Amendment.

Separation between church and state is obviously a worthy goal, an important part of the American conception of religious freedom. Separation will frequently be the best means of preserving religious autonomy. But separation is not, and cannot be, the central guiding principle. Too often in recent years, separation has come into conflict with the more central principle of religious freedom. When it does, the metaphor must give way to the substance.

Dean M. Kelley

Statism, not Separationism, is the Problem

Separation between church and state is a phrase often used to summarize, perhaps to sloganize, the relationship between religion and government envisioned by the founders and decreed by them in the religion clause of the First Amendment. ... We are often told in portentous tones that these words do not occur in the First Amendment (or anywhere else in the Constitution), that there has never been "absolute" separation of church and state (seemingly with the implication that therefore there shouldn't be *any* such separation), and that the concept has become outmoded with the demise of the quaint notion of limited government and the expansion of the activities of both governments and churches. ...

Rather than asking how close we can come to blurring the distinctions between religion and government without actually violating the First Amendment, we should ask how we can most fully differentiate the unique, important and very different functions of each so that each can be most fully itself rather than an imitation of, or interloper upon, the other.

The latter concern seems to be the thrust of Michael McConnell's argument. He recognizes some important values underlying the religion clauses but seems to view with alarm the course the Supreme Court has followed recently in applying those clauses. He represents the Court as having succumbed to a doctrinaire enthusiasm for "strict separation" that is pressing toward complete secularization of American public life. There *are* such pressures in American society, but the Court has not fallen captive to them, at least not since 1970, when Chief Justice Warren Burger spent many

106 *Christian Century* (January 18, 1989), 48–52. Used by permission of Christian Century Foundation.

words rejecting the earlier hard-line – though still not "absolute" – separationist stance of the Earl Warren court. Said Burger, "We will not tolerate either governmentally established religion or governmental interference with religion. Short of these expressly proscribed governmental acts there is room for play in the joints productive of a benevolent neutrality which will permit religious exercise to exist without sponsorship and without interference." "Benevolent neutrality" continues to be the goal of the Court today. "Separation between church and state" has not retained much currency in the Court's opinion since 1970. Therefore, it is puzzling to contemplate in 1989 a warning against making separation the key to church-state relations. It has not been the key for nearly 20 years. ...

Hyperseparationism is often a symptom of the fear of imperialistic faith groups (supposedly) seeking to dominate society and government (as most faith groups would like to do – in the sense of wanting their vision for all humankind to prevail). Prior to the 1960s the Roman Catholic Church may have aroused that anxiety; more recently Protestant fundamentalism has stirred it. Neither of these represents the real threat to optimum church-state relations, and both have served as distractions from the danger of the moment, which is not religious dominance – or even "secularism" – but *statism*. Lower court judges and the Justices of the Supreme Court have "failed to offer a principled or predictable alternative" to "strict separation" because they – like the American people – do not agree among themselves on the nature of the problem or how to resolve it. But in many recent cases they have tended to agree more readily on another thesis: that the free-exercise clause does not interpose protections of religious obligations and practices that it once did (from 1940 to 1981), and that the establishment clause does not have the force against government action that it once did (from 1948 to 1985).

Contrary to McConnell's contention, establishment-clause claims have not fared well in the Supreme Court lately. In the past five years the Court has upheld five such claims but has rejected six, one of them unanimously – not exactly a landslide for "separation." The unanimous 1987 decision in *Corporation of the Presiding Bishop v. Amos* reversed a lower court's holding that Congress violated the establishment clause when it permitted churches to hire their own members in preference to others for nonreligious jobs, a form of religious discrimination prohibited for other private employers. The Court stated:

A law is not unconstitutional simply because it *allows* churches to advance religion, which is their very purpose. For a law to have forbidden "effects" ... it must be fair to say that the *government itself* has advanced religion through its own activities and influence.

That is a far cry from separation and an encouraging sign for free exercise. But it may have another meaning: the court did not say that the free-exercise clause *required* this accommodation but only that if Congress *wished* to provide it, it was *permissible*. So the decision may be more a sign of deference to Congress than of solicitude for religion. A similar explanation may apply to the Court's rejection of seven free-exercise claims since 1982, during which time it upheld only one.

In those cases the Court deferred to the judgment of the Air Force that the free-exercise claim of a Jewish officer who wore his yarmulke on duty could not be accommodated; it deferred to the judgment of correctional authorities that the free-exercise claim of a Black Muslim to attend Friday afternoon religious services could not be accommodated; it deferred to the judgment of the Department of Agriculture's Forest Service that building a logging road through a national forest was necessary despite the damage to religious practices of Native American tribes in that area; it deferred to the Internal Revenue Service's ruling that Bob Jones University was not entitled to tax exemption because of its religiously motivated rule against interracial dating and marriage on campus; it deferred to the judgment of the secretary of labor that a religious community must pay its members the minimum wage for work they performed in the group's business although the members said they had religious objections to being paid for their work. The only free-exercise claim upheld was controlled by an earlier precedent from 1963.

I agree with what seems to be the implication of McConnell's argument: that most, if not all, of these rejections of free-exercise claims were wrongly decided. But the Court's resistance to those claims was not, in my view, because of any mindless fealty to "separation between church and state" – quite the contrary. The Court has been whittling back on both free-exercise and establishment-clause claims in favor of wider amplitude for the exercise of the powers of government. ...

Some of its members seem to feel that individuals should not have many rights that are judicially enforceable against the government. Apparently, individuals, minorities and courts should get out of the way and let the government – in its infinite wisdom – govern. That view, of course, would put the courts on the side of the strong against the weak and nullify the whole purpose of the Bill of Rights, which is to protect individual rights against government powers. Nevertheless, in some cases – and for various reasons – the more statist members of the Supreme Court are sometimes able to convince other justices to obtain such outcomes as those deplored above.

McConnell proposes "to replace 'separation' with the ideals of neutrality and accommodation." Those are good ideals, but so is separation. It does not need to be replaced, just reinterpreted, balancing it with free exercise – as the Supreme Court seems to be trying to do when not drawn into a statist stance. Neither religion clause should be subordinated to the other; each protects an important aspect of religious liberty. Under the free-exercise clause every person is entitled to respect for her or his religious commitments, and their free exercise should not be burdened by governmental interference except to secure "compelling state interests" (such as protection of public health and safety, not just public welfare or order) that can be served in no less burdensome way. Under the establishment clause every person is also entitled to government that does not sponsor, support or inculcate one religion, religion in general or all religions collectively; that does not prefer one religion over another; that does not build up the real estate or the personnel of a religious institution or set up religious proprietaries not required to supply state-impaired religious access; and that does not compose, initiate or promulgate official prayers, rites or liturgies, or otherwise "play church."

There are more ardent separationists than I who might disagree more extensively with McConnell. I tend to accept the two dicta by the Supreme Court quoted above – one defining an area of "benevolent neutrality" between governmental sponsorship of religion and governmental interference with religion, the other holding that it is not "establishment" for the government to get out of the way of religion by removing state-imposed barriers, so long as the government itself does not advance religion. Alas, the Court appears not always to have lived up to these good intentions.

My main area of disagreement with McConnell would be over the eligibility of church-related agencies for tax funds to perform ostensibly public services. This is admittedly a perplexing boundary area between the religious and the secular. When churches believe that their mission requires them to provide education, health care, social work, disaster relief, refugee resettlement, shelter for the homeless, food for the hungry, assistance to the aged, or whatever, they are often providing needed public services for which the public is willing, able and responsible to pay. Often the churches do so with skill, commitment and compassion that are of special worth to the public. Should they not be eligible for public funding available to nonreligious private agencies providing such services? Reasonably, they should, providing they do not become the only agencies providing such services. No people in need should have to go to or through a church agency to obtain public benefits to which they are entitled if they do not wish to do so – particularly if those public benefits are shaped to conform to the sponsoring churches' religious beliefs that are not shared by the recipients. (A case in point is that of a publicly supported, church-related hospital which is the only hospital in town and which refuses to permit certain medically accepted surgical procedures – such as abortion or tubal ligation – which are objectionable to the church but not to the patients of other faiths or no faith who depend upon that hospital for health care, and whose tax dollars support it.)

In accepting public funds for rendering public services, church-related agencies take on responsibilities to the public that reach beyond the church's faith community. In serving the public they cannot impose faith criteria or faith requirements upon members of the public who have not voluntarily accepted them. Though churches are entitled, unlike other private employers, to hire with their own money their own members in preference to others, they are not entitled to do so with the public's money. ...

Similarly, if teachers employed by the public are assigned to teach on parochial school premises, they tend to come under the administrative aegis of the parochial rather than the public school (not that they teach religion, but that they otherwise function to some degree as adjunct faculty, increasing with tax funds the staffing resources of the parochial school – a consideration apparently underlying two 1985 decisions but not well articulated by the Supreme Court.

On the other hand, much of the valued skill, commitment and compassion of such church-related agencies might be dissipated if they were to be completely "sanitized" of all religious influences or expression – made to "act as if they were secular," as McConnell trenchantly but rather pejoratively puts it. They are made to act – and should want to act – as agents of the public fisc who cannot rightfully use the tax funds paid under duress of law by all the people – of many faiths and no faith – for the imposition of the religious beliefs or for the institutional advantage or aggrandizement of the sponsoring church.

Whatever balance may be struck in these areas of mixed secular and religious services funded by tax money, the mixture is inherently unstable and will tend to move in one direction or the other, usually toward increased responsiveness to broader interests than those of the sponsoring church (which is often called "secularization") – a process seen in church-related colleges and hospitals even without tax funding, which merely makes it happen quicker and sometimes with the force of law. Since these "mixed" ventures may not always be the churches' most direct or effective way of fulfilling their central function of explaining the ultimate meaning of life to their adherents – and certainly not if muffled by the requirements of public fisc – perhaps churches should be less eager to enter into what can at best be but a very unequal partnership with the public, and less tenacious in clinging to "mixed" institutions rather than letting them spin off to non-sectarian auspices.

For these reasons McConnell's solicitude for the public funding of such mixed-service agencies of religious origin (and of inevitably attenuating religious affinity) may be to some degree misplaced.

Leo Pfeffer

Freedom and/or Separation: The Constitutional Dilemma of the First Amendment

The Relationship between Separation and Freedom

It is the premise of this Article that the religion clauses of the First Amendment encompass a unitary guarantee of separation and freedom. Notwithstanding instances of apparent conflict, separation guarantees freedom and freedom requires separation. The draftsmen of the amendment regarded freedom of religion and establishment as incompatible. American constitutional history and tradition do not justify an apportionment of values between disestablishment and freedom. The struggle for religious liberty and for disestablishment were portions of a single evolutionary process that culminated in the First Amendment. In the words of Justice Rutledge, "'[e]stablishment' and 'free exercise' were correlative and coextensive ideas, representing only different facets of the single great and fundamental freedom."

The history that leads up to the adoption of the First Amendment religion clauses amply supports Justice Rutledge's conclusion. Roger Williams, for example, opposed an "enforced uniformity of religion" (freedom concept) because it "confounds the Civil and Religious" (separation concept.) Madison opposed a bill establishing a provision for teachers of the Christian religion (separation concept) because it violated the "fundamental and undeniable truth, 'that Religion ... can be directed only by reason and conviction, not by force or violence'" (freedom concept). ...

In *Common Sense,* Thomas Paine noted ..."As to religion, I hold it to be the indispensible duty of government to protect all conscientious professors thereof, and I know of no other business which government hath to do

64 *Minnesota Law Review* 561 (1980).Used by permission.

therewith." The proposed versions of the First Amendment, submitted to the states and considered by Congress before it adopted the final form, combined both aspects of the dual prohibition without any indication that one was superior and the other subordinate. The first version of the Amendment submitted by James Madison and considered by Congress stated, "The civil rights of none shall be abridged on account of religious belief, nor shall any national religion be established, nor shall the full and equal rights of conscience in any manner be infringed." President Jefferson refused to proclaim days of fasting and prayer because of "the provision that no law shall be made respecting the establishment or free exercise of religion."

In an 1878 case involving a freedom clause attack on an antibigamy statute, the Supreme Court explicitly stated that the First Amendment was intended to erect "a wall of separation between church and State." Finally, the fact that all fifty states guarantee religious freedom and not one allows an establishment of religion would appear to be convincing evidence that in the American tradition, the concepts of free exercise and nonestablishment are correlative and unitary.

In *Everson v. Board of Education*, Justice Black, speaking for the majority of the Court, expressed the meaning of the Establishment Clause:

> The "establishment of religion" clause of the First Amendment means at least this: Neither a state nor the Federal Government can set up a church. Neither can pass laws which aid one religion, aid all religions, or prefer one religion over another. ... In the words of Jefferson, the clause against establishment of religion by law was intended to erect "a wall of separation between church and State." ...

The Court held that laws punishing disbelief or failure to attend church are forbidden by the Establishment Clause no less than by the Free Exercise Clause.

In numerous decisions during the past decade, the Court has phrased the meaning of the Establishment Clause in somewhat different language. The Court has formulated a three-part test to determine whether a law will "pass muster under the Establishment Clause": first, the statute "must reflect a clearly secular legislative purpose"; second, it "must have a primary effect that neither advances nor inhibits religion"; third, the statute "must avoid excessive government entanglement with religion." Advancing religion obviously constitutes establishment, but inhibiting religion means prohibiting its free exercise, and that, too, the Court has held, constitutes a violation of the Establishment Clause.

This view of the unity of the religion clauses is not shared by all constitutional lawyers and historians. ...

Except for occasional flights of rhetoric, no one contends either that absolute separation of church and state is required by the first amendment or that such a rule would be desirable. Nor does the concept of separation provide its own principle of limitation. In determining the limits of constitutional separation, it is the concept of religious freedom which provides the criterion. The principle of church-state separation is an instrumental principle. Separation ordinarily promotes religious freedom; it is defensible so long as it does so, and only so long.

These scholars are apparently not alone in discovering a dichotomy in the religion clauses. The majority of the current Supreme Court, unlike its predecessors, appears to find such a dichotomy in the First Amendment. In *Wisconsin v. Yoder,* Chief Justice Burger wrote for the majority:

The Court must not ignore the danger that an exception from a general obligation of citizenship on religious grounds may run afoul of the Establishment Clause, but that danger cannot be allowed to prevent any exception no matter how vital it may be to the protection of values promoted by the right of free exercise.

The same apparent conflict and preference was noted by Justice Brennan in his concurring opinion in *Abington School District v. Schempp.*

There are certain practices, conceivably violative of the Establishment Clause, the striking down of which might seriously interfere with certain religious liberties also protected by the First Amendment. Provisions for churches and chaplains at military establishments. ...[and] for chaplains in penal institutions may afford example(s). It is argued that such provisions may be assumed to contravene the Establishment Clause, yet be sustained on constitutional grounds as necessary to secure to the members of the Armed Forces and prisoners those rights of worship guaranteed under the Free Exercise Clause. Since government has deprived such persons of the opportunity to practice their faith at places of their choice, the argument runs, government may, in order to avoid infringing the free exercise guarantees, provide substitutes where it requires such persons to be. ...
    The State must be steadfastly neutral in all matters of faith, and neither favor nor inhibit religion. ... On the other hand, hostility, not neutrality, would characterize the refusal to provide the chaplains and places of worship for prisoners and soldiers cut off by the State from all civilian opportunities for public communion, or the withholding of draft exemptions for ministers and conscientious objectors.

Those who argue for a dualistic rather than a unitary interpretation of the First Amendment are faced with the task of determining which clause is superior in disposing of a situation where separation conflicts with freedom. Generally, their solution has been to allocate superiority to free exercise, a judgment that would probably receive the approval of all Americans, including members of the Supreme Court, except perhaps those who deem religion to be an enemy of the people. Nothing in the text of the First Amendment, however, supports such an allocation of supposedly competing constitutional values. The Amendment does not say, although it could easily have done so, that Congress shall make no law respecting an establishment of religion except when it conflicts with the free exercise thereof. Nothing in the text of the Amendment supports the view of John Courtney Murray, a view shared by many others, that "separation of church and state, ... put on its proper grounds ... in its true relation to the free exercise of religion [is] instrumental to freedom [and is] therefore ... a relative, not an absolute ... right."

It must be noted, however, that history reveals concerns other than or in addition to the protection of the free exercise of religion that impelled a prohibition of laws respecting an establishment of religion. Madison ... argued only a few years prior to the adoption of the Bill of Rights that religion, and not merely restraint on religion, was exempt from the authority of society and could not be subject to the authority of legislative bodies; he asserted that the state was not a competent judge of religious truth and had no authority to employ religion as even a willing engine of civil policy. Furthermore, nothing in Madison's other writings supports a theory of dualism or the assertion that the purpose of the Amendment was to protect free exercise, and that the prohibition of establishment was no more than a dispensable means to achieve that end.

The Supreme Court has not yet been faced with the need to definitively adjudicate conflicts between free exercise and establishment. In cases in which it appeared that the Court would be forced to make a choice, it has succeeded in finding a way to avoid having to do so. Nevertheless, in *Wisconsin v. Yoder,* the Court indicated that if it had to make a choice, free exercise would prevail over establishment. *Yoder,* however, was not the last word the Court has spoken on the question. In *Committee for Public Education and Religious Liberty v. Nyquist,* the Court held unconstitutional a law providing tuition grants for students attending church schools:

> Finally the State argues that its program of tuition grants should survive scrutiny because it is designed to promote the free exercise of religion. The State notes that only "low-income parents" are aided by this law, and without state assistance their right to have their children educated in a religious environment "is diminished or even denied." It is true, of course, that this Court has long recognized and main-

tained the right to choose nonpublic over public education. ... It is also true that a state law interfering with a parent's right to have his child educated in a sectarian school would run afoul of the Free Exercise Clause. But this Court repeatedly has recognized that tension inevitably exists between the Free Exercise and the Establishment Clauses, ... and that it may often not be possible to promote the former without offending the latter. As a result of this tension, our cases require the State to maintain an attitude of "neutrality," neither "advancing" nor "inhibiting" religion. In its attempt to enhance the opportunities of the poor to choose between public and nonpublic education, the State has taken a step which can only be regarded as one "advancing" religion. However great our sympathy ... for the burdens experienced by those who must pay public school taxes at the same time that they support other schools because of the constraints of "conscience and discipline," ... and ... notwithstanding the "high social importance" of the State's purposes, neither may justify an eroding of the limitations of the Establishment Clause now firmly emplanted.

Here, too, the Court's stated preference is only dictum, since the Court has never held, nor is it likely to hold, that a state's denial of tuition grants impinges upon the free exercise of religion. Nevertheless, in accepting the premise that such an impingement exists, the opinion, reasonably read, surprisingly indicates a choice favoring not the free exercise clause but rather the Establishment Clause.

The *Nyquist* case is one instance in which the Court was faced with an apparent, yet not unavoidable, need to choose between the two First Amendment mandates. The balance of this Article will consider in more detail other cases in which the Court was faced with the opportunity, though in no case the unavoidable necessity, of making such a choice.

Arenas of Conflict

Tax Exemption

In *Walz v. Tax Commission*, the Court was called upon to determine the constitutionality of exempting church properties from real estate taxation. The plaintiff claimed that exemption had both the purpose and effect of aiding religion, and thereby violated the Establishment Clause. With only Justice Douglas dissenting, the Court upheld the law on the ground that a major purpose of the Establishment Clause was to avoid excessive entanglement between church and state, and that exemption rather than taxation of church properties more effectively served that purpose. In a concurring opinion, Justice Brennan recognized that James Madison, after his retirement from the Presidency, had argued that tax exemptions for houses of worship was violative of the establishment clause. Nevertheless, the Court noted, both Congress and the states have historically exempted church properties from taxation, and all fifty states do so today – facts strongly indicating the constitutionality of tax exemption.

The amicus curiae brief submitted by the National Council of Churches of Christ in the *Walz* case argued that the First Amendment not only permits tax exemption but, in fact, mandates it: "The Free Exercise Clause in the First Amendment forbids taxation by the Federal or State governments of houses of worship or of other religious property used exclusively for religious purposes and owned by corporations organized exclusively for religious purposes." The Synagogue Council of America endorsed the claim:

> [P]roperty used for religious purposes, including the house of worship, the religious sanctuary, and all that is contained therein are so intimately connected with religious exercise that to levy a direct tax upon the value of such property would constitute a tax on the exercise of religion, having the same effect as that tax upon the itinerate evangelist which the Court found unconstitutional in *Murdock [v. Pennsylvania]*.

The progenitor of the theory that the free exercise clause requires tax exemptions for church properties appears to be Dean Kelley. ... The crux of the claim, set forth somewhat simplistically in Kelley's book, *Why Churches Should not Pay Taxes*, is that the power to tax is the power to destroy. Because the Free Exercise Clause forbids the government to destroy churches, the argument continues, it similarly forbids government to tax churches or their property, at least that part used for worship and prayer.

Because the Court determined that the exemption did not violate the Establishment Clause, there was no need to decide whether the Free Exercise Clause would require a finding of constitutionality even if the Establishment Clause were violated. Discretion being the better part of valor, the Court wisely refrained from indicating which way it would decide should there come a time when the Court could no longer avoid the troublesome question. Notwithstanding the present universality of tax exemption for church properties, that time may come sooner than most would expect. Today, more and more middle-income Americans are moving to the suburbs, where large estates are often purchased and converted to churches. Although the property is then removed from the tax rolls, the community must continue to provide costly services. Since, in the suburbs, real estate taxes are the major source of local finances, the increased burden on the homeowner can be significant. The discontent with this system is manifested not only by an increasing feeling among suburban homeowners that churches should pay property taxes, but also by the refusal of some town authorities to issue zoning permits for the establishment or expansion of churches.

Although it is a risky business to predict what the Court will do in any particular case, it seems likely that at least a majority of the Court would uphold the constitutionality of eliminating the exemption for church property, even that part used exclusively for religious purposes. When this happens, the Court will assuredly not conclude that free exercise is subordinate to the prohibition against establishment, but only that the former does not mandate exemption.

Aid to Parochial Schools

The current status of constitutional law respecting government support of church-related educational institutions may be summarized as follows: there is no constitutional barrier to the supply of health, nutritional, and similar noneducational services; although it is permissible to finance transportation and to loan secular textbooks at the elementary and secondary school levels, any other governmental supply of educational services would probably not be allowed, and the scope of permissible governmental financing is broader at the college or university level but is by no means as well defined as that at the lower levels.

Advocates of more substantial aid to parochial schools have frequently argued that such aid is not only constitutionally permissible, but that it is constitutionally required. That argument is based on the fact that a state law requiring attendance at *public* schools would violate the Free Exercise Clause.

There are many parents and children, the argument continues, whose religious conscience forbids public school attendance and requires that the children receive their secular as well as their religious education in parochial schools. Because state compulsory school attendance laws are applicable to all children, the argument concludes, the Free Exercise Clause requires states to make attendance at parochial schools possible by financing those schools so that the children of low-income parents can attend.

So formulated, the argument seems to present an unavoidable clash between the religion clauses. By barring aid to parochial schools and thereby precluding parochial school attendance by children of low-income families, the Supreme Court apparently decides in favor of nonestablishment and against free exercise.

The clash, however, is more apparent than real. The conflict is not between mandated governmental support of parochial schools and forbidden support, but rather between nonsupport and compulsory attendance. A true conflict of competing constitutional values would exist if the Constitution forbade the teaching of religion in public schools yet mandated attendance exclusively in those schools, even by students whose religious conscience requires that all instruction, including that generally designated as secular, be impregnated with religion. Because government support is constitutionally forbidden and compulsory attendance is purely statutory, however, there is no true clash of competing constitutional values.

In *Wisconsin v. Yoder*, the Supreme Court held that Amish parents have a constitutional right under the Free Exercise Clause not to send their children to school, even a church-related school, after they complete their elementary school education. The Court concluded that the constitutional mandate of free exercise is superior to the statutory obligation to send children to secondary schools. ... The conflict is not between nonestablishment and free exercise, but rather exclusively within the area of free exercise. Resolution of that conflict might require the Court to hold that compulsory school attendance laws are unconstitutional even at the elementary school level, but it would in no way require state support of parochial schools.

By the same reasoning, the constitutional barrier against religious teachings and practices in public schools does not present a conflict with the free exercise claim of those whose religious conscience impels them to pray in school. Rather, the conflict is between the constitutional mandate against prayer in public schools and the statutory mandate of school attendance. In other words, parents may have a first amendment right not to send their children to public schools in which prayer is forbidden, but they do not have a right to have prayer in those schools. ...

Religious Tests for Public Office

The latest Supreme Court case presenting a confrontation between the establishment and free exercise barriers, *McDaniel v. Paty,* involved a state provision barring clergy from public office. As noted earlier, by the time of the adoption of the Constitution, a majority of the states had enacted such provisions with the purpose of prohibiting an establishment of religion. By 1978, however, only one of these provisions remained in effect. The Tennessee provision that prohibited clergy from holding political office was the basis of a suit by a defeated candidate in a state election for delegates to a convention to revise the state constitution. The defeated candidate argued that the elected candidate was disqualified because he was an ordained minister. The Tennessee Supreme Court decided in favor of the defeated candidate, Paty, and the elected candidate, McDaniel, appealed to the United States Supreme Court. Although the eight participating Justices agreed that the Tennessee provision violated the Constitution, they could agree on little else.

The crux of Chief Justice Burger's plurality opinion was that, under the Court's decision in *Wisconsin v. Yoder,* "only those interests of the highest order and those not otherwise served can overbalance legitimate claims to the free exercise of religion." ... The Chief Justice argued that whatever may have been the situation in the eighteenth century, there is currently no persuasive support for the fear that clergymen elected to public office will be less careful of antiestablishment interests or less faithful to their oaths of civil office than their unordained counterparts. Absent such support, he concluded, the provision barring clergy from public office cannot withstand challenge under the Free Exercise Clause, since that clause "unquestionably encompasses the right to preach, proselyte, and ... to be a minister."

Justice Brennan, with the concurrence of Justice Marshall, also found no conflict in the case between the Free Exercise and Establishment Clauses. Rather, Brennan concluded that the challenged statute was invalid under both clauses. With respect to the latter, he stated that the Tennessee provision "manifests patent hostility toward, not nonneutrality in respect of, religion, forces or influences a minister or priest to abandon his ministry as the price of public office, and in sum, has a primary effect which inhibits religion."

Justice Stewart, in a concurring opinion, argued that the matter was settled by *Torcaso v. Watkins*, a case in which the Court invalidated a state law requiring public officials to take an oath that they believed in God. He noted, however, that the offense against the First Amendment "lay not simply in requiring an oath," (free exercise aspect) "but in 'limiting public offices to persons who have, or perhaps more properly profess to have, a belief in some particular kind of religious concept'" (establishment aspect).

In his concurring opinion, Justice White argued ... that the Free Exercise Clause did not invalidate the provision barring clergy from public office. He was not convinced that McDaniel would be deterred from the observance of his religious beliefs, since he was not compelled to abandon the ministry as a result of the challenged statute nor required to disavow any of his religious beliefs. Rather, Justice White concluded, he had been denied the equal protection of the laws and the provision should therefore have been invalidated on that ground. ...

The most significant aspect of the *McDaniel* case is what the Court did not say. As has been noted, the Chief Justice previously intimated that if the Court were faced with a factual situation requiring it to decide one way under the Free Exercise Clause and the opposite way under the Establishment Clause, it would rank free exercise over establishment and would decide the case accordingly. As has also been noted, the Court has never found it necessary to make the choice; the Justices have always been able to find under the particular facts of each case that a decision could be reached without sacrificing one clause to preserve the other.

Precisely the same thing happened in *McDaniel v. Paty*. Although basing their conclusions on different reasoning, all the Justices agreed that the Tennessee provision was unconstitutional. Furthermore, none of the Justices concluded that eliminating the provision – thereby permitting clergy to hold public office – violated the Establishment Clause. There was, therefore, no need for any of the Justices to indicate how they would have decided the case if it had presented an unavoidable collision between free exercise and nonestablishment. ...

The conclusion reached from an examination of these cases is that although the Supreme Court has stated that there may be instances in which the Establishment and Free Exercise Clauses conflict with each other, the Court will continue to find ways to decide such cases without definitely adjudicating which clause is superior and which subordinate. ...

Paul J. Weber

Strict Neutrality:
The Next Step in First Amendment Development?

In the world of Church-State scholarship writers are usually grouped into opposing camps called Absolute Separationists and Accommodationists. ... Yet there is another position gaining ground. In the 25 years since the concept of strict neutrality emerged success has come almost inadvertently. The Supreme Court, without adopting the concept of strict neutrality has begun to use the terminology of neutrality on occasion, and the major casebook in the field has the intriguing title, *Toward Benevolent Neutrality*. ...

To understand the strict neutralist position it is helpful to begin with two presuppositions. (a) When the Founders wrote the First Amendment they did not write with either the clairvoyance or the specificity that would make it easy to apply their principles to problems arising in contemporary church-state relations. There are various strands in the Founders thought which allow not only for conflicting interpretations but for contemporary adaptation. (b) We live almost two hundred years since the First Amendment Religion Clauses were penned and enormous changes have taken place. ...

Granted these presuppositions, the challenge in constitutional theorizing is to create a principle of interpretation which (1) remains as faithful as possible to the language of the Constitution and the intent of the Founders, (2) is realistic, i.e., acknowledges political and economic reality and which (3) resolves problems in a manner seen as just, fair and required by the Constitution. Before undertaking that challenge, further reflection on the presuppositions may be helpful.

Journal of Political Science (Spring 1988), 70–7. Used by permission.

Varieties of Separation

The term "separation of church and state" although never appearing in the Constitution, has become so enbedded in American consciousness that it seems to sum up what is meant by the First Amendment religion clauses. Small wonder. The term is so broad it can embrace a wide variety of beliefs and practices. … Our first task is to sort out the divergent meanings of the term "separation" and determine which best meet the challenges of constitutional theorizing.

Separation, in the First Amendment context, is a generic term which has at least five distinct meanings. The most fundamental is *structural separation,* and distinguishes most Western systems from such organic systems as exist in Iran, Saudi Arabia and other Muslim countries. The characteristics of structural separation are independent clerical and civil offices, separate organizations for government and religions, different personnel performing different functions, separate systems of law. … Jefferson, Madison and most of the other Founders accepted the need for structural separation, and where they found remnants of organic relationships, as in parts of common law, they worked to remove them. …

Absolute separation is a type vigorously pursued by some interest groups in this country. It is more of a financial separation than anything else, holding that no aid of any kind should flow from government to religion or churches, and no financial support should flow from religion or churches to the government. Absolutists would take as normative Justice Black's description of the Establishment Clause in *Everson v. Board of Education.*

> The "establishment of religion" clause of the first amendment means at least this: Neither a state nor the Federal Government can set up a church. Neither can pass laws which aid one religion, aid all religions, or prefer one religion over another. Neither can force nor influence a person to go to or to remain away from church against his will or force him to profess a belief or disbelief in any religion. … The clause against establishment of religion by law was intended to erect "a wall of separation between Church and State."

The difficulties facing the advocates of absolute separation are twofold. First, it is by no means clear that the Founders intended this specific a meaning of separation. Second, historical practice in the United States, including contemporary practice, has included enormous amounts of aid, both direct and indirect, flowing to religion from government in return for enormous amounts of mostly indirect aid from religion. This is a political and economic reality absolutists may rally against, but it is so imbedded in law and practice that it is unlikely to change in the forseeable future. Absolutists are left in the awkward position of claiming as constitutional principle – a law to be obeyed – something that has never existed and is never likely to. Absolute separation is an ideal, not a reality. Unfortunately for absolutists, the Constitution, unlike the Declaration of Independence, has the force of law and is meant to be obeyed as well as admired.

Transvaluing separation is less understood in the United States, but does have a devoted following. It holds that one objective of government is to secularize the political culture of the nation, that is, to reject as politically illegitimate the use of all religious symbols, or the appeal to religious values, motivations or policy objectives in the political arena. Transvaluing separation would deny all aid to religious organizations under any circumstances. It is this type of separation that [was] touted in the Soviet constitution and law. One statement from an American group that seems best to express this position is that of the American Humanist Association:

> To promote the "general welfare," a particular measure may be favored by church interests, and consequently pressure and influence are brought to bear on the state's political machinery to assure its passage. Or a measure may be viewed with disfavor by the church with a resultant pressure on the state's political machinery to assure its defeat. This type of activity by the church harks back to pre-Revolutionary days both here and in Europe, where there was "cooperation" between government and church. But it was just that sort of religion-political interplay that the Founding Fathers tried desperately to prevent on American soil by adopting the First Amendment and the corresponding state laws.

Thomas Jefferson's desire to provide access to the University of Virginia for neighboring schools of divinity is prima facie evidence that he did not favor this type of separation. I have argued elsewhere that Madison's Memorial and Remonstrance shows his opposition to this type separation. In any event, the Supreme Court has never accepted transvaluing separation and it does not appear to have much promise as a constitutional principle in the United States.

What has traditionally been called "accommodation" I would call *Supportive Separation*. Those who hold this position acknowledge the need for structural separation but would not drive the principle to the extremes of the absolute or transvaluing types. To the contrary, supportive separationists favor aid and support for religion, holding only that government

may not support one religion over another. This position takes as normative Justice William O. Douglas' dictum that

> We are a religious people whose institutions presuppose a Supreme Being. We
> guarantee the freedom to worship as one chooses. We make room for as wide a
> variety of beliefs and creeds as the spiritual needs of man deem necessary. We
> sponsor an attitude on the part of government that shows no partiality to any one
> group and that lets each flourish according to the zeal of its adherents and the
> appeal of its dogma. When the state encourages religious instruction and cooper-
> ates with religious authorities by adjusting the schedule of public events to sectar-
> ian needs, it follows the best of our traditions. For it then respects the religious
> nature of our people and accommodates the public service to their spiritual need.

Unfortunately for advocates of supportive separation the history of the
battle for religious liberty in Virginia and of the framing of the First
Amendment undermines any claim that this is what the Founders intended.
In addition, a whole series of decisions indicates very clearly that the
Supreme Court does not believe this is what the Constitution requires.
Finally, there has been strong political opposition to such a position
throughout American history.

Equal Separation is that type which rejects all political or economic
privilege, coercion or disability based on religious affiliation, belief or
practice, or lack thereof, but guarantees to religiously motivated or affiliated individuals and organizations the *same* rights and privileges extended
to other similarly situated individuals and organizations. It provides protection to religion without providing privilege. It treats the right to religious belief and practice as a human right to be protected along with other
human rights in an evenhanded manner. It protects the right of religiously
motivated groups and individuals to participate in the political process and
the economic system in the same manner and to the same extent as it
protects the rights of other similar groups and individuals to participate.

A difficulty facing proponents of equal separation is that it is a concept
only recently developed and therefore unfamiliar to most Americans. It has
been viewed suspiciously by advocates of other types of separation who
fear that it will lead to a decrease in protection for religious liberty or an
increase in aid to religion. Nonetheless it is the basis for the strict neutrality
approach to the religion clauses and will be further developed below. It has
been argued that equal separation is most consistent with the thought of
James Madison.

Historical Developments

Several developments of enormous proportions have made it impossible to apply the First Amendment religion clauses to contemporary problems in any simplistic fashion and still meet the requirements for constitutional theorizing posited above. … The first development is the application of the religion clauses to the states through the Due Process Clause of the Fourteenth Amendment by the Supreme Court. This is not something the Founders foresaw.

A second unforeseen development is the transformation of both federal and state governments from passive-protective, minimalist governments to active-expansive, pervasive administrative bureaucracies. This change from a laissez-faire to a bureaucratic state with broad taxing, regulatory and spending powers has enormous implications for church-state relations.

Parallel to the expansion of government has been the expansion of religious organizations in population, physical institutions, activities undertaken and sheer variety of denominations, sects and cults.

A fourth major change is … mass education, mass communication, massive impersonal solicitation of funds, the fabrication of mind altering drugs, and in the very near future, genetic manipulation.

Finally, the sheer growth in population density, mobility and diversity has profoundly altered the environment within which religious organizations and activities exist and the laws affecting them are made. Density and mobility are significant because it is no longer easy for individuals to live solely among their own kind or shelter their children from exposure to competing values.

Taken together, these five developments since the First Amendment was written pose such difficulties in terms of potential conflict, discrimination and entanglement that legal theories which ignore them are doomed to failure. The task of the original Founders was to protect religious liberty *from* government. The contemporary task is to protect religious liberty *in the midst of* government. The same is true for preventing establishment while not discriminating against religion.

The Theory of Strict Neutrality

Strict Neutrality was proposed a quarter century ago by Professor Philip Kurland of the University of Chicago:

> The thesis proposed here as the proper construction of the religion clauses of the first amendment is that the freedom and separation clauses should be read as a single precept that government cannot utilize religion as a standard for action or inaction because these clauses prohibit classification in terms of religion either to confer a benefit or to impose a burden.

... Some clarifications may be helpful. First, the purposes of the religion clauses can be summed up as freedom, separation and equality. The application of the clauses in conjunction is both possible and necessary. It can be done by reading the clauses as an equal protection doctrine, or as Kurland explains:

> For if the command is that inhibitions not be placed by the state on religious activity, it is equally forbidden the state to confer favors upon religious activity. These commands would be impossible of effectuation unless they are read together as creating a doctrine more akin to the reading of the equal protection clause than to the due process clause, i.e., they must be read to mean that religion may not be used as a basis for classification for purposes of government action, whether that action be the conferring of rights or privileges or the imposition of duties or obligations. ...

Acceptance of strict neutrality is not a denial that religion can be used as a classification to identify a significant personal interest or social unit. It would be incongruous to hold that the Constitution could recognize the existence of religion but that the government based on that Constitution could not. Recognition of an objective fact of personal value preference or of social organization would not be a violation of the neutrality principle. Examples might be recognition of the presence of a church or synagogue when planning traffic control signals or assigning personnel to expedite traffic. Such recognition implies that in relevant secular aspects individual religious interests and social groups are similar to other interests and groups, not based on religious content, but on the other public and secular aspects of a religion's social organization. ... Strict neutrality is committed to the proposition that there is seldom a *legally significant* characteristic of religion so unique that it is not shared by similar nonreligious individuals and groups. The conclusion to be drawn is that in most aspects, religious individuals and interests are subject to the same laws as other similarly situated individuals and groups.

But what happens when there is a claim based on a uniquely religious belief, e.g., when an Adventist cannot work on Saturday and requests unemployment compensation? ... Or a Baptist church requires all its employees to be members of the church? Or what happens when a purportedly neutral law in fact imposes a significant burden on a religion or even prohibits a religious activity, e.g., an ordinance that prohibits door to door solicitation on weekends? In such cases religion may be treated as a *suspect classification* subject to strict scrutiny by the courts. A suspect classification is one in which there is "a presumption of unconstitutionality against a law implying certain classifying traits." If religion is considered a suspect classification, any statute utilizing religion or specifically impacting on religion is automatically suspect, will demand a very heavy burden of justification, and will be subject to the most rigid scrutiny. More than just a rational connection to a legitimate public purpose will be required. Nevertheless, if the standards of proof are met, the religious interest will be protected.

The suspect classification concept is used most frequently to prohibit racial and sexual discrimination, but it can equally well be used to preserve government neutrality in respect to religion. The question immediately arises: what are the principles that justify such a classification and define its limits? Professor Donald Giannella several years ago offered two such principles. The first is the principle of free exercise neutrality that "permits and sometimes requires the state to make special provision for religious interests in order to relieve them of both direct and indirect burdens placed on the free exercise of religion by increased governmental regulation." Such a provision is consonant with the "protected civil right" nature of religious liberty, but in accordance with the general neutralist position such provisions must be extended to other similar groups if there are any.

The second principle is that of political neutrality. Its aim is "to assure that the Establishment Clause does not force the categorical exclusion of religious activities and associations from a scheme of governmental regulations whose secular purposes justify their inclusion." Several examples might clarify the concept: If a local government is distributing excess cheese and bread to the poor through neighborhood organizations, church groups could be neither given exclusive rights to distribute the foodstuffs nor excluded from doing so. If government rents neighborhood buildings as polling places, churches could be neither preferred nor excluded from participation. ...

Objections to the Strict Neutrality Principle

A number of objections have been raised to the neutrality principle. ... First is the objection that strict neutrality "guts" the religion clauses of any substantive meaning; this objection argues that if religious groups, individuals and interests are to be treated equally with others then the religion clauses are irrelevant – surely not a situation the Founders intended.

It is true that very much of religious activity and all of religious thought are fully protected in the speech, press, and assembly clauses of the First Amendment, as well as by the Due Process and Equal Protection Clauses, etc. Double protection serves no additional function. Unlike the speech, press and assembly clauses, however, the religion clauses are twofold, prohibiting the establishment of religion as well as guaranteeing its free exercise. The recognition of an independent liberty must be such that it offends neither one nor the other. Classification in terms of religion may tend to discriminate either by favoring religious interests at the expense of other similarly situated interests or by burdening religious interests in such a way as to have a "chilling effect" on religious liberty. The most equitable solution to this dilemma is to treat religious groups and interests like similar groups and interests. For example, a religious group seeking funds for its projects would have to conform to the same fundraising rules and accounting standards as other nonprofit groups.

Precisely because religious liberty is *an independent, substantive right,* it functions as an indicator of the need to protect other groups and limit government intrusion into their affairs as well as into its own. Religious liberty is a protected legal right, but not a uniquely privileged one, that is, it gives no rights on the basis of religious commitment that do not extend equally to similar interests. In that sense it is a qualified legal right – qualified by the Establishment Clause.

A second objection holds that strict neutrality will limit religious liberty, that is, religious groups will be required to live under the same government regulations, abide by such things as affirmative action goals, file informational tax returns, etc. in the same manner as other not-for-profit organizations. That objection is partially valid, and designedly so. There is a cost to be borne for living in an organized society and while that cost is not borne equally under the neutrality principle, churches and other religious groups ought to be paying the same price and sharing the same burdens as other similar groups. If they do not, they are in a uniquely privileged position which is not something the Founders intended and which is a major objective of the Establishment Clause to avoid. Does this mean churches would have to pay taxes under this principle? No, so long as other not-for-profit groups do not. ...

A third objection is that strict neutrality is only a smokescreen behind which to usher in massive aid to religious schools at the expense of the public schools. Several considerations are relevant. Religious schools seeking funds would need to conform to the same hiring, certification, accrediting, admissions and attendance standards, the same curriculum and textbook requirements and submit to inspections and oversight at the same level as other publically funded schools. This is not at all the Religious Right agenda or that of the parochial schools. Under such conditions there is unlikely to be a rush for funding. ...

A fourth objection is that acceptance of strict neutrality would undermine decades of court precedents and open the floodgates to a torrent of cases testing the limits of neutrality. The Supreme Court has increasingly been using the language of neutrality (although not consistently) and many of its holdings are consistent with the principle. Acceptance would not, for example, undermine the three-pronged test for Establishment Clause cases, except that entanglement would need to be refined. One advantage, if the principle were accepted, would be more consistently decided cases, a major dividend.

A fifth objection is that "similarly situated" is a vague term fraught with potential conflict and abuse. ... One model is nonprofit organizations under the I.R.S. 501(c)3 category, which includes charitable, literary, recreational, fraternal, scientific, social and educational groups. The neutrality principle is built on the realization that in most legally significant dimensions religiously motivated individuals and groups are similar to their secular counterparts. ...

The Values of Neutrality

1. The integration of free exercise and nonestablishment clauses into a coherent, consistent, comprehensible principle which is faithful to the intentions of the Founders, responsive to contemporary constitutional values of due process and equal protection, cognizant of current political and economic realities, and defensible as a fair and equitable rule of law.

2. Equal protection for nonreligious groups and individuals that are similar to religious groups and individuals.

3. Establishment of a principled reason for bringing the secular components of religious activities into conformity with the standards and procedures required for other not-for-profit groups and activities.

4. A stimulus for religious groups which currently seek to influence government policy to undertake protection of rights for society while they protect their own.

Chapter V

Secular Humanism as Religion:
The Great Debate

Background: Another battle over the relationship between God, the state, and moral values rages between traditional theistic (God-centered) religion and an anti-supernatural modernity influenced by secular humanism and its "worship" of man, reason, science and progress. For two centuries the advocates of established Protestantism, religious pluralism, and atheism (and "isms" in between these three) have vied for influence over American political and spiritual life.

According to one sociological theory, as America plunged into the post World War Two era, theistic religion lost its way and civil religion and secular humanism won the hearts and minds of the increasingly rational, tolerant, modern, and existential Americans. According to a theory of the Religious Right (see chapter VI), this process also marked the spiritual and cultural malaise that exploded in the radical counter-culture of the 1960s and the materialism and "me-ism" of the 1980s and 1990s. In a third neoconservative view, proponents doubt the degree of the secular trans-formation, see instead a religious revival, and insist that, while the struggle for hearts and minds continues, the law must treat non-theistic (secular humanism, for example) and theistic religion equally. In other words, both types of religions must be placed under the same separation of church and state restraints.

The struggle between humanists and theists for the hearts, minds and souls of Americans is uniquely American. It finds its historic roots in both vigorous professions of faith and reliance on God and equally vigorous declarations of independence and self-reliance. From the days of religious intolerance against non-believers, to the days of bend-over backwards relativism (all values are relative, as is truth because neither can be judged against a model of ultimate truth or value), Americans have alternated between faith in God and faith in rational discourse. More often than not Americans absorbed both faiths, and blithely accepted the risk of intellectual inconsistency. Ironically, the inconsistency has worked without excessive damage to the American soul or psyche. Americans seem to be both religious and rational, tolerant of pluralism yet insistent that their way is better, and accepting of the mix of the sacred and the secular in their religio-political culture. The authors in this section, a sociologist, a conservative Christian cleric, and a Jewish constitutional lawyer, explore the nature of this hodgepodge culture and the impact of religion and secular humanism on it.

Authors: James Davison Hunter, Professor of Sociological and Religious Studies at the University of Virginia, is the author of many works on religion, political philosophy, and religious liberty, including a definitive study on evangelicalism. In the selection below, he looks at the political debate over whether secular humanism is a religion, in any sociologically meaningful way, and thus protected *and* restricted by the religion clauses of the First Amendment. He begins by defining religion in contrast to its functional counterparts: belief and cultural systems, worldviews, and moral orders. Concluding that religion, as understood in the 20th century, includes non-theistic belief systems and movements, Hunter proposes that secular humanism is a cosmology or religion that holds humanity, rationalism, subjective experience, and human perfectibility sacred.

The important policy issue for Hunter is the extent to which this faith system infiltrates public education. He notes the stark contrast between this infiltration and the Supreme Court's efforts to exclude religion from the schools. He fears that the subjective, relativistic, and anti-supernatural ideology of humanism has already radically secularized the schools and the larger culture. While humanism is not "taught as religion," it subtly and by default monopolizes the moral and ideological atmosphere in the classroom and society, and thus threatens minority views and the principle of religious pluralism.

Richard John Neuhaus, a Lutheran pastor who converted to Roman Catholicism in 1990 and who earlier shifted from a liberal to a neoconservative view, is a prolific writer on church/state issues. He has been a religion editor for the *National Review*, a participant in several think tanks on religion and society, an appointed official in the Carter and Reagan administrations, and he now directs the Institute on Religion and Public Life. Neuhaus bases his views on church/state relations on the idea that the American experiment with democracy "derived from religiously grounded belief ... [and] continues to depend on such belief."

He insists that religion and traditional values persist, despite the on-slaught of secularism sponsored by the nation's intellectual elites who perpetuate the myth that America is increasingly and of necessity secular. According to Neuhaus their vision of a God-empty public square to "be filled by a state-promulgated civil religion" not only fails to recognize the persistence of religion, but also poses a threat to American democracy. This threat exists because law is not enough to protect against violations of human rights. In his view, the "only firm basis [of laws] is in their being perceived as a transcendent gift." The problem, for those concerned about the separation of church and state, is how to acknowledge a belief in the law as a transcendent gift "without running into the difficulties of a government establishment of a particular way of expressing that religious belief."

Like Hunter, Neuhaus sees a threat to religious freedom in the Supreme Court's denial of the right to religious exercise in schools. This exclusion, which strips the public square of "overarching meaning," is not neutrality, but hostility toward religion. Encroaching secularism in the larger culture poses another threat. "Without a transcendent or religious point of refer-ence, conflicts of values can't be resolved. ... [they] are viewed not as conflicts between contending truths but as conflicts between contending interests." This relativism frightens Neuhaus who fears that "in a thor-oughly secular society, notions of what is morally excellent or morally base are not publicly admissible ... as moral judgment." He concludes that such inadmissibility of moral judgments leads not to pluralism per se, but to "indifference to normative truth, an agreement to count all opinions about morality as equal." This would debase the public square by excluding from it the idea of virtue. In the meantime, there is a counter-revolution going on against the "naked public square" as people act to reinsert transcendent meaning into society. Neuhaus approves of this revolution.

Leo Pfeffer, who has labored long, hard and effectively in defense of a strict separation of church and state, first introduced the concept of secular humanism into Supreme Court documents in 1963. He argued then on behalf of equal constitutional protection for the free exercise of religion rights of non-believers. He subsequently waged a 30 year campaign to emphasize that secular humanism does not constitute a religion, quasi or otherwise, despite Supreme Court declarations to the contrary in *Torcaso v. Watkins, U.S. v. Seeger* and *Widmar v. Vincent.*

In these cases, the Court redefined religion to include "a sincere and meaningful belief which occupies in the life of its possessor a place parallel to that filled by ... God." In other words, all belief is religion and protected by the Free Exercise Clause. While Pfeffer approves of the Court decisions that reversed discrimination against "non-religion," he disapproves, as the conservative philosopher Sidney Hook did as well, of "conversion by definition." In other words, he approves the protection of free exercise rights for non-believers, but objects to the expanded definition of religion that encompasses secular humanism. Hunter discerns an inconsistency in this orientation that demands free exercise of religion rights for non-believers, like secular humanists, but rejects "no establishment" restrictions related to them and their beliefs and programs.

Pfeffer, on the other hand, cries foul since secular humanism is not a religion. He takes special umbrage, for example, at the fundamentalists. He accuses them of plotting to sneak their ideology back into public school life via a misleading demand for equal time with secular humanism, which they wrongly assume governs value making in the U.S. Pfeffer approves the Court's foiling of this plot in its recent rejection of the Fundamentalists' claim that creation science (religion) deserves equal time with evolution science (secular humanism as religion) in the schools. In sum, while Hunter and Neuhaus consider secular humanism as a philosophy that takes on the character of religion in terms of its impact on American values and society, Pfeffer holds that its non-theistic base exempts it from religious status.

Key Questions: Does the world view/ideology of Christianity or secular humanism (man is alone in the universe and the measure of all things) dominate American political and religious culture? How does the newly public battle between these views manifest itself in the issue of separation of church and state or in court cases involving prayer or the teaching of "creation science" in school? Has "enlightened" skepticism about religion guaranteed the victory of secularism, pluralism, and tolerance or contributed to spiritual and cultural malaise and a loss of transcendent values?

Richard John Neuhaus

The Naked Public Square:
Religion and Democracy in America

Most people allow that democracy's historical roots are somehow related to biblical religion. Most, but not all. Some textbook tellings of democracy's story attribute the whole idea to classical Greece. In this version, the influence of Christianity was entirely negative. Religion as the enemy of democratic freedom is epitomized, it is said, in the Inquisition. The classic period and our modern era of enlightenment are the opposite of everything represented by the Inquisition. Those who tell the story this way overlook the fact that in 300 years the Inquisition had fewer victims than were killed any given afternoon during the years of Stalin's purges and Hitler's concentration camps. Nonetheless, it is asserted that the modern era is uniquely friendly to democratic freedom.

The American experiment, which more than any other has been normative for the world's thinking about democracy, is not only derived from religiously grounded belief, it continues to depend upon such belief. In his first year as vice president under the new Constitution, John Adams said, "We have no government armed with power capable of contending with human passions unbridled by morality and religion. Our constitution was made only for a moral and a religious people. It is wholly inadequate for the government of any other."

Secular historians and social theorists typically assert that a new and different grounding is now necessary, for in a "secular society" religion cannot provide the cohesion required. [But] ... Americans, as a people, are as religious, probably more religious, than they have ever been. Their religious allegiances are identifiably Judeo-Christian. Dissent from a broadly defined religious orthodoxy is perhaps more marginal today than it was in the heyday of eighteenth-century deism. The militantly antireligious campaign of, for example, a Thomas Paine would likely have little influence today.

The discussion of religion's demise in "secular America" is a discussion carried on within a relatively small elite. All the while, ordinary people have gone along assuming that of course morality, public and private, is derived from religion. Most are mildly puzzled and a minority is outraged when told in textbooks and television that ours is a secular society.

Desire Disguised as Fact

Among the outraged, the suspicion grows that there is some kind of conspiracy afoot. It is said that certain elites declare things to be the way they want things to be. They declare the demise, or at least the decline, of religion because it is required for the kind of emancipation they seek. They declare the nuclear family to be moribund because the family is seen as repressive.

Meanwhile, however, the great majority of Americans, heedless of the wisdom imparted by their presumed betters, continue to go to church and to rate the "traditional" family as among life's highest goods. ...

For better and for worse, traditional values are very much alive in America. Some who view all tradition as oppressive earnestly desire that such values should die. Toward that end, they propagate "the fact" of their demise. However many there are who actively promote a revolutionary reevaluation of values, there are many more who quietly assimilate the dogmas of secularism.

Among those dogmas, few have been so widely assimilated as the proposition that ours is a secular society. Religion may be indulged in privacy, but it is no longer available for the reconstruction of the public ethic. What has happened in recent decades is a redefinition of what constitutes "the real world." Under the current guardians of public perceptions, religion only shows up on the screen when it impinges upon a real world defined apart from religion. We have all agreed, have we not, that ours is a secular society?

Media and Secularization

Those of us who received the grace of working with Martin Luther King, Jr., know how profoundly his life and work were empowered by religious faith. Following King's assassination, a television announcer spoke in solemn tones: "And so today there was a memorial service for the slain civil rights leader, Dr. Martin Luther King, Jr. It was a religious service and it is fitting that it should be, for, after all, Dr. King was the son of a minister."

How can we explain this astonishing blindness to the religious motive and meaning of King's ministry? The announcer was speaking out of a habit of mind that was quite unconscious. The habit of mind is that religion must be kept at one remove from the public square, that matters of public significance must be sanitized of religious particularity.

The misunderstanding of King is not an isolated instance but is symptomatic of the way our world is interpreted by prestige communicators. These interpreters are not the mastermind of a secular humanist conspiracy, but victims of the secularizing mythology of which they are hardly aware. Thus, were the mythical Man from Mars to watch television news and read the prestige press for many months, he would likely be quite oblivious to the role of religion in the society. He certainly would not know that, next to family and work, the things that Americans do most are called religion.

The point is not to excoriate the media. The point is that the widespread exclusion of religiously grounded values and beliefs is at the heart of the outrage and alienation of millions of Americans. They do not recognize their experience of America in the picture of it purveyed by cultural and communications elites. At the heart of this nonrecognition – which results in everything from puzzlement to crusading fever – is the absence of religion.

At one level, it can be said that the prevailing situation is extremely nondemocratic. At another level, more closely related to sociological theory, it must be said that the situation cannot be sustained. The emptiness of the public square will be filled by a state-promulgated civil religion, which poses a threat of totalitarianism. Or the emptiness will continue until the public square is finally invaded by one or another existing belief system, whether of the Left or the Right.

Church and State: Not a New Problem

... The role of religion and the democratization of public values have been problematic from the beginning of the American experiment. Thomas Jefferson was hardly a conventionally religious person. Unlike many of those who signed the Declaration of Independence, he thought one of its central purposes was to free people from "monkish ignorance and superstition."

Monkish ignorance and superstition, in his view, is what is ordinarily meant by Christian orthodoxy. Jefferson thought his "Bill for Establishing Religious Freedom" in Virginia one of the three greatest achievements in his life. The same Jefferson, however, had no illusions that democracy had resolved the religious question by establishing "the separation of church and state."

Consider, for example, his well-known reflection on the immorality of slavery: "And can the liberties of a nation be thought secure when we have removed their only firm basis, a conviction in the minds of the people that these liberties are the gift of God? That they are not to be violated but with his wrath? Indeed I tremble for my country when I reflect that God is just; that his justice cannot sleep forever. ..."

Jefferson understood that the naked public square is a very dangerous place. No constitution or written law is strong enough to defend rights under attack. Their "only firm basis" is in their being perceived as a transcendent gift. At the same time, the denial of such rights, as they were denied by slavery, cannot be sustained without invoking the dreadful judgment that follows upon the defiance of the moral basis.

Law and Secularization

Jefferson's understanding of the unstated religious foundation of this democracy has been seconded frequently by the Supreme Court. A problem has been, and continues to be, how to state the unstated. In other words, the goal is to acknowledge the "only firm basis" of democracy without running into the difficulties of a government establishment of a particular way of expressing that religious basis. The careful balancing and nuancing that is required is evident in *Zorach v. Clauson* (1952) in which the Court declared, ... "We are a religious people whose institutions presuppose a Supreme Being. We guarantee the freedom to worship as one chooses. We make room for as wide a variety of beliefs and creeds as the spiritual needs of man deem necessary. We sponsor an attitude on the part of government that shows no partiality to any one group and lets each flourish according to the zeal of its adherents and the appeal of its dogma. When the state encourages religious instruction or cooperates with religious authorities by adjusting the schedule of public events (such as "released time" in schools) to sectarian needs, it follows the best of our traditions. For it then respects the religious nature of our people and accommodates the public service to their spiritual needs. To hold that it may not would be to find in the Constitution a requirement that the government show a callous indifference to religious groups. That would be preferring those who believe in no religion over those who do believe."

A little over 10 years later, in 1963, *Abington* came before the Court. The quarrel then had to do with Pennsylvania's practice of Bible reading in government schools. Justice Clark wrote for the majority and attempted, as is required, to demonstrate that the decision was in agreement with prior Court pronouncements. Quoting from an earlier finding, he acknowledged that "the history of man is inseparable from the history of religion." He observed that many of the founding fathers believed in God and cited other instances in which the state continues to recognize religion.

Scholars have pointed out, however, that there is a significant shift from *Zorach* to *Abington*. In the second there is no affirmation that our institutions presuppose a Supreme Being. Nor is it said, as it was said in *Zorach* and earlier statements, that people do in fact have religious needs that the state must respect. Nor is there admission of the need for public encouragement of religion. As Prof. Glen Thurow writes: "All that is recognized [in *Abington*] is that our people do in fact participate in religious observances. ... The Court does not say whether it is good or bad that our national life reflects a religious people."

Abington is curious in another way. Historically, religious freedom was thought to be in the service of religious practice. Religious freedom was not primarily freedom *from* religion – although the freedom to espouse no religion or even to oppose all religion was carefully protected – but freedom to exercise religion in whatever way a person deems fit. In *Abington*, however, religious freedom is set against religious observance. Again Thurow: "Religion and the policy of freedom of religion are no longer seen as having a common root in recognition of presumed spiritual needs and institutional dependency on a Supreme Being. There is not one tradition, but two."

Abington set asunder what had been a unified tradition, as articulated in *Zorach* and innumerable other statements from our legal and political history. Some of the other justices recognized the ominous implications of *Abington.* When "religious freedom" is set against religious observance it tends to become the same thing as secularism. If, in addition to that, the burden of constitutional guarantees are put on the side of this version of religious freedom, the state's alleged neutrality to religion easily slides into hostility. Justice Stewart said as much in his dissenting opinion: "And a refusal to permit religious exercises thus is seen, not as the realization of state neutrality, but rather as the establishment of a religion of secularism, or at the least, as government support of the beliefs of those who think that religious exercises shall be conducted only in private."

Although agreeing with the decision, Justices Goldberg and Harlan also had grave misgivings: "But unilateral devotion to the concept of neutrality can lead to invocation or approval of results which partake not simply of that noninterference and noninvolvement with the religious ..., but of a brooding and pervasive devotion to the secular and a passive, or even active, hostility to the religious." In their reservations, the justices edge up to the insight that the naked public square cannot remain truly naked. The need for an overarching meaning, for a moral legitimation, will not go undenied. What is called neutrality toward religion is an invitation for a substitute religion. That substitute will be constructed from reasoning that is compatible with "a brooding and pervasive devotion to the secular."

While the 1952 decision is more satisfactory than that of 1963, Professor Thurow is correct, I believe, in arguing that both miss the public character of religion and of religiously based values. Thurow's point is worth quoting at some length:

"Justice Douglas asserts that our institutions presuppose a Supreme Being, but he discusses only the accommodation of *private* desires and needs. *Neither opinion raises directly the question of the public good involved.* As under the theory of *laissez faire* in economics, the theory of the Court is that it is the function of government to allow or facilitate and to harmonize the private religious or irreligious desires of individual citizens, without any explicit consideration of the public good. But we may wonder whether the conflicting private desires of citizens can be harmonized for the public good without considering what the public good as a whole requires" (emphasis added).

This supposed neutrality to religion is a novelty, a break with the one tradition of the republic. ... Before the tradition was split and religious freedom was set against religion, it was understood that reference to the transcendent was a public reference by which public purpose was defined and judged. To be sure, that way of speaking of God in public lingers on in presidential Thanksgiving Day proclamations and in inaugural ceremonies. But such references are thought to be no more than elements of a vapid and residual "civil religion."

Private Religion

As in the media, then, so also in the courts and centers of higher learning it is more or less taken for granted that ours is a secular society. When religion insists upon intruding itself into public space with aggressive force that cannot be denied, it is either grudgingly acknowledged, or alarms are raised about the impending return of the Middle Ages. Then the proposition becomes more explicit: if ours is not a secular society, it *should* be. Unless overwhelmingly countered by the evidence, the tendency is for that desire to be presented as fact. For an event to be *legitimately* public, it must be secular. If it is touched by religion, that is to be viewed as a private and somewhat idiosyncratic factor. ...

Public consideration of the religious beliefs of others is an invasion of privacy. The public assertion of one's own beliefs is an imposition upon carefully sterilized space. In the modern version of civility we agree not to lay uncomfortably ultimate burdens upon others. Our highest religious duty is not to offend those who might be offended by the idea of religious duty. There is much that is necessary and even admirable in this understanding of civility. But civility is vacuous when separated from the *civitas* of shared values. More than being vacuous, it is untenable; it inevitably results in the construction of values that are hostile to those values that might have given offense in the first place.

The democratic vitalities of America are today being stirred by those who were not consulted when it was decided that this is a secular society. Groups like the Moral Majority come to the public square not with the political religion of the republic but with the revivalist politics of the camp meeting. Confession of sin, repentance, decision, walking of the sawdust trail – all is transferred to political campaign and ballot box. Revivalist politics is also not new in American life. It is usually populist in nature and can erupt on the political Right or Left. In 1972, George McGovern accepted the presidential nomination in a ringing speech that catalogued America's iniquities, its wanderings from the path of righteousness. ...

The alliance between religion and the protest against perceived cultural directions is not accidental. That is, the protest could not have allied itself with some other institution, such as the university, or labor unions, or a political party. This is true because other institutions have narrower interests and lack a base in mass participation. But it is most importantly true because only religion must, by definition, insist upon moral truth that is transcendent, intersubjective, and therefore normative. True, science and the university that limits itself to scientific knowledge speak about normative truth; but, again by definition, scientific knowledge does not address the issue of moral purpose, not to mention the question of transcendent judgment.

Without a transcendent or religious point of reference, conflicts of values cannot be resolved; there can only be procedures for their temporary accommodation. Conflicts over values are viewed not as conflicts between contending truths but as conflicts between contending interests. If one person believes that incest is wrong and should be outlawed while another person believes incest is essential for sexual liberation, the question in a thoroughly secularized society is how these conflicting "interests" might be accommodated.

Since the person who practices incest can do so without denying the rights of the person who abhors incest, the accommodation will inevitably be skewed in favor of incest. Similarly, one person believes the government has an obligation to assist the poor through tax dollars while another denies that there is any such obligation. Since the "interests" of the first person cannot be accommodated without interfering with the "interests" of the second person (by imposing higher taxes), the accommodation will be skewed in favor of the second.

What the justices described as a "pervasive and brooding devotion to the secular" leads to the extreme forms of libertarianism that erupt from time to time on both the Left and the Right of the political spectrum. It is tenuously based upon the split in the one tradition by which historically our public life was held accountable to critical judgment. In a thoroughly secular society, notions of what is morally excellent or morally base are not publicly admissible. That is, they are not admissible as moral judgment: they have public status only as they reflect the "interest" of those who hold them. Only when we are forced to talk about morality within the context of the formal polity as, for example, in court cases, do we discover that the secular theory about our common life is frustrated by the moral and religious character of our common life.

In New York State a law has been passed forbidding the use of young children in the making of pornographic films. In order to protect it against challenges from extreme civil libertarians, it is specifically stated that the law is not based upon moral or religious reasons. The reasoning offered is that making pornographic films is injurious to the mental health of young children. ...

A secular polity requires that we profess more confidence in the "scientific" notions of psychiatry than in our moral judgment. In fact, while psychiatric and a host of other considerations might inform moral judgment, the law reflects the moral judgment of legislators who are responsive to the moral judgment of their constituencies. But they cannot admit that the law is based upon moral judgment. ...

Aristotle speaks of the impossibility of discussing virtue with people who are "handicapped by some incapacity for goodness." The notion of a secular society compels political actors to pretend to be more morally handicapped than they are. It might be argued that this is the price to be paid for a pluralistic society. The price is too high. What is meant by "pluralism", in such arguments is frequently indifference to normative truth, an agreement to count all opinions about morality as equal (equal "interests" to be accommodated) because we are agreed there is no truth by which judgment can be rendered. The result is the debasement of our public life by the exclusion of the idea – and consequently of the practice – of virtue.

Virtue and Politics

A familiar statement from Aristotle is pertinent: "Anything that we have to learn to do we learn by the actual doing of it: people become builders by building and instrumentalists by playing instruments. Similarly we become just by performing just acts, temperate by performing temperate ones, brave by performing brave ones. This view is supported by what happens in city-states. Legislators make their citizens good by habituation; this is the intention of every legislator, and those who do not carry it out fail of their object. This is what makes the difference between a good constitution and a bad one."

It is only in recent years that the Constitution of the United States has been interpreted to mandate that legislators fail, or at least pretend to fail, in carrying out their object. As "by habituation" we pretend not to be concerned for the good, we become what we pretend to be. The intervention of religiously based values in public affairs is a protest against the pretense. Whether that intervention speaks to our obligation for the hungry of the world or to the necessity of protection of the unborn and other endangered humans in our own society, it is a call for us to assume the dignity of being moral actors.

We are not merely atomistic individuals with interests to be accommodated but persons of reason and conviction whose humanity requires participation in the process of persuasion. From Aristotle through Jefferson, and up to the very recent past, politics was thought of as that process of persuading and being persuaded; a process engaged in by a community brought into being by its shared acknowledgement of the existence of truth beyond its certain grasp.

It is not that the greats of Western political philosophy did not understand the importance of accommodation. Burke, reflecting on the American experience, observed: "All government – indeed, every human benefit and enjoyment, every virtue and prudent act – is founded on compromise and barter." Persuasion often reaches its limits. It is one thing for you to propose a compromise when you realize that you will not persuade your neighbor of your understanding of the truth. It is quite another to conclude that there is no question of truth involved. In the first instance you remain a moral actor, acting according to the virtue of prudence. In the second instance, it is merely a matter of ciphers with conflicting interests splitting the difference.

Were the battle against a cabal of "secular humanists," as some would have it, there would be reason for greater optimism. They could be exposed and driven from their positions of influence, perhaps. Our difficulty is greater than that. It is the pervasive influence of ideas about a secular society and secular state, ideas that have insinuated themselves also into our religious thinking and that have been institutionalized in our politics.

The proposition that America is a secular society is contrary to sociological fact. The American people are more incorrigibly religious than ever before. The proposition is impossible in principle. The American experience is not self-legitimating; it requires what it has until recently possessed, some sense of transcendent meaning. And the proposition is politically unsustainable. There are simply too many people who are no longer prepared to pretend that we are not the kind of people we are.

Whatever he may have meant by it, and whatever he did with it, Jimmy Carter's intuition was democratically sound: the task is to provide government as good as are the American people. More precisely – since Americans are not necessarily more "good" in their behavior than others – a government responsive to the good to which most Americans aspire. Whatever our political persuasion, if we care about a democratic future, we have a deep stake in reconstructing a politics that was not begun by and cannot be sustained by the myth of secular America.

James Davison Hunter

America's Fourth Faith:
A Sociological Perspective on Secular Humanism

... One must start with the question of what constitutes religion. Contemporary sociology has inherited from the classical period (and has failed to improve substantially upon it) two analytically distinct approaches to the phenomenon of religion: the substantive approach (defining religion according to the "meaning contents of the phenomenon") and the functional approach (defining religion according to its role in social life). The former derives from the German idealistic tradition of the *Religionswissenschaften* (most notably developed by such intellectuals as Max Weber, Rudolf Otto ... and Peter Berger), while the functionalist approach derives from French and British structuralism (Emile Durkheim, Branislaw Malinowski, ... Robert Bellah ... and Mary Douglas) and German sociological materialism (Marx and Engels). ...

As Peter Berger makes plain, the differentia in the substantive definition is the category of the "sacred" or the "holy." Yet the sacred, from this perspective, is defined in fairly specific terms. The sacred is the realm of the supramundane or the transcendent – what Otto called the *mysterium tremendum*. It is a reality which humans experience as "wholly other," for it evokes feelings of ineffable wonder and awe. Religion is the meaning system which emanates from the sacred. Many who adopt this approach insist further that for a belief system to truly qualify as a religion, believers must view it as such. The social actors themselves must impute religious meaning to their beliefs.

This World (Fall 1987), 101–110. Used by permission.

A functional approach to religion is distinguished by concern for religion's role and consequences for individual and social existence. For the individual, religion provides a meaning system offering a sense of purpose and meaning, a stable set of moral coordinates to guide everyday life, as well as mechanisms to help the individual cope with the traumatic experiences of suffering, pain, and death. At the societal level, religion functions to justify institutional arrangements, thereby generating social integration (or in critical terminology, legitimating oppressive power structures). At this level, religion can also perform a prophetic function, delegitimating the status quo and calling for the establishment of a new social order. From this perspective, religion is also defined by the sacred, but the sacred in this case could be any ultimate value or concern (as Paul Tillich put it) or any orienting principle adhered to by a social group.

Few scholars have ever stridently rejected one of these approaches in exclusive favor of another, which has created problems for the legal debate necessitated by the First Amendment. In practice most sociologists implicitly operate out of a functional approach. One reason is that this approach is less Western-centric and, therefore, more inclusive of a wider variety of meaning systems. Another reason (probably the main one) is that it is a more purely sociological approach – the sacred is viewed as a "social fact," irreducible to the psychological state of the social actor. As a consequence, religion has, for analytical purposes, become largely (though not completely) synonymous with such terms as cultural system, belief system, meaning system, moral order, ideology, worldview, and cosmology.

A cultural system does not have to have a deity for it to be considered religious in character. Confucianism and Theravedin Buddhism, for example, contain no supernatural realm to speak of, yet few would eliminate them from the catalog of world religions. Other examples are less obvious, such as political ideologies or therapeutic techniques – the range of phenomena typically referred to as "quasi-religions" or "religion-surrogates" or "functional equivalents" of religion. Even those who are committed in principle to a more substantive approach to religion (including Weber and Berger) recognize the profoundly religious nature of these phenomena and employ these terms to describe them. Thus, a wide range of subjects have been analyzed, directly or indirectly, in terms that delineate how they function as religions. Among these have been radical Leftist political movements and ideologies, the environmental movement, science, bureaucracy, technology, individualism, and a large number of organizations in the human potential movement. ...

This well-established precedent for analyzing nontheistic ideologies and institutions in this way invites speculation about the religious nature of secular humanism, speculation which begins by looking at how secular humanism takes shape as a popular movement.

Onward, Humanist Soldiers

As a popular movement, the secular humanist movement is *institutionalized* in such organizations as the American Humanist Association, the Council for Democratic and Secular Humanism, the Unitarian Universalist Association, the Fellowship of Religious Humanists, the American Ethical Union, the United Secularists of America, the Washington Ethical Society, and the Association for Humanistic Psychology. Its creeds are *formalized* in such documents as the *Humanist Manifesto I* (1933), the *Humanist Manifesto II* (1973), and "A Secular Humanist Declaration" (1980) (among many others); and its interests are *articulated* by such periodicals as *Free Inquiry* (circulation: 10,325), *The Humanist* (circulation 11,000), and the *Progressive World* (circulation: 1,000). Such groups provide the network of organizations at the heart of the popular humanist movement in America. When examining Humanism in these formalized and institutionalized terms (hence the use of the upper case), it becomes immediately clear that it not only qualifies as a religion using functional criteria but, in many ways, it qualifies as a religion using substantive criteria as well.

Humanism at this level is clearly a meaning system or a cosmology. It is built upon certain unstated assumptions, as well as formal propositions about the nature of the universe (a closed, naturalistic system), the origin of the human race (evolutionary), the nature and origin of knowledge (scientistic if not positivistic), the nature of human values (relativistic, subjectivistic and, in part, scientifically derived), and the goal of human life (the full "realization" and "actualization" of human potentiality at both the individual and societal level). All of these positions are stated with extraordinary eloquence in any of the major humanist creedal statements including, of course, *The Humanist Manifesto I* and *II*, "A Secular Humanist Manifesto," *In Defense of Secular Humanism* (by Paul Kurtz, 1983), or "The Humanist Philosophy in Perspective" (*The Humanist*, January/February

1984, by Frederick Edwards). At the core of this meaning system is the assertion of ultimate value – in this case, humanity. Humanity as a symbol and as a reality is, for all practical purposes, sacralized, as is the chief mechanism for humanity's progress and development – science/technology. Indeed these elements define the essential soteriology of Humanism. As the *Humanist Manifesto II* puts it, "Using technology wisely, we can control our environment, conquer poverty, markedly reduce disease, extend our life-span, significantly modify our behavior, alter the course of human evolution and cultural development, unlock vast new powers, and provide humankind with unparalleled opportunity for achieving an abundant and meaningful life."

Thus, in its ideological content, Humanism is a far-reaching cosmology designed not only to provide individuals with a clear, alternate means of making sense of their everyday lives, but to provide a mechanism for legitimating the larger social order as well. As the *Humanist Manifesto II* puts it, "Humanism can provide the purpose and inspiration that so many seek; it can give personal meaning and significance to human life." Yet the functionally religious character of Humanism goes beyond the ideological to the institutional.

Humanism, in addition to its creeds, has a wide range of religious/ functionally religious institutions, most of which boast a 501(c)(3) status with the I.R.S. There are humanist churches known publicly as churches. ... These churches have credentialed "ministers" (in the Ethical Culture Society, they are called leaders; in the AHA, they are called humanist counselors and the latter enjoy the legal status of ordained pastors, priests, and rabbis). These churches have Sunday services (in the Ethical Culture Society, these are called platform meetings), Sunday schools for children, and collective rituals. ...

Simply using functional criteria, it is not difficult to make the argument that as a popular movement, Humanism is religious or quasi-religious. It is certainly no less religious than, say, Transcendental Meditation, est, psychosynthesis, Arica Training, Scientology, or any of the other organizations of the human potential movement. It is no less religious then ethical Confucianism or the "high road" tradition of Buddhism.

Humanism and Human Potential

It is possible to argue that this expression of Humanism could be understood as both a predecessor and a variant of the larger and more diverse human potential movement. It was a predecessor in that it became established organizationally decades before the proliferation of religious and quasi-religious experimentation of the mid to late 1970s, but it evolved into one organization among many human potential groups. The principal difference is that Humanism was and is primarily ethical and philosophical in concern, while most of the human potential groups were and are primarily therapeutic in orientation. Nevertheless, they are a part of the same cultural heritage. The ideological compatibility becomes obvious when humanists speak of the need for "self-actualization," the need for humans to "experience their full potentialities," or when they speak of the "ultimate goal" [of humanity as ...] "the fulfillment of the potential growth in each human personality." Humanism and the human potential movement thus share a common linguistic base. They also share a common ideological concern with the primacy of subjective experience.

In sum, Humanism clearly fits certain sociological criteria of religion. Would it matter if a group rejects the term "religion" as self-descriptive? Not particularly. Neo-orthodox Christian theology has rejected the term, as have a number of groups in the human potential movement (such as Transcendental Meditation). Yet this has not dissuaded most social scientists from regarding them theoretically and empirically as religions or quasi-religions. Even so it would be more difficult to use the term religion to describe Humanism if humanists rejected the term. The fact is, however, most do not reject the term. Ethical Culture, for example, officially describes itself as a "religious fellowship" as does the Fellowship of Religious Humanists – indeed, the preamble of the American Humanist Association states that the AHA is itself a "religious organization." Leaders in the popular movement (such as John Dewey in his book, *A Common Faith*; Corliss Lamont in his book, *The Philosophy of Humanism*; Paul Kurtz in his book, *In Defense of Secular Humanism*; and Paul Beattie in his 1985 *Free Inquiry* article, "The Religion of Secular Humanism") have repeatedly identified humanism as a religion. Likewise, the *Humanist Manifesto I* is replete with references and inferences that Humanism is a religion. Indeed, in this document it is implied that Humanism is the highest realization of man's religious aspirations. ...

All social movements have vested interests. These are invariably related to the expansion of power and privilege. Curiously, in the 1961 *Torcaso v. Watkins* case, it served the interests of humanists for Humanism to be recognized as a religion and so they pressed for such recognition. In that case, the Supreme Court adopted a functional approach (relying expressly on Tillich) for *free exercise purposes* and included secular humanism among those non-theistic faiths that qualified. The present judicial debate surrounding the recognition of Humanism as a religion for *establishment purposes* would clearly undermine their vested interests as a movement. Thus it is not surprising to learn of some humanists who now reject the label as descriptive of their movement. Such efforts to redefine Humanism as something other than religion could and should be viewed with a measure of skepticism.

Back to School

The obvious and important question remains: secular humanism may be a sectarian faith for a marginal, sometimes eminent, but certainly powerless minority. But what does that have to do with the public school curricula and the larger culture? Few people would be so facile as to suggest the votaries or even leaders were at all influential in setting curricular policy in public schools or that they had any direct influence in any American institution. Yet it would seem equally simplistic to maintain that there is absolutely no relation between the formal ideology of the popular movement and developments in the larger culture – or that the relationship between Humanism and the ideology of public education (if one exists) is purely coincidental. But what is the nature of the relationship? ...

Public education as secular education. What virtually all Americans insist upon is that no one theism or combination of theisms be propagated to the exclusion of others in the public schools. Virtually all, then, accept secular education of a limited nature. Yet there is evidence that the secularization of public education has gone beyond that. The radicalization of this secularization comes in the "censorship" (by neglect or omission) of almost any reference to theistic religion in the description of American life and culture or of its role in American history. These patterns are documented summarily in an National Institute of Education study ("Equity in Values Education") conducted by Paul Vitz of New York University and, ironically and unexpectedly, in two other studies – one sponsored by People for the American Way called *Looking at History* and the other by Americans United for the Separation of Church and State entitled "Teaching About Religious Liberty in American Secondary Schools." To the extent that such censorship exists it not only distorts the historical record, it also unjustifiably prejudices the educational process against theistic faiths. As one commentator put it: "It is a fallacy to suppose that by omitting a subject you teach nothing about it. On the contrary you teach that it is to be omitted, and that it is therefore a matter of secondary importance. And you teach this not openly and explicitly, which would invite criticism; you simply take it for granted and thereby insinuate it silently, insidiously, and all but irresistibly."

Public education as humanistic education. This anti-theistic bias is certainly consistent with the formal ideology of the popular humanistic movement. According to studies conducted by Richard Baer of Cornell University, there is also evidence to support the hypothesis that the public school curricula (particularly as embodied in the textbooks) reflect an emphasis on the individual as the measure of all things and on personal autonomy, on feelings, personal needs and subjectively-derived values, all independent of a transcendent standard. To the extent that this is true, then public education arguably shares a common ethical orientation with modern popular movement as well. It is not as though public school textbooks should discuss these matters from the perspective of a particular set of transcendent standards. They most certainly should not. But neither should they assert what may comprise a subjectivistic and implicitly relativistic approach to values, needs, emotions and the nature of the individual a) uncritically, b) without detachment, or c) without respect to cultural traditions that would strongly dissent.

In sum it would appear that some evidence supports the notion that a secular humanism of a sort does comprise a dominant moral ideology of public education. If this is ultimately true, it is certainly *not* as a *formal* ideological system (e.g., in the sense that it is formalized in the popular humanist movement). Neither is it taught *as* religion. It is less crystalized than that – more diffused. It lacks the self-consciousness and articulation of a formal ideology. One could even call it a reflexive or "folk" ideology – even, as Robert Coles put it, a cultural ethos. But is this a religion – the same kind of relgion as embodied in the popular movement? Perhaps not. Nevertheless, the late Harvard sociologist, Talcott Parsons called secular humanism (in this latent form) "America's fourth faith." Legal scholar Leo Pfeffer, also of Harvard (and one whose "separation" credentials are beyond question), also wrote of "humanism as a religion along with the three major theistic faiths." What, then, does this folk ideology have in common with the formal tenets of Humanism? I would argue that there is a general "isomorphism" between the two. That is, they share a common ideological structure.

Interestingly, the drafters and signers of the *Humanist Manifesto I* and the *Humanist Manifesto II* seem to recognize this. Charles Francis Potter, one of the signers of the *Humanist Manifesto I*, wrote in his book, *Humanism: A New Religion:* "Education is thus a most powerful ally of Humanism and every American public school is a school of Humanism. What can the theistic Sunday schools, meeting for an hour once a week, and teaching only a fraction of the children, do to stem the tide of a five-day program of humanistic teaching?" Likewise, in an essay in *The Humanist* (March/April, 1976), Paul Blanshard wrote: "I think the most important factor moving us toward a secular society has been the educational factor. Our schools may not teach Johnny to read properly, but the fact that Johnny is in school until he is sixteen tends toward the elimination of religious superstition."

Bureaucratization and Disenchantment

But from what does this latent ideology derive? At the risk of disappointing the conspiritorially minded, we can safely reject the theory that the editors of *The Humanist* deserve all the credit. At one level, this ideology derives from the intellectual traditions of the secular Enlightenment – an ideological revolution which eventuated in the debunking of medieval and Reformational cosmologies and undermining of feudal forms of political authority and theistic forms of moral authority. Enshrined in their place were the commitments to scientific rationality and utopian visions of human progress and perfectibility – commitments that were embedded within the assumptions of philosophical naturalism.

But the secular Enlightenment was not just a solitary event generated by French, English and German intellectuals in the eighteenth century. These intellectual traditions have been "carried" through to succeeding generations even to the present, *institutionalized* within certain sectors of post-

Enlightenment society. The main "carriers" have been the intellectual classes, broadly understood – those who derive their livelihood from the
knowledge sector – whether they be professors, journalists, media elites,
lawyers or educators. This sector of the population is distinguished by their
access to higher education and thus, to the institutions of intellectual rationality. They are also distinguished, as public opinion surveys indicate, by a
posture of general indifference toward traditional theistic beliefs and
practices (if not outright secularity) and by a social and political liberalism
(at least as compared to the general population). Sociologist Peter Berger
has himself called the ideology of the knowledge classes "secular humanism"; while Alvin Gouldner (on the Left) has called it "the culture of critical
discourse" – two terms essentially describing the same reality. It is here also
where we can locate, sociologically, the popular humanist movement. Its
advocates occupy only a tiny fraction of the intellectual classes; their ideology represents only a formalization and crystallization of these more diffuse ideological themes.

At still another level are broader trends within the larger structure of
modern life. One of those trends involves the increasing "rationalization"
of the major institutional bureaucracies of contemporary society. ... A
second trend concerns the changing nature of life in the private sphere, the
sphere of personal and family life, of personal relationships, and so on.
These developments have been variously discussed as a tendency toward
narcissism ... hedonism ... subjectivism ... the therapeutic mentality ...
antinomianism ... and expressive individualism (Bellah, et al.). As Daniel
Yankelovich has shown, these latter tendencies are particularly prominent
in the highy educated upper-middle classes. If social science has described
these cultural tendencies, even in their general contours, with any accuracy,
then they could also be seen as isomorphic with the ideology of naturalistic
humanism. What this means is that the structure of contemporary culture
provides a "plausibility structure" or a social context within which humanistic ideology, both formal and "folk," becomes credible if not "com-
mon-sensical."

But how does all of this relate to the latent ideology of a secularistic
humanism in the public schools? First of all, public education is simply one
of the massive public bureaucracies of modern society and, as such, has
been subject to the same "disenchantment" as other public bureaucracies.
A second reason, perhaps one that is even more important than the first, has
something to do with a certain *affinity* between the ideological content of

public education and the interests of certain cultural elites and the state. The public school system in the United States represents a government monopoly over mass education and therefore represents education grounded in a particular cluster of institutional interests. In various private schools, education would more closely reflect the interests of the paying-clientele. These institutions depend directly on the capital resources of that clientele, who, if dissatisfied, withdraw their children, destroying these institutions altogether. Public schools, on the other hand, are not so directly dependent and, therefore, not so directly beholden to their local constituencies. Public education, then, is more likely to reflect the interests of the secular bureaucracy of the modern state from which it derives. It is also more likely to reflect the vested interests and cultural orientation of a larger category of cultural elites – not only those who design educational curricula, but other arbiters of social taste and opinion (i.e., the professoriat, journalists, lawyers, etc.).

Clearly, one should be cautious about making quick and direct linkages between Humanism (the formal ideology and movement) and humanism (the folk ideology as it exists either in the public schools or in the larger culture). Though the relationships among these phenomena are complex, they do exist. The advocates of Humanism themselves seem to recognize and even celebrate this as a statement from the *Humanist Manifesto II* suggests: "Many kinds of humanism exist in the contemporary world. The varieties and emphases of naturalistic humanism include 'scientific,' 'ethical,' 'democratic,' 'religious,' and 'Marxist' humanism. Free thought, atheism, agnosticism, skepticism, deism, rationalism, ethical culture, and liberal religion all claim heir to the humanist tradition." To the extent that expressive individualism, subjectivism, radical secularism (as described above), and the like are institutionalized in the public schools (even in a more latent form), they also are heirs to the humanist tradition.

If a naturalistic humanism is the dominant (albeit, latent) ideology of public education, not only should traditional Jews, Catholics, and Protestants be uneasy. In principal, so should humanists. In "A Secular Humanist Declaration," Paul Kurtz writes: "The lessons of history are clear: wherever one religion or ideology is established and given a dominant position in the state, minority opinions are in jeopardy." There is much to be gained by all parties in an intensely pluralistic society heeding that lesson.

Leo Pfeffer

The Religion of Secular Humanism:
A Judicial Myth

Every calling has a lexicon that makes little or no sense to the noninitiated. Neither religion nor law is an exception. Roman Catholic clergy can be secular or religious, but to the outsider all are religious and none are secular – else they would not be priests. Lawyers speak of "irrebuttable presumptions," even though to the nonlawyer that which cannot be rebutted is a fact, not a presumption.

These are words of art, and no doubt are useful or perhaps even indispensable to the trade or profession that uses them. When, however, a court, and particularly the Supreme Court of the United States, uses a term in a sense that even to other courts and to lawyers generally seems self-contradictory, the unanticipated consequences may turn out to be quite harmful. This, I suggest, may be the case in respect to the term "Secular Humanism," used by the Supreme Court in the 1961 decision in the case of *Torcaso v. Watkins*.

Research indicates that in the United States courts, the term does not appear in any judicial opinion prior to that decision. Beginning in 1776 our states adopted written constitutions as independent political entities. These set forth the powers and duties of the executive, legislative, and judicial branches and prescribed the qualification for election or appointment to governmental offices. Basically these were the same as those later to be set forth in the U.S. Constitution adopted in 1787, with however, one major difference that is relevant to this essay.

The closing words of the Constitution provide that "no religious test

---

Free Inquiry (Spring 1982) 24–27. Used by permission.

shall ever be required as a qualification to any office or public trust under the United States." On its face this seems to apply only to federal offices, leaving states free to decide for themselves whether to impose a religious test, manifested by an oath of belief in God or Jesus Christ or the Trinity, in respect to state offices, and indeed at the time the Constitution was drafted and adopted, most of the states did impose some religious qualifications for holding public office. In Rhode Island, Roger Williams had argued the irrelevancy of a religious test and urged that to limit civil magistrates to church members was like permitting only church members to assume "the office of a Doctor of Physic, a Master or a Pilot of a Ship, or a Captain or a Commodore of a Band or Army of men." Nevertheless by the beginning of the eighteenth century, even Rhode Island had adopted the pattern prevailing among the other colonies and had enacted a law that limited eligibility for public offices to Protestants.

As time went on, the states became more multi-religious and the oath progressed from Protestantism to Christianity and ultimately to belief in God. Typical of these was Article 37 of the Maryland Constitution, which provided that "no religious test ought ever to be required as a qualification for any office of profit or trust in this State, other than a declaration of belief in the existence of God."

It was not until 1961 that the United States Supreme Court had occasion to pass on the validity of these provisions under the federal constitution. Roy Torcaso, a resident of Maryland, had been appointed to the office of notary public by the governor of Maryland, but was refused a commission to serve because he would not take an oath or declare that he believed in the existence of God. He then brought suit to compel the issuance of the commission on the ground that the state's requirement that he declare this belief violated the First Amendment, which bans laws respecting an establishment of religion or prohibiting the free exercise thereof, and the Fourteenth Amendment, which had on numerous occasions been interpreted by the Supreme Court as making the provisions of the First Amendment applicable against the states. ... In a unanimous decision the Court upheld Torcaso's contentions and declared the Maryland religious oath requirement to be unconstitutional. While the language of the opinion is not precise as to the exact basis of its decision, it seems reasonably clear that the Court relied on both clauses in relation to religion in the Amendment, the one forbidding establishment of religion and the other banning laws prohibiting its free exercise.

The relevancy of the establishment clause guaranteeing the separation of church and state is quite obvious, but since Roy Torcaso was an avowed atheist, the same is not true in respect to the free exercise guarantee since Torcaso was not demanding any right to exercise religion. However, this invocation of the Free Exercise Clause was not unprecedented. In a case decided in 1943, *West Virginia Board of Education* v. *Barnette*, the Court had ruled that the clause guaranteeing freedom of speech encompasses as well freedom of nonspeech, and accordingly Jehovah's Witnesses pupils could not be expelled from public school for refusal to pledge allegiance to the flag of the United States. The fact that to the noninitiated the concept that speech encompasses silence, which is its direct opposite, might appear to be strange, yet it must be recognized that the Court's linguistic legerdemain in that case represented a great step forward in the protection of individual rights.

Our concern in this essay, however, is not a question of whether the guarantee of the free exercise of religion encompasses the practice or promulgation of atheism, but rather the Court's definition of "Secular Humanism" and its implications in respect to the ban on religious establishment. In their brief to the Supreme Court, counsel for Torcaso noted that the Court had previously interpreted that ban to encompass not only laws preferring some religions over others, but no less those preferring any or all religions over nonreligion or even anti-religion. It was really the latter that was relevant in the case, but cautious lawyers generally present all reasonable arguments support of their case, even if not entirely relevant. It is for this reason that Torcaso's brief argued:

> The requirement of a belief in the existence of God prefers some religions over others, specifically theistic religions over those which are non-theistic.
> It is frequently assumed that all religions are founded upon a belief in the existence of a personal God or at least some "God" no matter how that term is defined. This is not so. So great a religion as the Buddhist religion with over 150 million adherents throughout the world including the United States (World *Almanac*, 1959, p. 715) is not founded upon a belief in the existence of God. ...)

The Amendment, the brief concluded, "protects the Buddhists, Ethical Culturist and other non-theists no less than the Protestant, the Roman Catholics and Jew."

This paragraph of the brief is reflected in the following extract from the Supreme Court's opinion, set forth as footnote 11.

"Among religions in this country which do not teach what would generally be considered a belief in the existence of God are Buddhism, Taoism, Ethical Culture, Secular Humanism and others." ...

As previously noted, this is the first time a court of law in the United States characterized "Secular Humanism" as a "religion."

The Constitution secures the free exercise of religion and forbids laws respecting its establishment but does not undertake to define what is meant by the term "religion." In 1890, the Supreme Court did essay a definition in the case of *Davis v. Beason*. "The term 'religion,'" the Court said, "has reference to one's views of his relations to his Creator, and to the obligations they impose of reverence to His being and character, and of obedience to His will." The Court reached what it considered the quite logical conclusion that since the Creator would obviously not have sanctioned, much less commanded, polygamous marriages, what called itself the Church of Jesus Christ of Latter Day Saints was obviously not a religion, and hence Mormons were not within the protection secured by the First Amendment to the free exercise of "religion."

If the Court could spell out its definition of "religion," so also could Congress, and it too exercised the privilege within accepted conventional or majoritarian limitations. And like the Court, Congress was not eager to expand the definition to encompass unfavored or unconventional commitments. In 1948, Congress amended the Selective Service Act to limit the privilege of exemption from military service for conscientious objection by defining religion as belief in a "Supreme Being," and excluding those whose objection to war was based on "essentially political, sociological or philosophical views or a merely personal code."

The constitutional issue was presented to the Supreme Court in cases involving three draftees each of whom was denied exemption by his local draft board because he did not believe in God or a Supreme Being within the common understanding of those terms. One of the draftees refused to answer "yes" or "no" to the question as to his belief in a Supreme Being but asserted that his "skepticism or disbelief in the existence of God" did "not necessarily mean lack of faith in anything whatsoever"; that his was a "belief in and devotion to goodness and virtue for their own sakes, and a religious faith in a purely ethical creed." He cited such personages as Plato, Aristotle, and Spinoza for support of his ethical belief in intellectual and moral integrity "without belief in God, except in the remotest sense."

Another of the draftees defined religion as the "sum and essence of one's basic attitudes to the fundamental problems of human existence"; he said that there was a relationship to Goodness in two directions, "vertically towards Godness directly," and "horizontally towards Godness through Mankind and the World," and he accepted the latter.

The third draftee quoted with approval the Reverend John Haynes Holmes's definition of religion as "the consciousness of some power manifest in nature which helps man in the ordering of his life in harmony with its demands ... [It] is the supreme expression of human nature; it is man thinking his highest, feeling his deepest, and living his best."

Unanimously the Supreme Court held that all three draftees did indeed believe in a "Supreme Being" in the sense intended by Congress. By using that term rather than "God" Congress indicated its intent not to limit the exemption to persons believing in an anthropomorphic deity but intended to include all who possess "a sincere and meaningful belief which occupies in the life of its possessor a place parallel to that filled by the God of those admittedly qualifying for the exemption." Accordingly, all three draftees were entitled to exemption as religious objectors.

One can express some doubt that this was what Congress intended or that it wanted to exempt such young men as the three draftees involved in these cases. Nevertheless, by reading this intent into the minds of the congressmen who enacted the law, the Court was able to avoid passing upon the challenge that the law was unconstitutional since it granted a privilege to religious conscience which it denied to secular conscience, thereby preferring religion over nonreligion. What, in effect, the Court did in this case (*United States v. Seeger*) was what it had done four years earlier in *Torcaso v. Watkins,* that is, it made a religion out of secular humanism, a term that quite clearly characterizes what motivated the three draftees.

Civil libertarians were quite naturally gratified with the decision in the Seeger case, as they were with that in *Torcaso.* But for all things there is a price, and for the equalization of secular humanism and religion a price must be paid. Champions of prayer and religious instruction in the public schools and of governmental financing of religious schools were not long in recognizing the implications of the Court's decisions in these cases. We all know that what the public schools teach is "Secular Humanism," and if that religion may be taught there, so too may other religions, such as Protestantism, Catholicism, and Judaism, among others. This is dictated not only by the Constitution but also by the concept of equal-time fairness.

Indeed, these protagonists go even further. The First Amendment forbids preferential treatment of some religions over others, and if the government finances the teaching of Secular Humanism in the public schools, as of course it does, it must accord the same treatment to other religious instruction in both public and private schools. Logic might dictate that the remedy for the unconstitutional teaching of the religion of Secular Humanism in the public school is the termination of the practice, but since this is patently impractical, the appropriate remedy is to accord equal treatment to the more conventional religions.

On a number of occasions, this argument was presented to the courts, and was uniformly rejected. Take, for example, the recently decided case of *Brandon* v. *Board of Education*. New York law does not allow public school premises to be used for prayer, and accordingly the authorities in the community of Guilderland rejected a request by a group of high school students that they be allowed to use a classroom for congregational prayer in the half-hour just before regular classes begin. Since, they argued, such use was permitted for purposes other than prayer – purposes that might well be called Secular Humanist – they had a constitutional right to equal treatment for prayer.

The lower federal courts rejected this argument and the Supreme Court refused to hear the students' appeal. But what appears to be a directly contrary result was reached by the Supreme Court just about the same time in the case of *Widmar* v. *Vincent*. There the Court held it unconstitutional for Missouri state authorities to deny students the right to use a college student-center building for prayer and worship services while it allowed such use for secular purposes, such as political, cultural, educational, and recreational events. The obvious difference between these two cases is that one involved college students and the other high school students, who, presumably, are more vulnerable to sectarian pressures and hence require more stringent constitutional protection. Nevertheless, a reasonable interpretation of the decision can be cast in the terms of Secular Humanism as a religion, if college premises can be used for Secular Humanism, so too can they be used for Christian prayer or instruction.

A case that most starkly presents the issue relating to the religiosity of Secular Humanism involves the question of evolution in the public school curriculum. In the past, at least two legislative attempts, one in Tennessee and the other in Arkansas, were made to forbid the teaching of evolution in the public schools. In the first of these, the famous Scopes case of 1925, a state court upheld a law enacted by the Tennessee legislature that prohibited instruction contrary to the explanation of creation as set forth in the book of Genesis. In the second, *Epperson* v. *Arkansas* (1968), the United States Supreme Court ruled that the Arkansas anti-evolution law violated the First Amendment's mandate of the separation of church and state.

Not long after the Epperson decision was handed down, a suit was started in a federal court in Texas for an injunction against the teaching of evolution on the ground that it amounted to the support of the "Religion of Secularism" and thus violated the same establishment clause that barred Genesis in the Epperson case.

This proved unsuccessful, as did another law suit ... which sought either an injunction against the federally funded Smithsonian Institute from explaining and advocating the theory of evolution on the ground that it supported the "religion of Secular Humanism," or a judgment requiring the Institute to give equal treatment to the Genesis account of creation.

Actually the Constitution does not bar entrance of Genesis or any other part of the Bible into public school classrooms. Teaching the Bible as literature or the Missa Solemnis as music or the Last Supper as art is perfectly permissible so long as they are taught with secular objectiveness and considered as the works of man rather than the word of God.

This, however, is not what the anti-evolutionists want; on the contrary, they would oppose any teaching that Genesis might be only literature, as are the works of Homer or Dante. (In this respect, they would undoubtedly be right, since the First Amendment commands neutrality rather than hostility in respect to religion.) What they do want is that creationism in the teaching of science be as acceptable as is Darwinism. And while they would undoubtedly prefer the literal Genesis version, many of them realize that the best they can get is what has become known as Scientific Creationism, or, as in Arkansas, Creation Science. ...

Arkansas' Act 590 was declared unconstitutional by Federal District Judge William Overton on January 5. It is fairly certain that the case will be appealed, ultimately to the Supreme Court. That tribunal may well then be called upon to adjudge whether Secular Humanism is a religion, entitled to equal but not preferential treatment in the public schools. ...

Chapter VI

The Rise of Fundamentalism

Background: This chapter explores the phenomenon of Christian fundamentalism. Reichley defines it, Falwell preaches it, Wilcox measures its political influence, Corbet fears its puritanical and theocratic tendencies, and Glazer dismisses these fears as unwarranted. The authors, fundamentalist and non-fundamentalist Christians, a secular humanist, and a Jew all identify the rise of fundamentalism and the New Christian Right as a major political, cultural, and religious event in the latter half of the 20th century. This event has already influenced the American party system and its electoral strategies, and re-opened the issue of original intent regarding the religion clauses of the First Amendment. Christian fundamentalists now compete with secular humanists over legal, social, economic, and moral issues and values, in an attempt to influence American cultural, spiritual, and intellectual character. While critics worry about a threat to civil liberty and an improper religious militancy, fundamentalists see their increased political mobilization as a legitimate and necessary response to their threatened lifestyle and interests. In their view, the secular elite's campaign to capture the moral/cultural agenda demands an activist response.

This brief introduction, which raises more questions than it answers, reveals substantial differences of opinion by advocates, activist participants, outside observers, and outraged opponents. Despite the partisan flavor of some of the selections, the reader is invited to evaluate, rather than to choose sides.

Authors: Baptist Minister Jerry Falwell, along with professional political conservatives, founded the Moral Majority in 1979. This "born-again" preacher intended to create a national and non-denominational organization to lobby the government for causes of interest to the "religious right." He also sought to mobilize the moral majority in America, which he believed feared secular threats to traditional values, into a cohesive interest group. While the less active Liberty Federation replaced the Moral Majority in the late 1980s, Falwell's participation in the public arena, like Martin Luther King's breakthrough efforts on behalf of civil rights, was a major step in establishing the legitimacy of religion-based political movements. He used his book, *The Fundamentalist Phenomenon*, excerpted below, to identify enemies (secular humanism and liberal Protestantism), and to set the agenda for his newly formed interest group.

He begins by explaining fundamentalism, its purposes and beliefs, its legitimacy as an interest group organized to influence but not control government, and its contributions to "moral sanity" in America. Falwell's list of vital concerns is a litany of conservative moral causes: pro-life, pro-family, pro-defense, and pro-Israel. His Moral Majority opposes homosexuality, the Equal Rights Amendment, pornography, drugs, and an absolute or inflexible separation of church and state. He believes that fundamentalists should get "out of the pew and into the precinct" and seek to influence public policy as liberals and secular humanists do. Finally, he recruits evangelicals to the cause, after first chiding them about their reticence about reembracing the fundamentals of the faith along with their fundamentalist bretheran. Falwell has little tolerance for their hesitancy, disgust for the secular and churched elite and liberals of any ilk, and dismay at "the pitiful philosophies of unregenerate mankind." On the other hand, he declares the commitment of the Moral Majority to First Amendment rights, political and religious pluralism, and separation of church and state.

A. James Reichley, Senior Fellow in the Governmental Studies Program at the Brookings Institution, has written extensively on religion in America and served on Gerald Ford's White House staff. In the article excerpted below, Reichley looks at the influence of evangelicals (a term he prefers over fundamentalists) on American politics; the social, ideological, and theological nature of the religious right; distinctions between fundamentalists and evangelicals; the rise and political potential of the religious right; the Pat Robertson phenomenon; and the moderating influence of American pluralism on the religious right.

As he describes the character and make-up of evangelicals, Reichley paints a non-threatening picture of the coming of political age of conservative evangelicals and fundamentalists. This newly mobilized minority interest group, which first embraced President Jimmy Carter, the born-again co-religionist, and then Ronald Reagan, showed enough consistency in political engagement and tenacity in pursuing its social agenda to convince Reichley "that evangelicals will continue to be a force in national politics, predominantly on the conservative side." On the other hand, their tendency to ideological rigidity and fragmentation might limit their influence. In general, Reichley believes that the active conservative core of the religious right has changed its social and political tactics and moved toward the mainstream in a successful effort to gain and hold influence over the Republican party and American political life. He concludes that the more the evangelicals move toward the mainstream, the less chance there is that they "will misuse whatever political power the electoral tides bring their way."

Clyde Wilcox, Associate Professor of Government at Georgetown University, is a specialist on American religious interest groups, political parties, and elections. His most recent work, *God's Warriors: The Christian Right in 20th Century America* (1991), provides an expanded version of the article excerpted below. In this article, Wilcox discusses the theological and moral concerns of Christian Right groups in the 20th century and their efforts to influence the surrounding political culture.

He looks first at the fundamentalist revolt against theological liberalism and modernism at the turn of the century. Wilcox then traces fundamentalist battles against communism and the teaching of evolution, the fundamentalist hibernation in the 1930s and 1940s, and its political ressurection in the 1970s. He compares these events with the recent rise of the Pentecostal and Charismatic Right, which reflects an expanded political agenda and greater public recognition and status. Like Nathan Glazer, Wilcox argues that the uprisings of the new and old Christian Right groups occurred as defensive responses to a perceived hostile political and social environment. On the other hand, he also discerns the offensive character of the movement's attack on the teaching of evolution in the schools, communism, and secular humanism in the 1920s, 1950s, and 1980s.

Despite the limited past success of Christian Right groups in capturing the American domestic agenda and in attracting widespread public support, Wilcox points out that both liberal Democrat Jimmy Carter and conservative Republican Ronald Reagan targeted and won evangelical and fundamentalist votes. Bush also gathered in many of these votes when Pat Robertson withdrew from the 1988 presidential race. While Wilcox notes the decline of organizations like the now defunct Moral Majority, he argues that the conservative and spiritual message of the New Christian Right is popular among fundamentalists, evangelicals, pentecostals, conservative Catholics, and even secular conservatives. The Christian Right awaits only a more cohesive vehicle than that so far provided by the fundamentalists. Wilcox suggests that the Pentecostal/Charismatic Right, showcased in Robertson's race, might have been a preview of that vehicle, since it created a broad alliance of Christian conservatives.

Julia Mitchell Corbett, Associate Professor of Philosophy at Ball State University, is the author of several recent books and articles on religion in American culture. She equates "the religious political right" and proponents like Jerry Falwell with the stern and unenlightened puritanism of the 17th and 18th century. Corbett fears that a narrow neo-puritanism, with its focus on one universal truth (the reality of a judging Christian God) and its crusading objective to force society to embrace its moral code of behavior, threatens religious pluralism. In her view, early American puritans intended to create and maintain a theocracy (a state run on biblical foundations) to purify the church and civil government. With a similar objective in mind, 20th century puritans or right-wing fundamentalists take on humanists, church liberals, and those who follow the secular gospels of socialism, relativism, absolute separation of church and state, and modern Ben Franklins. (Ben Franklin ripped out sections of the Bible he did not like, and reinterpreted Scripture to fit his enlightened view of man and Deist view of a distant, not very demanding or judgmental God.)

Corbett urges Americans to say "no" to the new puritans, who she described as narrow-minded, intolerant, fanatical, tyrannical, unreasoning, sin-obsessed, blind to human potential for perfectibility, and apparently possessing few redeeming qualities. This creation of a "straw-man" reconstructionist believer, who is compelled to impose conservative Christian values on all mankind, provides a one-sided portrait of the religious right. It imitates the one-sidedness of the portrait of "godless amoral humanists," who worship only man and reason rather than God, painted by extremist members of the religious right. (Falwell bemoans the depravity of American society run by elites who turn their backs on traditional values, and open their arms to an "anything goes," and is equally valid or true, philosophy.) In response to Falwell, Corbett worries that God-fearing neo-puritans seek to foist functionalist Christianity on American laws and society. Such a fate would lead Americans to turn their backs on humanist principles that affirm the freedom of individuals to choose from, and tolerate, many points of view in a secular, pluralistic, and open society.

Nathan Glazer is an editor of the *Public Interest*, a Professor of Education at Harvard University, and an author who has written extensively on
religion, especially on Judaism, for over 40 years. In the work included
below, he comments on the upsurge of fundamentalism and the unwarranted fears about its possible threat to civil liberty. Glazer attempts to alleviate
the fear and trembling of secular and Protestant liberals and "cosmopolitan
elites;" all of whom oppose the resurgence of fundamentalism and traditional Protestantism in the 1970s because of their reputed assault on freedom, religious pluralism, and modern social values. He dismisses these
anxieties as exaggerated, and observes that the modern secular and liberal
assault on traditional values of importance to "the conservative heartland"
inspired a legitimate fundamentalist reaction.

Glazer characterizes this reaction as a "defensive offensive" with limited
aims. Despite being driven off by modern culture, " the once dominant
culture of middle America" seeks not a theocracy but a counter-revolution
"to protect some enclaves for traditional religion." Since America is, in
Glazer's words, a land of many cultures, there should be room for both
modern and traditional cultures. Unfortunately, conflict between these
cultures permeates the political arena as they take opposite positions on
legal, social, and economic issues. The conflict centers on the Supreme
Court's finding of a constitutional protection of the right to privacy that
allowed women freedom to choose abortions, the national ban on school
prayer, eroding laws against pornography and obscenity, exempting religious organizations from taxation, and court-imposed restrictions on state
aid to private and religious schools.

Glazer argues that most of these issues should be handled at the state and
local level, and not at the national level via the Supreme Court. By allowing
local regulations to govern, local opinion and values (and diversity) could
be protected and honored. Glazer hopes that the evolution in the make-up
of the Supreme Court will reverse decisions, especially regarding local
opinion in morality, that so offended fundamentalists. This need not threat-
en, in his view, the "cosmopolitan elite," which has already attempted to
impose its values and beliefs on the whole country.

Key Questions: Who are the fundamentalists and what drives their cultural
and moral agenda? What has been the role of secularism in galvanizing the
"New Christian Right?" To what extent is it legitimate for groups like the
Moral Majority to pursue their moral objectives in the public arena? Are

they dangerous to civil liberties, or are they just new interest groups, albeit with a powerful patron? Should moral issues, such as abortion and prayer in public schools, be decided at the state and local level or at the national level by way of the U.S. Supreme Court?

A. James Reichley

Pietist Politics

Socially conservative Protestants – whether they be labeled "fundamental-ists," "evangelicals," or the religious new right" – have already significantly shifted the balance of American politics. Movement of large numbers of white evangelical Protestants from the Democratic to the Republican side of the partisan lineup, and change from political passivity to at least sporad-ic bursts of electoral activity, were major contributors to the social and political swing to the right that characterized most of the 1980s.

White evangelicals used to be a reliable, though usually quiescent, pillar of the dominant Democratic coalition that came out of the 1930s. This was partly because evangelicals were concentrated in the South, where the Democrats monopolized virtually all political power until the 1960s. But even in the northern industrial states with sizable evangelical populations in their rural areas, such as Pennsylvania, Ohio, Indiana, and Illinois, evangeli-cals seem to have been more Democratic than other Protestants, probably because they were found disproportionately in relatively low-income groups. The political impact of the white evangelicals, who make up about one-fifth of the national population, was limited by their low level of electoral participation, caused in part by theological aversion to social action outside their church communities.

All of this has now dramatically changed. White evangelicals, after sup-porting Jimmy Carter, himself an evangelical Baptist, for president in 1976, switched in 1980 to give Ronald Reagan 60 percent of their vote. Four years later, white evangelicals went even further, supporting Reagan by a major-

From *The Fundamentalist Phenomenon*, Norman J. Cohen ed., Eerdmans, 1990. Used by permission.

ity of slightly more than 80 percent. ... White evangelicals gave George Bush about four-fifths of their vote. ...

In presidential years, the evangelicals' shift in partisan allegiance has been accompanied by a substantial increase in voter participation. In 1980, 1984, and 1988, white evangelicals appear to have voted at levels not far below those of other major groups in the electorate. In the midterm elections of 1982 and 1986, however, evangelicals returned to their old pattern of participating well below the national average.

If evangelicals continue to produce Republican majorities ... and *if* they vote at the level of their recent participation in presidential elections, the Republican party will have taken an important step toward regaining the national majority status it lost at the beginning of the 1930s.

[On the other hand] support from the evangelicals, while so far a net electoral plus for the Republicans, has already produced some negatives and could cause considerably more in future elections. The evangelicals, while a sizable group within the electorate, remain very much a minority. The Republicans will have to attract several other major groups, as well as retaining most of the traditional Republican base, to achieve their goal of becoming again the national majority party. Some of the participants in the coalitions that elected Reagan and Bush, including many traditional Republicans, are decidedly put off by both the tone of the political utterances from some leaders of the religious right and by the content of some of the issues that have helped draw evangelicals toward the Republicans. If the Republican party were to appear to be dominated by its new evangelical recruits, as already seems to have happened in some parts of the country, and if the evangelicals were to press for strict loyalty to their social agenda, the electoral losses suffered by the Republicans among other supporters or potential supporters could in the long run more than offset the gains brought to them by the religious right.

Second, the evangelicals, while for the most part socially conservative – in fact, attracted to the Republicans by their social conservatism – have by no means given up all the other attitudes and dispositions that for many years kept them loyal to the Democrats. ... As the evangelicals have begun to acquire political confidence, some have shown signs of doubting that there is a necessary connection between traditional morality and, say, supplyside economics or an aggressively interventionist foreign policy. Older themes of economic populism and foreign policy noninterventionism, even isolationism, have begun to reappear.

Nevertheless, the switch by the evangelicals in partisan and ideological attachments, if it continues, will certainly profoundly affect national politics. There are some, moderates as well as liberals, who hold that the results of this change will be extremely negative. The evangelicals' new political role, they argue, will create a shrill and divisive social atmosphere, introduce elements of dogmatism and intolerance and even bigotry into political life, and move the nation not merely in a conservative direction but toward outright social reaction. To determine how seriously one should take these predictions, it is necessary to arrive at some understanding of the social and ideological and even theological nature of the religious right, as well as of its political potential.

Fundamentalists and Evangelicals

... The term "evangelical" has been used at times to designate all Protestants or even all Christians. ... In the United States, however, this term has generally been used to describe those denominations and sects and independent churches that descend from the pietist branch of the Reformation. Baptists and Methodists were formerly the two major denominational representatives of evangelicalism in the United States; evangelicalism has also been powerfully represented within the Presbyterian and Lutheran denominations, and to a lesser extent among Episcopalians.

In a general way, evangelicals have been viewed as those Protestants who put particular emphasis on establishing a direct relationship between the individual and God, and on the conversion experience – the event of being "born again," which many evangelicals hold is a necessary prerequisite for salvation for all Christians. ... Evangelicals concentrate on spiritual inspiration of the individual, rather than on church doctrine, [ritual], and the moral reform of society. ... Evangelicals generally became associated with the inerrancy side in the debate that developed among Protestants in the latter part of the nineteenth century over the degree of literal truth to be assigned to the Bible.

When several of the major Protestant denominations joined in 1908 to form the Federal Council of Churches, evangelicals were for the most part skeptical of this move toward church unity – engineered, as they saw it, by theological and social liberals who aimed to use the churches for social action, while glossing over doctrinal differences and shifting emphasis away from individual spiritual experience. The denominations that participated in the Federal Council of Churches and in its successor, the National Council of Churches, ... including the Methodists as well as the Presbyterians, Episcopalians, and some Lutherans, have come to be designated the "mainline" Protestant churches. Those who stayed outside these ecumenical bodies, including most Baptists and many Lutheran as well as many smaller sects, are generally termed "evangelicals." Many individual members and some ministers in the "mainline" denominations remain "evangelical" in their theological and cultural, and more recently political, outlooks.

During the 1920s, the label "fundamentalist," derived from a series of theological volumes, *The Fundamentals,* was applied to conservative evangelicals, at times by the conservatives themselves, but even more by their political and cultural opponents. In the 1930s and 1940s evangelicalism went into relative decline, and fundamentalism became a kind of national joke. ... When conservative evangelical Protestantism enjoyed a modest revival, led by Billy Graham and others, in the early 1950s, its participants generally avoided the fundamentalist label.

At the present time, some conservative evangelicals, such as Jerry Falwell, identify themselves as fundamentalists. But many others, including many who are doctrinally fully as conservative as the avowed fundamentalists, prefer the older term, "evangelical." Thus "fundamentalist" has become a label used by outsiders, usually pejoratively, to characterize a group, many of whose members do not use it themselves. ...

Fundamentalists, like other evangelicals, have numerous theological and cultural divisions among themselves. ...

The most important division among fundamentalists is between those, like Pat Robertson, who are "charismatics," believing in faith healing and other exercises of miraculous power by chosen individuals, and those, like Falwell, who are not. Many noncharismatic fundamentalists regard the religious claims of charismatics as socially dangerous and theologically preposterous.

For social or political analysis, neither evangelicals nor fundamentalists are easy to identify. They cannot be located simply by denominational designation, since they are found in many denominations, including some of the mainline denominations, and some belong to local churches (like Falwell's church in Lynchburg, Virginia) that are not affiliated with any organized denomination. ...

The two questions that most clearly separate evangelicals from nonevangelicals are those regarding the inerrancy of the Bible and the born-again experience. Those who answer both these questions affirmatively may fairly be considered evangelicals. White Protestants who meet this criteria make up about 20 percent of the total population of the United States.

Many black Protestants are also evangelicals, but since their political and social experience has been so different, they are best regarded ... as a separate group. Some Catholics meet the evangelical criteria, but come out of a quite different social tradition. Though some of them have recently established political ties with evangelical Protestants, they are more usefully considered politically with their fellow Catholics.

For many kinds of social and cultural analysis, it is worthwhile to divide white Protestant evangelicals into fundamentalists and nonfundamentalists. There is, however, no reliable statistical tool for distinguishing within evangelical ranks between fundamentalists and nonfundamentalists. Fundamentalists are generally considered to make up about one-third of white evangelicals, or about seven percent of the total population, but this estimate is to some extent conjectural. The most that can be safely said is that there are more intense evangelicals, who may be called fundamentalists, and relatively moderate evangelicals.

... Whatever the cultural and social differences between fundamentalists and other evangelicals – and they are important – both groups seem to respond similarly to political stimuli. The religious new right, which became active as a political force around 1978, has won its most active adherents among fundamentalists (though a portion of fundamentalists have vigorously opposed it), but the issues that it has emphasized have also been among those drawing other evangelicals toward political conservatism and Republicanism. Obviously, the impact of the larger body on national politics, if it may be considered analytically as a distinguishable group, is more important than that of the more extreme fundamentalists only. ...

Evangelicals in Politics

American evangelicalism, including fundamentalism, carries on the tradition of pietism* in the U.S. ...Evangelicalism has usually expressed the tendency of pietism to regard civil society as largely irrelevant to the spiritual welfare of the individual, if not inherently and irredeemably corrupt (contrasting in this respect with Calvinism, which regards civil society as flawed instrument but nevertheless as a proper arena for realizing a part of God's purpose; and with Lutheranism, which has tended to view civil society as a necessary corrective within the individual). At the same time, when evangelicalism is drawn to participation in civil politics, it is likely to speak with the conviction of absolute moral authority.

The political expression of personalism, when it enters civil society, may be radical. Its aspiration to spiritual perfection for the individual may lead it, once it is persuaded that social involvement is in any way appropriate, to aim for social perfection as well. Such a direction may well place it on a collision course with established social authority, formed by pragmatic compromise among dominant social and economic interests. This happened in Germany in the sixteenth century, when radical pietists rose against the feudal nobility ... . It happened in England in the seventeenth century, when the pietists formed the radical cutting edge of the Puritan Revolution. And it is happening today among the small minority of radical pietists, such as the Sojourners group in Washington, who campaign for egalitarian populism and pacifism.

Pietism, however, may also take a conservative turn in politics. Several factors attract some pietists, often the majority, toward social conservatism. First, emphasis on belief in original sin, which is a usual though not invariable element in pietist theology, often persuades pietists that stern social authority, even authority exercised by pagans, is needed to deal with natural corruption (The thirteenth chapter of Paul's epistle to the Romans is often cited in support of this belief.) Second, the ascetic behavior associated with pietism often leads, paradoxically, as John Wesley pointed out, to

---

* Editor's note: Reichley explains that pietism is a form of personalism, which is a religious orientation based on a belief that each human individual may communicate directly with God; i.e., have a direct personal experience with transcendence. He asserts that this pietist/Personalism tradition is "highly absolutist in its moral expression" and places absolute reliance on the authority of the Bible.

worldly success. Many pietists, therefore, acquire an economic stake in maintenance of the existing order (and are tempted, as Wesley warned, to slip away from the faith that shaped their characters). Third, the leading opponents and critics of the established social order in the West since the French Revolution have often attacked not only traditional social authority or the existing economic system but also all institutions linked to a religious view of reality, pietist as well as legalist or hierarchical. Social and political radicalism has therefore been linked for many pietists with antagonism toward their most cherished associations and beliefs.

All of these factors have contributed to the recent shift of evangelicalism toward political conservatism. But there is another, perhaps even more basic, reason, not tied directly to religion.

Evangelicalism in the United States has maintained its greatest strength among those groups, predominantly rural but also substantially represented in some urban areas, that have remained most closely attached to what I would call traditional social structures. ... I would suggest, without here trying to prove, that its general characteristics have normally included hierarchical order within the family and the community, ... dictation of different social and economic roles for men and women, maintenance of rigid though somewhat varied sexual taboos, intense local patriotism, mutuality among insiders, suspicion of outsiders, identification with the local natural environment, and resistance to change. This tradition also includes religion, in the sense of belief in a transcendent moral order that reinforces the authority of its internal order. ...

In the United States, social traditionalism (family oriented, patriotic, culturally conservative) has in recent times felt itself under intense pressure from destabilizing forces rising from the dynamic economic, political, and cultural systems that have created and shaped the modern world. These varying forces of modernity have often been in combat with each other (capitalist industrializers against egalitarian collectivizers, both against bohemian aesthetes), but have held in common the tendency, whether or not intended, to undermine the traditional social system. Since evangelicalism happened to be the prevailing religious faith in some sectors of society where traditionalism has remained strong (in other sectors it has been Catholicism), evangelicalism has been enlisted in defense of traditional social structures.

... There has also been the issue of race. Before the Civil War, southern pietists, most of whom were small farmers or mechanics, were probably less implicated in support of slavery than were practitioners of the more hierarchical forms of religion. Nevertheless, most white evangelicals adhered to strict social distinction between the races (most emphatically within their churches, leading to the founding of separate black evangelical denominations). After the abolition of slavery, white evangelicals, tending to come from lower-income groups, were the group most subject to direct economic competition with blacks. ... White evangelicals ... became among the most intransigent supporters of racial segregation.

When the national Democratic party in the 1960s became a major participant in the drive to dismantle the machinery of official racial segregation, many southern white evangelicals were shaken loose from their traditional loyalty to the Democrats – first to vote for Barry Goldwater in 1964, then for George Wallace in 1968, and finally to normal support for Republican candidates in national elections. Some commentators have argued that racial prejudice is the major ... factor motivating the political shift among white evangelicals. Historical evidence and survey research do not, I think, support this claim, but certainly racial feeling has been a contributing cause.

Rise of the Religious Right

In the middle of the 1970s, all of these factors came together among evangelicals in a national society undergoing severe strain. At the national level, dissension over the Vietnam War and disgust caused by the Watergate scandals had left wounds in the social fabric. At more intimate levels of experience, increase in violent crime, spreading use of drugs, rising divorce, weakening of family ties, assault on traditional sexual distinctions, and virtually unchecked availability of pornography contributed to a general sense of social unease, especially among, though not limited to, social traditionalists. Evangelicals in particular, along with many conservative Catholics, associated these social developments with a series of Supreme Court decisions, beginning with the 1962 decision prohibiting organized prayer in the public schools, and reaching a kind of climax with the 1973 decision establishing essentially, a constitutional right for a woman to have an abortion.

Popular television preachers like Jerry Falwell and Pat Robertson told their audiences that these judicial decisions grew from a conspiracy by secular humanists – persons hostile to any religious faith – to take over the national political system. Many evangelicals became convinced that if they were to turn back the tides of destructive cultural and social change, they would have to give up their traditional avoidance of politics and become active players in the political system.

The first major beneficiary of the changing attitude among evangelicals toward politics was Jimmy Carter in 1976. The evangelicals' support for Carter, their co-religionist, not only enabled him to be the first Democratic presidential candidate since 1964 to sweep most of the South, but also brought him enough backing in the rural areas of northern states like Pennsylvania and Ohio to capture these states' crucial blocs of electoral votes. In a close national election, evangelicals could fairly claim to have supplied Carter with his margin of victory. ...

After taking office, Carter failed to support the evangelical's social agenda and promoted some measures they regarded as hostile, such as the women's Equal Rights Amendment. ... He also did not appoint evangelical leaders to positions in his administration. ...

During the early 1970s, increasing numbers of white evangelical congregations, partly in response to court-ordered stripping of religious associations from the public schools, and partly as a result of racial desegregation, began setting up independent Christian academies in which students could be indoctrinated in traditional values. One result of this development was to relax the evangelicals' historic opposition against state financial aid to private schools. Another was to give the churches sponsoring schools a direct interest in resisting what they regarded as excessive government regulation of private education.

In 1978, the Carter administration tightened standards for tax exemptions for church operated schools, requiring that the percentage of their student bodies coming from racial minorities be at least one-fifth of the percentage of such minorities in the local population. A group of the Christian academies reacted by forming a national association to look after their interests in Washington.

Meanwhile, a number of veteran champions of right-wing causes, such as Paul Weyrich, director of the Committee for the Survival of a Free Congress, and Howard Philips, founder of the Conservative Caucus, a grassroots conservative coalition, had begun scouting the aggrieved evangelicals as a potential mass base for a national militant conservative movement. Weyrich and Philips held a series of meetings with evangelical leaders, including Falwell, from which emerged agreement that the association representing Christian academies should be converted into a more broadly based national political organization promoting restoration of traditional moral values. In June, 1979, Falwell announced formation of the Moral Majority.

At first, the Moral Majority was not much more than a letterhead organization. ... But the Moral Majority, partly because of its catchy title and partly because of Falwell's skills as a publicist, was adopted by the national media as a kind of surrogate for the entire movement.

The election of Ronald Reagan as president in 1980, and the Republican's capture of control of the U.S. Senate for the first time in twenty-six years, was a political earthquake that called for explanation by the news media. Shift of white evangelicals from support of Carter in 1976 to a 60 percent margin for Reagan in 1980 was certainly part of the cause for the triumph of conservative Republicanism. ... The religious right in general, and the Moral Majority in particular, were given sensational media attention. Some liberals began to warn that know-nothing fundamentalists were on the verge of taking over the United States. ...

Assertive remarks by some of the television preachers and their political allies were quoted to fuel the alarm. Pat Robertson bragged, "We have enough votes to run the country." Jim Bakker, formerly Robertson's protégé, and then his rival in religious broadcasting, chimed in: "Our goal is to influence all visable candidates on issues important to the church. We want answers. We want appointments in government." Paul Weyrich went even further than his clerical associates: "We're radicals working to overturn the present structure in this country – we're talking about Christianizing America."

Reagan was careful not to repeat Carter's political error of seeming to turn against the evangelicals once he was in office. Though the legislative agenda of the religious right, calling for constitutional amendments to prohibit abortion and permit organized prayer in the public schools, achieved little headway, Reagan made what most evangelicals, at the grassroots level if not among the leadership, regarded as good faith efforts. A number of key players in the religious right were given posts in the Reagan administration at secondary and tertiary levels. Appointments to the federal judiciary, though by no means drawn mainly from the ranks of rightwing fundamentalists, began to reflect more conservative social attitudes.

In the 1982 congressional elections, occurring toward the end of that year's deep economic recession, the Republicans lost 26 seats in the House of Representatives. The religious right was relatively inactive and seemed to have little success at dissuading economically pressed evangelicals from returning to their traditional support for the Democrats. ...

In 1984, however, the religious right was more active than ever. Evangelical groups appeared better organized and helped the Republicans win an easy victory in the fight for new registrants. Jesse Jackson's candidacy for the Democratic nomination for president produced a large outpouring of new black registrants, most of whom voted for Walter Mondale in November; but registration drives among evangelicals helped the Republicans do even better. A study by the nonpartisan Committee for the Study of the American Electorate found that new registrants voted for Reagan over Mondale by a majority of more than two to one. White evangelicals cast ballots for Reagan by a margin of four to one, and gave Republican candidates for the House of Representatives 65 percent of their vote.

A study by James Guth showed, significantly, that while in 1980 41 per cent of Southern Baptist ministers had considered themselves Democrats and only 29 percent Republicans, by 1984 this distribution had altered to 66 percent Republican and 25 percent Democrat. ... In 1980, evangelical voters, despite their strong support for Reagan, were 56 percent Democratic, 16 percent Republican, and 28 percent independent. By 1984, this balance had shifted to 40 percent Democratic, 23 percent Republican, and 37 percent independent.

The Robertson Campaign

In the 1986 midterm elections, the Republicans made a net gain of eight governorships, many in states with large evangelical constituencies, but suffered a net loss of eight seats in the U. S. Senate, many also from states heavily populated by evangelicals. The Democrats recaptured majority control of the Senate. Electoral turnout was down steeply among most voter groups from 1984, but the decline was particularly sharp among evangelicals. Exit polls indicated that white evangelicals, who had made up about 17 percent of the total electorate in 1984, composed only 12 percent in 1986 – a change which by itself probably cost the Republicans at least five Senate seats.

Besides failing to halt the Democratic takeover of the Senate, the religious right suffered some notable losses in contests for the House of Representatives. Mark Siljander, a Republican representing the largely rural fourth congressional district in southwestern Michigan, had been the religious right's most outspoken supporter in Congress. Early in 1986, Siljander sent a taped message to evangelical ministers in his district urging: "We need to break the back of Satan and the lies that are coming our way." In the primary election he was defeated 55 to 45 percent by a more moderate Republican. ...

Despite these setbacks, Pat Robertson in 1987 found sufficient evidence of evangelical surge in recent elections, and enough indicators that a large share of the electorate hold conservative social attitudes, to declare his own candidacy for the Republican nomination for president. Running on a platform pledging to restore the nation to traditional morality, Robertson scored startling successes in early tests in Michigan and Iowa. The media again sounded the alarm that the religious right was threatening to capture the Republican party, if not to take over the country.

Robertson continued to do well in Republican party caucuses and county conventions, where participation was small and an effective organization mobilizing dedicated supporters, even if relatively few in numbers, could often carry the day. But once the race for the Republican nomination moved to states where national convention delegates are elected through primaries, Robertson was easily overwhelmed by the candidacy of George Bush. In the Super Tuesday primaries on March 8, held mainly in the South, where evangelicals are most numerous, Robertson was wiped out by the Bush avalanche. In every state holding a primary, Bush received more votes *among evangelicals* than Robertson, not to mention among nonevangelical Republicans, whose negative ratings of Robertson were exceptionally high.

Robertson's accomplishment in 1988 should not be underestimated. While he did poorly in primaries, his ability to carry caucuses enabled his followers to take over or win powerful roles in party organizations in such states as Iowa, Texas, Michigan, Louisiana, Nevada, Washington, Oklahoma, Alaska, Hawaii, and Georgia. ... In some nonprimary states like Washington, most delegates selected by party caucuses favored Robertson, but shifted to Bush at the convention following their candidate's recommendation.

During the struggle for the nomination, many Robertson backers had the experience of being resisted in Republican caucuses, sometimes to the point of being physically excluded, by agents of established party organizations wearing Bush buttons. ... Nevertheless, ordinary Robertson delegates from Georgia and the state of Washington whom I interviewed at the Republican convention in New Orleans indicated almost without exception that they intended to pitch into the fight to elect Bush, and that, although most of them had no previous political experience, they planned to remain politically active. ... In the end, evangelicals voted almost as heavily for Bush in 1988 as they had for Reagan in 1984, helping Bush carry every southern state and pile up large majorities in the rural areas of northern states like Pennsylvania, Ohio, and Indiana.

Perhaps most significantly, Republican candidates made impressive break throughs in 1988 at the state and local levels in some of the southern states where evangelicals are most heavily concentrated. In North Carolina, Governor James Martin became the second Republican in history to win a second term and Republicans gained three seats in the state senate and ten in the house of representatives. In Texas, Republican candidates for the first time won statewide offices below the office of governor. ...

Evangelicals in a Pluralist Society

... Evangelicals will continue to be a force in national politics, predominantly on the conservative side. They have come to enjoy the power that goes with political participation. They like being courted by national political leaders. ... And they have an unfulfilled social agenda which they remain most determined to enact. ...

How politically effective the evangelicals will be in the future remains questionable. If they behave like a rigid political sect, they will turn off many voters. ... Early impressionistic reports indicate that in many places they are developing the usual tendency of most politicians, whatever their ideological origins, to subsume their particular programmatic goals to their party's interest in winning elections. It should be remembered that many of the regular Republican organizations the evangelicals are now entering, or challenging, are controlled, not by moderate or "Rockefeller" Republicans, but by devoted conservatives who themselves achieved dominance during the Reagan uprisings of 1976.

Even if the evangelicals acquire some of the pragmatic attitudes that most political analysts believe are needed to enhance political effectiveness, their influence within the Republican party may be limited by their tendency to fragment, which in the past has usually been one of their characteristics in politics as well as in religion. In 1980 and 1984, they were remarkably united in support of Reagan. ... But in 1988 they failed to come together on a single candidate for the Republican nomination for president. Some evangelical leaders supported Robertson, but Falwell and some others aligned themselves with Bush, and others backed Senator Bob Dole of Kansas or Representative Jack Kemp of New York.

Robertson's failure to rally a majority of evangelicals to his cause is instructive. ... The southern strongholds of evangelicalism were the very places where Robertson's identification with the charismatic brand of religion, and his long-standing rivalries with other televison preachers like Falwell and Bakker, could be expected to limit his appeal. A leader like Reagan, who projects sympathy for the values of the movement but has not risen through its ranks, actually has a better chance than one of its own leaders to get its united support. As matters turned out, Robertson ran behind Bush in every southern primary.

The Republicans may be able to assemble an enduring national majority coalition sometime in the 1990s. If a stable conservative majority emerges, conservative evangelicals will be one of its most important constituencies. Certainly evangelical leaders, or politicians identified with their cause, will be rewarded with some role in the national government and some implementation of their social agenda, whether through legislation or judicial decisions. Person who oppose the evangelicals' agenda will understandably be displeased if it is put into effect, even to a limited extent. But some tightening of moral regulation would probably be accepted without extreme protest by most liberals, just as most conservatives, however unhappily, accèpted loosening of restraints in the 1960s and 1970s.

... The main source of worry about evangelicals holding access to political power is that some evangelical activists do not seem to grasp that the American polity, as it was designed by the Founders, and as it has evolved, is not merely majoritarian, but also requires a considerable degree of consensus. The party that elects its candidate president, which in a nation as diverse as the United States must always represent a coalition, has won the right to direct administration of the executive branch and to nominate federal judges. But groups that do not form part of the majority in any given election, or even in a series of elections, must also be able to feel that their rights and interests will be respected. If the numerical majority seeks to run roughshod over the rights of minorities, the American system ...

will not work. Some utterances by some of the evangelical leaders and their allies – "We have enough votes to run the country," "We need to break the back of Satan," "We're radicals working to overthrow the present structure in this country" – suggest that they do not fully subscribe to this principle.

Fortunately, our constitutional and political systems are to a great extent self-corrective against incursions by extremist groups. ... The American political system has an inherent tendency to require that governmental authority be based not merely on majoritarian rule but also on widely extended public acceptance. In a pluralist society like the United States, no single group is able, by itself, to form a majority. A group that finds itself in a majority coalition after one election must expect to be part of the minority at some future time. ... Every group, therefore, has a vested interest in maintaining the principle of respect for minority rights and interests.

One of the qualities that distinguishes leaders of the current religious right from earlier political enterprises by evangelicals or fundamentalists is that some of them seem to have learned at least part of this lesson. At earlier times, fundamentalists were cut off from potential allies by their identifications with anti-Catholicism, anti-Semitism, and racism. These tendencies have not totally disappeared, particulary at the grassroots level, from the current evangelical movement. But evangelical leaders like Falwell and Robertson have taken pains to ally themselves with Catholics in opposition to abortion, and to cultivate friendly relation with Jews through support for Israel (for which they also have theological justifications, troubling to many Jews). Conservative evangelicals have never been in the forefront of the struggle to extend civil rights, but most of their leaders are now careful to avoid any connection with racism. Some of them, in fact, have taken Martin Luther King as a role model for expressing moral protest.

This change in social tactics by conservative evangelicals has had two effects: first, it has made them politically more formidable; and second, it has drawn them more into the mainstream of American life. The first gives those who oppose the social agenda of the religious right cause for alarm. But the second reduces the danger that evangelicals will misuse whatever political power the electoral tides may bring their way.

Jerry Falwell

The Fundamentalist Phenomenon

Fundamentalism was born out of a doctrinal controversy with Liberalism. The ultimate issue is whether Christians who have a supernatural religion are going to be overpowered by Christians who have only a humanistic philosophy of life. Fundamentalism is the affirmation of Christian belief and a distinctively Christian lifestyle as opposed to the general secular society. It is the opposite of radical liberal Protestantism, which has attempted both to secularize Christianity and to Christianize secularism at the same time. Viewed from the standpoint of supernaturalism vs. secularism, Barr is right when he observes that there is ultimately very little difference between the theological framework of Fundamentalists and that of Evangelicals. While acknowledging that a difference of attitude does exist between the two, he nevertheless exposes the Evangelical Movement for attempting to hide its Fundamentalism behind the "conservative Evangelical" label. ..."It is not clear that modernized and updated Evangelicalism has yet attained to any conceptual framework that is intrinsically different from the Fundamentalist one, or that it has even tried. ..."

Most people trace the basics of Fundamentalism back to the five fundamentals that became crucial in the fundamentalist-modernist controversy. These are usually expressed as:

1. The inspiration and infallibility of Scripture.
2. The deity of Christ (including His virgin birth).
3. The substitutionary atonement of Christ's death.
4. The literal resurrection of Christ from the dead.
5. The literal return of Christ in the Second Advent.

This list of Christian essentials has been expanded and amplified many times, including such issues as the doctrine of the Holy Spirit, the depravity of humankind, belief in a literal heaven and hell, the importance of soul-winning and evangelism, the existence of the person of Satan, and the importance of the local church. Nevertheless, it is more correct to limit the definition of doctrinal Fundamentalism to the essential fundamentals that have been the heart of the movement for nearly a century now.

Organizing the Moral Majority

Facing the desperate need in the impending crisis of the hour, several concerned pastors began to urge me to put together a political organization that could provide a vehicle to address these crucial issues. ... They urged that we formulate a nonpartisan political organization to promote morality in public life and to combat legislation that favored the legalization of immorality. Together we formulated the Moral Majority, Inc. Today Moral Majority, Inc., is made up of millions of Americans, including 72,000 ministers, priests, and rabbis, who are deeply concerned about the moral decline of our nation, the traditional family, and the moral values on which our nation was built. We are Catholics, Jews, Protestants, Mormons, Fundamentalists – blacks and whites – farmers, housewives, businessmen, and businesswomen. We are Americans from all walks of life united by one central concern: to serve as a special-interest group providing a voice for a return to moral sanity in these United States of America. Moral Majority is a political organization and is not based on theological considerations. We are Americans who share similar moral convictions. We are opposed to abortion, pornography, the drug epidemic, the breakdown of the traditional family, the establishment of homosexuality as an accepted alternate lifestyle, and other moral cancers that are causing our society to rot from within. Moral Majority strongly supports a pluralistic America. While we believe that this nation was founded upon the Judeo-Christian ethic by men and women who were strongly influenced by biblical moral principles, we are committed to the separation of Church and State.

Here is how Moral Majority stands on today's vital issues:

1. *We believe in the separation of Church and State.* Moral Majority, Inc. is a political organization providing a platform for religious and nonreligious Americans who share moral values to address their concerns in

these areas. Members of Moral Majority, Inc., have no common theological premise. We are Americans who are proud to be conservative in our approach to moral, social, and political concerns.

2. *We are pro-life.* We believe that life begins at fertilization. We strongly oppose the massive "biological holocaust" that is resulting in the abortion of one and a half million babies each year in America. We believe that unborn babies have the right to life as much as babies that have been born. ...

3. *We are pro-traditional family.* We believe that the only acceptable family form begins with a legal marriage of a man and a woman. We feel that homosexual marriages and common-law marriages should not be accepted as traditional families. We oppose legislation that favors these kinds of "diverse family form," thereby penalizing the traditional family. We do not oppose civil rights for homosexuals. We do oppose "special rights" for homosexuals who have chosen a perverted life-style rather than a traditional life-style.

4. *We oppose the illegal drug traffic in America.* ...

5. *We oppose pornography.* While we do not advocate censorship, we do believe that education and legislation can help stem the tide of pornography and obscenity that is poisoning the American spirit today. Economic boycotts are a proper way in America's free-enterprise system to help persuade the media to move back to a sensible and reasonable moral stand. We most certainly believe in the First Amendment for everyone. We are not willing to sit back, however, while many television programs create cesspools of obscenity and vulgarity in our nation's living rooms.

6. *We support the state of Israel and Jewish people everywhere.* It is impossible to separate the state of Israel from the Jewish family internationally. Many Moral Majority members, because of their theological convictions, are committed to the Jewish people. Others stand upon the human and civil rights of all persons as a premise for support of the state of Israel. ...

7. *We believe that a strong national defense is the best deterrent to war.* We believe that liberty is the basic moral issue of all moral issues. The only way America can remain free is to remain strong.

8. *We support equal rights for women.* We agree with President Reagan's commitment to help every governor and every state legislature to move quickly to ensure that during the 1980s every American woman will earn as much money and enjoy the same opportunities for advancement as her male counterpart in the same vocation.

9. *We believe ERA is the wrong vehicle to obtain equal rights for women.*
   We feel that the ambiguous and simplistic language of the Amendment
   could lead to court interpretations that might put women in combat,
   sanction homosexual marriages, and financially penalize widows and
   deserted wives. ...

We have been labeled by our critics as arrogant, irresponsible, and simplistic. They accuse us of violating the separation of Church and state. However, the National Council of Churches (NCC) has been heavily involved
in politics for years, and virtually no one has complained. Since many moral
problems, such as abortion, require solutions that are both legal and political, it is necessary for religious leaders to speak on these matters in order to
be heard.

What Moral Majority is Not

1. *We are not a political party.* We are committed to work within the
   multiple-party system in this nation. We are not a political party and do
   not intend to become one.
2. *We do not endorse political candidates.* Moral Majority informs American citizens regarding the vital moral issues facing our nation. We have no
   "hit lists." While we fully support the constitutional rights of any special
   interest group to target candidates with whom they disagree, Moral
   Majority, Inc., has chosen not to take this course. We are committed to
   principles and issues, not candidates and parties.
3. *We are not attempting to elect "born-again" candidates.* We are committed to pluralism. The membership of Moral Majority, Inc., is so totally
   pluralistic that the acceptability of any candidate could never be based
   upon one's religious affiliation. Our support of candidates is based upon
   two criteria: (a) the commitment of the candidate to the principles that we
   espouse; (b) the competency of the candidate to fill that office.
4. *Moral Majority, Inc., is not a religious organization attempting to control
   the government.* Moral Majority is a special-interest group of millions of
   Americans who share the same moral values. We simply desire to influence government – not control government. ...
5. *We are not a censorship organization.* We believe in freedom of speech,
   freedom of the press, and freedom of religion. Therefore while we do not
   agree that the Equal Rights Amendment would ultimately benefit the

cause of women in America, we do agree with the right of its supporters to boycott those states that have not ratified the amendment. Likewise, we feel that all Americans have the right to refuse to purchase products from manufacturers whose advertising dollars support publications and television programming that violate their own moral code.

6. *Moral Majority, Inc., is not an organization committed to depriving homosexuals of their civil rights as Americans.* While we believe that homosexuality is a moral perversion, we are committed to guaranteeing the civil rights of homosexuals. We do oppose the efforts of homosexuals to obtain special privileges as a bona fide minority. And we oppose any efforts by homosexuals to flaunt their perversion as an acceptable lifestyle. We view heterosexual promiscuity with the same distaste which we express toward homosexuality.

7. We do not believe that individuals or organizations that disagree with Moral Majority, Inc., belong to an immoral minority. However, we do feel that our position represents a consensus of the majority of Americans. This belief in no way reflects on the morality of those who disagree with us who are not involved in our organizational structures. ...

Out of the Pew and into the Precinct

Many Christians are raising the question of whether or not they should be involved in politics at all. Some raise the question of the separation of Church and State; others feel that politics is the devil's arena and Christians should stay out; and others say politics requires compromising and Christians should not compromise. Many liberal church people are also claiming that Evangelicals are violating the separation of Church and State. Recently Richard Dingman said: "As one who has held local public office for 10 years and worked in congress for 11 years, it is my opinion that it is not only proper for Christians to become involved, but it is absolutely biblical and absolutely necessary."

The recent emergence of the Fundamentalists and Evangelicals into politics in no way violates the historical principles of this nation. The incorporation of Christian principles into both the structures and the basic documents of our nation is a matter of historical fact. ...Separation of Church and State simply means that the state shall not control religion and religion shall not control the state. It does not mean that the two may never work together.

Here is how Moral Majority, Inc., is contributing to bringing America back to Moral Sanity

1. *By educating millions of Americans concerning the vital moral issues of our day. ...*
2. *By mobilizing millions of previously "inactive" Americans.* We have registered millions of voters and reactivated more millions of frustrated citizens into a special-interest group who are effectively making themselves heard in the halls of Congress, in the White House, and in every state legislature.
3. *By lobbying intensively in Congress to defeat any legislation that would further erode our constitutionally guaranteed freedom* and by introducing and/or supporting legislation that promotes traditional family and moral values, followed by the passage of a Human Life Amendment, which is a top priority of the Moral Majority agenda. We support the return of voluntary prayer to public schools while opposing mandated or written prayers. We are concerned to promote acceptance and adoption of legislation that keeps America morally balanced.
4. *By informing all Americans about the voting records of their representatives so that every American, with full information available, can vote intelligently following his or her own convictions. We are nonpartisan. ...*
5. *By organizing and training millions of Americans who can become moral activists. ...*
6. *By encouraging and promoting non-public schools in their attempt to excel in academics while simultaneously teaching traditional family and moral values. ...*

Moral Majority, Inc., does not advocate the abolition of public schools. Public schools will always be needed in our pluralistic society. We are committed to helping public schools regain excellence. That is why we support the return of voluntary prayer to public schools and strongly oppose the teaching of the "religion" of secular humanism in the public classroom.

The First Amendment says: "Congress shall make no law respecting an establishment of religion, or prohibiting the free exercise thereof." This does not rule out church influence in government. Presbyterian theologian John Gerstner has said: "Establishment of religion is not the same thing as no influence of religion. I think Moral Majority is right in stating that the church should seek to have influence in political matters."

California pastor Dr. Tim La Haye, believes that the pulpit must be active in resisting encroaching federal bureaucracy that threatens both the Church and the traditional family. He has stated: "God founded the government to protect the home against external enemies. The prophet of God is derelict if he does not, in God's name, rebuke government when it fails to protect the family."

Catholic theologian and journalist Father Robert Burns, C.S.P., stated in the national Catholic weekly *The Wanderer*: "If our great nation collapses, it will not be because of the efforts of some foreign power, Soviet or otherwise, but rather for the same reason that ancient Rome collapsed because it was morally rotten to the core." He further comments: "The members of Moral Majority believe in fighting for the basic moral values on which this nation was built and upon which its strength rests. They are determined to prevent materialists, secular-humanists, and non-believers from destroying these values by replacing them with a valueless, amoral society."

Christians are now realizing that governmental actions directly affect their lives. They are questioning the government's right to carry out such programs. They are beginning to realize that the only way to change the actions of government is to change those elected to govern. ...

Clyde Wilcox

The Christian Right in Twentieth Century America: Continuity and Change

The Fundamentalist Revolt: Religious Conflict at the Turn of the Century

Fundamentalism developed out of evangelicalism early in the twentieth century. Its theological roots were firmly planted in millenarianism. The doctrinal heritage of fundamentalism included three main tenets: pre-millennialism, dispensationalism, and biblical inerrancy. Protestants at the turn of the century were widely involved in a debate involving the timing of the second coming of Christ. For the post-millennialists, Christ would come after the millennium, a thousand year period of perfect peace and tranquility. The pre-millennialists, on the other hand, believed that Christ would return prior to the millennium, and defeat the Antichrist in a major battle. The second coming, also known as the Rapture, was widely believed to be imminent, and it was commonly believed that it would be triggered by a worsening of the world situation, and the growing successes of the Antichrist in the world.

These doctrinal disputes had important political consequences. If Christ's return is to be preceded by a period of perfect peace, then politics may be a viable means of improving the world. If on the other hand, Christ's return is triggered by the success of the Antichrist, and this return is imminent, then political solutions to the world's problems are not possible. Turmoil and discord are to be expected, and in fact may signal the end of the world.

Review of Politics (Fall 1988), 659–679. Used by permission.

The second doctrinal element of millenarianism which is important in fundamentalist thought is dispensationalism. Essentially, this doctrine argued that God has dealt with mankind through different means over the centuries. History unfolds under different dispensations, or covenants between God and man. The most accepted variant on this theme was that there were seven dispensations, and that the world is now in the sixth. Because the seventh and final dispensation was the kingdom, this doctrine served to reinforce the notion that the second coming was imminent.

Finally, the fundamentalists drew upon the millenarianist belief in the inerrancy of the Scriptures. Most accepted an even stronger view – that the Bible was literally true. This doctrine, which originated in the nineteenth century, has become an important component of the creed of contemporary fundamentalism.

The latter part of the nineteenth century and the early years of the twentieth were times of great strain within Protestantism. Revivalists of the pietistic tradition and denominational conservatives of the Calvinist tradition who accepted these doctrinal positions were concerned with the growing liberalism of the clergy. Theological modernists, who sought to make religious teachings consistent with contemporary understanding of science and culture, were making impressive gains within the denominations. With the publication of *The Fundamentals* in 1910, the conservatives went on the offensive. These volumes of collected writings were largely ignored by liberals and academics, but provided a rallying point for conservative Protestants. Throughout the decade, the split between conservatives and the liberals widened. In 1919, the formation of the World's Christian Fundamentals Association (WCFA) marked the beginning of a bitter religious battle. Fundamentalism had emerged as a distinct movement within evangelicalism. ...

Although the fundamentalist-modernist dispute was the most important religious battle of the period, another development would have some later importance. The turn of the century not only marked the origins of fundamentalism, but also the birth of the pentecostal movement in America. Unlike the contemporary charismatic movement, this early manifestation was largely confined to newly formed denominations, such as the Church of God, the Church of God in Christ, and the Pentecostal Holiness Church which emerged from the revivalist tradition. ...

Although there are important doctrinal differences between them, the pentecostal, holiness and charismatic churches share a belief in the importance of the gifts of the Holy Spirit. The most frequent manifestations of these gifts are in glossolalia, or speaking in tongues, and in faith healing. The pentecostals shared with the fundamentalists an opposition to modernism and a belief in the inerrancy of the Scriptures, and considered themselves to be fundamentalists, but the fundamentalist response to pentecostalism was strongly negative. ... The doctrinal debate between the two camps centered on dispensationalism. While the pentecostals felt that the early 1900's were the "Age of the Spirit," the fundamentalists believed that the gifts of the Spirit were part of an earlier dispensation, ending with the age of the apostles.

The pentecostals did not play an important role in the political actions of the 1920's or the 1950's, but are an important part of the contemporary Christian Right.

The Fundamentalist Revolt: Political Battles over Evolution in the 1920's

Although the fundamentalists joined their liberal colleagues in support of Prohibition, the two camps were deeply divided by the teaching of evolution in public schools, an issue which marked the formation of the first set of Christian Right groups in this century. Fundamentalist leaders saw the teaching of evolution as striking at the heart of their doctrine of biblical literalism, and representing the worst excesses of the modernist movement. A variety of political organizations were formed by fundamentalist elites around the evolution issue. ...WCFA led the fight, but other organizations were quite active.

These groups had mixed success, winning in some northern states which today would seem unlikely candidates for Christian Right influence, but losing in a number of southern and border states. Between 1920 and 1925, the movement seems to have had fairly broad backing among conservative Protestants, but by 1926, support was limited to the extreme fundamentalists. As support for the anti-evolution campaign waned, the leaders began to shift their emphasis to anticommunism. ...

Anticommunism was a natural cause for the fundamentalists for several reasons. First, the pre-millennialist teachings concerning the second coming of Christ were often interpreted as predicting a final battle between the forces of God and the Antichrist, in which the latter forces would come from the geographic area now occupied by the Soviet Union. Second, the atheism which communist leaders professed made it seem likely that communism was the doctrine of the Antichrist in the world. Finally, the tendency of fundamentalist leaders to see world history as an arena for battle between good and evil was conducive to interpreting the contemporary world as a battleground between a nation of God and one opposed to God, from which the forces of the Antichrist were to come.

It should be noted that although fundamentalists became politicized in the 1920's, "this politicization was haphazard." Their consensus did not extend much beyond opposition to the teaching of evolution and to communism. Fundamentalist doctrine steered its adherents away from politics, and admonished them to remain separate from the sinful secular world. Indeed, Marsden has argued that fundamentalists developed no coherent political theory during this period, and so were more easily swayed by conspiracy theories and extremist politics after World War I.

Political Retreat and Religious Turmoil: The 1930's and 1940's

During the next two decades, many of the fundamentalist political organizations of the 1920's continued to exist, albeit without widespread support. Many of the leaders of these organizations began adopting the language of racism, anti-Semitism, and anti-Catholicism. This language was often imbedded in some description of a larger conspiracy. Some of the early leaders of the fundamentalist movement, such as Gerald Winrod, openly advocated fascist ideas.

The Great Depression fit well with the pre-millennialist prediction of a collapse of the social and political order that would precede the second coming, and many prominent preachers foresaw an immediate end to the world. Opposition to the New Deal provided a focus to the efforts of these fundamentalists leaders, but proved an unpopular position. Indeed, rival religious leaders, such as Gerald L. K. Smith, preached a populist fascism which advocated radical redistribution of wealth. Among all of these leaders, however, a strident anticommunism remained a major theme. Although fundamentalist and other religious figures attracted a good deal of attention during these two decades, they do not seem to have attracted widespread support among rank-and-file fundamentalists, evangelicals or pentecostals. Moreover much of the attention which these leaders attracted was quite negative. ...

It may seem that these fundamentalist leaders should have been able to attract widespread support during this period. Not only did the Depression fit well with pre-millennialist theology, but the suffering it caused was consistent with teaching that spiritual salvation, not the pursuit of worldly goods, was of paramount importance. Hunter has argued that the religious tendencies of fundamentalists during this period became "privatized," that is, religion became a private matter of spiritual concern. Revivals were the preferred form of expression of the fundamentalist impulse, not political action. Indeed, perhaps the perceived immanence of the second coming made political action seem all the more futile.

Although fundamentalism was relatively quiet on the political front during this era, on the religious front the fundamentalists continued to make progress. Bible colleges were built, and fundamentalist churches grew. In 1941, fundamentalist leaders organized the American Council of Christian Churches (ACCC). Designed to be an organization which represented the independent and separatist fundamentalist churches, the organization was headed by the fiery anticommunist Carl McIntire. McIntire roundly attacked liberal Protestants, Roman Catholics, and pentecostals in preaching a militant separatism. Alienated by the intolerance of the ACCC, more moderate fundamentalist leaders in 1942 formed the National Association of Evangelicals (NAE). This neo-evangelical movement shared a common doctrine with the fundamentalists, but was considerably more moderate. The new evangelicals rejected the anti-intellectualism of the fundamentalists, and welcomed cooperation with pentecostals and liberal Protestants. This evangelical-fundamentalist split is still present among conservative Christians, and has important political ramifications, as will be seen below.

The Second Fundamentalist Crusade: Anticommunism in the 1950's and 1960's

... Many prominent fundamentalist leaders preached vigorously against the communist menace in the latter part of the 1940's, but it was not until the McCarthy campaign began in earnest that Christian Right organizations began to form. Fundamentalist leaders cooperated closely with McCarthy, and urged investigation of prominent modernist religious leaders as possible communists or fellow travelers.

Sociologists have stressed the role of sympathetic organization in mobilizing resources into social action. The resource mobilization theory fits well the establishment of the Christian Right of the 1950's. By 1953, all of the future leaders of the anticommunist organization were associated with the ACCC. Even as McCarthy began to self-destruct, these leaders were forming, with the aid of the ACCC, organizations which would constitute the Christian Right of the 1950's. ...

The fundamentalist efforts did not attract widespread support, even within the conservative Christian community. Evangelical leaders, while sharing a general anticommunist orientation, were critical of the tactics of these fundamentalist groups. Moreover, the public seems to have been largely unaware of these groups. Even among those who attended fundamentalist churches, for example, less than a third were aware of the Christian Anti-Communism Crusade. Only 5 percent of the white population supported the Crusade in 1964.

The activists in the Christian Right during this period were, like all political activists, well educated, wealthy individuals. Although they were strongly anticommunist, they were not doctrinate conservatives. Predictably, they were overwhelmingly Republican. The anticommunist message seems to have appealed not only to fundamentalists, but to more secular rightists as well. Wolfinger et al. reported that among activists in the Christian Anti-Communism Crusade, the fundamentalists were actually less conservative than other supporters. Wilcox ... noted that fully 11 percent of the Crusaders appeared to have no real religious attachments, and that only half attended church regularly.

Similarly, researchers have found that mass support for the Crusade was highest among fairly well-educated fundamentalists. As was the case among the activists, a set of secular supporters could be identified, and when these were excluded from the analysis, the Crusade supporters were quite moderate on most issues, although strongly anticommunist.

In 1964, the Christian Right organizations shed their separatist tendencies and allied themselves with more secular organizations in open support of Barry Goldwater. Goldwater's repudiation in the election seems to have dealt a major blow to the Christian Right, whose financial base soon began to evaporate. ...

The Third Coming of the Fundamentalist Right: the 1970's and Beyond

The period between 1965 and 1976 was marked by a good deal of change in the political behavior of evangelicals and fundamentalists. A sizable bloc of evangelicals moved towards the left of the political spectrum, and in 1972 endorsed McGovern. Although evangelical and fundamentalist elites had previously accepted a doctrine which indicated that Christians should remain separate from the secular world, evangelical elites began to pay increasing attention to politics, as the content of their publications demonstrates. In 1976 the Carter candidacy mobilized the evangelicals as no candidate had done before. Carter was a confessed "born-again" Christian, and a Southern Baptist. ...

Fundamentalist elites were less favorable to Carter, and responded negatively to his *Playboy* interview in which he admitted to having committed adultery in his heart. Nevertheless, substantial numbers of fundamentalists joined their evangelical brethren in casting their votes for the first avowedly evangelical candidate in over fifty years.

The Carter candidacy had two important consequences for the future of the Christian Right. First, the mobilization of previously apolitical evangelical voters by the campaign demonstrated to secular political elites the existence of a new potential voting bloc. Leaders of the secular New Right began to devise strategies to further mobilize these evangelicals and woo them to Republican activism. Second, because Carter argued that Christians had an obligation to participate in politics, his candidacy helped to break down the long-standing feeling among evangelicals and fundamentalists that electoral politics was not the proper realm for Christian activity.

The period between 1965 and 1976 was also marked by the development of a number of networks which improved the communications between fundamentalists. Christian bookstores grew rapidly during this period, and stimulated the sale of books by fundamentalist religious and political leaders. ... Christian magazines also grew in circulation. Christian radio and television stations were established, giving fundamentalist, evangelical, and pentecostal preachers access to wider audiences.

Fundamentalist Christian schools also grew rapidly during this decade. Spurred in part by school desegregation efforts, but also by the increased teaching of evolution that was part of the increased emphasis on science that followed Sputnik, and by the changing content of public school textbooks in the area of history, politics and sex roles, the number of students enrolled in fundamentalist academies increased markedly. ...

During the late 1970's, the organizations of the New Christian Right were formed. The two most important organizations, Christian Voice and the Moral Majority, were both officially founded in 1979. Christian Voice was established to extend the work of several local anti-gay and antipornography groups in California. ...

The Moral Majority was formed by Falwell after he had been approached by leaders of the secular New Right and promised support in the form of direct mail lists, organizational support, and training of state and regional leaders. Unlike the Christian Voice, the Moral Majority did attempt to build state organizations, primarily through the networks of Falwell's denomination, the Bible Baptist Fellowship. Although Falwell claimed organizational success in nearly every state, actual organizations were established in fewer than twenty, and some of these were quite small. Although Falwell publicly sought to forge a coalition between fundamentalists, evangelicals, pentecostals, and conservative Catholics, Jews, and other Protestants, this effort floundered on the relative intolerance of the fundamentalist pastors who headed the state and local organizations. ...

The New Christian Right was headed by fundamentalist ministers who relied on existing religious and political organizations to build their groups. While the organizations of the 1950's spread their message through radio, the new organizations used television and direct mail to communicate with their followers. ... These organizations were fairly well funded. Their message included a vehement anticommunism, as well as a rejection of modernism in the classroom, this time in the form of an attack on the teaching of "secular humanism." Unlike these earlier organizations, however, the New Christian Right took positions on a range of issues, from South Africa and the contras to the balanced budget amendment and the gold standard to gay rights and the Equal Rights Amendment (ERA).

The New Christian Right attracted a good deal more media attention than had the earlier manifestations of the fundamentalist Right. The new communication channels that the fundamentalists had established, particularly the televised sermons of sympathetic preachers, served to alert potential converts. Moreover, new technology such as computerized direct mail enabled the organizations to more accurately target sympathetic individuals and approach these individuals with carefully designed messages. The net result of all of these factors was that the general public was significantly more aware of the existence and message of the New Christian Right than it had been of its predecessors.

Studies suggest that support for the Christian Right in the 1970's and 1980's was not widespread, however. Among the general public, support hovered between 10 percent and 15 percent of the population. Among white evangelicals, support was somewhat higher, but limited to around 25 percent.

... Studies of the supporters of the New Christian Right have suggested that support is strongest among evangelicals and fundamentalists who attend church regularly. Unlike the supporters of the Christian Right in the 1950's, however, they tend to be Republican, and conservative on economic, social and foreign policy issues. Studies of the activists of the Moral Majority suggest that they are remarkably similar in demographic profile to those of the Christian Anti-Communism Crusade some twenty years earlier. Unlike the Crusaders, however, the Moral Majority activists were fairly consistent conservatives. Moreover, unlike the Christian Right of the 1950's the New Christian Right did not attract a sizable secular group of supporters.

The 1980 election brought a good deal of attention to the leadership of the Christian Right, and in particular to Jerry Falwell. The results of this scrutiny were not positive. ... Although the New Christian Right played a visible role in the 1984 Republican convention, by 1987 the fundamentalist right was in retreat. Falwell had retired as head of the Moral Majority, which had been incorporated into an umbrella organization known as the Liberty Federation as its financial base eroded. ...

The collapse of the organizations of the new fundamentalist right should not be taken as an indication that their message was not popular among fundamentalists, evangelicals, and pentecostals, however. A number of studies have suggested that the platform of the New Christian Right had substantially more support than did the organizations themselves, particularly among evangelicals. The potential support for the Christian Right in the 1980's, then, was not fully tapped by the fundamentalist Right.

The Rise of the Pentecostal Right:
Pat Robertson's Presidential Campaign

During the 1960's a second wave of pentecostal and charismatic activity occurred. Unlike the earlier movement, which was confined to a set of newly created splinter denominations, in the 1960's charismatic activity grew within mainstream Protestant churches such as the Methodists, Presbyterians, and Lutherans, and among Roman Catholics as well. In addition, this latter movement was not confined to poor whites and blacks, but was largely a middle-class and suburban phenomenon. ...

Charismatic ministers, like their fundamentalist colleagues, took their message to the airwaves. The Bakkers, Jimmy Swaggart, and Pat Robertson preached the blessings of baptism of the Holy Spirit on their respective television programs. Swaggart and Robertson included in their programs a healthy dose of conservative politics.

The 1980's witnessed the first flowering of a new type of Christian Right activity – this time by pentecostal Christians. Pat Robertson, the Baptist minister who hosted the televised 700 Club, in 1987 declared his candidacy for president. During his career on the 700 Club, Robertson clearly established himself as a pentecostal. ... He also endorsed a pre-millennialist view of the future, and often interpreted contemporary political events as harbingers of the Rapture.

Although most polls showed that Robertson lacked widespread support, his campaign showed considerable muscle in Michigan and in early straw polls, where the degree of dedication of a candidate's followers could influence the results. His early fundraising was immensely successful. ... Robertson won the endorsement of several prominent charismatic leaders, but the fundamentalist and evangelical response was lukewarm. The two major organizations of the fundamentalist Right did not spring to his support, and Falwell endorsed George Bush despite earlier feelers from Robertson. Moreover, studies suggested that Robertson's support among evangelical pastors was weak. One early study of the major financial contributors to the Robertson campaign found that nearly half came from charismatic and pentecostal churches, especially the Assemblies of God, and that only 4 percent came from fundamentalist churches.

Robertson's political platform was quite similar to that of the fundamentalist Right. He called for the elimination of the vestiges of secular humanism from the classroom, and condemned the teaching of evolution. His foreign policy was strongly anticommunist. He took conservative positions on economic issues as well. This expanded issue agenda was evident in the issue positions of his early contributors, who were consistently conservative.

As the campaign unfolded, Robertson had considerable success in states which selected their delegates by caucuses. Because caucuses typically have very low levels of public participation, small groups of committed activists who turn out in large numbers can dominate the process. Robertson surprised Bush by finishing second in Iowa, and went on to win or do well in several other caucus states, from Hawaii to Alaska.

His campaign began to develop problems around the time of the New Hampshire primary. Over a period of a few weeks, Robertson charged that the Soviets had missiles hidden in the caves of Cuba, claimed to have known where hostages were held in the Mideast, and accused the Bush campaign of masterminding the troubles of fellow charismatic Jimmy Swaggart. These events reinforced doubts which conservative Republicans had about Robertson's judgment. ...

In assessing the successes and failures of the campaign, however, two points must be made. First, Robertson did fairly well for a novice politician. He raised more money than any candidate except George Bush, won several states, and got around 20 percent of the vote in each of the Southern primaries. Moreover, his campaign succeeded in establishing footholds in state party committees throughout the country – presumably with another bid for the presidency in mind. ...

Exit polls indicated that Robertson drew some support from Catholic voters. Unlike the fundamentalists, the pentecostals have generally welcomed cooperation from like-minded conservative Protestants. The charismatic movement has welcomed Catholics into its ranks, and sees fundamentalists and evangelicals as kindred spirits. The pentecostals therefore have the potential to accomplish what Falwell claimed to seek: a coalition of conservative Christians united in common political action.

The Christian Right in the 20th Century:
Continuity and Change

... Political scientists who seek to explain the formation of interest groups have generally offered two sets of explanations. The pluralist theories, best articulated by Truman, sees interest group formation as a response to disturbances in the equilibrium between groups, both active and latent. In contrast, the entrepreneur theory articulated by Salisbury sees group formation as the result of the efforts of political leaders who see a potential market for the issue positions and benefits of a group, and form a group to offer these goods. The theories need not be viewed as mutually exclusive: disturbances in the equilibrium may create the market which entrepreneurs seek to mobilize.

Both sets of theories offer explanations for the creation of the Christian Right of the 1920's, the 1950's, and the 1980's. The activity in the 1920's was preceded by a marked liberalization among the clergy in the mainstream Protestant denominations. Thus the anti-evolution groups are usually perceived as a response to the creeping modernism which was evident in many Protestant churches. The activity of the 1950's was facilitated, not by an upset to the equilibrium against the fundamentalists, but rather by one in their favor. McCarthyism made the anticommunist message which many of the fundamentalist preachers had espoused for decades suddenly popular, and made the formation of political organizations profitable. The fundamentalist and pentecostal activity of the 1980's was preceded by a period of rapid social change, including changes in the role of women and the national legalization of abortion. In each era, the potential market created by these changes was exploited by dynamic preachers, who headed the organizations.

Sociologists, on the other hand, have stressed the role of resources in the creation of social movement organizations. The resource mobilization theory suggests that such organizations are more likely to form when they have access to resources from sympathetic organizations. There is considerable support for this theory in each wave of Christian Right activity as well. The groups in the 1920's relied on the resources of the fundamentalist religious organizations to launch themselves. During the 1950's, the ACCC provided an organizational umbrella [for] the fledgling Christian Right. ... In the 1980's, the secular New Right leaders supplied Moral Majority and the Christian Voice with the technology of direct mail to help fund the organizations. Moreover, the Moral Majority built its grassroots efforts around the already existing network of pastors of the Baptist Bible Fellowship. Robertson achieved name recognition through the 700 Club, and in late 1987 the Federal Election Commission was investigating the possibility that his Christian network has channeled resources to his presidential campaign.

It is often argued that Christian Right and other conservative crusades seek to preserve the lifestyles and/or status of their constituencies. These explanations suggest that these movements are essentially defensive, and occur in times when the prestige or status of the lifestyles in question are declining. An argument can be made that the Christian Right movements of the 1920's and the 1980's occurred when modern and secular forces were in ascendancy. Although there is a strong element of lifestyle defense in the emphasis of the Christian Right on education (discussed below), a careful reading of the history of the Christian Right, however, suggests that this explanation is not entirely accurate. The formation of the Christian Right organizations in the 1920's occurred when the fundamentalists were on the offensive. Similarly, the anticommunist groups of the 1950's formed while McCarthy was leading his crusade. Finally, the fundamentalist and charismatic organizations of the 1980's were formed after a decade of growth in evangelical, fundamentalist, and pentecostal churches, bookstores, and television ministries.

The similarities between the Christian Right do not end at their formation. Two prominent themes echo throughout each crusade. The first, anticommunism, has been present in the message of each Christian Right organization. ... The second common theme throughout this century is one of education policy. The first crusade in this century was centered on the teaching of evolution in the schools, the organizations of the 1950's were concerned with sex education in the schools, and the fundamentalist and pentecostal movements of the 1980's opposed the teaching of secular humanism in the classroom. ... The wave of fundamentalist schools in the 1970's and 1980's was in part a response of fundamentalist activists to the teaching in public schools of doctrines which they believed contradicted their faith. The activities by many state school boards to certify or deny certification to these fundamentalist schools gave impetus to the formation of the Christian Right organizations in the 1980's. In many states, the Christian school organizations were markedly stronger than any other Christian Right group.

In many ways, however, the organizations of the 1980's were different in kind from those which preceded them. While the organizations of the 1920's confined their messages primarily to evolution ... and the organizations of the 1950's rarely strayed from the anticommunist theme, those of the 1980's took position on a broad range of public policy issues. As a consequence, while research has shown that the activists and supporters of the anticommunist groups were not consistently conservative, the activists and supporters of the Christian Right of the 1980's were.

Moreover, the new technologies of television and direct mail made the groups of the 1980's a more visible part of public life. ... The Moral Majority of the 1980's was widely known. As a consequence, it had a somewhat larger support base than had the earlier organizations, but it also aroused more heated and organized opposition.

There are also similarities between the organizations of the 1920's and the 1980's, which do not apply to those of the 1950's. Like the anti-evolution groups of the 1920's, the New Christian Right has attempted to influence government by lobbying the legislature, as well as through electoral politics. Although the anticommunist groups in the 1950's were involved in electoral politics, they made no appreciable effort to influence legislation. Moreover, the groups in the 1920's often worked at the grassroots level, building local organizations to attempt to influence the state legislatures. Similarly, the New Christian Right attempted to build grassroots organizations in the early 1980's, although these attempts were largely unsuccessful. Like the anti-evolution groups, and unlike the anticommunist organizations, the New Christian Right seems to appeal almost entirely to highly religious evangelicals and fundamentalists.

Finally, the new charismatic Right ... differs in one potentially important way. By embracing the support of evangelicals, conservative Catholics and other Christians, the charismatic Right has the potential to build a coalition of conservative Christians that the intolerance of the fundamentalists has prevented. Smidt has noted that the contemporary charismatic movement is the most ecumenical religious movement in recent history. ... Moreover, although the fundamentalist leaders continue to condemn the pentecostals, Ammerman suggests that fundamentalist members may view charismatic Christians as potential allies. If the rank-and-file fundamentalism begin to see the many similarities between the charismatics and themselves, then the possibility of a truly important Christian Right may emerge. This possibility might be further enhanced by Robertson's popularity among blacks, probably due in part to his choice of a black as cohost of the 700 Club.

If the charismatic Right could gain the support of white evangelicals, some white fundamentalists, and a portion of the black evangelical and charismatic movement, it would constitute a sizable political force. There are several barriers to the formation of this larger movement, however. First, there are important religious differences between the various original pentecostal churches and the charismatic movement in mainstream Protestant and Catholic congregations. Whereas the original pentecostal churches splintered from the mainstream denominations, the new charismatic movement is one of renewal of faith within established denominations. Doctrinal differences have long been a source of disunity among conservative Protestants, and doctrinal differences between Catholic and mainstream Protestant charismatics, and the separate pentecostal denominations might prevent the formation of a unified Christian Right. Yet Poloma notes that "the spirit of unity among charismatics bridges both denominational and interdenominational differences."

Moreover, like evangelicals, pentecostals are not consistently conservative. Indeed, Smidt found that self-identified charismatics were more moderate than evangelicals, although other studies contradict this result. Poloma has argued, however, that one wing of the charismatic movement is quite similar in its political outlook to the fundamentalist Right, calling Pat Robertson "[the] Moral Majority in charismatic dress." It is from this wing of the charismatic movement that support for the Christian Right comes.

The fundamentalist Christian Right of the 1920's faded from view after the Scopes verdict, and the fundamentalist Right of the 1950's likewise faded after the defeat of Goldwater in 1964. Recent scandals involving prominent televangelists have weakened the fundraising power of the contemporary movement, and may likewise undermine the current charismatic and fundamentalist Right.

Julia M. Corbett

The New Puritanism:
We Must Say "No" Again

The new religious-political right is, in many ways, the puritanism of the eighties. Its *goals* are the same as those of its early forebears, its *methods* are strikingly similar when we account for the differences brought about by the severing of official ties between church and state, and its *theological rationales* are virtually identical.

That puritanism left a legacy for future generations has been pointed out frequently. For example, in *A Religious History of the American People*, Sidney E. Ahlstrom, the undisputed dean of American religious historians, compares the impact of puritanism's legacy in America with that of Martin Luther's in Germany. It is a legacy of stern morality applied to every aspect of life – both public and private – without regard for persons or conditions, reinforced insofar as possible by the power of the civil government, and unmoved by advances brought about by human reason. Puritanism is again alive and well in Lynchburg, Virginia, the site of Jerry Falwell's Thomas Road Baptist Church. ... Robert T. Handy, in comparing the earlier crusades for a "Christian America" with the current new right movement in his book, *A Christian America: Protestant Hopes and Historical Realities,* emphasizes the differences between them, the disjunctures occasioned largely by the pluralism of our own era. In general, Handy does a first-rate job of documenting the historical dialogue between the "Protestant hopes" for a Christian nation and the "historical realities" of ever-expanding pluralism. But, although the new religious and political right formally acknowledges the pluralistic nature of our present situation, the ideas and methods

The Humanist (Sept./Oct. 1988) 19–23, 38. Used by permission.

that its members advocate would take us back to an era in which pluralism was seriously compromised. It is for this reason that America must say "no" to puritanism.

America said "no" to puritanism in the early days of statehood. The history of religious liberty legislation is a record of increasing support for pluralism and for the clear separation of the roles of religion and government. State establishments of religion, carried over from the colonial period, were gradually eliminated. Freed from the restraints of establishment, religion has flourished in the United States, developing a nearly infinite variety of forms to best meet the religious needs of a diverse population. Humanism was instrumental in creating this climate and itself became a significant element in American life and thought in the climate which it had helped to create. These developments could occur because America said "no" to puritanism. To protect them, it is time to say "no" again.

In the first place, the *goals* of the puritans and the new religious and political right are very similar. Like the puritans, the new religious and political right sees itself as the "purifier" of both church and state and, like them also, seeks to make of America a "commonwealth holy unto God."

The puritans sought to purify both the church and the civil government. The church had to be rid of any surviving elements of Catholicism, which puritans often derogatorily called "popery," and conformed to the principles of biblicist Calvinism. The civil government, on the other hand, had to be purified of the influence of the ungodly – read nonpuritan – whose depravity made them unfit to lead.

There has been a fairly persistent taint of anti-Catholicism among at least a segment of the Protestant fundamentalist right, but Catholicism has generally been supplanted as the unsavory element from which the church must be purged. The new enemy within the walls of the church itself is liberalism – social, political, moral, religious – often referred to as the "social gospel" and the "socialist" and "communist" clergy who advocate it. It is also referred to repeatedly as "humanism." The liberal apostasy perceived by the new religious and political right is social, with the involvement of the church in the advocacy of everything from welfare programs to ecology. It is political. As in the 1950s, the enemy today is communism, specifically Soviet communism. Communism is the looming threat to the church as well as to the government. Jerry Falwell, for example, pictures that threat in terms of the possibility that to be a Christian in America might one day be a threat to life. It is moral, as in the support of the National Council of Churches for the

Equal Rights Amendment, church support for homosexual rights, and the ordination of women to ministry. And it is religious, with the departure from "the fundamentals" of biblical inerrancy and literalism and the emphasis on human sinfulness in favor of a "humanistic" gospel of human possibility.

The second goal of the puritans – the creation of a holy commonwealth – also has its counterpart in the battle waged by the new religious and political right. The puritans sought to establish civilizations in the New World that would be covenanted together to advance the Christian religion and be a continual witness to God's glory, omnipotence, and providence. Official documents, such as the Mayflower Compact, and unofficial records, such as John Winthrop's sermon, "A Modell of Christian Charity," delivered in 1630, point unanimously toward this goal. Their model, of course, was Calvin's masterful if misguided Genevan theocracy, and they sought to establish something very similar on the soil of the New World.

The spokesmen – and they are spokes*men* – for the new religious and political right repeatedly sound the theme that only God-fearing men should be in positions of leadership in the United States. The leaders are in their positions of authority, because these powers are ordained by God. Thus, only godly men, should exercise those powers. Separation of church and state, which circumstances have forced the new religious and political right to accept as a given of the American situation, does not mean the separation of "godliness and government". That the God of Christianity should be intimately involved in the affairs of state is a touchstone of both puritanism and the new religious and political right.

In the second place, the *methods* by which the puritans sought to reach their goals and those advocated by the new religious and political right are strikingly similar. The use of the legislative process and the laws of the land to bring about their goals and the enlistment of the public school system to inculcate their point of view from an early age characterize the methods of both groups.

For the puritans, of course, the use of the legislative process was largely a matter of law. Church membership was usually made a condition of candidacy for public office and for voting. Non-puritans were clearly second-class citizens in the early colonial era. Also, the church was made responsible for the oversight of government, at least in some instances, and at the same time government was to exercise control over the church. In Virginia, for instance, the civil authorities had the right and the obligation to determine the fitness of the church's ministers.

The role of the new religious and political right vis-à-vis government must be one with greater influence in the marketplace of competing religious views. However, it is influence with a very clear goal: to have legislation enacted which supports the new right's religious agenda and makes it, in effect, the law of the land. The new religious and political right disclaims that it is seeking any sort of religious establishment. New right literature claims support for religious liberty, and, further, its members insist that theirs is a *moral* rather than a religious crusade. The extent to which morality is itself a central feature of this religious outlook makes such a separation of the moral and the religious impossible. Tim LaHaye, for example, developed a twenty-one-item checklist of moral values, dictated by his view of the Bible, which has been used to evaluate candidates' fitness for office. Even a cursory examination of this list reveals its close interweaving of the moral and the religious and also clearly shows that its real basis is religious and firmly lodged in a specific interpretation of the Christian Bible.

Both the puritans and the new religious and political right want to use the public schools as a primary·vehicle for advocating their point of view. In 1701 in Massachusetts, for example, a law required the approval of schoolmasters by no fewer than three ministers. There were good reasons for this, since among the duties of schoolmasters were prayer and Bible reading with their young charges, catechetical instruction, and instruction in moral and religious subjects, according to a 1789 ordinance passed in Boston.

A key feature of the new religious and political right campaign for its way of life also involves the public schools. Its supporters have called for the reinstatement of voluntary prayer in public schools. They have fought long and hard for laws that would require the teaching of the Genesis account of creation alongside the study of evolution. They are currently working for the elimination of textbooks with language or concepts offensive to their beliefs and life-style and have routinely encouraged the removal of such books from school library shelves. They would exempt Christian schools and the teachers in them from the licensing requirements by which public schools and educators must abide.

The motivation behind the goals and the methods is a set of religious and theological rationales that are drawn straight and unaltered from those which guided the puritan forebears of the new religious and political right. Four clusters of these rationales are particularly significant. …

The puritans were very much the "people of the book." The Bible was central; its truth was infallible and applied equally to every arena of life –

both public and private. Its word was final on matters of cosmology as well as conscience, science as well as sin. The puritans read their Bible, knew it well, and turned the searchlight of scripture into every nook and cranny. Its word judged the truth or falsity of every other word, while it, in turn, was judged by nothing.

Likewise, the movement we have come to call the new religious and political right has been a "back to the Bible" movement from its inception. Jerry Falwell's "Agenda for the Eighties" is, in his opinion, a thoroughly biblical agenda. The Bible is taken to be without error and infallible in all matters – scientific and historical as well as religious. To vary from it in the slightest is to invite dire consequences. It is held to be the foundation of virtually everything American and the source of America's greatness and stability.

But there is a further, related attitude that the new religious and political right shares with the puritans. Truth is absolute. There can be no compromise, and toleration of other ways of living and believing is tantamount to compromise. The new religious and political right, like the puritans who came before it, believes that its members are the sole possessors of this one truth of orthodox, fundamentalist, Protestant Christianity. This means, according to one important new religious and political right leader, that any person who is not a Christian is "inherently a failure." It also means, according to the same source, that the new religious and political right is qualified to define and legislate "sin" for each and every American, since their definition is, in fact, God's own. Truth is not to be compromised, even to create space for doing right. It is here as much as anywhere that the profoundly inhumane character of the new right's program emerges.

The power and sovereignty of God, and obedience to him as the only proper human response, is a second shared cluster of ideas. Calvin and the puritans who followed him read the Bible as the record of God's sovereignty and omnipotence. Their compelling interest in upholding God's monarchical sovereignty was largely what led Calvin to formulate the doctrine of predestination, or election, a teaching which comes very close to describing God as an arbitrary tyrant. The new religious and political right often uses the phrase "God Almighty" when referring to deity. The emphasis on God's power often means a corresponding emphasis on God's judgment much more so than on his mercy. ... The threat of God's impending judgment and descriptions of past events as the fulfillment of that judgment abound.

Given the emphasis on God's power and sovereignty and the constant sounding of warnings about judgments past, present, and yet to come, there is only one reasonable human response: obedience motivated largely by fear. It is an unthinking obedience, an acceptance of authority without question, an abdication of the use of reason.

The puritan emphasis on moralism, purity, and the fruits of faith as evidenced in obedience has led over the course of history to puritans embracing a variety of causes, such as the abolition movement, temperance crusades, pacifism (as well as pro-military, anti-communist advocacies), and civil rights. Today's puritanism has given birth to the new religious and political right with its moral program and to the Liberty Federation (formerly Moral Majority) as its flagship organization, stressing a traditional code of public and private morality. "We must be obedient, lest God turn his back on America and we fall even further from divine favor" is a theme that is sounded again and again. ...

This theme is significant throughout the ... new religious and political right. ...

America is at a critical juncture, a fork in the road, a time of apocalypse. The choice is between obedience and destruction, and that choice must be made *now*. For the puritans, crossing unfriendly seas to establish the new Israel, the urgency was a positive one: God was calling them to begin a great new embodiment of the kingdom of God on Earth. For the new religious and political right, the urgency is essentially negative: unless America turns around, God has run out of patience.

Another central idea in the thought of the new religious and political right – that all of humanity since the fall of Adam and Eve is depraved and equally deserving of hellfire – comes directly from Calvin. The puritans' letters and diaries are replete with accounts of their acutely painful awareness of deep and abiding unworthiness before the Almighty. The sermons of their ministers focus upon sin and guilt and, again, on God's judgment via disease, hard winters, Indian wars, and any number of other disasters. "Examine yourself!" was preached very frequently. And there was absolutely no doubt about what the faithful puritan would encounter upon such honest self-scrutiny. He or she was a morass of sin and evil, held in check only by obedience.

Nothing has changed, says the new religious and political right. People are still evil, sinful, wicked, and incapable of doing any good apart from God's intervention. Attacks on humanism for its more optimistic view of human nature abound. Advice on rearing children is frequently concerned with curbing their "natural" wickedness. Sin lurks around every corner, and Sodom or Gomorrah is every crossroads town on the map. This overarching vision of an evil, corrupt, and depraved humanity again marks the underlying value system and presuppositions of the new right as anti-humanistic at the core.

Yet another point of similarity is that both yesterday's and today's puritans tend to focus much more upon personal than on social sins. Greed, avarice, sloth, laziness, and pride concerned the puritans, according to their letters and diaries. The larger problems of the world are infrequently mentioned. This is true also of the new religious and political right. In *Listen, America!* for example, Falwell deals with communism and national defense in the first section of the book, but his harsher criticism comes in the second section when he describes the changing structure of the family, the Equal Rights Amendment, the National Organization for Women, abortion, and homosexuality. The personal and social are collapsed into each other; the explanation for the menace of communism and the threat of a Soviet takeover, aided and abetted by humanism, is ultimately put in terms of people's personal lives. Matters often thought very private are said to have sweeping public ramifications – a characteristic also of puritan ethics.

Both share the belief that every individual must undergo an explicit "conversion experience." A complete conversion – a turning around – of the nation as a whole is necessary for national survival, and the fate of the entire nation hangs upon the rebirth of each and every citizen in it. Individual as well as national conversion appears as both the condition and the guarantee of national survival and prominence in material and political as well as spiritual matters. In other words, the new religious and political right maintains that national survival is dependent not upon the United States being a diverse community in which a wide range of opinion, belief, and practice can find respect but upon the elimination of that diversity.

A final theme in which the new religious and political right embodies its puritan heritage is the sense of America as having a special mission ... in God's plan for the world. John Winthrop ... strongly believed that America had a special mission, given by God, on behalf of the Christian faith. ...

To William Bradford of Plymouth, America was a kind of last hope for humankind, and the pilgrims were the carriers of that hope. It was a stirring vision, as well it needed to be to enable them to endure the hardship they would encounter.

The new religious and political right is also very explicit in its claim that the United States has a special place in God's overall plan. According to its spokesmen, because America has a government based upon biblical principles, it has enjoyed a greatness unknown to other nations, and God's leading in the development of the Constitution has given America freedom. In the early days of the young nation, adherence to scriptural principles called down God's blessings and could again do so. For what divine purpose did God bless the fledgling nation, and why would God yet restore America to greatness? The answer given by the new religious and political right is clearly stated: the United States is the logical springboard from which to launch the campaign to convert the entire world to its version of Christianity.

The new religious and political right, along with other very conservative to fundamentalist forms of Christianity, clearly appeals to a significant number of people today. ... As Americans shift their religious loyalties, it is fairly obvious that the fundamentalists and conservatives are gaining at least some ground. What is the attraction of this new puritanism of the 1980s? What do we, in our era, share with the pilgrims of Plymouth? ...

Like the early settlers, our lives are beset by vast insecurities, and we are called upon to live creatively in the face of those uncertainties. Given that, the puritanism of the 1980s represents for some people a solution or a way to carry on.

The new religious and political right seems to offer answers as well as a framework which helps to make sense of the questions. No matter how overwhelmingly complex the issue may seem – nuclear holocaust, balancing the nation's budget, AIDS – it ultimately reduces to one common denominator, depressing perhaps in its persistence but not as frightening because it is the same enemy who has been there all along: Satan.

The solution is equally direct. Conversion, turning around, and repentance will solve the problems-turned-problem. Alternatives and partial answers to be weighed in the balance do not exist, nor do tentative solutions that might or might not work out. Initially hopeful attempts that drag with them yet another set of problems are nonexistent. Conversion comes with the promise that it *will* work. It will result in an improvement in conditions in this life and avoidance of hellfire in the next. And – perhaps most important for the appeal of this line of thought – each and every individual has the capacity to make a difference, since the fate of the nation and the world ultimately hangs on the sum of individuals' decisions for or against God. It eliminates the paralyzing despair reflected in the lament, "But what difference can *I* make?"

The present turmoil finds its place, say the new religious and political right advocates, in a much larger scheme of things. It is another chapter in the long record of the battle between God Almighty and that foremost fallen angel, Satan. Its frightening element of strangeness is diluted, if not eliminated entirely. Those on the side of right are assured that they play a key role in winning this eons-old struggle and thus find the strength to carry on.

The appeal of puritanism – whether in the sixteenth or the twentieth century – is the appeal of simplicity and of the assurance of being "in the right" in perilous and emotionally unnerving times. It is the appeal of being part of something much larger than our human fears and efforts. It is the guarantee of playing on what ultimately *must* be the winning team.

But America must again say "no" to that appeal. The price to be paid is far too high for the security offered. It is a security based upon a drastic narrowing of our field of vision and an ever-tighter restriction of the humane principles we have affirmed. It is a security purchased for the price of accepting as the one truth the perspective of one point of view within one religion. It is a security for which we would pay by accepting a view of humankind as weak and sinful, turning our backs on the rich heritage of both religious and secular humanism. And it is a security that would require us to see ourselves sharply divided into opposing groups – like those in possession of "the truth" and those who have chosen falsehood and "the lie." To be beguiled by the simplistic security offered by the new religious and political right – the puritanism of the 1980s – would require that we deny as a central aspect of that falsehood most of the rich and varied experience of humankind, both religious and nonreligious.

Nathan Glazer

Fundamentalism

We are now buried in an avalanche of publicity and journalistic commentary, and even a moderate degree of analysis, regarding an upsurge of Fundamentalism. We have been told again and again about Fundamentalism's potential threat to civil liberties, to a healthy diversity of opinion, and to the hope that we can conduct public affairs free of the divisiveness of religious factionalism.

Of course, we have been plagued through most of our history by religious-based conflicts. Catholics, from the time when they increased in numbers in the United States owing to Irish and German immigration in the 1840s, often have been seen as a danger. They have been subjected to prejudice, and have felt forced to create their own distinctive institutions, particularly schools and colleges. In the regions where they were numerically dominant – in the cities and states of the Northeast – Catholics have been feared as a danger to diversity and secularism by Protestants and Jews. Jews have struggled with the anti-Semitism aroused by their ethnic and national differences, and with intolerance directed against their religion, its public practice, and the special arrangements in work, education, and dietary matters that its practice requires.

But these religious conflicts had seemed to be declining rapidly in intensity and significance in the 1960s and 1970s. The modernization of the Catholic Church, which created serious conflicts among Catholics, reduced conflict between Catholics and their non-Catholic neighbors. There had been fierce divisions between Catholics on the one hand, and Protes-

This World, Summer 1982. Reprinted with permission of the Rockford Institute (Rockford, Illinois).

tants and Jews on the other, during the 1930s, 1940s, and 1950s. Many of us were surprised and pleased to see divisive issues simply evaporate in the 1960s. Sadly, a distinctive Catholic culture also seemed rapidly to evaporate. Many Catholic schools closed because of the difficulty of financing in the absence of public funds; Catholic colleges became less and less distinctive, and less and less religious. Meanwhile, Catholic public opinion became more and more similar to the opinion of other Americans of the same class and education. Two issues still remain even after the 1960s to divide Catholics from Protestants and Jews – support of parochial schools, and attitudes to abortion. But even these issues are today no longer distinctively *Catholic* issues, and certainly not as distinctively Catholic as they were twenty years ago. The Moral Majority is not Catholic, and those who support tuition tax credits and education vouchers, while they certainly include Catholics, have non-Catholics among their dominant voices. ...

It is hardly necessary to go through this recital to make the point that the new rising tide of religious issues has nothing to do with traditional Catholic/Protestant, or Jewish/Gentile splits and divisions: Rather, it pits Fundamentalist and resurgent traditional Protestantism against liberal Protestantism. Jews and Catholics, both traditional and liberal, are involved – but now not as representatives of embattled faiths, but as citizens, because major public issues have been raised. In terms of current conflicts involving religion, Jews, Catholics, and Protestants are no longer the principal combatants – the combatants are, rather, traditionalists against liberals of whatever religious background.

If some have been caught by surprise ... that is because we have forgotten a great deal of American history. And perhaps even more important, we have ignored a great deal of existent and still potent American reality. This nation has been, if anything, a *religious* republic, and we are still, to a surprising degree for the modern, industrialized or post-industrialized world, a *religious* people. Ours is also, of course, a law-ridden republic and people. We are committed to elaborate legal processes to come to conclusions, and those conclusions are sometimes rather bizarre. And finally, paralleling our involvement in religion and our commitment to legal processes, we are committed to the market – to the free development of goods and services, which must inevitably undermine anything traditional in our society.

What has been happening in recent years is that law and the market have created a situation in which it was inevitable that the more religious elements of the population would react with anger and with vigor. They have done so, and put a fright into those who have forgotten our religious past. ...

Nationalizing Morality

It is worth pointing out ... that intense religious-based beliefs have often directly inserted themselves, for good or ill, into American politics. We are reminded of this in Paul J. Weber's interesting article on ... two major movements in American life that were fueled primarily by religious senti-ment. One was abolitionism. While this encompassed a much wider band of American opinion and power than that represented by the clergy of various Protestant denominations, Weber argues that "no other segment of the population pursued the issue with such intensity or tenaciousness. No other groups had the opportunity and facilities to raise consciousness to the extent religious groups did."

Weber's second example is more ambiguous, but still shows the power of religion in American public life: the temperance movement. Once again, not only religious groups were involved. There were "progressive" el-ements who saw in the wiping out of the saloon the salvation of the working man and his family. There was also more than a touch of anti-Catholicism, for Catholics in no way shared the fervor of Protestants, and in particular of the churches of the Protestant lower-middle classes, in opposing drink. But at the heart of the movement were religious groups. The manpower and womanpower, the contributions, and the publications, were animated primarily by a religious sentiment, rather than any prag-matic or rational analysis. This was also preeminently a "single-issue" movement, parallel to today's anti-abortion, pro-prayer, and other efforts. And it won. It resulted in the 18th Amendment banning drink, an astonish-ing victory, which eventually had to be repealed by yet another amendment to the Constitution.

What explains the recent resurgence of the Religious Right? It is worth looking at the issues that most agitate them. ... One was the Supreme Court decision *Roe v. Wade* of 1973 that thrust aside the abortion laws of fifty states. A second issue is the concern with a rising tide of nontraditional attitudes toward sexual and family roles, and the almost casual references to pre-marital sex, homosexuality, and drug use in television and the mass media. A third is the ban on school prayer. *In other words, it is the great successes of secular and liberal forces, principally operating through the specific agency of the courts, that has in large measure created the issues on which the Fundamentalists have managed to achieve what influence they have. ...*

Abortion was not a national issue until the Supreme Court, in *Roe v. Wade,* set national standards for state laws. Abortion did *not* become an issue because Fundamentalists wanted to *strengthen* prohibitions against abortion, but because liberals wanted to abolish them. Equal rights for women did *not* become an issue because Fundamentalists wanted to *limit* women's rights, but because the proposed Equal Rights Amendment raised fears, both rational and irrational, that all traditional distinctions between men's and women's roles would be overturned. (That these fears were not so irrational is evidenced by the litigation against a military draft for men only.) Pornography in the 1980s did *not* become an issue because Fundamentalists wanted to *ban* D. H. Lawrence, James Joyce, or even Henry Miller, but because, in the 1960s and 1970s under-the-table pornography moved to the top of the newsstands. Prayer in the schools did *not* become an issue because Fundamentalists wanted to *introduce* new prayers or sectarian prayers, but because the Supreme Court ruled against all prayers. Freedom for religious schools became an issue *not* because of any legal effort to *expand* their scope, but because the Internal Revenue Service and various state authorities tried to impose restrictions on them that private schools had not faced before. (Only tuition tax credits, it can be argued, is a case of an aggressive attempt to overthrow an old arrangement – but tuition tax credits are less a concern of Fundamentalists than of Catholics and conservative Protestants and Jews.)

... I rehearse this story to make a simple point that is much forgotten in the rising tide of fear: Dominant power – measured by money, access to the major media, influence, the opinion of our educated, moneyed, and powerful elites – still rests with the secular and liberal forces that created, through court action, the changes that have aroused Fundamentalism. What we are seeing is a defensive reaction of the conservative heartland, rather than an offensive that intends to or is capable of really upsetting the balance, or of driving the United States back to the nineteenth century or early twentieth century.

The two court decisions that have most sharply focused the anger of the heartland date back only to 1963 – the school prayer decision, and 1973 –

the abortion decision. The court decisions that have made it so difficult for states to assist private (and religious) schools date back only to the early 1970s. The court decisions that have made it all but impossible for states, cities, and communities to control pornography do not go much further back.

A Defensive Offensive

We are in a strange political posture, indeed, one in which both liberals and Fundamentalists see themselves as embattled and endangered, in which both see themselves as playing a defensive role, as protecting some important value or institution against an attack which is upsetting a stable balance. It needs no argument to demonstrate that this is the posture of secular and liberal forces. ...

But I would argue that this is also the posture of the now-resurgent Fundamentalists. They may be on the offensive, but it is, if I may use the phrase, a "defensive offensive," meant to get us back to, at worst, the 1950s, and even that is beyond the hopes, or I would think the power, of Fundamentalist faith. This "defensive offensive" itself can be understood only as a response to what is seen as aggression – the aggression that banned prayer from the schools, or, most recently, the Ten Commandments from schoolhouse walls, that prevented states from expressing local opinion as to the legitimacy of abortion, and that, having driven religion out of the public schools, now is seeking to limit the schools that practice it, or to prevent any assistance to the private schools in which many parents – who want a religious atmosphere and education for their children – have sought refuge.

We are very far from the time when we might have legitimately feared the power of narrow-mindedness and bigotry as embodied in Fundamentalist and traditional religion. Not that there is not enough bigotry and narrow-mindedness to be found there, as elsewhere. But we must make a distinction between a powerful and self-confident movement that would hope to reshape America in its image, and a defensive one that wants to protect some enclaves for traditional religion. ...

First, in an organizational sense, the Fundamentalist movement is weaker than its opponents. It is sobering ... to see how weak the major Fundamentalist, traditionalist, or conservative religious lobbies are in terms of money and manpower and prestige. Paul Weber has done yeoman service in trying to characterize the religious lobbies. He has located no less than seventy-four in Washington, of which twenty-seven are conservative Protestant. Of all seventy-four organizations, only nine had budgets of more than $1 million a year. Only three had staffs of more than thirty – and all three were liberal. The Fundamentalist lobbies are truly tiny, compared to many Washington lobbies.

Second, the conservative groups are for the most part quite new. The great majority were created in the 1970s. ...

Third, the new conservative religious movements show less bias and bigotry against other religions or minority racial groups than did some religious groups in the past. They define as their enemies not Catholics, Jews or Negroes, but secular liberals who have introduced changes which the Fundamentalists believe undermine religion and the family. ... The new movement is perhaps the first major Fundamentalist Protestant movement that is not anti-Catholic. Indeed, it has many interests in common with Catholics, such as opposition to abortion and the concern for the independence of religious schools. ...

One reason for this refusal to embrace bigotry is that Fundamentalist Protestantism is no longer dominant in the country, and therefore seeks allies everywhere – and allies can be found even among conservative Jews and blacks. In fact, blacks are still on the whole more religious than whites, and share, in a larger degree than white opinion generally, some of the positions of the Fundamentalist Protestant movements, such as opposition to abortion.

In any case, there is nothing in the issues embraced by Fundamentalist Protestants that is implicitly anti-Catholic, anti-Jewish, or anti-black, whatever the degree of these feelings that one may still find among some of the movement's supporters. ...

Fourth, the new Fundamentalist movement expresses points of view and attitudes that the dominant mass media – the national newspapers, weeklies, and television networks – for the most part reject, and that dominant elites also reject. Evangelists' television audiences are much exaggerated; they do not appear on the television networks or the national newsmagazines – only their critics do. It is interesting to compare the attitudes on religion and religious issues of American public opinion generally and elite opinion, as we find in the important Connecticut Mutual Life Insurance Company-sponsored survey of American values. In this survey, 65 percent of the public believed abortion to be morally wrong, but only 36 percent of society's leaders. Seventy-one percent of the public believed homosexuality to be morally wrong, but only 42 percent of the leaders. Fifty-seven per cent of the public considered smoking marijuana to be wrong, but only 33 percent of the leaders. If the surveyors had asked, a much greater percentage of the leaders probably would have supported the Supreme Court on prayer and aid to private schools than would the public. ...

The Counter-Revolution

But the strongest argument for seeing the new movement as defensive and with limited aims is that we saw in the 1960s and 1970s a real revolution, and that what we are seeing now is an attempt at a counter-revolution. ...

[The first] revolution encompassed sex, dress, and drugs. One need recall only that in the late 1960s it was still possible for Harvard to debate passionately parietal rules – when boys could visit girls, and vice versa. The revolution encompassed women's roles. ... The revolution encompassed the schools, once a place where traditional morality and religion were taught by teachers who were authoritative, and authoritarian – and were backed-up or disciplined by self-confident authorities. The driving forces of the revolution were two: The expanded reach of constitutional litigation, based on the model of civil rights litigation; and the power of the free market, in goods and ideas, to diffuse minority and unconventional models of behavior. The second faced a reduced resistance from community norms because of the power of the first.

But what both the legal revolutionaries and the marketing experts forgot is that we are not one culture, but many cultures. The once-dominant culture of middle America had been driven from television screens, mass magazines, universities, and opinion-molding circles. But it still existed. The Fundamentalists had suffered crushing defeats in the 1920s in their fight against revolution and modernism in the churches. They had been reduced to irrelevance in the Depression of the 1930s and the war against Nazism in the 1940s. In the family-building period of the 1950s, there had been little to arouse them. But the cultural revolution of the 1960s and 1970s did.

We are presently in a phase not dissimilar to that described by George M. Marsden in his interesting book, *Fundamentalism and American Culture: The Shaping of Twentieth Century Evangelicism, 1870–1925.* ...

The Fundamentalists' most alarming experience was that of finding themselves living in a culture that by the 1920s was openly turning away from God. "Christendom," remarked H. L. Mencken in 1924, "may be defined briefly as that part of the world in which, if any man stands up and solemnly swears he is a Christian, all the auditors will laugh." The "irreligion of the modern world," concurred Walter Lippman in his *Preface to Morals,*" ... is radical to a degree for which there is, I think, no counterpart."

"The American Christians [Fundamentalists]," Marsden asserts, "underwent a remarkable transformation in their relationship to the culture. Respected 'evangelicals' in the 1870s, by the 1920s they had become a laughingstock, ideological strangers in their own land ... The philosophical outlook that had graced America's finest academic institutions came to be generally regarded as merely bizarre."

It all came crashing down in the Scopes trial in Dayton, Tennessee, in 1925. After that, Fundamentalism, insofar as the national mass media were concerned, went underground, though it still existed on a vast scale and represented the outlook on religion and life of a substantial section of the American population. In a second period of sexual license and of changing sex roles, and with a new expansion of the mass media and mass markets, now supported by the actions of an activist bar and a responsive Federal judiciary (neither of which we had in the 1920s), Fundamentalism reawakened, too, the dormant fear of theocracy. This fear is much exaggerated. It ignores the primarily defensive character of the new Fundamentalist movement. The aim of the new movement is basically to protect enclaves of literal, Fundamentalist faith and the practices that accompany it. ...

The protection of enclaves is best accomplished, not by sweeping national decisions, but by practice, law, and custom adapted to the enormous variety of our country. The temperance movement ... went too far when it imposed one section's view of drink on the rest of the country. But when that dispute was finally settled by the repeal of the 18th Amendment, it did not bother most people that in one section of the country or another, one could not get a drink on Sunday. In the same way, liberalism went too far when it imposed on the whole country the views of one part of the population regarding abortion, or school prayer, or support for religious schools, through major cases that led to sweeping Supreme Court decisions that set national standards. These major decisions made what should have been state and local issues, such as abortion and school prayer, national issues. ...

Is it possible to define the switches that are necessary to moderate Fundamentalist anger, and that may yet be acceptable to the cosmopolitan elite? I would like to suggest a theme for these switches: It is local option in morality, as we have local option in drink. Imagine the uproar if the Supreme Court were to take seriously an argument ... that restriction of drink in public places is as much an invasion of privacy ... as prohibition on the use or sale or advertisement of contraceptive devices, or prohibition of abortion. There would be an uproar, and a painfully forged compromise would have been upset, and a new round of national conflict over morality opened. Local option, by states and communities, on such matters as abortion, Bible reading in schools (one can switch from one translation to the other, and add the Bhagavad Gita and the Koran as school composition changes), public assistance to private schools, and a number of other matters, could do wonders, and would simply and honestly reflect the reality that we are a diverse country. Nor would the Constitution be violated, even if undoubtedly many professors of constitutional law would be outraged. After all, the constitutional principles that permitted national prohibitions in these areas were found lurking in the Constitution only 180 years or so after it was adopted. ...

Fundamentalism is not an anachronistic remnant doomed to disappear rapidly, but neither is the world about to be saved, once and for all. Our policy must adapt to this reality. Fundamentalists must recognize that at least half of us are and will remain skeptical and unsaved; and secular liberals must accept the fact that their outlook will not gain universal acquiescence.

The arrangements that permit us to survive are those in which neither side imposes on the other its vision of the good society. Working out the details is not simple in a society in which there is no ruling elite, and any view, no matter how eccentric, may find itself law if it finds the right judge. But if we withdraw from imposing the views and beliefs of the cosmopolitan elite on the whole country, we will find the new Fundamentalism returning to its modest role in the American kaleidoscope.

Chapter VII
War, Peace, and Pacifism

Background: This chapter covers in four separate sections the issues of war, peace, and justice in the context of Christian realism and idealism. The first section consists of excerpts from the theological superstars of the Christian church as they argue about the nature of Just and Unjust Wars and the duties of Christians to God and the state. These themes continue in section two, which compares Reinhold Niebuhr's realism about conflict, politics, the "will to power," and human nature to Lyman Abbott's pacifist commitment to non-violence. While Niebuhr and the early "realists" emphasize the inevitability of war and injustice and the resulting need for defense and redress of grievances, Abbott and the early pacifists follow Christ's example from the Sermon on the Mount (Matt. 5:9, 39–41, 43–45 – The Gideons International King James Version)

> Blessed are the peacemakers: for they shall be called the children of God. ... But I say unto you, That ye resist not evil: but whosoever shall smite thee on thy right cheek, turn to him the other also. And if any man will sue thee at the law, and take away thy coat, let him have thy cloak also. And whosoever shall compel thee to go a mile, go with him twain. ... Ye have heard that it hath been said, Thou shalt love thy neighbor, and hate thine enemy. But I say unto you, Love your enemies, bless them for them which despitefully use you, and persecute you; That ye may be the children of your Father ...

The discussion of nuclear deterrence in the third section may seem out of place at the end of the Cold War where the threat of nuclear conflict between the superpowers all but disappeared with the disintegration of the Soviet empire. However, nuclear weapons still exist and proliferate, as do conflicts between nation-states, ethnic groups, and terrorist offshoots of both of these. In addition, there is no assurance that, in the "new world order," nations and peoples will draw appropriate lessons from the 45 year balance of terror that underlay the Cold War. Uncertainty and instability remain, as does the following moral question: Does the strategy of nuclear deterrence, based on the threat to annihilate the enemy (Mutual Assured Destruction or MAD), constitute a legitimate strategy, since it appears that the threat of annihilation succeeded in stopping the U.S. and the Soviet Union from starting a nuclear war? In other words, is MAD moral because the threat produces peace (a moral effect)? Or, is it immoral because of the appalling paradox pointed out by the American Catholic Bishops – the threat to use nuclear weapons against human hostages, if implemented, would be the ultimate immorality?

Moralists and pacifists conclude that MAD is immoral for several reasons. The Methodist Bishops, for example, note the violations of the Just War "rules" inherent in the lack of distinction between threatening and using nuclear weapons. They also condemn the pseudo-moral facade of the ends/means dynamic in which the end (peace) justifies the means (threatening and preparing for massive destruction.) On the other hand, if a threat of MAD causes no death and deters war because of the fear of retaliation, then MAD is profoundly moral in result (no war.) Charles Krauthammer, who is not Methodist but Jewish, uses the ends/means dynamic to rationalize his conditional approval for the Cold War balance of terror stabilized by the mutual fears of the U.S. and the Soviet Union. He sees MAD as the moral alternative to strategies more likely to trigger war and thus world wide destruction.

The last section continues the discussion of the Just War tradition as it affected the evaluation of the legitimacy of using force in the U.S./United Nations war against Iraq in 1991. While legal scholars and theologians since Augustine have attempted to persuade governments to comply with Just War limits on the initiation and conduct of war, pacifists reject the whole discussion of Just Wars because it undermines the New Testament's unconditional prohibition against all use of force. They believe, along with Tertullian (c. 155–c. 240), that Jesus, "in disarming Peter, unbelted every soldier."

In the Gulf War case, Professor Yoder and Journalist Geyer maintain the strict pacifist line, as do the American "Peace Churches" like the Mennonites and Quakers. The Methodist and Catholic Bishops (and the leaders of other religious groups), while gravitating to the Just War theory that moral principles should govern the use of force, oppose its application in the Gulf. Professors Langan and Johnson, following Augustine and Niebuhr, accept the use of force against Iraqi aggression in this imperfect world still well short of the Kingdom of God.

Authors: Augustine (354–430) is recognized by both Catholics and Protestants as one of the greatest Christian theologians of all time. His work includes commentaries on scripture, heresy, history, ethics, society, and war. In the selection here, Augustine criticizes Christian pacifists. He reminds his readers of the differences between just and unjust wars (actions, "in obedience to God or some lawful authority," to defend public safety or to pursue peace versus action of lust for violence, revenge, or power), the requirements of just cause and rightful authority, and the call to both a personal attitude of peaceful living and to war. He views war as a necessity forced on man living in a sinful world. He uses God's call on Moses and David to war on Israel's enemies as examples of Just Wars.

Thomas Aquinas (1225–1274) is also universally recognized as one of the great Christian theologians. His works, influenced by Aristotelian and Pauline philosophy, covered scriptural exegesis and the study of God, man, ethics, and the law of nature. Like Augustine, he also accepts the necessity of war and soldiering. Aquinas then notes three prerequisites for a just war: the war must be authorized by the sovereign, have a just cause, and be fought for "the advancement of good, or the avoidance of evil."

Martin Luther (1483–1546) expounds the doctrines of unfree will, God's righteousness, salvation in Christ (grace), and evangelicalism. This great leader of the Reformation criticizes the superstitions and deformities of the medieval Catholic Church. He also rejects the pacifist objection that the New Testament commands God's people only to suffer and endure, rather than to fight or resist evil. Luther believes in fighting for (and obeying) the institutions of the state, which are "instituted by God to punish the evil, protect the good, and preserve peace." Like Augustine and Aquinas, he distinguishes between Just and Unjust Wars. Just Wars (or lawful self-defense) are those intended to preserve peace and obey God, to defend and deter, and to resist rebellion (even by mistreated and oppressed subjects.) Just Wars "should be fought in the fear of God" and under the temporal authority of a sovereign acting rightly. In sum, a world plagued by war, cruelty and injustice requires counterwars to force aggressors into peace and justice.

John Calvin (1509–1564), an early convert to the Reformation and soon its theological director, teaches total reliance on the inerrant word of God-inspired Scripture, the necessity of a prayerful personal encounter with Jesus, the fallen nature of man, the redeeming grace of Christ, and the bonds of predestination. Regarding the individual's obligations to the state, he teaches obedience to civil authority. Like Luther, he defends the right of soldiers and "magistrates to shed blood" in pursuing justice, executing God's judgment, avenging the afflicted, deterring the wicked, guarding law and territory, and suppressing the seditious. Calvin believes in submitting to even tyrannical and unjust authority. He also warns princes not to be unjust, and thus to invite God's wrath. He then warns citizens that commanded obedience to men does not extend to following impious commands that "seduce us from obedience" to God. Like Luther, Calvin also rejects pacifism based solely on examples of Christ's suffering. He notes the difference between Christ's plan for the spiritual and peaceable kingdom of God and the public's need to organize and defend civil government in an unpeaceable world.

Menno Simons (1496–1561) opposes the same sedition that Luther and Calvin do. This includes the sedition by the Dutch theologian's fellow religionists, the Anabaptist, some of whom called for Holy Wars against infidels and rebellion against oppressive regimes. But Menno Simons, whose followers would take the name Mennonites, goes further than medieval reformers or founding elders in rejecting all wars and violence as the work of Satan and not Christ, the Prince of peace. He teaches obedience to Christ's commands to sheathe the sword, love and forgive enemies, return good for evil, turn the other cheek, "not know vengeance," and to beat swords into ploughshares. In a dramatic statement of absolute pacifism, Simons concludes that true Christians "are prepared to forsake country, goods, life, and all for the sake of peace."

Desiderius Erasmus (1496–1536) was a Dutch Catholic priest of enormous theological influence on both the Catholic church and the Reformation. He differed with Luther on key issues that split the Catholic Church apart (free will vs. predestination, for example), yet he also joined in Luther's critique of the abuses of the medieval church. In the selection here, Erasmus opposes the use of force almost as absolutely as does Simons. While he reluctantly accepts that a prince may go to war if "he cannot possibly avoid it," Erasmus doubts that any war may be called just. He asks why Christians listen to Augustine rather than to Christ and the apostles, who teach specifically against war. Erasmus especially regrets internecine wars between Christian peoples. He also opposes crusades against Turks and Saracens which bring few converts and risk "that we degenerate into Turks."

Reinhold Niebuhr (1892–1971) brings the classical debate over the justness of war into the 20th century. An eclectic scholar, Niebuhr taught social justice and power politics at Union Theological Seminary, published widely in the tradition of Augustine and Calvin, embraced both Christian Marxism and neo-orthodoxy at different times in his life, and dominated Western Christian political theology in the 20th century. In the excerpts below, he first provides background on the Christian doctrines of "the law of love," forgiveness and justification, atonement, and divine mercy. He then explains why the church is not pacifist. In a still hauntingly relevant essay on the ills of man, the state and war, Niebuhr maintains that sin is a permanent factor in human history and destroys humankind's ability to follow the "law of love." He believes that sinfulness and selfishness enslave human beings, who achieve salvation, not through their actions, but through Christ's forgiveness (redeeming grace). He thus criticizes secularized versions of Christianity that "believe there is some fairly simple way out of the sinfulness of human history."

In the world where sin and human egoism make conflict inevitable and persistent, the Christian has responded to war by denial, engagement (realism), or abstention (pacifism.) Niebuhr does not regard traditional Christian pacifism as unrealistic or heresy. It "is simply a version of Christian perfectionism" that takes "the law of Christ seriously." Traditional pacifism "did not give itself to the illusion that it had discovered a method for eliminating the element of conflict from political strategies." It pursued individual unselfishness and peace, but knew that political conflict was "beyond its power of solution." However, modern Christian pacifism is heretical and foolish, in Niebuhr's view, because of its faith in man (to achieve peace and perfection) rather than God, its rejection of the doctrine of original sin, and its belief that "there is some fairly easy way out of the human situation."

In this diatribe against liberal pacifism, Niebuhr also reveals the fundamentals of Christian realism. According to this theory, the law of love, which Christians strive for but fail to follow fully even in their personal lives, is "not immediately applicable to the task of securing justice in a sinful world."

Since God's people live in an uncooperative world where the "will-to-power" dominates and tyranny grows if not restricted, they must sometimes fight for social justice. In other words, "it is because men are sinners that justice can be achieved only by a certain degree of coercion, on the one hand, and by resistance to coercion and tyranny on the other."

Reverend Lyman Abbott (1835–1922) is a polar opposite to Niebuhr. He abandoned theological conservatism for liberal Protestantism and pacifism, but he believed, as did Niebuhr, that World War I was a just war. In the selection below, Abbott notes that Jesus taught passive non-resistance with one qualification: defense of others may demand a resort to force. Abbott also maintains that, while in certain circumstances war is legitimate ("when there is no law to which an appeal can be made, and when the law ... is defied"), Christianity and wars "are absolutely inconsistent." Therefore the objective of Christianity is "to abolish trial by battle between nations, as it has already abolished trial between individuals, – not merely to mitigate the horrors of war, not merely to reduce occasions of war ... but to put an end to public war absolutely."

According to Abbott, when Christianity has achieved this objective and people submit "controversies to an impartial tribunal, ... nations also will go unarmed." He also hypothesizes that the "power in public opinion" will enforce decisions of international tribunals and eliminate the need for armies. Where Niebuhr emphasizes the persistence of sin and conflict, Abbott trusts that Christianity can overcome war, once "law is substitute for war, reason for force, the spiritual for the animal, Christianity for barbarism."

The United Methodist Bishops' statement on the nuclear crisis, *In Defense of Creation*, brings the debate over Just Wars into the nuclear age. The Bishops respond to the moral dilemma of war in the nuclear age: should the U.S. base its defense on nuclear deterrence and the threat of all-out war? Since implementing such a threat would violate the Just War rules against indiscriminate and unproportional bombing, they seek to persuade Christians and governments that the proper answer is no. To explain their position, the Bishops rely on Christian scripture. They stress that, while struggle with sin makes government, law, and defense against enemies warranted, peace is the "natural state of humanity birthed by God." They argue that Christ calls for "a new kingdom, a new order of love, and justice," and that his crucifixion and resurrection testify "to the transcendent power of forgiving love and nonviolence." Given these doctrines and the new convenant of Christ, the Bishops believe that human beings can transcend their sinful nature by becoming new creations in Christ. Christ requires his new creations to be peacemakers.

As to the latter role, the Bishops review and critique three Christian traditions which address the ethics of war. The early pacifist tradition opposed "all killing, military service, and warfare." The Just War tradition accepted war as inevitable, given the fallen nature of mankind. It attempted to impose moral boundaries on the conduct of war and on when, and under what conditions, states might legitimately resort to war. The crusade tradition went in the opposite direction and "assume[d] that an unrestrained conduct of war is a religious obligation." The Bishops offer a new Just Peace tradition as the most appropriate theological tradition for the nuclear age.

In this effort to create a Just Peace doctrine, the Bishops wrote a statement of guiding principles that juxtaposes traditional anti-war themes with their opposition to nuclear weapons. In this statement, they reject nuclear pacifism that leaves the door open to non-nuclear wars, "yes/no deterrence" that allows possession but no use of nuclear weapons, and other strategies that envision limited use of nuclear weapons. They condemn "the idolatry of deterrence" in which the U.S. "presumes the power of ultimate judgment and destruction of other nations." The Bishops also disparage the unstable core of nuclear deterrence: "the contradiction between inordinate confidence in the rationality of decision makers and the absolute terror of annihilation." In sum, they question a strategy that depends on a suicidal nuclear retaliation, and a hope that fear of such an irrational retaliation would deter a rational enemy from striking first. The Bishops believe this system is both immoral and irrational.

Charles Krauthammer, an editor for the NEW REPUBLIC and a former speech writer for Walter Mondale (Presidental candidate in 1984), writes on international relations. In "On Nuclear Morality," he responds to attacks on the morality and logic of deterrence. Krauthammer first compares deterrence based on MAD – a threat to retaliate against civilians – to deterrence based on a "counterforce" strategy – a threat to retaliate against strategic weapons with sufficient capacity to defeat an opponent's first strike plan, win a limited nuclear war, and prevent escalation. He then responds to the moral and strategic objections to these two forms of deterrence by the American Catholic Bishops, secular populist critics like Jonathan Schell, and former government officials like Robert McNamara.

Krauthammer objects to the American Catholic Bishops' "nuclear bluff" strategy of possessing, but never using, nuclear weapons. Deterrence, in his view, depends on "a combination of possession [of nuclear weapons] and the will to use them. If one side renounces, for moral or other reasons, the intent of ever actually using nuclear weapons, deterrence will cease to exist." He sees no alternative to the strategy of deterrence (MAD), which has kept the peace for 40 years. Krauthammer also argues that deterrence is moral because it prevents great evil (nuclear war) and "keep(s) us free." After thus stating his preferences, he attacks the nuclear freeze movement and the campaign to end America's "First Use" strategy, which extended deterrence to Europe via a threat to use nuclear weapons if the Soviets launched a nuclear or conventional attack against Western Europe.

The last section in this chapter brings the Just War issue back to the land of the early Christian church, the Middle East. It begins with James Turner Johnson, Professor of Religion and Director of International Programs at Rutgers, The State University of New Jersey. Johnson, a well-known American authority on the ethics of war, argues that the military action to drive Iraq out of Kuwait in 1991 met all of the seven conditions of the Just War tradition.

John Langan, Professor of Christian Ethics at Georgetown University, lacks Johnson's assurance. He views the Just War tradition as only an instrument to sharpen our "critical and questioning attitude toward any war." In the process of questioning the war in the Gulf, he argues that it was an "Imperfectly Just War." There was just cause for intervention because Iraq's seizure of Kuwait violated a basic principle of international law requiring respect for state sovereignty. In addition, sovereign authorities, the U.S. and the United Nations, initiated the intervention and, due to their combined strength, could assume a reasonable prospect of success. Thirdly, the American-led coalition, which intervened only after diplomatic and economic sanctions failed to induce Iraqi withdrawal from Kuwait, met the criterion of proportionality between means and ends (resort to force to resist Iraqi aggression). Finally, the coalition maintained limited objectives. Despite meeting these criteria of the Just War doctrine, Langan questions whether the amount of casualties inflicted on Iraqi civilians and troops fully met the criterion of proportionality.

John H. Yoder, Professor of Theology at Notre Dame and a leading Mennonite pacifist and scholar, not only doubts the justness of the war, but also the 20th century relevance of the Just War tradition. In his view, the latter serves only as "a checklist of questions which it is fitting to ask in considering war." In the process of questioning the war against Iraq, Yoder notes the impossibility of determining "justness." This is due to the confusion over the facts of the case, the looseness of the definitions of the Just

War criteria, and the difficulty in weighing proportionality between attack and response, given the technological wizardry of modern American weapons. All of these prove, in his view, "the incapacity of the [Just War] system to yield a clear and commonly accessible adjudication of contested cases." Given this incapacity, the Just War tradition may only be good for identifying and denouncing the dominant political view that no holds are barred in war. Yoder fears that the Just War discourse on moral accountability has not superseded this view and has, in fact, served to disguise the persistence of the dominant "realist" view. He therefore prefers the less compromised pacifist tradition which says no to all war because it violates the laws of God and man.

Alan Geyer, editor of the liberal journal *Christian Century,* shares Yoder's doubts and fears. He holds the U.S. and the coalition as partially responsible for the outbreak of hostilities in the Gulf. The issue of American innocence is not clear to him when he recalls American arms aid to the volatile Middle East region, an undisciplined energy policy that drives the U.S. to military action to safeguard resources, inconsistent attitudes toward the claims of Israelis and Palestinians, unclear political signals to Iraq, and double standards on nuclear proliferation – OK for allies of the U.S., but not for Arabs. Geyer joins with Yoder in blaming the U.S. as much as Iraq for the sparks that ignited the war, and in calling for greater reliance on negotiations rather than force of arms.

Key Questions: Must the Christian choose pacifism to honor Christ's example of brotherly love and peace? Or, given the imperfect nature of the world, may the Christian resort to force to defend self, others, and values? As Niebuhr asks, may the Christian "give his devotion to the highest values he knows; defend those citadels of civilization of which necessity and historic destiny have made him the defender; ... [and] enter the affairs of men to bring good out of evil?" Are strategies based on deliberately targeting innocent civilians morally acceptable if they deter nuclear war? Or are they unacceptable because they threaten what would otherwise be an immoral act?

Augustine

Letter 189

Do not think that it is impossible for any one to please God while engaged
in active military service. Among such persons was the holy David, to
whom God gave so great a testimony; among them also were many righteous men of that time; among them was also that centurion who said to the
Lord: "I am not worthy that Thou shouldest come under my roof, but
speak the word only, and my servant shall be healed: for I am a man under
authority, having soldiers under me: and I say to this man, Go, and he
goeth; and to another, Come, and he cometh; and to my servant, Do this,
and he doeth it"; and concerning whom the Lord said: "Verily, I say unto
you, I have not found so great faith, no, not in Israel." Among them was
that Cornelius to whom an angel said: "Cornelius, thine alms are accepted,
and thy prayers are heard," when he directed him to send to the blessed
Apostle Peter, and to hear from him what he ought to do, to which apostle
he sent a devout soldier, requesting him to come to him. Among them were
also the soldiers who, when they had come to be baptized by John – the
sacred forerunner of the Lord, and the friend of the Bridegroom, of whom
the Lord says: "Among them that are born of women there hath not risen a
greater than John the Baptist" – and had inquired of him what they should
do, received the answer, "Do violence to no man, neither accuse any falsely;
and be content with your wages." Certainly he did not prohibit them to
serve as soldiers when he commanded them to be content with their pay for
the service. …

Trans. J. G. Cunningham, in *The Nicene and Post-Nicene Fathers* (1st series) 1,
Wm. B. Eerdmans. Used by permission.

Peace should be the object of your desire; war should be waged only as a necessity, and waged only that God may by it deliver men from the necessity and preserve them in peace. For peace is not sought in order to the kindling of war, but war is waged in order that peace may be obtained. Therefore, even in waging war, cherish the spirit of a peacemaker, that, by conquering those whom you attack, you may lead them back to the advantages of peace. ...

Reply to Faustus the Manichean 22

The real evils in war are love of violence, revengeful cruelty, fierce and implacable enmity, wild resistance, and the lust of power, and such like; and it is generally to punish these things, when force is required to inflict the punishment, that, in obedience to God or some lawful authority, good men undertake wars, when they find themselves in such a position as regards the conduct of human affairs, that right conduct requires them to act, or to make others act in this way. Otherwise John, when the soldiers who came to be baptized asked, What shall we do? would have replied, Throw away your arms; give up the service; never strike, or wound, or disable any one. But knowing that such actions in battle were not murderous, but authorized by law, and that the soldiers did not thus avenge themselves, but defend the public safety, he replied, "Do violence to no man, accuse no man falsely, and be content with your wages." But as the Manichaeans are in the habit of speaking evil of John, let them hear the Lord Jesus Christ Himself ordering this money to be given to Caesar, which John tells the soldiers to be content with. "Give," He says, "to Caesar the things that are Caesar's."

For tribute money is given on purpose to pay the soldiers for war. ...

A great deal depends on the causes for which men undertake wars, and on the authority they have for doing so; for the natural order which seeks the peace of mankind, ordains that the monarch should have the power of undertaking war if he thinks it advisable, and that the soldiers should perform their military duties in behalf of the peace and safety of the community. When war is undertaken in obedience to God, who would rebuke, or humble, or crush the pride of man, it must be allowed to be a

---

Trans. R. Stothert, in *The Nicene and Post-Nicene Fathers* (1st series) 4.

righteous war; for even the wars which arise from human passion cannot harm the eternal well-being of God, nor even hurt His saints; for in the trial of their patience, and the chastening of their spirit, and in bearing fatherly correction, they are rather benefited than injured. No one can have any power against them but what is given him from above. For there is no power but of God, who either orders or permits. Since, therefore, a righteous man, serving it may be under an ungodly king, may do the duty belonging to his position in the state in fighting by the order of his sovereign – for in some cases it is plainly the will of God that he should fight, and in others, where this is not so plain, it may be an unrighteous command on the part of the king, while the soldier is innocent, because his position makes obedience a duty – how much more must the man be blameless who carries on war on the authority of God, of whom every one serves Him knows that He can never require what is wrong?

If it is supposed that God could not enjoin warfare, because in after times it was said by the Lord Jesus Christ, "I say unto you, That ye resist not evil: but if any one strike thee on the right cheek, turn to him the left also," the answer is, that what is here required is not a bodily action, but an inward disposition. The sacred seat of virtue is the heart, and such were the hearts of our fathers, the righteous men of old. But order required such a regulation of events, and such a distinction of times, as to show first of all that even earthly blessings (for so temporal kingdoms and victory over enemies are considered to be, and these are the things which the community of the ungodly all over the world are continually begging from idols and devils) are entirely under the control and at the disposal of the one true God. ...

The City of God 19.5–7

But who can enumerate all the great grievances with which human society abounds in the misery of this mortal state? Who can weigh them? Hear how one of their comic writers makes one of his characters express the common feelings of all men in this matter: "I am married; this is one misery, Children are born to me; they are additional cares." What shall I say of the miseries of love which Terence also recounts – "slights, suspicions, quar-

Trans. M. Dods, in *The Nicene and Post-Nicene Fathers* (1st series) 2.

rels, war today, peace tomorrow?" Is not human life full of such things? Do they not often occur even in honorable friendships? On all hands we experience these slights, suspicions, quarrels, war, all of which are undoubted evils; while, on the other hand, peace is a doubtful good, because we do not know the heart of our friend, and though we did know it today, we should be as ignorant of what it might be tomorrow. Who ought to be, or who are more friendly than those who live in the same family? And yet who can rely even upon this friendship, seeing that secret treachery has often broken it up, and produced enmity as bitter as the amity was sweet, or seemed sweet by the most perfect dissimulation? …

For it is the wrongdoing of the opposing party which compels the wise man to wage just wars; and this wrongdoing, even though it gave rise to no war, would still be matter of grief to man because it is man's wrongdoing. Let every one, then, who thinks with pain on all these great evils, so horrible, so ruthless, acknowledge that this is misery. And if any one either endures or thinks of them without mental pain, this is a more miserable plight still, for he thinks himself happy because he has lost human feeling. …

From *The City of God* 19.12–27.

Whoever gives even moderate attention to human affairs and to our common nature, will recognize that if there is no man who does not wish to be joyful, neither is there any one who does not wish to have peace. For even they who make war desire nothing but victory – desire, that is to say, to attain to peace with glory. For what else is victory than the conquest of those who resist us? and when this is done there is peace. It is therefore with the desire for peace that wars are waged, even by those who take pleasure in exercising their warlike nature in command and battle. And hence it is obvious that peace is the end sought for by war. For every man seeks peace by waging war, but no man seeks war by making peace. For even they who intentionally interrupt the peace in which they are living have no hatred of peace, but only wish it changed into a peace that suits them better. They do not, therefore, wish to have no peace, but only one more to their mind. And in the case of sedition, when men have separated themselves from the community, they yet do not effect what they wish, unless they maintain some kind of peace with their fellow conspirators. And therefore even robbers take care to maintain peace with their comrades, that they may with greater effect and greater safety invade the peace of other men. … And thus all men desire to have peace with their own circle whom they wish to govern as suits themselves. For even those whom they make war against they wish to make their own, and impose on them the laws of their own peace. ... and force them to, either through love or fear, yield themselves to peace with them. It is thus that pride in its perversity apes God. It abhors equality with other men under Him; but, instead of His rule, it seeks to impose a rule of its own upon its equals. It abhors, that is to say, the just peace of God, and loves its own unjust peace; but it cannot help loving peace of one kind or other. For there is no vice so clean contrary to nature that it obliterates even the faintest traces of nature.

He then, who prefers what is right to what is wrong, and what is well-ordered to what is perverted, sees the peace of unjust men is not worthy to be called peace in comparison with the peace of the just. And yet even what is perverted must of necessity be in harmony with, and in dependence on, and in some part of the order of things, for otherwise it would have no existence at all. ...

But as this divine Master inculcates two precepts – the love of God and the love of our neighbor – and as in these precepts a man finds three things he has to love – God, himself, and his neighbor – and that he who loves God loves himself thereby, it follows that he must endeavor to get his neighbors to love God, since he is ordered to love his neighbor as himself. He ought to make this endeavor in behalf of his wife, his children, his household, all within his reach, even as he would wish his neighbor to do the same for him if he needed it; and consequently he will be at peace, or in well-ordered concord, with all men, as far as in him lies. And this is the order of this concord, that a man, in the first place, injure no one, and, in the second, do good to every one he can reach. ... But in the family of the just man who lives by faith, and is as yet a pilgrim journeying on to the celestial city, even those who rule serve those whom they seem to command; for they rule not from a love of power, but from a sense of the duty they owe to others – not because they are proud of authority, but because they love mercy. ...

If we are to accept the definitions laid down by Scipio in Cicero's *De Republica*, there never was a Roman republic; for he briefly defines a republic as the weal of the people. And if this definition be true, there never was a Roman republic, for the people's weal was never attained among the Romans. For the people, according to his definition, is an assemblage associated by a common acknowledgement of right and by a community of interests. And what he means by a common acknowledgement of right he explains at large, showing that a republic cannot be administered without justice. Where, therefore, there is no true justice there can be no right. For that which is done by right is justly done, and what is unjustly done, cannot be done by right. For the unjust inventions of men are neither to be considered nor spoken of as rights; for even they themselves say that right is that which flows from the fountain of justice, and deny the definition which is commonly given by those who misconceive the matter, that right is that which is useful to the stronger party. Thus, where there is not true justice there can be no assemblage of men associated by a common acknowledgment of right, and therefore there can be no people, as defined by Scipio or Cicero. ...

But if we discard this definition of a people, and, assuming another, say that a people is an assemblage of reasonable beings bound together by a common agreement as to the objects of their love, then, in order to discover the character of any people, we have only to observe what they love. Yet whatever it loves, if only it is an assemblage of reasonable beings and not of beasts, and is bound together by an agreement as to the objects of love, it is reasonably called a people; and it will be a superior people in proportion as it is bound together by higher interests, inferior in proportion as it is bound together by lower. According to this definition of ours, the Roman people is a people, and its weal is without doubt a commonwealth or republic. But what its tastes were in its early and subsequent days, and how it declined into sanguinary seditions and then to social and civil wars, and so burst asunder or rotted off the bond of concord in which the health of a people consists, history shows, and in the preceding books I have related at large. And yet I would not on this account say either that it was not a people, or that its administration was not a republic, so long as there remains an assemblage of reasonable beings bound together by a common agreement as to the objects of love. But what I say of this people and of this republic I must be understood to think and say of the Athenians or any Greek state, of the Egyptians, of the early Assyrian Babylon, and of every other nation, great or small, which had a public government. For, in general, the city of the ungodly, which did not obey the command of God that it should offer no sacrifice save to Him alone, and, which, therefore, could not give to the soul its proper command over the body, nor to the reason its just authority over the vices, is void of true justice. ...

Thomas Aquinas

Summa Theologica 2–2, Q

FIRST ARTICLE

Whether it is Always Sinful to Wage War

... Augustine says in a sermon on the son of the centurion: *If the Christian Religion forbade war altogether, those who sought salutary advice in the Gospel would rather have been counselled to cast aside their arms, and to give up soldiering altogether. On the contrary, they were told: "Do violence to no man; ... and be content with your pay." If he commanded them to be content with their pay, he did not forbid soldiering.*

I answer that, In order for a war to be just, three things are necessary. First, the authority of the sovereign by whose command the war is to be waged. For it is not the business of a private individual to declare war, because he can seek for redress of his rights from the tribunal of his superior. Moreover it is not the business of a private individual to summon together the people, which has to be done in wartime. And as the care of the common weal is committed to those who are in authority, it is their business to watch over the common weal of the city, kingdom or province subject to them. And just as it is lawful for them to have recourse to the sword in defending that common weal against internal disturbances, when they punish evildoers, according to the words of the Apostle (Rom. 13: 4): *He beareth not the sword in vain: for he is God's minister, an avenger to execute wrath upon him that doth evil;* so too, it is their business to have recourse to the sword of war in defending the common weal against

Trans. Fathers of English Dominican Province. Used by permission of Benziger/ Glencoe (Macmillan/McGraw-Hill.)

external enemies. Hence it is said to those who are in authority (Ps. 81: 4): *Rescue the poor: and deliver the needy out of the hand of the sinner;* and for this reason Augustine says (*Contra Faust.* 22.75): *The natural order conducive to peace among mortals demands that the power to declare and counsel war should be in the hands of those who hold the supreme authority.*

Secondly, a just cause is required, namely that those who are attacked, should be attacked because they deserve it on account of some fault. Wherefore Augustine says (*QQ. in Hept., qu. 10, super Jos.*): *A just war is wont to be described as one that avenges wrongs, when a nation or state has to be punished, for refusing to make amends for the wrongs inflicted by its subjects, or to restore what it has seized unjustly.*

Thirdly, it is necessary that the belligerents should have a rightful intention, so that they intend the advancement of good, or the avoidance of evil. Hence Augustine says (*De Verb. Dom.*): *True religion looks upon as peaceful those wars that are waged not for motives of aggrandizement, or cruelty, but with the object of securing peace, of punishing evildoers, and of uplifting the good.* For it may happen that the war is declared by the legitimate authority, and for a just cause, and yet be rendered unlawful through a wicked intention. Hence Augustine says (*Contra Faust.* 22.74): *The passion for inflicting harm, the cruel thirst for vengeance, an unpacific and relentless spirit, the fever of revolt, the lust of power, and such like things, all these are rightly condemned in war.*

Reply Obj. 1. As Augustine says (*Contra Faust.* 22.70): *To take the sword is to arm oneself in order to take the life of anyone, without the command or permission of superior of lawful authority.* On the other hand, to have recourse to the sword (as a private person) by the authority of the sovereign or judge, or (as a public person) though zeal for justice, and by the authority, so to speak, of God, is not to *take the sword,* but to use it as commissioned by another, wherefore it does not deserve punishment. And yet even those who make sinful use of the sword are not always slain with the sword, yet they always perish with their own sword, because, unless they repent, they are punished eternally for their sinful use of the sword.

Reply Obj. 2. Such like precepts, as Augustine observes (*De Serm. Dom. in Monte* 1.19), should always be borne in readiness of mind, so that we be ready to obey them, and, if necessary, to refrain from resistance or self-defense. Nevertheless it is necessary sometimes for a man to act otherwise for the common good, or for the good of those with whom he is fighting. Hence Augustine says (*Ep. ad Marcellin.* 138): *Those whom we have to punish with a kindly severity, it is necessary to handle in many ways against their will. For when we are stripping a man of the lawlessness of sin, it is good for him to be vanquished, since nothing is more hopeless than the happiness of sinners, whence arises a guilty impunity, and an evil, like an internal enemy.*

Reply Obj. 3. Those who wage war justly aim at peace, and so they are not opposed to peace, except to the evil peace, which Our Lord *came not to send upon earth* (Matt. 10:34). Hence Augustine says (*Ep. ad Bonif.* 189): *We do not seek peace in order to be at war, but we go to war that we may have peace. Be peaceful, therefore, in warring, so that you may vanquish those whom you war against, and bring them to the prosperity of peace. ...*

Summa Theologica 2–2, Q. 41

FIRST ARTICLE

Whether Strife is always a Sin?

… While contention implies a contradiction of words, strife denotes a certain contradiction of deeds. Wherefore a gloss on Gal. 5:20 says that *strifes are when persons strike one another through anger.* Hence strife is a kind of private war, because it takes place between private persons, being declared not by public authority, but rather by an inordinate will. Therefore strife is always sinful. In fact it is a mortal sin in the man who attacks another unjustly, for it is not without mortal sin that one inflicts harm on another even if the deed be done by the hands. But in him who defends himself, it may be without sin, or it may sometimes involve a venial sin, or sometimes a mortal sin; and this depends on his intention and on his manner of defending himself. For if his sole intention be to withstand the injury done to him, and he defended himself with due moderation, it is no sin, and one cannot say properly that there is strife on his part. But if, on the other hand, his self-defense be inspired by vengeance and hatred, it is always a sin. It is a venial sin, if a slight movement of hatred or vengeance obtrude itself, or if he does not much exceed moderation in defending himself: but it is a mortal sin if he makes for his assailant with the fixed intention of killing him, or inflicting grievous harm on him. …

Summa Theologica 2–2, Q. 42

FIRST ARTICLE

Whether Sedition is a Special Sin Distinct from Other Sins?

... Sedition is a special sin, having something in common with war and strife, and differing somewhat from them. It has something in common with them, in so far as it implies a certain antagonism, and it differs from them in two points. First because war and strife denote actual aggression on either side, whereas sedition may be said to denote either actual aggression, or the preparation for such aggression. Hence a gloss on II Cor. 12:20 says that *seditions are tumults tending to fight,* when, to wit, a number of people make preparations with the intention of fighting. Secondly, they differ in that war is, properly speaking, carried on against external foes, being as it were between one people and another, whereas strife is between one individual and another, or between few people on one side and few on the other, while sedition, in its proper sense, is between mutually dissentient parts of one people, as when one part of the state arises in tumult against another part. Wherefore, since sedition is opposed to a special kind of good, namely the unity and peace of a people, it is a special kind of sin.

Reply Obj. 1. A seditious man is one who incites others to sedition, and since sedition denotes a kind of discord, it follows that a seditious man is one who creates discord, not of any kind, but between the parts of a multitude. And the sin of sedition is not only in him who sows discord, but also in those who dissent from one another inordinately.

Reply Obj. 2. Sedition differs from schism in two respects. First, because schism is opposed to the spiritual unity of the multitude, viz., ecclestical unity, whereas sedition is contrary to the temporal or secular unity of the multitude, for instance of a city or kingdom. Secondly, schism does not imply any preparation for a material fight as sedition does, but only a spiritual dissent. ...

Now Augustine says (*De Civ. Dei* 2. 21) that *wise men understand the word people to designate not any crowd of persons, but the assembly of those who are united together in fellowship recognized by law and for the common good.* Wherefore it is evident that the unity to which sedition is opposed is the unity of law and common good: whence it follows manifestly that sedition is opposed to justice and the common good. Therefore by reason of its genus it is a mortal sin, and its gravity will be all the greater according as the common good which it assails surpasses the private good which is assailed by strife.

Accordingly the sin of sedition is first and chiefly in its authors, who sin most grievously; and secondly it is in those who are led by them to disturb the common good. Those, however, who defend the common good, and withstand the seditious party, are not themselves seditious, even as neither is a man to be called quarrelsome because he defends himself, as stated above (Q. 41, A. 1). ...

Reply Obj. 3. A tyrannical government is not just, because it is directed, not to the common good, but to the private good of the ruler, as the Philosopher states (*Polit.* 3. 5; *Ethic.* 8. 10). Consequently there is no sedition in disturbing a government of this kind, unless indeed the tyrant's rule be disturbed so inordinately, that his subjects suffer greater harm from the consequent disturbance than form the tyrant's government. Indeed it is the tyrant rather that is guilty of sedition, since he encourages discord and sedition among his subjects, that he may lord over them more securely; for this is tyranny, being conducive to the private good of the ruler, and to the injury of the multitude.

Martin Luther

Whether Soldiers Too, Can Be Saved

I am dealing here with such questions as these: whether the Christian faith, by which we are accounted righteous before God, is compatible with being a soldier, going to war, stabbing and killing, robbing and burning, as military law requires us to do to our enemies in wartime. Is this work sinful or unjust? Should it give us a bad conscience before God? Must a Christian only do good and love, and kill no one, nor do any harm?

... The very fact that the sword has been instituted by God to punish the evil, protect the good, and preserve peace [Rom. 13...1–4; I Pet. 2: 13–14] is powerful and sufficient proof that war and killing along with all the things that accompany wartime and martial law have been instituted by God. What else is war but the punishment of wrong and evil? Why does anyone go to war, except because he desires peace and obedience?

... When I think of a soldier fulfilling his office by punishing the wicked, killing the wicked, and creating so much misery, it seems an un-Christian work completely contrary to Christian love. But when I think of how it protects the good and keeps and preserves wife and child, house and farm, property, and honor and peace, then I see how precious and godly this work is; and I observe that it amputates a leg or a hand, so that the whole body may not perish. For if the sword were not on guard to preserve peace, everything in the world would be ruined because of lack of peace. Therefore, such a war is only a very brief lack of peace that prevents an everlasting and immeasureable lack of peace, a small misfortune that prevents a great misfortune.

From *Luther's works* 46, H. T. Lehman, ed., © 1967 Fortress Press. Used by permission of Augsburg Fortress.

What men write about war, saying that it is a great plague, is all true. But they should also consider how great the plague is that war prevents. If people were good and wanted to keep peace, war would be the greatest plague on earth. But what are you going to do about the fact that people will not keep the peace, but rob, steal, kill, outrage women and children, and take away property and honor? The small lack of peace called war or the sword must set a limit to this universal, worldwide lack of peace which would destroy everyone.

This is why God honors the sword so highly that he says that he himself has instituted it [Rom. 13...1] and does not want men to say or think that they have invented it or instituted it. For the hand that wields this sword and kills with it is not man's hand, but God's; and it is not man, but God, who hangs, tortures, beheads, kills, and fights. All these are God's works and judgments.

To sum it up, we must, in thinking about a soldier's office, not concentrate on the killing, burning, striking, hitting, seizing, etc. This is what children with their limited and restricted vision see when they regard a doctor as a sawbones who amputates, but do not see that he does this only to save the whole body. So, too, we must look at the office of the soldier, or the sword, with the eyes of an adult and see why this office slays and acts so cruelly. Then it will prove itself to be an office which, in itself, is godly and as needful and useful to the world as eating and drinking or any other work.

There are some who abuse this office, and strike and kill people needlessly simply because they want to. But that is the fault of the persons, not of the office, for where is there an office or a work or anything else so good that self-willed, wicked people do not abuse it? ... Indeed, they themselves are a part of that universal lack of peace which must be prevented by just wars and the sword and be forced into peace. It always happens and always has happened that those who begin war unnecessarily are beaten. Ultimately, they cannot escape God's judgment and sword.

... If the waging of war and the military profession were in themselves wrong and displeasing to God, we should have to condemn Abraham, Moses, Joshua, David, and all the rest of the holy fathers, kings, and princes, who served God as soldiers and are highly praised in Scripture because of this service, as all of us who have read even a little in Holy Scripture know well, and there is no need to offer further proof of it here.

Perhaps someone will now say that the holy fathers were in a different position because God had set them apart from the other nations by choosing them as his people, and had commanded them to fight, and that their example is therefore not relevant for a Christian under the New Testament because they had God's command and fought in obedience to God, while we have no command to fight, but rather to suffer, endure, and renounce everything. This objection is answered clearly enough by St. Peter and St. Paul, who both command obedience to worldly ordinances and to the commandments of worldly rulers even under the New Testament [Rom. 13: 1–4; I Pet. 2: 13–14]. And we have already pointed out that St. John the Baptist instructed soldiers as a Christian teacher and in a Christian manner and permitted them to remain soldiers, enjoining them only not to use their position to abuse people or to treat them unjustly, and to be satisfied with their wages. Therefore even under the New Testament the sword is established by God's word and commandment, and those who use it properly and fight obediently serve God and are obedient to his word.

Just think now! If we gave in on this point and admitted that war was wrong in itself, then we would have to give in on all other points and allow that the use of the sword was entirely wrong. For if it is wrong to use a sword in war, it is also wrong to use a sword to punish evildoers or to keep the peace. Briefly, every use of the sword would have to be wrong. For what is just war but the punishment of evildoers and the maintenance of peace? ... Romans 13 calls the sword "the wrath of God."

As for the objection that Christians have not been commanded to fight and that these examples are not enough, especially because Christ teaches us not to resist evil but rather suffer all things. ... Christians do not fight and have no worldly rulers among them. Their government is a spiritual government, and, according to the Spirit, they are subjects of no one but Christ. Nevertheless, as far as body and property are concerned, they are subject to worldly rulers and owe them obedience. If worldly rulers call upon them to fight, then they ought to and must fight and be obedient, not as Christians, but as members of the state and obedient subjects. Christians therefore do not fight as individuals or for their own benefit, but as obedient servants of the authorities under whom they live. This is what St. Paul wrote to Titus when he said that Christians should obey the authorities. ...

For God has established two kinds of government among men. The one is spiritual; it has no sword, but it has the word, by means of which men are to become good and righteous, so that with this righteousness they may attain eternal life. He administers this righteousness through the word, which he has committed to the preachers. The other kind is worldly government, which works through the sword so that those who do not want to be good and righteous to eternal life may be forced to become good and righteous in the eyes of the world. He administers this righteousness through the sword. And although God will not reward this kind of righteousness with eternal life, nonetheless, he still wishes peace to be maintained among men and rewards them with temporal blessings. He gives rulers much more property, honor, and power than he gives to others so that they may serve him by administering this temporal righteousness. Thus God himself is the founder, lord, master, protector, and rewarder of both kinds of righteousness. ...

Whoever starts a war is in the wrong. And it is only right and proper that he who first draws his sword is defeated, or even punished, in the end. This is what has usually happened in history. Those who have started wars have lost them, those who fought in self-defense have only seldom been defeated. Worldly government has not been instituted by God to break the peace and start war, but to maintain peace and to avoid war. Paul says in Romans 13 [:4] that it is the duty of the sword to protect and punish, to protect the good in peace and to punish the wicked with war. God tolerates no injustice and he has so ordered things that warmongers must be defeated in war. ...

Self-defense is a proper ground for fighting and therefore all laws agree that self-defense is innocent in the eyes of all man. ...

No war is just even if it is a war between equals, unless one has such a good reason for fighting and such a good conscience that he can say, "My neighbor compels and forces me to fight, though I would rather avoid it." In that case, it can be called not only war, but lawful self-defense, for we must distinguish between wars that someone begins because that is what he wants to do and does before anyone else attacks him, and those wars that are provoked when an attack is made by someone else. The first kind can be called wars of desire; the second wars of necessity. ...

Every lord and prince is bound to protect his people and to preserve the peace for them. That is his office; that is why he has the sword, Romans 13 [:4]. This should be a matter of conscience for him. And he should on this basis be certain that this work is right in the eyes of God and is commanded by him. I am not now teaching what Christians are to do, for your government does not concern us Christians; but we are rendering you a service and telling you what you are to do before God, in your office of ruler. A Christian is a person to himself; he believes for himself and for no one else.

But a lord and prince is not a person to himself, but on behalf of others. It is his duty to serve them, that is, to protect and defend them. It would indeed be good if he were also a Christian and believed in God, for then he would be saved. However, being a Christian is not princely, and therefore few princes can be Christians; as they say, "A prince is a rare bird in heaven." But even if princes are not Christians, they nevertheless ought to do what is right and good according to God's outward ordinance. God wants them to do this.

But if a lord or prince does not recognize this duty and God's commandment and allows himself to think that he is prince, not for his subject's sake, but because of his handsome, blond hair as though God had made him a prince to rejoice in his power and wealth and honor, take pleasure in these things, and rely on them. If he is that kind of prince, he belongs among the heathen; indeed, he is a fool. That kind of prince would start a war over an empty nut and think of nothing but satisfying his own will. God restrains such princes by giving fists to other people, too. There are also people on the other side of the mountain. Thus one sword keeps the other in the scabbard. ...

The third question is whether overlords have the right to go to war with their subjects. We have, indeed, heard above that subjects are to be obedient and are even to suffer wrong from their tyrants. Thus, if things go well, the rulers have nothing to do with their subjects except to cultivate fairness, righteousness, and judgment. However, if the subjects rise up and rebel, as the peasants did recently, then it is right and proper to fight against them. That, too, is what a prince should do to his nobles and an emperor to his princes if they are rebellious and start a war. Only it must be done in the fear of God, and too much reliance must not be placed on being in the right, lest God determine that the lords are to be punished by their subjects, even though the subjects are in the wrong. ...

"Suppose my lord were wrong in going to war." I reply: If you know for sure that he is wrong, then you should fear God rather than men, Acts 4 [5:29], and you should neither fight nor serve, for you cannot have a good conscience before God. "Oh, no," you say, "my lord would force me to do it; he would take away my fief and would not give me my money, pay, and wages. Besides, I would be despised and put to shame as a coward, even worse, as a man who did not keep his word and deserted his lord in need." I answer: You must take that risk and, with God's help, let whatever happens, happen. ...

John Calvin

Institutes of the Christian Religion 4.20

If by the law of God all Christians are forbidden to kill, and the prophet
predicts respecting the Church, that "they shall not hurt nor destroy in all
my holy mountain, saith the Lord," how can it be compatible with piety for
magistrates to shed blood? But if we understand, that in the infliction of
punishment, the magistrate does not act at all from himself, but merely
executes the judgments of God, we shall not be embarrassed with this
scruple. The law of the Lord commands, "Thou shalt not kill"; but that
homicide may not go unpunished, the legislator himself puts the sword into
the hands of his ministers, to be used against all homicides. *To hurt* and *to
destroy* are incompatible with the character of the godly; but to avenge the
afflictions of the righteous at the command of God, is neither *to hurt* nor *to
destroy*. Therefore it is easy to conclude that in this respect magistrates are
not subject to the common law; by which, though the Lord binds the hands
of men, he does not bind his own justice, which he exercises by the hands of
magistrates. So, when a prince forbids all his subjects to strike or wound
any one, he does not prohibit his offices from executing that justice which is
particularly committed to them. I sincerely wish that this consideration
were constantly in our recollection, that nothing is done here by the
temerity of men, but every thing by the authority of God, who commands
it, and under whose guidance we never err from the right way. For we can
find no valid objection to the infliction of public vengeance, unless the
justice of God be restrained from the punishment of crimes. But if it be
unlawful for us to impose restraints upon him, why do we caluminate his
ministers? Paul says of the magistrate, that "He beareth not the sword in

Trans. T. Lane and H. Osborne, ed., Baker House and Hodder and Stoughton. Used
by permission.

vain; for he is the minister of God, a revenger to execute wrath upon him that doeth evil." Therefore, if princes and other governors know that nothing will be more acceptable to God than their obedience, and if they desire to approve their piety, justice, and integrity before God, let them devote themselves to this duty. This motive influenced Moses, when, knowing himself to be destined to become the liberator of his people by the power of the Lord, "he slew the Egyptian"; and when he punished the idolatry of the people by the slaughter of three thousand men in one day. The same motive actuated David. ...

Now, if it be true justice for them to pursue the wicked with a drawn sword, let them sheathe the sword, and keep their hands from shedding blood, while the swords of desperadoes are drenched in murders; and they will be so far from acquiring the praise of goodness and justice by this forbearance, that they will involve themselves in the deepest impiety. There ought not, however, to be any excessive or unreasonable severity. ...

XI. Now, as it is sometimes necessary for kings and nations to take up arms for the infliction of such public vengeance, the same reason will lead us to infer the lawfulness of wars which are undertaken for this end. For if they have been intrusted with power to preserve the tranquillity of their own territories, to suppress the seditious tumults of disturbers, to succour the victims of oppression, and to punish crimes – can they exert this power for a better purpose, than to repel the violence of him who disturbs both the private repose of individuals and the general tranquillity of the nation; who excites insurrections, and perpetrates acts of oppression, cruelty, and every species of crime? If they ought to be the guardians and defenders of the laws it is incumbent upon them to defeat the efforts of all by whose injustice the discipline of the laws is corrupted. And if they justly punish those robbers, whose injuries have only extended to a few persons, shall they suffer a whole district to be plundered and devastated with impunity? For there is no difference, whether he, who in a hostile manner invades, disturbs, and plunders the territory of another to which he has no right, be a king, or one of the meanest of mankind: all persons of this description are equally to be considered as robbers, and ought to be punished as such. It is the dictate both of natural equity, and of the nature of the office, therefore, that princes are armed, not only to restrain the crimes of private individuals by judicial punishments, but also to defend the territories committed to their charge by going to war against any hostile aggression; and the Holy Spirit, in many passages of Scripture, declares such wars to be lawful.

XII. If it be objected that the New Testament contains no precept or example, which proves war to be lawful to Christians, I answer first, that the reason for waging war which existed in ancient times, is equally valid in the present age; and that, on the contrary, there is no cause to prevent princes from defending their subjects. Secondly, that no express declaration on this subject is to be expected in the writings of the apostles, whose design was, not to organize civil governments, but to describe the spiritual kingdom of Christ. Lastly, that in those very writings it is implied by the way, that no change has been made in this respect by the coming of Christ. "For," to use the words of Augustine, "if Christian discipline condemned all wars, the soldiers who inquired respecting their salvation ought rather to have been directed to cast away their arms, and entirely to renounce the military profession; whereas the advice given them was, 'Do violence to no man, neither accuse any falsely; and be content with your wages.' An injunction to be content with their wages was certainly not a prohibition of the military life." But here all magistrates ought to be very cautious, that they follow not in any respect the impulse of their passion. ...

They must not suffer themselves to be carried away by any private motive, but be wholly guided by public spirit; otherwise they grossly abuse their power, which is given them, not for their own particular advantage, but for the benefit and service of others. ...

Submit to the government, not only of those princes who discharge their duty to us with becoming integrity and fidelity, but of all who possess the sovereignty, even though they perform none of the duties of their function. For, though the Lord testifies that the magistrate is an eminent gift of his liberality to preserve the safety of men, and prescribes to magistrates themselves the extent of their duty, yet he at the same time declares, that whatever be their characters, they have their government only from him; that those who govern for the public good are true specimens and mirrors of his beneficence; and that those who rule in an unjust and tyrannical manner are raised up by him to punish the iniquity of the people; that all equally possess that sacred majesty with which he has invested legitimate authority. I will not proceed any further till I have subjoined a few testimonies in proof of this point. It is unnecessary, however, to labour much to envince an impious king to be a judgment of God's wrath upon the world, as I have no expectation that any one will deny it: and in this we say no more of a king than of any other robber who plunders our property; or adulterer who violates our bed; or assassin who attempts to murder us;

since the Scripture enumerates all these calamities among the curses inflicted by God. But let us rather insist on the proof of that which the minds of men do not so easily admit; that a man of the worst character, and most undeserving of all honour, who holds the sovereign power, really possesses that eminent and Divine authority, which the Lord has given by his word to the ministers of his justice and judgment; therefore, that he ought to be regarded by his subjects, as far as pertains to public obedience, with the same reverence and esteem which they would show to the best of the kings. ...

XXX. And here is displayed his wonderful goodness, and power, and providence; for sometimes he raises up some of his servants as public avengers, and arms them with his commission to punish unrighteous domination, and to deliver from their distressing calamities a people who have been unjustly oppressed: sometimes he accomplishes this end by the fury of men who meditate and attempt something altogether different. Thus he liberated the people of Israel from the tyranny of Pharaoh by Moses. ...

XXXI. But whatever opinion be formed of the acts of men, yet the Lord equally executed his work by them, when he broke the sanguinary sceptres of insolent kings, and overturned tyrannical governments. Let princes hear and fear. But, in the meanwhile, it behoves us to use the greatest caution, that we do not despise or violate that authority of magistrates, which is entitled to the greatest veneration, which God has established by the most solemn commands, even though it reside in those who are most unworthy of it, and who, as far as in them lies, pollute it by their iniquity. For though the correction of tyrannical domination is the vengeance of God, we are not, therefore, to conclude that it is committed to us, who have received no other command than to obey and suffer. ...

XXXII. But in the obedience which we have shown to be due to the authority of governors, it is always necessary to make one exception, and that is entitled to our first attention – that it do not seduce us from obedience to him, to whose will the desires of all kings ought to be subject, to whose decrees all their commands ought to yield, to whose majesty all their sceptres ought to submit. And, indeed, how preposterous it would be for us, with a view to satisfy men, to incur the displeasure of him on whose account we yield obedience to men! ... On this principle Daniel denied that he had committed any crime against the king in disobeying his impious decree; because the king had exceeded the limits of his office. ...

Erasmus

On Beginning War

A good prince should never go to war at all unless, after trying every other means, he cannot possibly avoid it. If we were of his mind, there would hardly be a war. Finally, if so ruinous an occurrence cannot be avoided, then the prince's main care should be to wage the war with as little calamity to his own people and as little shedding of Christian blood as may be, and to conclude the struggle as soon as possible. The really Christian prince will first weigh the great difference between man, who is an animal born for peace and good will, and beasts and monsters, who are born to predatory war; [he will weigh also] the difference between men and Christian men. Then let him think over how earnestly peace is to be sought and how honorable and wholesome it is; on the other hand [let him consider] how disastrous and criminal an affair war is and what a host of all evils it carries in its wake even if it is the most justifiable war – if there really is any war which can be called "just." Lastly, when the prince has put away all personal feelings, let him take a rational estimate long enough to reckon what the war will cost and whether the final end to be gained is worth that much – even if victory is certain, victory which does not always happen to favor the best causes. ...

Among such great and changing vicissitudes of human events, among so many treaties and agreements which are now entered into, now rescinded, who can lack a pretext – if there is any real excuse – for going to war? But the pontifical laws do not disapprove all war. Augustine approves of it in some instances, and St. Bernard praises some soldiers. But Christ himself

The Education of a Christian Prince, trans. and ed. L. K. Born (1965), Columbia University Press. Used by permission.

and Peter and Paul everywhere teach the opposite. Why is their authority less with us than that of Augustine or Bernard? Augustine in one or two places does not disapprove of war, but the whole philosophy of Christ teaches against it. There is no place in which the apostles do not condemn it; and in how many places do those very holy fathers, by whom, to the satisfaction of some, war has been approved in one or two places, condemn and abhor it? Why do we slur over all these matters and fasten upon that which helps our sins? Finally, if any one will investigate the matter more carefully, he will find that no one has approved the kind of wars in which we are now commonly involved. ...

The Christian prince should first question his own right, and then if it is established without a doubt he should carefully consider whether it should be maintained by means of catastrophes to the whole world. Those who are wise sometimes prefer to lose a thing rather than to gain it, because they realize that it will be less costly. Caesar, I think, would prefer to give up his rights rather than seek to attain the old monarchy and that right which the letter of the jurisconsults conferred on him. But what will be safe, they say, if no one maintains his rights? Let the prince insist by all means, if there is any advantage to the state, only do not let the right of the prince bear too hard on his subjects. But what is safe anywhere while everyone is maintaining his rights to the last ditch? We see wars arise from wars, wars following wars, and no end or limit to the upheaval! It is certainly obvious that nothing is accomplished by these means. Therefore other remedies should be given a trial. ...

If you are not moved by devotion, nor by the calamity of the world, surely you will be stirred by the honor of the term "Christian." What do we think the Turks and Saracens are saying about us when they see that for century after century there has been no harmony between Christian princes; that no treaties have secured peace; that there has been no end to bloodshed; and that there has been less disorder among the heathen than among those who profess the most complete accord in following the teachings of Christ? ...

If the whole teachings of Christ do not everywhere inveigh against war, if a single instance of specific commendation of war can be brought forth in its favor, let us Christians fight. The Hebrews were allowed to engage in war, but only by consent of God. Our oracle, which we hear steadily in the Gospels, restrains us from war, and yet we wage war more madly than they. David was most pleasing to God for various good qualities, and yet

He forbade His temple to be built by him on the one ground that he was tainted with blood; that is, he was a warrior. He chose the peaceful Solomon for his task. If these things were done among the Jews, what should be done among us Christians? They had a shadow of Solomon, we have the real Solomon, the Prince of Peace, Christ, who conciliates all things in heaven and earth.

Not even against the Turks do I believe we should rashly go to war, first reflecting in my own mind that the kingdom of Christ was created, spread out, and firmly established by far different means. Perchance then it is not right that it should be maintained by means differing from those by which it was created and extended. We see how many times under pretexts of wars of this kind the Christian people have been plundered and nothing else has been accomplished. Now, if the matter has to do with faith, that has been increased and made famous by the suffering of martyrs and not by forces of soldiery; but if it is for ruling power, wealth, and possessions, we must continuously be on guard lest the cause have too little of Christianity in it. But on the contrary, to judge from some who are conducting wars of this kind, it may more readily happen that we degenerate into Turks than that they become Christians through our efforts. First let us see that we ourselves are genuine Christians, and then, if it seems best, let us attack the Turks.

Menno Simons

Reply to False Accusations

We have heard the word of peace, namely, the consoling gospel of peace. We, by His grace, have believed and accepted it in peace and have committed ourselves to the only, eternal, and true Prince of peace, Christ Jesus, in His kingdom of peace and under His reign, and are thus by the gift of His Holy Spirit, by means of faith, incorporated into His body. And henceforth we look with all the children of His peace for the promised inheritance and reward of peace.

Such exceeding grace of God has appeared unto us poor, miserable sinners that we who were formerly no people at all and who knew of no peace are now called to be such a glorious people of God, a church, kingdom, inheritance, body, and possession of peace. Therefore we desire not to break this peace, but by His great power by which He has called us to his peace and portion, to walk in this grace and peace, unchangeably and unwaveringly unto death.

Peter was commanded to sheathe his sword. All Christians are commanded to love their enemies; to do good unto those who abuse and persecute them; to give the mantle when the cloak is taken, the other cheek when one is struck. Tell me, how can a Christian defend scripturally retaliation, rebellion, war, striking, slaying, torturing, stealing, robbing and plundering and burning cities, and conquering countries?

... True Christians do not know vengeance, no matter how they are mistreated. In patience they possess their souls (Luke 21:18). And they do not break their peace, even if they should be tempted by bondage, torture,

In The Complete Writings of Menno Simons (trans. L. Verduin and J. C. Wenger, 1956). Reprinted by permission of Herald Press.

poverty, and besides, by the sword and fire. They do not cry, Vengeance, vengeance, as does the world; but with Christ they supplicate and pray: Father, forgive them; for they know not what they do (Luke 23:34; Acts 7:60).

According to the declaration of the prophets they have beaten their swords into plowshares and their spears into prunning hooks. They shall sit every man under his vine and under his fig-tree, Christ; neither shall they learn war any more (Isa. 2:4; Mic. 4:3).

They do not seek your money, goods, injury, nor blood, but they seek the honor and praise of God and the salvation of your souls. They are the children of peace; their hearts overflow with peace; their mouths speak peace, and they walk in the way of peace; they are full of peace. They seek, desire, and know nothing but peace; and are prepared to forsake country, goods, life, and all for the sake of peace.

Reinhold Niebuhr

Why the Christian Church is not Pacifist

The thesis is, that the failure of the Church to espouse pacifism is not apostasy, but is derived from an understanding of the Christian Gospel which refuses simply to equate the Gospel with the "law of love." Christianity is not simply a new law, namely, the law of love. The finality of Christianity cannot be proved by analyses which seek to reveal that the law of love is stated more unambiguously and perfectly in the life and teachings of Christ than anywhere else. Christianity is a religion which measures the total dimension of human existence not only in terms of the final norm of human conduct, which is expressed in the law of love, but also in terms of the fact of sin. It recognizes that the same man who can become his true self only by striving infinitely for self-realization beyond himself is also inevitably involved in the sin of infinitely making his partial and narrow self the true end of existence. It believes, in other words, that though Christ is the true norm (the "second Adam") for every man, every man is also in some sense a crucifier of Christ.

The good news of the gospel is not the law that we ought to love one another. The good news of the gospel is that there is a resource of divine mercy which is able to overcome a contradiction within our own souls, which we cannot ourselves overcome. This contradiction is that, though we know we ought to love our neighbor as ourself, there is a "law in our members which wars against the law that is in our mind," so that, in fact, we love ourselves more than our neighbor.

The grace of God which is revealed in Christ is regarded by Christian faith as, on the one hand, an actual "power of righteousness" which heals

Reprinted in *The Essential Reinhold Niebuhr*, by Robert M. Brown, ed., 1990. Used by permission of Yale University Press.

the contradiction within our hearts. In that sense Christ defines the actual possibilities of human existence. On the other hand, this grace is conceived as "justification," as pardon rather than power, as the forgiveness of God, which is vouchsafed to man despite the fact that he never achieves the full measure of Christ. In that sense Christ is the "impossible possibility." Loyalty to him means realization in intention, but does not actually mean the full realization of the measure of Christ. In this doctrine of forgiveness and justification, Christianity measures the full seriousness of sin as a permanent factor in human history. Naturally, the doctrine has no meaning for modern secular civilization, nor for the secularized and moralistic versions of Christianity. They cannot understand the doctrine precisely because they believe there is some fairly simple way out of the sinfulness of human history. ...

It is not possible to regard pacifism simply as a heresy. In one of its aspects modern Christian pacifism is simply a version of Christian perfectionism. It expresses a genuine impulse in the heart of Christianity, the impulse to take the law of Christ seriously and not to allow the political strategies, which the sinful character of man makes necessary, to become final norms. In its profounder forms this Christian perfectionism did not proceed from a simple faith that the "law of love" could be regarded as an alternative to the political strategies by which the world achieves a precarious justice. These strategies invariably involve the balancing of power with power; and they never completely escape the peril of tyranny on the one hand, and the peril of anarchy and warfare on the other.

In medieval ascetic perfectionism and in Protestant sectarian perfectionism (of the type of Meno Simons, for instance) the effort to achieve a standard of perfect love in individual life was not presented as a political alternative. On the contrary, the political problem and task were specifically disavowed. This perfectionism did not give itself to the illusion that it had discovered a method for eliminating the element of conflict from political strategies. On the contrary, it regarded the mystery of evil as beyond its power of solution. It was content to set up the most perfect and unselfish individual life as a symbol of the Kingdom of God. It knew that this could only be done by disavowing the political task and by freeing the individual of all responsibility for social justice.

It is this kind of pacifism which is not a heresy. It is rather a valuable asset for the Christian faith. It is a reminder to the Christian community that the relative norms of social justice, which justify both coercion and resistance to coercion, are not final norms, and that Christians are in constant peril of forgetting their relative and tentative character and of making them too completely normative.

There is thus a Christian pacifism which is not a heresy. Yet most modern forms of Christian pacifism are heretical. Presumably inspired by the Christian gospel, they have really absorbed the Renaissance faith in the goodness of man, have rejected the Christian doctrine of original sin as an outmoded bit of pessimism, have reinterpreted the Cross so that it is made to stand for the absurd idea that perfect love is guaranteed a simple victory over the world. ... This form of pacifism is not only heretical when judged by the standards of the total gospel. It is equally heretical when judged by the facts of human existence. There are no historical realities which remotely conform to it. It is important to recognize this lack of conformity to the facts of experience as a criterion of heresy. ...

No religious faith can maintain itself in defiance of the experience which it supposedly interprets. A religious faith which substitutes faith in man for faith in God cannot finally validate itself in experience. If we believe that the only reason men do not love each other perfectly is because the law of love has not been preached persuasively enough, we believe something to which experience does not conform. If we believe that if Britain had only been fortunate enough to have produced 30 per cent instead of 2 per cent of conscientious objectors to military service, Hitler's heart would have been softened and he would not have dared to attack Poland, we hold a faith which no historic reality justifies.

Such a belief has no more justification in the facts of experience than the communist belief that the sole cause of man's sin is the class organization of society and the corollary faith that a "classless" society will be essentially free of human sinfulness. All of these beliefs are pathetic alternatives to the Christian faith. They all come finally to the same thing. They do not believe that man remains a tragic creature who needs the divine mercy as much at the end as at the beginning of his moral endeavors. They believe rather that there is some fairly easy way out of the human situation of "self-alienation." ...

The common element in these various expressions of faith in man is the belief that man is essentially good at some level of his being. They believe that if you can abstract the rational-universal man from what is finite and contingent in human nature, or if you can only cultivate some mystic-universal element in the deeper levels of man's consciousness, you will be able to eliminate human selfishness and the consequent conflict of life with life. These rational or mystical views of man conform neither to the New Testament's view of human nature nor yet to the complex facts of human experience.

In order to elaborate the thesis more fully, that the refusal of the Christian Church to espouse pacifism is not apostasy and that most modern forms of pacifism are heretical, it is necessary first of all to consider the character of the absolute and unqualified demands which Christ makes and to understand the relation of these demands to the gospel.

The injunction "resist not evil," "love your enemies," "if ye love them that love you what thanks have you?" "be not anxious for your life," and "be ye therefore perfect even as your father in heaven is perfect," are all of one piece, and they are all uncompromising and absolute. Nothing is more futile and pathetic than the effort of some Christian theologians who find it necessary to become involved in the relativities of politics, in resistance to tyranny or in social conflict, to justify themselves by seeking to prove that Christ was also involved in some of these relativities, that he used whips to drive the money-changers out of the Temple, or that he came not to bring peace but a sword. ...

Those of us who regard the ethic of Jesus as finally and ultimately normative, but as not immediately applicable to the task of securing justice in a sinful world, are very foolish if we try to reduce the ethic so that it will cover and justify our prudential and relative standards and strategies. To do this is to reduce the ethic to a new legalism. The significance of the law of love is precisely that it is not just another law, but a law which transcends all law. Every law and every standard which falls short of the law of love embodies contingent factors and makes concessions to the fact that sinful man must achieve tentative harmonies of life with life which are less than the best. It is dangerous and confusing to give these tentative and relative standards final and absolute religious sanction.

Curiously enough the pacifists are just as guilty as their less absolutist brethren of diluting the ethic of Jesus for the purpose of justifying their position. They are forced to recognize that an ethic of pure non-resistance can have no immediate relevance to any political situation; for in every political situation it is necessary to achieve justice by resisting pride and power. They therefore declare that the ethic of Jesus is not an ethic of non-resistance, but one of non-violent resistance; that it allows one to resist evil provided the resistance does not involve the destruction of life or property.

There is not the slightest support in Scripture for this doctrine of non-violence. Nothing could be plainer than that the ethic uncompromisingly enjoins non-resistance and not non-violent resistance. Furthermore, it is obvious that the distinction between violent and non-violent resistance is not an absolute distinction. If it is made absolute, we arrive at the morally absurd position of giving moral preference to the non-violent power which Doctor Goebbels wields over the type of power wielded by a general. ...

One may well concede that a wise and decent statesmanship will seek not only to avoid conflict, but to avoid violence in conflict. Parliamentary political controversy is one method of sublimating political struggles in such a way as to avoid violent collisions of interest. But this pragmatic distinction has nothing to do with the more basic distinction between the ethic of the "Kingdom of God," in which no concession is made to human sin, and all relative political strategies which, assuming human sinfulness, seek to secure the highest measure of peace and justice among selfish and sinful men.

If pacifists were less anxious to dilute the ethic of Christ to make it conform to their particular type of non-violent politics, and if they were less obsessed with the obvious contradiction between the ethic of Christ and the fact of war, they might have noticed that the injunction "resist not evil" is only part and parcel of a total ethic which we violate not only in war-time, but every day of our life, and that overt conflict is but a final and vivid revelation of the character of human existence. This total ethic can be summarized most succinctly in the two injunctions "Be not anxious for your life" and "love thy neighbor as thyself."

In the first of these, attention is called to the fact that the root and source of all undue self-assertion lies in the anxiety which all men have in regard to their existence. ... The fact is that anxiety is an inevitable concomitant of human freedom, and is the root of the inevitable sin which expresses itself in every human activity and creativity. Not even the most idealistic preacher who admonishes his congregation to obey the law of Christ is free of the sin which arises from anxiety. ...

That is the tragedy of human sin. It is the tragedy of man who is dependent upon God, but seeks to make himself independent and self-sufficing.

In the same way there is no life which is not involved in a violation of the injunction, "Thou shalt love thy neighbor as thyself." No one is so blind as the idealist who tells us that war would be unnecessary "if only" nations obeyed the law of Christ, but who remains unconscious of the fact that even the most saintly life is involved in some measure of contradiction to this law. ...

Do we not know that the sinful will-to-power may be compounded with the most ideal motives and may use the latter as its instruments and vehicles? The collective life of man undoubtedly stands on a lower moral plane than the life of individuals; yet nothing revealed in the life of races and nations is unknown in individual life. The sins of pride and of lust for power and the consequent tyranny and injustice are all present, at least in an inchoate form, in individual life. ...

The pacifists do not know human nature well enough to be concerned about the contradictions between the law of love and the sin of man, until sin has conceived and brought forth death. They do not see that sin introduces an element of conflict into the world and that even the most loving relations are not free of it. They are, consequently, unable to appreciate the complexity of the problem of justice. They merely assert that if only men loved one another, all the complex, and sometimes horrible, realities of the political order could be dispensed with. They do not see that their "if" begs the most basic problem of human history. It is because men are sinners that justice can be achieved only by a certain degree of coercion on the one hand, and by resistance to coercion and tyranny on the other hand. The political life of man must constantly steer between the Scylla of anarchy and the Charybdis of tyranny.

Human egotism makes large-scale co-operation upon a purely voluntary basis impossible. Governments must coerce. Yet there is an element of evil in this coercion. It is always in danger of serving the purposes of the coercing power rather than the general weal. We cannot fully trust the motives of any ruling class or power. That is why it is important to maintain democratic checks upon the centers of power. It may also be necessary to resist a ruling class, nation or race, if it violates the standards of relative justice which have been set up for it. Such resistance means war. It need not mean overt conflict or violence. But if those who resist tyranny publish their scruples against violence too publicly the tyrannical power need only threaten the use of violence against non-violent pressure to persuade the resisters to quiescence. (The relation of pacifism to the abortive effort to apply non-violent sanctions against Italy in the Ethiopian dispute is instructive at this point.)

The refusal to recognize that sin introduces an element of conflict into the world invariably means that a morally perverse preference is given to tyranny over anarchy (war). If we are told that tyranny would destroy itself, if only we would not challenge it, the obvious answer is that tyranny continues to grow if it is not resisted. If it is to be resisted, the risk of overt conflict must be taken. The thesis that German tyranny must not be challenged by other nations because Germany will throw off this yoke in due time, merely means that an unjustified moral preference is given to civil war over international war, for internal resistance runs the risk of conflict as much as external resistance. Furthermore, no consideration is given to the fact that a tyrannical State may grow too powerful to be successfully resisted by purely internal pressure, and that the injustices which it does to other than its own nationals may rightfully lay the problem of the tyranny upon other nations. ...

One of the most terrible consequences of a confused religious absolutism is that it is forced to condone such tyranny as that of Germany in the nations which it has conquered and now cruelly oppresses. It usually does this by insisting that the tyranny is no worse than that which is practised in the so-called democratic nations. Whatever may be the moral ambiguities of the so-called democratic nations, and however serious may be their failure to conform perfectly to their democratic ideals, it is sheer moral perversity to equate the inconsistencies of a democratic civilization with the brutalities which modern tyrannical States practise. If we cannot make a distinction here, there are no historical distinctions which have any value. All the distinctions upon which the fate of civilization has turned in the history of mankind have been just such relative distinctions. ...

The gospel is something more than the law of love. The gospel deals with the fact that men violate the law of love. The gospel presents Christ as the pledge and revelation of God's mercy which finds man in his rebellion and overcomes his sin.

The question is whether the grace of Christ is primarily a power of righteousness which so heals the sinful heart that henceforth it is able to fulfill the law of love; or whether it is primarily the assurance of divine mercy for a persistent sinfulness which man never overcomes completely. ...

Perhaps St. Paul could not be quite sure about where the emphasis was to be placed, for the simple reason that no one can be quite certain about the character of this ultimate peace [in Christ.] There must be, and there is, moral content in it, a fact which Reformation theology tends to deny and which Catholic and sectarian theology emphasizes. But there is never such perfect moral content in it that any man could find perfect peace through his moral achievements, not even the achievements which he attributes to grace rather than the power of his own will. This is the truth which the Reformation emphasized and which modern Protestant Christianity has almost completely forgotten.

We are, therefore, living in a state of sorry moral and religious confusion. In the very moment of world history in which every contemporary historical event justifies the Reformation emphasis upon the persistence of sin on every level of moral achievement, we not only identify Protestant faith with a moralistic sentimentality which neglects and obscures truths in the Christian gospel. ... but we even neglect those reservations and qualifications upon the theory of sanctification upon which classical Catholicism wisely insisted.

We have, in other words, reinterpreted the Christian gospel in terms of the Renaissance faith in man. Modern pacifism is merely a final fruit of this Renaissance spirit, which has pervaded the whole of modern Protestantism. We have interpreted world history as a gradual ascent to the Kingdom of God which waits for final triumph only upon the willingness of Christians to "take Christ seriously." There is nothing in Christ's own teachings, except dubious interpretations of the parable of the leaven and the mustard seed, to justify this interpretation of world history. ...

The New Testament does not, in other words, envisage a simple triumph of good over evil in history. It sees human history involved in the contradictions of sin to the end. That is why it sees no simple resolution of the problem of history. It believes that the Kingdom of God will finally resolve the contradictions of history; but for it the Kingdom of God is no simple historical possibility. The grace of God for man and the Kingdom of God for history are both divine realities and not human possibilities.

The Christian faith believes that the Atonement reveals God's mercy as an ultimate resource by which God alone overcomes the judgment which sin deserves. If this final truth of the Christian religion has no meaning to modern men, including modern Christians, that is because even the tragic character of contemporary history has not yet persuaded them to take the fact of human sinfulness seriously.

The contradiction between the law of love and the sinfulness of man raises not only the ultimate religious problem how men are to have peace if they do not overcome the contradiction, and how history will culminate if the contradiction remains on every level of historic achievement; it also raises the immediate problem how men are to achieve a tolerable harmony of life with life, if human pride and selfishness prevent the realization of the law of love. ...

To look at human communities from the perspective of the Kingdom of God is to know that there is a sinful element in all the expedients which the political order uses to establish justice. That is why even the seemingly most stable justice degenerates periodically into either tyranny or anarchy. But it must also be recognized that it is not possible to eliminate the sinful element in the political expedients. They are, in the words of St. Augustine, both the consequence of, and the remedy for, sin. If they are the remedy for sin, the ideal of love is not merely a principle of indiscriminate criticism upon all approximations of justice. It is also a principle of discriminate criticism between forms of justice.

As a principle of indiscriminate criticism upon all forms of justice, the law of love reminds us that the injustice and tyranny against which we contend in the foe is partially the consequence of our own injustice, that the pathology of modern Germans is partially a consequence of the vindictiveness of the peace of Versailles, and that the ambition of a tyrannical imperialism is different only in degree and not in kind from the imperial impulse which characterizes all of human life.

The Christian faith ought to persuade us that political controversies are always conflicts between sinners and not between righteous men and sinners. ... It cannot be denied that the Christian conscience failed terribly in restraining vengeance after the last war. It is also quite obvious that the natural inclination to self-righteousness was the primary force of his vengeance (expressed particularly in the war guilt clause of the peace treaty). The pacifists draw the conclusion from the fact that justice is never free from vindictiveness, that we ought not for this reason ever to contend against a foe. This argument leaves out of account that capitulation to the foe might well subject us to a worse vindictiveness. It is as foolish to imagine that the foe is free of the sin which we deplore in ourselves as it is to regard ourselves as free of the sin which we deplore in the foe.

The fact that our own sin is always partly the cause of the sins against which we must contend is regarded by simple moral purists as proof that we have no right to contend against the foe. They regard the injection "Let him who is without sin cast the first stone" as a simple alternative to the schemes of justice which society has devised and whereby it prevents the worst forms of anti-social conduct. This injunction of Christ ought to remind every judge and every juridical tribunal that the crime of the criminal is partly the consequence of the sins of society. But if pacifists are to be consistent they ought to advocate the abolition of the whole judicial process in society. ... Yet we cannot dispense with it; and we will have to continue to put criminals into jail. There is a point where the final cause of the criminal's anti-social conduct becomes a fairly irrelevant issue in comparison with the task of preventing his conduct from injuring innocent fellows.

The ultimate principles of the Kingdom of God are never irrelevant to any problem of justice, and they hover over every social situation as an ideal possibility; but that does not mean that they can be made into simple alternatives for the present schemes of relative justice. The thesis that the so-called democratic nations have no right to resist overt forms of tyranny, because their own history betrays imperialistic motives, would have meaning only if it were possible to achieve a perfect form of justice in any nation and to free national life completely of the imperialistic motive. This is impossible; for imperialism is the collective expression of the sinful will-to-power which characterizes all human existence. The pacifist argument on this issue betrays how completely pacifism gives itself to illusions about the stuff with which it is dealing in human nature. ...

Justice is basically dependent upon a balance of power. Whenever an individual or group or a nation possesses undue power, and whenever this power is not checked by the possibility of criticizing and resisting it, it grows inordinate. The equilibrium of power upon which every structure of justice rests would degenerate into anarchy but for the organizing center which controls it. One reason why the balances of power, which prevent injustice in international relations, periodically degenerate into overt anarchy is because no way has yet been found to establish an adequate organizing center, a stable international judicatory, for this balance of power.

A balance of power is something different from, and inferior to, the harmony of love. It is a basic condition of justice, given the sinfulness of man. Such a balance of power does not exclude love. In fact, without love the frictions and tensions of a balance of power would become intolerable. But without the balance of power even the most loving relations may degenerate into unjust relations, and love may become the screen which hides the injustice. ...

There is no perfectly adequate method of preventing either anarchy or tyranny. But obviously the justice established in the so-called democratic nations represents a high degree of achievement; and the achievement becomes the more impressive when it is compared with the tyranny into which alternative forms of society have fallen. The obvious evils of tyranny, however will not inevitably persuade the victims of economic anarchy in democratic society to eschew tyranny. When men suffer from anarchy they may foolishly regard the evils of tyranny as the lesser evils. Yet the evils of tyranny in fascist and communist nations are so patent, that we may dare to hope that what is still left of democratic civilizations will not lightly sacrifice the virtues of democracy for the sake of escaping its defects. ...

Any social structure in which power has been made responsible, and in which anarchy has been overcome by methods of mutual accommodation, is preferable to either anarchy or tyranny. If it is not possible to express a moral preference for the justice achieved in democratic societies, in comparison with tyrannical societies, no historical preference has any meaning. This kind of justice approximates the harmony of love more than either anarchy or tyranny.

If we do not make discriminate judgments between social systems we weaken the resolution to defend and extend civilization. Pacifism either tempts us to make no judgments at all, or to give an undue preference to tyranny in comparison with the momentary anarchy which is necessary to overcome tyranny. ... The defeat of Germany and the frustration of the Nazi effort to unify Europe in tyrannical terms is a negative task. It does not guarantee the emergence of a new Europe with a higher level of international cohesion and new organs of international cohesion and new organs of international justice. But it is a negative task which cannot be avoided. All schemes for avoiding this negative task rest upon illusions about human nature. Specifically, these illusions express themselves in the failure to understand the stubbornness and persistence of the tyrannical will, once it is fully conceived. ...

A simple Christian moralism is senseless and confusing. It is senseless when, as in the World War, it seeks uncritically to identify the cause of Christ with the cause of democracy without a religious reservation. It is just as senseless when it seeks to purge itself of this error by an uncritical refusal to make any distinctions between relative values in history. The fact is that we might as well dispense with the Christian faith, entirely if it is our conviction that we can act in history only if we are guiltless. This means that we must either prove our guiltlessness in order to be able to act; or refuse to act because we cannot achieve guiltlessness. Self-righteousness or inaction are the alternatives of secular moralism. If they are also the only alternatives of Christian moralism, one rightly suspects that Christian faith has become diluted with secular perspectives.

In its profoundest insights the Christian faith sees the whole of human history as involved in guilt, and finds no release from guilt except in the grace of God. The Christian is freed by that grace to act in history; to give his devotion to the highest values he knows; to defend those citadels of civilization of which necessity and historic destiny have made him the defender; and he is persuaded by that grace to remember the ambiguity of even his best actions. If the providence of God does not enter the affairs of men to bring good out of evil, the evil in our good may easily destroy our most ambitious efforts and frustrate our highest hopes.

… It is a terrible thing to take human life. The conflict between man and man and nation is tragic. If there are men who declare that, no matter what the consequences, they cannot bring themselves to participate in this slaughter, the Church ought to be able to say to the general community: We quite understand this scruple and we respect it. It proceeds from the conviction that the true end of man is brotherhood, and that love is the law of life. We who allow ourselves to become engaged in war need this testimony of the absolutist against us, lest we accept the warfare of the world as normative, lest we become callous to the horror of war, and lest we forget the ambiguity of our own actions and motives and the risk we run of achieving no permanent good from this momentary anarchy in which we are involved. …

[But] a pacifism which really springs from the Christian faith, without secular accretions and corruptions, could not be as certain as modern pacifism is that it possesses an alternative for the conflicts and tensions from which and through which the world must rescue a precarious justice. …

Lyman Abbott

Christianity and Social Problems

The first principle finds its clearest statement in the following passage: "But I say unto you that ye resist not evil; but whosoever shall smite thee on thy right cheek, turn to him the other also. And if any man will sue thee at the law and take away thy coat, let him have thy cloak also. And whosoever shall compel thee to go a mile, go with him twain."

A careful scrutiny of this direction makes it clear that it covers the three forms of wrong under which men suffer, – personal violence, legal injustice, governmental oppression. To smite on the right cheek is an act of personal violence; to attempt by law to take away one's coat is an act of legal injustice; to impress one to go a mile in public service without compensation is an act of governmental oppression. Such impressment, permitted by modern society only in times of war, was formerly allowed to the government in time of peace. Christ, referring to these forms of wrong, – personal violence, legal injustice, governmental oppression, – bids his followers oppose to them only a passive non-resistance. He sets in operation a new force in the world, what Milton has well called "the irresistable might of meekness." This might was before Christ's time almost absolutely unknown.

If these instructions were not in themselves perfectly clear, they are made so by the interpretation which he has put upon them by his life. The despotic government under which he lives sends out its officers to arrest him. He surrenders himself and is led away. And when one of his own disciples would resist the band, though he says, "I could have twelve legions of angels to rescue me," he will not. He condemns resistance. "They

---

Johnson Reprint Corporation, 1970. Used by permission.

that take the sword shall perish with the sword." He is brought into the court. ... The High Priest calls Jesus to the stand and administers the oath to him: "I adjure thee by the living God that thou tell us whether thou be the Son of God or no." He protests: "If I tell you, you will not believe me." Yet he submits, testifies under oath that he is the Son of God, and is led away to his death. In this trial, and following it, he is beaten, spit upon, scourged. He protests, but does not resist. To each of these three forms of wrong he submits, – the wrong of a despotic government, the wrong of a court of law, the wrong of personal violence. ... Yet Christ sometimes did resist wrong-doing. When he went up to the Temple, a corrupt and wicked government had put cattle in the one court, where the Gentiles might go. He did not merely utter a verbal protest against it; he wove a whip of small cords of the straw that was at his feet and drove the frightened traders from the Temple, and with them the cattle, and overturned the money-changers' tables, and left the money to roll about the floor. When the Temple band came to arrest him, and his disciples were asleep before the gate, he went forward and put himself between the band and the disciples. They fell backward to the ground, it is said. For the moment he confronted the guard and held it at bay, that his disciples might escape, and then, and not till then, surrendered himself. Christ used force to defend others, but never to defend himself. The fundamental principle in Christ's teaching is this: Love may use force; selfishness may not. ...

Christianity, then, and war are absolutely inconsistent. Christianity proposes, as the method of settling all contests, an appeal to reason: first, in the contestants; then, if that fails, in an impartial tribunal. War prefers appeal to force. For war is not mere chance quarreling. It is the publicly recognized method of settling quarrels between nations. It is provided for and brought under the regulation of international law. ... Legitimate war is carried on under the sanction of international law. This law determines measureably what is a proper occasion for war; what notice of war should be given before the first offensive act; how that notice should be given; who are combatants and who are non-combatants; what are the rights of non-combatants, and under what rules and regulations the war may be prosecuted. ... International law determines ... the conditions under which war may be declared and carried on; and the avowed object of this war between nations is to establish justice between them. ...

It is the object of Christianity to abolish trial by battle between nations, as it has already abolished trial by battle between individuals, – not merely to mitigate the horrors of war, not merely to reduce the occasions of war, not merely to lessen the preparations for war, but to put an end to public war absolutely, as it has put an end to private war absolutely. Fights there still are between individuals, but the right to fight is not recognized by law. Fights there may still continue to be between nations, but the right to fight will not be recognized by international law when Christianity has wrought among the nations what it has wrought within the nations. ... When Christianity has achieved its mission, nations also will go unarmed. They will also submit their controversies to an impartial tribunal, and trust for their protection to the coöperation of the nations of Christendom. ... Law gives might to right; war gives might for right; law establishes justice, war simply demonstrates power; law evokes the judgment, war organizes the passions; law is civilization, war is barbarism. ...

How shall the decisions of such a court be enforced? How have the decisions of courts of international arbitration been enforced? Not by authority from above, but by authority from below. As Daniel Webster eloquently pointed out, there is a power in public opinion. Neither the United States nor Great Britain would be sustained by its own people in refusal to abide by the decision of an impartial tribunal in which an issue between the two countries had once been submitted by mutual agreement. ...

Two causes provoke war, – one, human passion, too hot and hasty to pause for consideration; law restrains such passion, and calls on the reason to act; the other, the absence of any other remedy for real or fancied injustice; law provides such other remedy, and the passion dies for want of fuel to feed it. ...

The issue between war and law has been decided by civilization in favor of law for settlement of all personal controversies. War has been brought under law in international controversies, but the consummation of Christian progress will not be attained until law is substituted for war, reason for force, the spiritual for the animal, Christianity for barbarism.

United Methodist Bishops

In Defense of Creation

Shalom in Creation, Covenant, and Community

At the heart of the Old Testament is the testimony to *shalom*, that marvelous Hebrew word that means peace. ... *Shalom* is positive peace: harmony, wholeness, health, and well-being in all human relationships. It is the natural state of humanity as birthed by God. It is harmony between humanity and all of God's good creation. All of creation is interrelated. Every creature, every element, every force of nature participates in the whole of creation. If any person is denied *shalom*, all are thereby diminished.

To speak of the sovereignty of God over all nations and peoples is to testify to this ordering of the whole creation by the goodness and peaceable will of God. It is therefore to discern the inescapable reality of moral law in the universe. The creation is not a realm of chaos or meaninglessness, however much persons or nations may cause anarchy by their own behavior. This cosmic drama of moral struggle among the nations has been a persistent biblical theme in Methodist teaching about the fallenness of sinful human creatures. ... Human sinfulness is, according to Scripture, a warrant for government, law enforcement, and defense against enemies – and also a warning against the iniquity of governors themselves.

Throughout both Testaments, there is a dual attitude toward political authority. The powers of government are legitimate expressions of the creation's natural order of political community among God's children, as well as constraints upon human sinfulness. Their authority is thus from

---

In Defense of Creation: The Nuclear Crisis and a Just Peace, 1986, 24–48. Used by permission.

God – at least provisionally. Rulers are ordinarily to be obeyed. Taxes are ordinarily to be paid. But the moral law implanted in creation transcends the laws of any state or empire. When governors themselves become oppressive and lawless, when they presume to usurp the sovereignty that belongs to God alone, they are rightly subject to criticism, to correction, and ultimately, to resistance.

For love of his own nation and people, Jeremiah speaks boldly against his kings for their false gods, religious pride, militaristic adventures, and forced labor to build luxurious palaces. For that he is seized by priests, called a traitor, beaten, jailed, and thrown into a slimy cistern. Through such faithful prophets, we know that patriotism is not only to be found on a battlefield against the enemies of one's nation but can also be courageously expressed in a struggle of resistance against the inhumanities of one's own government. Jeremiah foreshadows another prophet, a prophet of a new convenant, who, six centuries later, for the love of his people, would warn his followers that they too would be dragged before governing authorities, even as he would be – a prophet who would be beaten and nailed to a cross.

The Old Testament speaks of God's sovereignty in terms of *covenant*, more particularly the "covenant of peace" with Israel, which binds that people to God's *shalom* (Isaiah 54:10; Ezekiel 37:26). In the covenant of *shalom*, there is no contradiction between justice and peace or between peace and security or between love and justice (Jeremiah 29:7). In Isaiah's prophecy, when "the Spirit is poured upon us from on high," we will know that these laws of God are one and indivisible:

Then justice will dwell in the wilderness,
    and righteousness abide in the fruitful field.
And the effect of righteousness will be peace. ... (Is. 32:16)

Shalom, then, is the sum total of moral and spiritual qualities in a community whose life is in harmony with God's good creation. It indicates an alternative community – alternative to the idolatries, oppressions, and violence that mark the ways of many nations. Israel's mission is to live out that alternative pattern of life in the world.

When the rulers fulfill the covenant of *shalom*, they will know that there is no true security without peace and no true peace without justice. When, on the contrary, they seek unjustly to enhance their own security and tell lies to justify their military ambitions, they will bring down violence and devastation instead of security or peace:

You have plowed iniquity, you have reaped injustice ...
Because you have trusted in your chariots
   and in the multitude of your warriors,
therefore the tumult of war shall arise among your
   people. (Hosea 10:13–14)

The sovereignty of God means that vengeance in human hands is evil.
When in the Song of Moses Yahweh proclaims "vengeance is mine," the
message is not that God is violent but rather that the people of God have no
right to usurp God's powers of ultimate judgment (Deuteronomy 32:35).
We believe that particular biblical truth is directly relevant to ethical attitudes toward nuclear weapons.

To be sure, the Old Testament tells of much violence and warfare. In
Israel's earliest traditions Yahweh is often portrayed as a warrior. God's
victory over Pharaoh and the Egyptians to liberate Hebrew slaves discloses
God's implacable opposition to oppression and injustice, which violate
shalom. Exodus is liberation.

But liberation from oppression is hardly on the same moral plane as the
building up of standing armies for nationalistic expansion and the oppression of weaker nations. It is when the elders of Israel forsake their moral
covenant for warrior-kings that the nation begins its dismal descent into
generations of exploitation, repression, and aggression – and then into
chaos and captivity. Yahweh, the Creator, the Sovereign One, the transcendent God of the Covenant, becomes reduced to a domesticated and nationalistic idol. ... Destruction and exile come upon Jerusalem precisely as
God's judgment upon nationalistic pride, religious arrogance, and excessive
confidence in military power. Exile in Babylon is more than the loss of a
war; it is the collapse of an illusion that military power, unrestrained by
shalom, can offer security, peace, and prosperity.

We must look to the great prophets of that bitter period of Exile for the
renewed vision of *shalom.* If Exodus is liberation, Exile is renewal. Ezekiel
and Isaiah reaffirm God's creation and redemption as universal in scope.
Narrow nationalism is repudiated. Servanthood is exalted. ... Swords into
plowshares, arms converted to food and death to life, no more wars or
training for wars, peaceable kingdoms. ... These are the radiant images of
shalom at the visionary heights of Old Testament prophecy. With these
images we know that the Bible is really one Book. The images forecast the
coming of One who will be the Prince of Peace. ...

He invokes the most special blessings upon peacemakers. He exalts the humanity of aliens. He commands us to love our enemies; for he knows, even if we do not, that if we hate our enemies, we blind and destroy ourselves. *Shalom*, after all, is the heart of God and the law of creation. ...

New Testament faith presupposes a radical break between the follies, or much so-called conventional wisdom about power and security, on the one hand, and the transcendent wisdom of *shalom*, on the other. Ultimately, New Testament faith is a message of hope about God's plan and purpose for human destiny. ...

Paul's letters announce that Jesus Christ is "our peace." It is Christ who has "broken down the dividing wall of hostility," creating one humanity, overcoming enmity, so making peace (Ephesians 2:14–19). It is Christ who ordains a ministry of reconciliation. Repentance prepares us for reconciliation. Then we shall open ourselves to the transforming power of God's grace in Christ. Then we shall know what it means to be "in Christ." Then we are to become ambassadors of a new creation, a new Kingdom, a new order of love and justice (2 Corinthians 5:17–20). It is Christ who has "disarmed the principalities and powers and made a public example of them, triumphing over them in him" (Colossians 2:15). To be citizens of this new Kingdom means that Christians are subject to conflicting loyalties – loyalty to one's nation and its government and a transcending loyalty to the "Governor of the whole universe" (John Wesley's term), whose laws may compel us to challenge our nation and its policies.

In Jesus Christ we know, when confronted with such conflicting loyalties, how costly the grace of God can be. This "only begotten Son" is sacrificed in a controversy with imperial and religious authorities so that we may know the full measure of God's love for us, even in our sinfulness, even when we crucify the Christ in our brothers and sisters. Yet we may still come to know that life never really ends but is transformed by eternal grace. Jesus never resorted to violence in his own defense. Somehow he had the power to forgive even his own killers. The Crucifixion is an eternal testimony to the transcendent power of forgiving love and nonviolence.

The Crucifixion was initially a political event – and a seeming defeat at that – but it quickly became transformed into a theological event, the ultimate act of our redemption. Christ is forever "making peace by the blood of his cross" (Colossians 1:19–20). Beyond all brutality, suffering, and death, God's costly gift of peace awaits us. Peace is the ultimate victory. ...

The Diversity of Traditions

Despite the biblical heritage of *shalom*, there has been a conspicious lack of harmony among Christians, especially since the fourth century, concerning the ethics of war and peace. Disharmonies have not simply represented the varied opinions of biblical scholars and theologians; they have reflected national, cultural, and class perceptions and prejudices. They have been expressed in public controversy and civil strife, even to the repression and persecution of Christian dissenters. They have been most horribly invoked in murderous crusades and bloody Wars of Religion.

Over the centuries three classical positions developed among Christian thinkers and church bodies: pacifism, "just-war" doctrine, and the crusade. ...

The early church of the first four centuries was predominantly pacifist. For most Christians, being pacifist meant opposition to all killing, military service, and warfare. Their scriptural seriousness and their historical proximity to Jesus and his immediate followers have remained a persuasive warrant for the pacifist witness ever since.

Justin Martyr (about A.D. 100–165) announced that Jesus Christ was the fulfillment of Isaiah's promise of peace. Christians, therefore, have "in every part of the world converted our weapons of war into implements of peace – our swords into plowshares, our spears into farmers' tools. ..." This unwillingness of Christians to fight in the military campaigns of the Roman Empire evoked a severe scolding in A. D. 178 from Celsus, a pagan critic: "If everyone were to do the same as you, there would nothing to prevent [the king] from being abandoned, alone and deserted, while earthly things would come into the power of the most lawless and savage barbarians. ..."

There were surely other reasons for this early pacifism, reasons such as rejection of the idolatry of emperor-worship, which was required in the military oath of allegiance; the generally sectarian, nonpolitical orientation of church life within the empire; and an apocalyptic expectation of the end of the world.

However, the pacifist tradition outlived the Roman Empire and the Constantinian establishment of Christianity in the fourth century. ... Renaissance Christianity, was graced with the pacifist testimony of the brilliant Erasmus of Rotterdam (1466–1536). His tract, *The Complaint of Peace*, marveled at the peaceableness of subhuman creatures among their own kind, in contrast to the warring tendencies of humans, even Christians.

Among Erasmus's recommendations were procedures for peaceful arbitration and clergy abstention from military rituals.

The Protestant Reformation, like the fifteen preceding centuries, bequeathed a mixed legacy concerning peacemaking. Though neither Luther nor Calvin, nor Zwingli could be called pacifist, the Reformation eventually generated several new religious communities that have come to be known collectively as the "historic peace churches" because of their pacifist founders and credos. Among them are Mennonites, the Church of the Brethren, and the Society of Friends (Quakers). ...

Pacifism in this century has received powerful reinforcement from nonwhite, non-Western, and non-Christian sources. While not exclusively identified with pacifism, the nonviolent philosophies of Mahatma Gandhi, Toyohiko Kagawa, Martin Luther King, Jr., Albert Luthuli, and Desmond Tutu have helped make pacifism more credible to our generation. Nonviolent strategies of social change, civilian defense, and conflict resolution have become increasingly sophisticated and systematic, inviting the most serious attention from academic, governmental, and religious leaders. ...

The courage and endurance of the pacifist tradition have not prevented most Christians and virtually all governments from appealing to nonpacifist principles in support of military establishments and the resort to war. For many Christians the principle that matters most has been obedience to whatever their government commands. ...

We believe it is a serious mistake to identify just-war doctrine with the "blank-check" option. It is surely true that just-war principles (and even pacifist language) have all too frequently rationalized unjust wars and brutal policies. We are also persuaded that just-war morality provides too narrow a base from which to discern many of the most salient issues in the nuclear crisis.

We cannot agree, however, with those who claim that nuclear weapons have simply nullified the just-war tradition altogether. That tradition remains a morally earnest restraint on the resort to war, a summons to peaceful settlement, and a guide to humane conduct in the event of war. Just-war criteria provided many young nonpacifist Americans with an ethical basis for challenging US policies in Indochina and for formulating a position of selective conscientious objection, which has been repeatedly validated in United Methodist pronouncements. ...

The principal criteria of the just-war tradition evolved over many centuries, beginning with Saint Ambrose and Saint Augustine in the fourth and fifth centuries, and were elaborated by Saint Thomas Aquinas and other moral philosophers in the medieval and modern periods. A distinction was made between principles concerning the *just resort to war (jus ad bellum)* and those concerning *just conduct in war (jus in bello)*.

The five most common *jus ad bellum* principles are:

(1) Just cause. A decision for war must vindicate justice itself in response to some serious evil, such as an aggressive attack.

(2) Just intent. The ends sought in a decision for war must include the restoration of peace with justice and must not seek self-aggrandizement or the total devastation of another nation.

(3) Last resort. The tradition shares with pacifism a moral presumption against going to war – but is prepared to make exceptions. Every possibility of peaceful settlement of a conflict must be tried before war is begun.

(4) Legitimate authority. A decision for war may be made and declared only by properly constituted governmental authority.

(5) Reasonable hope of success. A decision for war must be based on a prudent expectation that the ends sought can be achieved. It is hardly an act of justice to plunge one's people into the suffering and sacrifice of a suicidal conflict.

The two main *jus in bello* principles are:

(6) Discrimination. Justice in the actual conduct of war requires respect for the rights of enemy peoples, especially for the immunity of non-combatants from direct attack. Such respect also rules out atrocities, reprisals, looting, and wanton violence.

(7) Proportionality. The amount of damage inflicted must be strictly proportionate to the ends sought. Small-scale injuries should not be avenged by massive suffering, death and devastation. The war's harm must not exceed the war's good. (Proportionality is also a criterion to be applied to *jus ad bellum* – the decision whether to resort to war in the first place. …)

First, we are convinced that no actual use of nuclear weapons offers any *reasonable hope of success* in achieving a just peace. Whether the "mere" possession of such weapons, with an explicit or implicit threat to use them, is morally justifiable again raises the topic of deterrence, which we shall be discussing in Chapter 2.

Second, we believe that the principle of *discrimination*, whatever the intention of political and military leaders, is bound to be horribly violated in any likely use of nuclear weapons not only because of the widespread effects of blast, fire, fallout, and environmental damage but also because of the unlikelihood that any resort to nuclear weapons by major powers can result in a strictly controlled or "limited" nuclear war. The consequences are likely to be global.

Third, we cannot imagine that the norm of *proportionality* can be meaningfully honored in a nuclear war, since such a war could not be waged with any realistic expectation of doing more good than harm.

These considerations posed by the still-valuable just-war tradition require us to say *No*, a clear and unconditioned *No*, to nuclear war and to any use of nuclear weapons.

But our *No* to nuclear war and weapons is more than a matter of ethical calculation. It is a refusal to participate in that nuclear idolatry that presumes to usurp the sovereignty of the God of *shalom* over all the nations and peoples. Vengeful judgment and mass destruction are clearly contrary to the will of God and to the moral order of creation. ...

The fusion of political and religious authority in the Middle Ages fostered a third Christian tradition in matters of war and peace: crusades against infidels. The capture of Jerusalem's holy places by the Turks at the end of the eleventh century was cited to make warfare itself a holy cause. ... Unlike the pacifist and just-war traditions, which share a moral presumption against war, the crusade assumes that an unrestrained conduct of war is a religious obligation. A holy war need not stop to count the casualties on either side; "higher" values are at stake. The sixteenth century's Wars of Religion turned the crusade tradition inward and produced Christian massacres by fellow Christians.

If the crusade tradition seems today like a quaint relic of past centuries, we forget the excess of self-righteousness and the barbarism with which almost all modern wars have been waged. Moral restraints have been overwhelmed; and poison gas, fire raids, nuclear weapons, and napalm have been used. ...

A Theology for a Just Peace: Guiding Principles. ...

1. Perfect peace is beyond human power; it is that grace that is the whole of God's love in action. For Christians, that grace is ultimately the gift of God through Jesus Christ.

2. Every person of every race in every nation is a sacred being, made in God's image, entitled to full participation in the *shalom* of God's good creation – to life and peace, health and freedom.

3. Peacemaking is a sacred calling of the gospel, especially blessed by God, making us evangelists of *shalom* – peace that is overflowing with justice, compassion, and well-being.

4. God's gift of genuine freedom to humanity includes the possibility of humanity's self-destruction.

5. Peacemaking in the nuclear age, under the sovereignty of God, requires the defense of creation itself against possible assaults that may be rationalized in the name of "national defense."

6. Government is a natural institution of human community in God's creation as well as a requirement for the restraint of human evil.

7. Every policy of government must be an act of justice and must be measured by its impact on the poor, the weak, and the oppressed – not only in our own nation but in all nations.

8. Loyalty to one's own government is always subject to the transcendent loyalty that belongs to the Sovereign God. ...

9. Security is not only a legitimate concern but also an imperative responsibility of governments for the protection of life and well-being. But the security of which biblical prophets speak cannot be separated from the moral imperatives of justice and peace and the full range of basic human needs.

10. Security is indivisible in a world threatened with total annihilation. Unilateral security is impossible in the nuclear age.

11. The transformation of our conflict-ridden nation-state system into a new world order of common security and interdependent institutions offers the only practical hope for enduring peace.

12. No nation may presume the powers of ultimate judgment on the fate of other nations, even to their destruction.

13. The Gospel command to love enemies is more than a benevolent ideal; it is essential to our own well-being and even to our survival. ...

16. All Christians, pacifists and nonpacifists alike, ought to share a strong moral presumption against violence, killing, and warfare, seeking every possible means of peaceful conflict resolution.

17. Any just resort to coercive force must seek the restoration of peace with justice, refrain from directly attacking noncombatants, and avoid causing more harm than good.

18. No just cause can warrant the waging of nuclear war or any use of nuclear weapons. ...

Traditional Pacifism

Those who conscientiously repudiate all warfare and weapons of war have a clear answer to the question of nuclear weapons: No – no production, no possession, no deployment, no use. From this perspective, nuclear deterrence is illegitimate and immoral because it rationalizes the possession, if not the use, of the weapons themselves ... the endurance of this tradition among a sizable minority of Christians point to a fundamental question of the nuclear age: Can any major war remain non-nuclear? If not, hasn't rejection of war itself become an imperative for all our churches? . ...

We therefore reject war as an instrument of national foreign policy and insist that the first moral duty of all nations is to resolve by peaceful means every dispute that arises between or among them; that human values must outweigh military claims as governments determine their priorities; that the militarization of society must be challenged and stopped; that the manufacture, sale, and deployment of armaments must be reduced and controlled; and that the production, possession, or use of nuclear weapons be condemned.

Nuclear Pacifism

Some Christians support conventional military forces and remain open to the possible justice or necessary evil of some wars or revolutions but say No to all nuclear wars and weapons. For them the "nuclear threshold" is an absolute moral boundary that must never be crossed. They may appeal to the historic prerequisites of a "just war" in Christian tradition, such as proportionality and civilian immunity, in judging that nuclear weapons are too destructive ever to serve the ends of justice. Or, oppositely, they may come to the conviction that the just-war tradition itself has been made obsolete by the enormity of any nuclear conflict.

A position of virtual nuclear pacifism ... was set forth by the World Council of Churches in 1983: We believe that the time has come when the churches must unequivocally declare that the production and deployment

as well as the use of nuclear wepons are a crime against humanity and that
such activities must be condemned on ethical and theological grounds. [The
WCC] rejected the doctrine of nuclear deterrence as "morally unacceptable
and as incapable of safeguarding peace and security in the long-term."

Yes/No Deterrence

While nuclear pacifists draw the moral line between conventional and
nuclear weapons, others draw the line between possession of nuclear
weapons and their actual use. They say Yes to having them but No to
using them. They are prepared to maintain a nuclear arsenal for its presumed deterrent effect but they have absolute scruples against using the
weapons. ...

Critics of this position have dubbed it "bluff deterrence" (or even "clergy
deterrence") because its proponents are not really prepared to retaliate. The
credibility of yes/no deterrence is therefore a vexing question.

No First Use/Deterrence

Another moral boundary is drawn by those who approve of the possession
and possible use of nuclear weapons, but absolutely oppose any use of
them against a conventional attack. This restriction of nuclear retaliation to
only a nuclear attack is termed a "no-first-use" policy. ...

In June 1982, Pope John Paul II offered an extraordinary moral justification for nuclear weapons:

> In current conditions "deterrence" based on balance, certainly not as an end in itself
> but as a step on the way toward a progressive disarmament, may still be judged
> morally acceptable. Nonetheless in order to ensure peace, it is indispensable not to
> be satisfied with this minimum which is always susceptible to the real danger of
> explosion. ...

Charles Krauthammer

On Nuclear Morality

The contemporary antinuclear argument takes two forms. There is, first, the prudential argument that the nuclear balance is inherently unstable and unsustainable over time, doomed to breakdown and to taking us with it. ...
There has been a subtle shift in emphasis to a second line of attack, from a concern about what nuclear weapons might do to our bodies to a concern about what they are doing to our souls. Medical lectures on "the last epidemic" have been replaced by a sharper, and more elevated, debate about the ethics of possessing, building, and threatening to use nuclear weapons. (The most recent and highly publicized document on the subject is the Pastoral Letter of the U.S. Bishops on War and Peace.) ... The moral antinuclear argument is based on the view that deterrence, the central strategic doctrine of the nuclear age, is ethically impermissible. ...

The Argument against Deterrence

The doctrine of deterrence holds that a nuclear aggressor will not act if faced with a threat of retaliation in kind. It rests, therefore, on the willingness to use nuclear weapons in response to attack. The moral critique of deterrence holds that the actual use of such weapons, even in retaliation, is never justified. As the bishops put it, simply, one is morally obliged to "say no to nuclear war." But the issues are not so simple. There are different kinds of retaliation, and different arguments (often advanced by different proponents) for the inadmissibility of each.

From R. James Woolsey, *Nuclear Arms: Ethics, Strategy, Politics*, Institute for Contemporary Studies, 1984, 11–21. Used by permission.

The popularly accepted notion of deterrence (often mistakenly assumed to be the only kind) is "countervalue" retaliation – an attack on industrial and population centers aimed at destroying the society of the aggressor. The threat to launch such retaliation is the basis of the doctrine of "mutual assured destruction," also known as MAD, massive retaliation or the balance of terror. It is a balance constructed of paradox: weapons are built in order never to be used; purely defensive weapons, like antiballistic missile systems, are viewed as more threatening to peace than offensive weapons; weapons aimed at people are thought to lessen the risk of war while weapons aimed at weapons are thought to increase it.

For [the Bishops], MAD is unequivocally bad. Deliberate attacks on "soft targets" grossly violate the just war doctrine of discrimination. They are inadmissible under any circumstance because they make no distinction between combatants and noncombatants; indeed, they are aimed primarily at innocent bystanders.

The bishops, however, reject not just a countervalue strategy, but also a counterforce strategy of striking military targets. Since military targets are often interspersed with civilian population centers, such an attack would kill millions of innocents and thus violate the principle of proportionality, by which the suffering inflicted in a war must not outweigh the possible gains of conducting such a war. "It would be a perverted political policy or moral casuistry," write the bishops, "which tried to justify using a weapon which 'indirectly' or 'unintentionally' killed a million innocent people because they happened to live near a 'militarily significant target.'" The bishops also reject, in a second sense, the idea that a counterforce war would be limited. They share the widespread conviction that limited nuclear war is a fiction – that counterforce attacks must inevitably degenerate into countervalue warfare, and thus bring us full circle back to the moral objections to MAD and all-out nuclear war.

That doesn't leave very much. If a countervalue strategy is rejected for violating the principle of discrimination, and a counterforce strategy is rejected for violating the principle of proportionality (and also for leading back to total war), one runs out of ways of targeting nuclear weapons. That suits the bishops: they make a point of insisting that their doctrine is "no-use-ever." The logic, and quite transparent objective, of such a position is to reject deterrence *in toto*.

However, ... Pope John Paul has declared that "in current conditions 'deterrence' based on balance, certainly not as an end in itself but as a step on the way toward a progressive disarmament, may still be judged morally acceptable." What to do? The bishops settle for the unhappy compromise of opposing not deterrence in itself, but simply what it takes to make deterrence work. Accordingly, they do not in principle oppose the possession of nuclear weapons when its sole intention is to deter an adversary from using his; they oppose only any plan, intent, or strategy to use these weapons in the act of retaliation. You may keep the weapons, but you may not use them. In sum, the only moral nuclear policy is nuclear bluff.

It is a sorry compromise. ... It is not coherent because it requires the bishops to support a policy – deterrence – that their entire argument is designed to undermine. And it is not convincing because the kind of deterrence they approve is no deterrence at all. Deterrence is not inherent in the weapons. It results from a combination of possession and the will to use them. If one side renounces, for moral or other reasons, the intent of ever actually using nuclear weapons, deterrence ceases to exist.

Pacifists unencumbered by papal pronouncements are able more openly to oppose deterrence. ... Jonathan Schell's argument goes like this: biological existence is the ultimate value; all other values are conditional upon it; there can be neither liberty nor democracy nor any other value in defense of which Western nuclear weapons are developed, if mankind itself is destroyed; and after nuclear war the earth will be "a republic of insects and grass." (Schell too rejects the possibility of limited nuclear war.) Therefore nothing can justify using nuclear weapons. Deterrence is more than a hoax; it is a crime.

Schell's argument enjoys a coherence that the bishops' case lacks, but it is still unsatisfying. Judged on its own terms – of finding a policy that best serves the ultimate and overriding value of biological survival – it fails.

For one thing, it willfully ignores history. Deterrence has a track record. For the entire postwar period it has maintained the peace between the two superpowers, preventing not only nuclear but conventional war as well. Under the logic of deterrence, proxy and brushfire wars are permitted, but not wars between the major powers. As a result, Europe, the central confrontation line between the two superpowers, has enjoyed its longest period of uninterrupted peace in a century. And the United States and the Soviet Union, the two most powerful nations in history, locked in ideological antagonism and engaged in a global struggle as profound as any in history, have not exchanged so much as smallarms fire for a generation.

This is not to say that deterrence cannot in principle break down. It is easy to say that when a system that has kept the peace for a generation is to be rejected, one is morally obliged to come up with a better alternative. It makes no sense to reject deterrence simply because it may not be infallible; it makes sense to reject it only if it proves more dangerous than the alternatives. And a more plausible alternative has yet to be offered. Schell's recommended substitute is a call for a new world order in which all violence, nuclear and conventional, is renounced. ... Of the job of re-making politics and man, he says, "I have left to others those awesome, urgent tasks."

There is one logical alternative to deterrence, and it does not require remaking man or politics, though neither Schell nor the bishops are quite willing to embrace it: unilateral disarmament. (The bishops' position that one may possess but never use nuclear weapons, however, is unilateralist in all but name.) It has something of a track record, too. The only nuclear war ever fought was as one-sided as it was short. It ended when the nonnuclear power suffered the destruction of two cities. ...

We have evidence also of a bacteriological war, the one going on today in Southeast Asia, where yellow rain falls on helpless tribesmen. The same Vietnamese forces in the same place a decade before never used these weapons against a far more formidable American enemy. The reason is obvious. The primitive Hmong, technologically disarmed, cannot retaliate; the Americans could. ...

Far from being a guarantor of survival, unilateralism is a threat to it. ... The breakdown of deterrence would lead to a catastrophic increase in the probability of precisely the inadmissible outcome its critics seek to avoid. The bishops unwittingly concede that point in a subsidiary argument against counterforce when they speak of such a strategy "making deter-rence unstable in a crisis and war more likely."

The critics argue that no ends can justify such disproportionate and nondiscriminatory means as the use of nuclear weapons. That would be true if the ends of such use were territory, domination, or victory. But they are not. The sole end is to prevent a war from coming into existence in the first place. That the threat of retaliation is the best available this-world guarantee against such a war is a paradox the bishops and other pacifists are unwilling to face. As Michael Novak writes, "The appropriate moral prin-ciple is not the relation of means to ends but the choice of a moral act which prevents greater evil. Clearly, it is a more moral choice and occasions lesser evil to hold a deterrent intention than it is to allow nuclear attack." Or recklessly to increase the danger of such an attack.

Nevertheless, moral debate does not end with the acceptance of the necessity, and thus the morality, of deterrence. Not everything is then permitted. There is a major argument between proponents of countervalue and counterforce deterrence. The former claim that counterforce threats lower the nuclear threshold and make nuclear war more likely because it becomes "more thinkable." The latter argue that to retaliate against defenseless populations is not only disproportionate and nondiscriminatory but dangerous as well, since it is not credible and thus actually lowers the nuclear threshold. Note that the debate among nonpacifists is over the relative merits of different kinds of retaliation, and not, as is sometimes pretended, between a "party of deterrence" and a "war-fighting party." The latter distinction is empty: all deterrence rests on the threat of nuclear retaliation, i.e., "war fighting"; and all retaliatory (i.e., nonlunatic) war-fighting strategies from McNamara to today are designed to prevent attack in the first place, i.e., for deterrence. ... The "war fighters" are willing to spell out the retaliatory steps that the "deterrers" rely on to prevent war but prefer not discuss in public.

Whichever side of the intramural debate among deterrence advocates one takes, it seems to me that deterrence wins the debate with its opponents simply because it is a better means of achieving the ultimate moral aim of both sides – survival.

There is another argument in favor of deterrence, though in my view it carries less weight. ... It holds that (1) there are values more important than survival, and (2) nuclear weapons are necessary to protect them. The second proposition is, of course, true. The West is the guarantor of such fragile historic achievements as democracy and political liberty; a whole constellation of ideals and values ultimately rests on its ability to deter those who reject these values and have a history of destroying them wherever they dominate. To reject deterrence unilaterally is to surrender these values in the name of survival.

The rub comes with the first proposition. Are there values more important than survival? Sidney Hook was surely right when he once said that when a person makes survival the highest value, he has declared that there is nothing he will not betray. But for a civilization, self-sacrifice is senseless, since there are no survivors to give meaning to the sacrificial act. For a civilization, survival may be worth betrayal. If indeed this highly abstract choice were the only one, it would be hard to meet Schell's point that since all values hinge on biological survival, that is to forfeit everything. It is thus simply not enough to say (rightly) that nuclear weapons, given the world as it is today, keep us free; one must couple that statement with another, equally true: they keep us safe. A nuclear policy – like unilateralism – that forces us to choose between being dead or Red is morally dubious. A nuclear policy – like deterrence – that protects us from both calamities is morally compelling. ...

The Nuclear Freeze

The moral attack on the weapons themselves takes two curiously contradictory approaches. The first, a mainstay of freeze proponents, is that beyond existing levels new weapons are simply redundant, that we are wasting billions of dollars on useless weapons that will do no more than make the rubble bounce, to borrow another memorable Churchian formulation. The moral crime, it is alleged, is that these monies are being taken away from human needs, like housing and health care and aid to poorer countries. ...

It is extraordinary that an argument so weak can enjoy such widespread currency. Compared to other types of weapons, strategic nuclear weapons are remarkably cheap. In the U.S. they account for less than 10 percent of the military budget, and for about 5 percent of the gross national product. ... A shift away from strategic to conventional weapons would be extremely expensive. That is precisely why the West decided in the 1950s and 1960s to rely so heavily on nuclear weapons and to permit the current conventional imbalance in Europe. Rather than match the Soviet bloc tank for tank, plane for plane, the West decided to go nuclear because nuclear weapons offered in John Foster Dulles's immortal phrase, "more bang for the buck." ...

On the other hand, freeze advocates often argue that these weapons are not useless but dangerous, destabilizing, and likely to precipitate a nuclear war. The more weapons we build, the closer we come to nuclear war. The assumption is that high weapons levels *themselves* increase the likelihood of war. That reverses cause and effect. Weapons are a result of tensions between nations and not their primary cause. It is true that distrust can be a dangerous by-product of an uncontrolled arms race. And yet arms control agreements like SALT can reduce the risk of war by building mutual confidence and trust, while at the same time permitting higher weapons levels. Historically, nuclear tension simply does not correlate well with weapons levels. The worst nuclear crisis took place in October 1962, when the level of nuclear arms was much lower than it is today. And nuclear tensions were probably at their lowest during the heyday of détente in the mid-1970s; at that time U.S.–Soviet relations were at their peak, while each side had by then vastly increased its capacity for multiple overkill.

There is an understandable built-in prejudice against new weapons. Even those willing grudgingly to grant the need for minimal deterrence recoil from building and deploying new weapons. ... What is ignored in this critique of the weapons themselves is that deterrence has requirements, and one is survivability (the ability of one's weapons to sustain a first strike and still deliver a second strike). And survivability, in an era of technological innovation, requires modernization. ... Thus the new American bomber, whether it be the B-1 or the Stealth, will be better able to elude destruction on the ground and Soviet defenses in the air. It will not be any more destructive – or immoral – than the B-52. Similarly for the Trident submarines, which are quieter and (because they have longer-range missiles) can hide in larger areas of the ocean than Poseidons. In short, mainstream nonunilateralist freeze proponents are caught in the position of accepting the fundamental morality of deterrence but rejecting the addition of any new weapons for preserving it.

"No-First-Use"

The penchant for providing ends without means also characterizes the final flank attack on deterrence: the rejection of the doctrine of "extended deterrence," "the threat to use nuclear weapons, if necessary, in response to an attack (even a conventional attack) by the Soviet Union on NATO. That policy, which derives ultimately from Western unwillingness to match Soviet conventional strength in Europe, has long troubled many Americans. But since the alternatives are massive conventional rearmament or abandonment of our European allies, it has had to serve ... as the guarantor of the Western alliance.

The campaign waged against this policy has [called for] a "no-first-use" policy on nuclear weapons. This position has found an echo in many quarters, including, not surprisingly, the bishops' Pastoral Letter. It, too, doubts the possibility that limited nuclear war can remain limited, and resolutely opposes ever crossing the line separating conventional from nuclear war. Therefore any nuclear retaliation against any conventional attack is rejected in principle.

Leave aside the consideration that the impossibility of limited nuclear war is both historically unproven and by no means logically necessary. Assume that limited nuclear war is indeed a fiction. We are still faced with the central problem of the no-first-use approach. Its intent is to prevent any war from becoming nuclear, but its unintended consequence is to make that eventuality more likely. For thirty years war between the superpowers has been deterred at its origin: the prospect that even the slightest conventional conflict might escalate into a nuclear war has been so daunting that neither has been permitted to happen. Current policy sets the "fire break" at the line dividing war from peace; a no-first-use policy moves it to the line dividing conventional war from nuclear war. No-first-use advocates are prepared to risk an increased chance of conventional war (now less dangerous and more "thinkable") in return for a decreased chance of any such war going nuclear. But a no-first-use pledge is unenforceable. Who will guarantee that the loser in any war will stick to such a pledge? A conventional European war would raise the risk of nuclear war to a level infinitely higher than ever before. Thus, any policy, however pious its intent, that makes such a conventional war more thinkable makes nuclear war more likely.

And that is the fundamental flaw in both this argument and the general attack on deterrence. ... It ignores the fact that rejecting these policies forces the adoption of more dangerous alternatives, and makes more likely the calamities we are trying to avoid. ...

Nuclear weapons are useful only to the extent that they are never used. But they are more likely to fulfill their purpose, and never be used, if one's adversary believes that one indeed has the will to use them in retaliation for attack. That will to use them is what the moralists find unacceptable. But it is precisely on that will to use them that the structure of deterrence rests.

James Turner Johnson

The Use of Force: A Justified Response

What moral judgment – as opposed to political, economic and other kinds of judgment – should be made on the use of force by the U.S. and the other members of the multilateral force to drive Iraq out of Kuwait? I want to address this question in terms of the just war tradition of Western culture, or more specifically, by means of the seven criteria that must be satisfied to justify use of military force according to that tradition: just cause, right authority, right intention, overall proportionality of the good to be done over the evil, a reasonable hope of success, a situation of last resort, and the goal of restoring peace. These seven categories are deeply rooted in both Christian tradition and international law, and they are commonly used in contemporary moral debate, even by people who will not share the conclusions I am about to draw on the basis of these categories.

In my judgment these seven conditions were all met prior to the beginning of air attacks against Iraqi forces on January 16. Lacking Iraqi action to pull its forces out of occupied Kuwait and make amends for its invasion and systematic rape of that country, the United Nations – sanctioned coalition reached the position where the use of such force was the only remaining resort.

A *just cause* for use of force against Iraq has existed since last August, when Iraq militarily invaded Kuwait and then declared the area that was "formerly Kuwait" to be thereafter part of Iraq. Morally speaking, and in terms of international law, this was the crucial action: a flagrant case of aggression, violating the most fundamental norm of the international order.

Christian Century (Feb. 6–13, 1991), 134–5. Used by permission of The Christian Century Foundation.

It was not the first time that Iraq under Saddam Hussein had been guilty of aggression against another country: we should not forget that Iraq, acting in the same way, started the lengthy and bloody war with Iran only recently settled. Iran then responded by using force in self-defense: what was different in August 1990 was that Kuwait was in no position to defend itself against Iraq, and so it called for help from the international community. That help came in the form of the mulitnational coalition of forces placed in Saudi Arabia and the United Nations Security Council resolutions authorizing first the imposition of economic sanctions against Iraq and then the use of military force if Iraq still did not reverse its action of violence against international peace and order. These are responses in defense of both a tiny country and of the fundamental moral and legal norms that outlaw such aggression.

Historically, just war tradition held that just cause for the use of force exists whenever it is necessary either to repel an unjust attack, to retake something wrongly taken, or to punish evil. International law has justified use of force only in response to aggressive attack. By either standard Iraq's attack against Kuwait was unjust and constitutes just cause for use of force to undo it.

The remaining six moral conditions have also been satisfied. In the international context, *right authority* was provided by the Security Council's resolution authorizing force. In the U.S., right authority consists in the powers granted to the president by the Constitution and by the War Powers Act and by the congressional resolutions decisively adopted on January 12 and 13 authorizing use of force against Iraq.

Right intention in this case consists in the aims of turning back and undoing aggression. There are no aggressive aims against the territory or people of Iraq. Right intention here also consists in deterring such aggression in the future, restoring the shattered peace of the Persian Gulf region, and attempting to set in place safeguards to protect that peace in the future. This right intention also satisfies the criterion of *the end of peace*.

As to the question of *proportionality* between the good such use of force would do and the evil that would result from allowing Iraq's violent aggression to stand, it must not be forgotten that Iraq has already brought great evil into being, and it is promising more. That country has already violated the rights of innocent people and caused great suffering and loss of life and resources by invading two of its neighbors, first Iran and then Kuwait. It has launched deliberate attacks on population centers in both

Israel – which is not even a member of the coalition of nations seeking to enforce the UN resolutions against Iraq – and Saudi Arabia. It has developed chemical and biological weapons and is seeking to develop nuclear arms, and it has shown no hesitation in using its chemical weaponry both in war and in attacks against its own citizens.

By loosing crude oil into the Persian Gulf it has shown flagrant disregard for the fragile ecology of that region and the people who depend on the Gulf for food, water, and livelihood. Saddam Hussein has openly threatened to do more such damage, as well as to use weapons of mass destruction in the war. Coupled with all this, Iraq's militaristic aggressiveness, backed up by the most powerful military forces of any nation in the region, if left unchecked constitutes an unspoken but real threat to other neighboring countries. Allowing Iraq's aggression to stand in condoning an evil in itself and opening the door to yet further evil by a restless and aggressive Iraq. These are the issues in determining the existence of proportionality – not simply the costs expected from the use of the UN-sanctioned forces against Iraq.

Is there reasonable hope of success in the use of force by the coalition allied against Iraq? The aim of satisfying this concern justifies the vigorous buildup of American and other military might in the region. ...

Finally, was resort to military force a *last resort*? Iraq's intransigence and continued belligerence sadly left no choice. Efforts to negotiate an Iraqi withdrawal failed. The sanctions imposed by the UN, even if they had worked more effectively, in themselves were the source of moral harm. Such sanctions, and not only military force, cause human suffering and loss of life. Moreover, the more effective sanctions are, the greater their inherent impact on those persons most remote from the wrongdoing of their nation's leaders and least able to bring about change: the poor, the aged, children, the infirm. These are exactly the people who, in war, are regarded most clearly as noncombatants. By contrast, the coalition's use of military force against Iraq aims at the military power behind Iraq's aggression: its combatant forces, its military resources and the leaders who have led it into aggressive wrongdoing. This is a more moral course than either condoning Iraq's aggression or continuing economic sanctions against the Iraqi people.

All the above considerations have to do with the decision to resort to use of military force and why I am convinced that, by the moral criteria of just war tradition, that decision was justified. Just war concerns require also that the means used in war be moral: specifically, that these means be discriminate and tactically proportionate.

Discrimination is the moral principle that seeks to protect noncombatants in war by prohibiting their being directly and intentionally targeted by military force. There is a vast difference, in terms of this moral principle, between the actions thus far of the coalition air forces and the actions of Iraq. The former have been directed at military targets and have employed weapons that by their nature are extremely accurate. By contrast, Iraq's Scud missile attacks have been direct, intentional attempts to harm the noncombatant inhabitants of Israeli and Saudi cities. Also by contrast, the flooding of oil into the Persian Gulf is an action inherently indiscriminate in its nature, with little direct military impact.

As for the principle of *proportionality,* when the noncombatants are directly and intentionally targeted, any means at all are grossly disproportionate; Iraq's Scud attacks against population centers and its pouring of oil into the Persian Gulf thus fail the test of proportionality of means as well as that of discrimination. Only when the principle of discrimination is met does the question of proportionality of means come into play. In this regard it is important to note that the ability to make closely targeted strikes against military installations or associated support systems has produced a very different kind of war than was possible only a relatively short time ago, before contemporary guidance systems were available. A single "smart" bomb or cruise missile can do what, in Vietnam or Korea or World War II, it took an entire bombing raid to accomplish. Accordingly, the accuracy of contemporary weapons used by coalition forces means that the total damage done by an attack on a particular target can be much less than in earlier wars. The development of targeting technology shows that it is simply wrong to argue, as many people have argued in America in recent years, that contemporary war must of necessity be grossly and disproportionately destructive in its conduct. Rather, the means of war now available and in use by coalition forces against Iraq are inherently both more discriminate and more proportionate than means previously used. …

Alan Geyer

Just War and the Burdens of History

Christian reconnaissance of the hellish war in the Middle East would do well to recall the plenitude of biblical perspectives shared by both pacifists and nonpacifists. An ineluctable imperative for nations as well as persons – so say the Hebrew prophets and Jesus and Paul – is that repentance is usually the precondition of reconciliation.

Repentance over the Persian Gulf War is in very short supply just now. Indignation over the brutalities of Saddam Hussein, inordinate pride in the newest wonders of military technology, and sanctimonious "new world order" rhetoric all conspire to overwhelm any confessional impulse. Not only the burdens of the distant past (such as centuries of Christian assaults on both Islam and Judaism) now compel a confessional stance by American Christians. What must not be lost to memory are the specific entanglements of U.S. policy in the events leading up to Saddam Hussein's August 2 assault on Kuwait, as well as the U.S. course of escalation between August 2 and January 15.

The invocation of just war criteria in the present conflict can be truly an exercise of justice only if the burdens of history are taken seriously. Too often those criteria have rationalized military reactions to only the last in a series of events steeped in moral ambiguities.

There are surely enough iniquities on the part of the Saddam Hussein regime to commend the justice of a firm response. But the case for a just cause is made morally ambiguous by recalling these things:

- the tens of billions of dollars of U.S. arms poured into almost every country in the Middle East, the most combustible region in the world;

Christian Century (Feb 6–13, 1991) 135. Used by permission.

- the U.S. double-standard concerning nuclear proliferation, with the Middle East presenting the most likely scenario for nuclear war;
- the lack of a disciplined energy policy in the 1980s, making the U.S. more driven to military action to safeguard oil resources;
- backsliding on promises of a homeland for the Palestinians, thus handing Saddam Hussein his most powerful political weapon;
- neglect of any serious effort in the past 20 years to develop a genuinely multinational United Nations peacekeeping force;
- the July 25 assurance by the U.S. ambassador to Iraq that the U.S. would not take sides in Iraq's disputes with Kuwait.

The norm of *just intent* has been scrambled since the November elections by the escalation of U.S. objectives: from 1) defense of Saudi Arabia and economic sanctions, to 2) deployment of an offensive force of a halfmillion troops, to 3) massive assault on Iraqi cities that has destroyed not only military facilities but the infrastructures of energy, communications and transportation upon which civilian life depends, to 4) the demand for unconditional surrender.

The administration's claim that offensive military action was a *last resort* is highly questionable on two grounds. With regard to economic sanctions, two former chairmen of the Joint Chiefs of Staff, six former secretaries of defense, and a near-majority of the U.S. Senate had urged a much more patient and protracted sanctions campaign while voicing grave reservations about the costs and ultimate consequences of military action. With regard to diplomacy, the administration's claim that it had gone "the last mile for peace" is belied by the fact that Iraqi leaders were offered only threats and no incentives, even to the point of denying them any possibility of "face-saving." This macho style, along with the refusal to accept European proposals for a wider conference in the Middle East, hardly amounts to constructive diplomacy.

The criterion of *legitimate authority* was finally finessed by United Nations and congressional resolutions. However, the UN mantle and repeated invocation of a "new world order" are tainted not only by the unilateralism of military decision and command but by a long list of U.S. defaults concerning the authority and efficacy of the UN. That list includes U.S. repudiation of the jurisdiction of the World Court, its crippling nonpayment of dues, and its obstruction of a consensus on most global issues.

Prior to January 15, some of us argued against offensive military action on consequential grounds, appealing to the traditional requirements of a *reasonable hope of success, discrimination* and *proportionality.* Without making confident predictions, we nevertheless imagined the dangers of a wider war enveloping Israel, the collapse of restraints on targeting and weapons, massive casualties, the mounting hostility of Palestinians and other Arab peoples, millions of refugees, the bankruptcy of the U.S. economy, the shattering of our body politic, and protracted terrorism. Since January 15 these imaginings have not become less credible.

There are enormous public and even pastoral pressures to suspend political debate and support the president and U.S. forces. Our churches would indeed do well to maintain a more compassionate ministry to military personnel and their families, both now and after this war, than was the case in the Vietnam tragedy. But the very definition of pastoral ministry must be stretched to include the recovery of our own involved history through congregational and ecumenical forums, the counteracting of stereotypes, and the anticipation of policies and ministries for the huge tasks of postwar reconstruction. Even more, ministry must make public witness for a ceasefire, to stop the killing and start genuine negotiations at last. ...

John Langan

An Imperfectly Just War:
Part of the Uncertainty is Factual

The conflict in the Persian Gulf has been a war of mixed signals and contrary intentions; a war that many people feel need not have been fought; a war that is unlikely to resolve the problems of the Middle East. Both proponents and critics have attempted to evaluate it in moral terms. President George Bush assured the American people that this conflict was indeed a just war, a conflict between good and evil, right and wrong. The U.S. Congress debated the morality and the timeliness of the war and gave it less than resounding approval.

The critics of the war have had a hard time staking out a counterposition. It is not possible to offer a convincing apologia for Saddam Hussein, who has shown considerable ingenuity in finding ever novel ways to outrage world public opinion, from mistreating the citizens of Kuwait, to exhibiting prisoners of war on television, to polluting the waters of the Gulf, torching Kuwait's oil industry, and, most recently, crushing the Shiites and the Kurds. Saddam Hussein is a serial aggressor, a man ready to use lethal force against his opponents, a man who has invested large sums for a long time in building a war machine meant to bully and abuse his neighbors. In the face of the vast array of military personnel and technology that the coalition assembled, he refused to give up his hold on Kuwait. This combination – a bloodthirsty and tyrannical adversary and the mobilization of vast forces by a diverse coalition led and orchestrated by the United States – left much of the religious leadership of the United States in a quandary

118 Commonweal (1 June 1991), 361–365. Used by permission.

about whether to accept or to condemn our use of force against him. More broadly, an entire generation of Americans who acquired a deep distrust of government and the military from the sad experience of Vietnam were left searching for an appropriate framework for interpreting this very different situation.

The analogies that critics of the Gulf War tried to make to Vietnam and the war of attrition on the Western Front between 1914 and 1918 were rendered useless by the rapid pace and conclusion of the war. But so was Bush's comparison of Saddam Hussein to Hitler, which came to seem overdrawn as the weakness of the Iraqi forces became apparent. No doubt, such analogies provided orientation and legitimation for advocates of alternative policies as they confronted the uncertainties of the Gulf conflict, but finally they did not prove useful or convincing.

Just-war theory is the primary instrument that ethicists have for surmounting conflicting perceptions, analogies, and claims that naturally develop in any debate over a violent conflict. It commits us to a critical and questioning attitude to any war. Though the theory itself offers neither a blanket condemnation nor a blanket endorsement of this most dangerous and destructive human activity, it operates with a strong presumption against the use of violence. It includes elements that require the exercise of sophisticated and informed political judgment, and it recognizes the complexity of political disputes.

From August 2, 1990, when Hussein's troops seized Kuwait and converted it into the nineteenth province of Iraq, there was a strong basis for arguing that a war for the liberation of Kuwait was morally justified. A basic principle of international law requiring respect for the sovereignty of states was violated without warning. The brutal occupation of Kuwait, the seizure of its assets, the dispersal of large numbers of its citizens and residents compounded the original crime. Kuwait was entitled to wage a war of self-defense and to ask for help both from its allies and from states concerned over the threat to international order presented by Iraq. From the beginning the requirement that there be a just cause for hostilities was present.

But the course of events ensured that this factor counted for less than it would normally. First, whether as a result of the speedy response of the United States to the Saudi request for troops or because Hussein's original plans had not extended beyond Kuwait, it quickly became apparent that the Iraqis were not going to invade Saudi Arabia or to annex its oil-producing areas. Second, the Kuwaiti government was not able to mount a sustained resistance against the Iraqi invasions and occupation, which was carried out with overwhelming force. There is no evidence that any significant element of Kuwaiti society with the exception of some Palestinians, preferred Iraqi occupation to the rule of the al-Sabah family. Third, once the occupation of Kuwait was complete and overt hostilities ceased, Iraq settled in to exploit its victim and to integrate Kuwait into its territory. ... All of these factors obscured reality: the fundamental act of war had been committed by Iraq with little provocation or warning. Then, it took several months for the coalition to assemble sufficient forces to make threats that would be plausible to Hussein, a guileful and unyielding leader. During that time, the allies and other concerned powers had time and opportunity to explore alternative ways of resolving the dispute without resorting to war. That interval was lengthy, but it makes more difference for political perception than for moral analysis.

It is true that the brutal character of Saddam Hussein's regime did not prevent various powers from collaborating with him before the invasion of Kuwait. France, Germany, the Soviet Union, and the United States had all in different ways provided support for what the world now agrees was a murderous, tyrannical, and aggressive regime. The history of Western dealing with Saddam Hussein's regime over the years before 1990 exhibits a mixture of wishful thinking and willful ignorance, of economic greed and legalistic formalism that Western governments often adopt when they find themselves facing a distasteful despotism with which, for various reasons (good and bad), they think they have to deal and which they think they are powerless to alter. It is true that large portions of the West, including governments and the media, have come relatively late to a clearheaded recognition of Saddam Hussein's threat to peace and order in the Middle East. But the failure to see this point early does not invalidate a policy that attempts to reverse a mistaken judgment before its consequences become catastrophic.

Another requirement that a just war must meet is that the war must be conducted by competent authority. In this regard, it is extremely important that the war on Iraq was authorized by the UN Security Council on behalf of the international community, by several states in the Middle East, and by the U.S. Congress. The Bush administration, which had unwisely attempted to operate on the principle that the war did not need congressional authorization, fortunately agreed to the congressional debate that took place before the January 15 deadline. Congress took its share of the responsibility for the decision, and the possibility that the war would lead sooner or later to a constitutional crisis was avoided. ...

Just-war theory also includes a requirement that the war being considered must have a reasonable prospect of success. ... The main uncertainty was not about ultimate victory but about the level of casualties that would be required to achieve this result and therefore about the willingness of the American public to sustain the war effort. The Iraqi army, while technologically inferior to the allies, was a large and experienced force. The key step for the allies was to convert their air superiority into a decisive edge in the ground war. This was done by hammering the ground forces from the air, by misleading the Iraqi command about our plan of battle, and by encouraging desertions from the relatively inexperienced troops near the frontier.

From another angle, the prospect of ultimate success was, and remains, uncertain. If we move beyond defining success only in terms of military victory and think of it as including significant progress toward making the Middle East a more secure and peaceful region, then we have to admit that our technological superiority and our ability to win battles in the air and on land can do little more than buy time for working out a settlement that the major players (including popular movements as well as governments) are prepared to live with for the short- and medium-term future. It may well be that "winning" in the present crisis does little more than preserve us and our allies from disasters that would have undermined our entire position in the Middle East if we had not successfully resisted Saddam Hussein.

Questions about success and objectives were given many different answers during the months from August to January. The lack of clear answers made it difficult to determine whether the military option met the just-war criterion of proportionality. Were the objectives sufficiently urgent and important to make war both necessary and plausible as a course that would prevent serious evils and were they likely to produce a better outcome than nonviolent alternatives? President Bush and the military leadership repeatedly spoke of our objectives as: (1) the eviction of Iraqi forces from Kuwait and (2) the enforcement of the relevant UN resolutions. ...

In the public discussion there was a certain inevitable escalation of objectives; these included the removal of Saddam Hussein and his regime as well as the removal of the weapons of mass destruction that the Iraqi military had been accumulating. The first of these more ambitious objectives would be attained, it was hoped, either as a consequence of defeat or as the result of an internal coup. It is a matter of regret to nearly everyone that this did not happen. The second objective is one that the coalition has chosen to pursue by limited means that fall between the complete occupation and demilitarization of the country, and a tortuous and lengthy process of arms control negotiation. Including the disarmament requirements within the cease-fire provisions was a positive move in that it combined two morally compelling objectives: the end of hostilities and restrictions on Iraq's ability to develop more weapons of mass destruction. Further objectives such as the territorial dismemberment of Iraq and the destructions of its people and culture were ruled out by President Bush. They were seen to be morally unacceptable and davastating for the long-term stability of the Middle East and for the future of American relations with the people of the region. At least this seemed to be the view that would have drawn general assent before the revolts in northern and southern Iraq. These revolts raised the troubling question of whether the unity of Iraq could be preserved without enormous human suffering or without reliance on dictatorial methods.

Clarifying the war's objectives came relatively late in the public debate, which made it difficult to determine whether the war could meet the just-war criterion of proportionality. My own judgment is that taken together the following factors justified the resort to war: (1) protecting the principle of the inviolability of sovereignty (especially in an area that contains a number of very vulnerable states); (2) preventing Iraq from achieving a weapons capability that would enable it to attack the major population centers of the region; (3) thwarting Saddam Hussein from achieving a predominant position in the world oil market; and (4) terminating the grave human rights abuses that his regime inflicted on the people of Kuwait and Iraq. I am not claiming that the United States and its allies have consistently defended these values in their foreign policy, only that these and related considerations about attainable objectives and values to be protected against an aggressor provide a reasonable basis for affirming that the test of proportionality between the means and the end was met in this decision to go to war.

Though the oil supply was a common theme of analysts and cartoonists, of commentators and protesters, no serious moralist regards the U.S. maintenance of gasoline at $1 per gallon as a justifying reason for any use of violence, much less for a fullscale war. ... Industrial economies have shown that they can make the adjustments required to pay for increased oil prices.

Nonetheless, there was a morally serious reason for being concerned about higher oil prices: their negative effect on the nations of Eastern Europe and the third world. The history of OPEC shows that, even while the world depends heavily on a small number of producers in one highly volatile region, the direction of oil prices is not simply up and that the forging of a consistent policy within the oil cartel is extraordinarily difficult. What Saddam Hussein's seizure of Kuwait threatened to do was to start a chain of events that would give him both enormous wealth for carrying out further aggressions as well as a decisive voice in allocating one of the world's most essential commodities, particularly if he were to control, directly or indirectly, Saudi supplies.

The norm in just-war theory that has probably been most prominently invoked by critics of the Gulf War is that of last resort. This requires that alternatives to war be tried and found wanting and that the only way to maintain justice – and the values that are wrongfully threatened by the adversary – is to fight. ...

There is no doubt that alternatives to fighting were offered to the Iraqi government and that the coalition would not have fought a war if Kuwait had been evacuated. But it also became clear that Saddam Hussein was not inclined to pull out of Kuwait even when the threat of war became credible and imminent. ... The key question about last resort is whether less coercive measures, particularly sanctions, would have been sufficient over time, and whether the diplomatic process was pursued with sufficient vigor and commitment from August through January.

We can see that the primary task of U.S. diplomacy was to build and maintain the coalition against Saddam Hussein. It was particularly important to cut the connections between Iraq and the Soviet Union, which had long been its primary source of weapons and military and technical expertise. On closer inspection, the worldwide coalition against Saddam Hussein is really divided into two coalitions. The first, a very broad coalition of states concerned about Iraq's violation of Kuwaiti sovereignty, was likely to be satisfied by achieving the minimal objective of evicting Iraq from Kuwait. The second, far narrower coalition demanded a decisive reorientation in Iraq's external policy, for which the defeat or removal of Saddam Hussein was an indispensable requirement. This coalition is unstable, since it agrees on the need to alter the direction of Iraq's foreign and military policies while its members disagree on how they understand this need and what they would put in place of Hussein's regime. Such disagreement is not surprising since this narrow coalition includes Kuwait, Saudi Arabia, Israel, Egypt, Syria, the United Arab Emirates, the United Kingdom, and the United States. It thus includes states that are not keen about being seen in public agreement with each other as well as states that have fought wars with each other in the recent past. The narrow coalition presents us with a situation in which nations are willing to take very strong measures against a common adversary but cannot be relied on to cooperate over an extended period of time. ...

The United States had to function as the leader of both. To maintain the broad coalition, Saddam Hussein was offered a no-frills deal: withdrawal from Kuwait without a retaliatory attack. But this left many observers unsatisfied, presumably not because they thought it unjust but because they thought it unlikely to be acceptable to a leader with his ambitions. At the same time, the United States had to avoid agreeing to concessions that would shatter the confidence of key members of the narrow coalition that the United States really was prepared to use force against Iraq. The Israelis, in particular, had strong and understandable objections to allowing linkage between the Gulf dispute and the claims of the Palestinians.

It is clear that no lasting peace in the Middle East is possible without a resolution of the Palestinian issue. Those who had been hoping for an international conference or some other process requiring the Israelis to deal with the Palestinians were too inclined to think that a complex negotiation aimed at a peaceful settlement of both Kuwait and Palestinian demands was an avenue worth exploring. This overlooked the possibility, indeed the likelihood, that the conference would fail on both counts with a consequent shattering of the coalition and with the Iraqis more deeply entrenched than ever in Kuwait. Of course, even an unsuccessful conference is less a disaster than war; but not if it ends in a way that makes a war on less favorable terms even more likely. It also overlooks the point that, precisely because there are important elements of justice in the Palestinian cause, it is important not to allow them to be captured and exploited by an unscrupulous demagogue like Saddam Hussein, whose interest in the Palestinians is secondary and manipulative. ...

What about the sanctions? ... Clearly, it would have been a great sin for international order to have this kind of crisis solved with nonlethal measures. The best hope for sanctions did not turn on a general slowing down of the Iraqi economy or on the denial of essential food and medicine to the Iraqi people (which were not included in the embargo), but on the denial of spare parts and military supplies. But such a denial would only constitute serious pressure on Hussein if there were a powerful military force in the region capable of making the shortage of supplies a starkly urgent priority. Enforcing the embargo over a period of time, particularly since this would have meant maintaining the narrow coalition on a war-ready footing while preventing major evasions of the embargo, would have meant that U.S. allies in the region would have had to carry considerable stress in a situation of continuing tension. Given the requirement for a continuing deployment of substantial forces and the constraints that the climate and the religious calendar would have put on military operations and thus on the plausible threat to Iraq, a strong case can be made that the January 15 deadline was a reasonable decision.

I have grave reservations about the major increase in U.S. forces after the November congressional elections. But this is primarily a problem about the administration's lack of candor in dealing with the American people. On the one hand, this deployment made our threats of military action against Iraq considerably more credible. Yet it inevitably created more pressure for a shorter timetable for the working of sanctions and other measures.

... But I believe that in the last analysis, the decisive judgment is one that was reached by most of the Middle East powers and that has been confirmed by Hussein's behavior during the last nine months. That judgment is that (1) Iraq under his rule was deeply committed to an aggressive and destructive policy; (2) Iraq posed a threat to almost all of its neighbors; (3) war with Iraq was inevitable at some point; and (4) such a war was best conducted before Iraq's arsenal was capable of dealing catastrophic blows to its neighbors. Those who hoped that this war could be averted or, at least, postponed did so in the honorable belief that better ways of resolving this dispute and others like it should be tried. This was not a false or foolish belief; the point is that the nature of this particular adversary and what we could reasonably expect from his regime made it inapplicable.

The course of the war made it clear that we had underestimated the tenacity and obduracy of the Iraqis and that we had overestimated their effective fighting power. This double error cuts two ways. In the first instance, it underlines the enormous difficulty that sanctions would have encountered in changing Iraq's policy. In the second, it undermines some of the more dramatic claims about what Iraq could have done to its neighbors and enemies. One important sign of progress is that a serious and conscientious effort was made to observe the principle of discrimination or noncombatant immunity. ...

After the fact, more questions have been raised about whether the war was conducted in a proportionate way or, whether the allies inflicted excessive or unnecessary casualties and damage on Iraq. Granted that the electricity and communications systems are legitimate targets, was it possible to restrict the damage to Iraq's infrastructure so that the civilian population would be less at risk than it now seems to be? ... I would argue that more care should be taken to protect civilians from the consequences of a catastrophic demolition of the infrastructure that modern societies rely on to sustain life. In this matter, however, the Iraqi people are as much the victims of their own government's intransigence (which makes humanitarian aid both hard to offer and hard to deliver) as they are victims of the coalition's bombs.

I have grave doubts about whether it was really necessary to bomb the Iraqi troops retreating from Kuwait as intensively as we did. Certainly, as the stories of their occupations of Kuwait made clear, many of them were no innocents. Later events also made it clear that Iraqi military power was far from totally destroyed. While retreating troops who have not indicated an intention to surrender are a legitimate military target, they did not constitute an immediate or serious threat to our own troops or military operations. Given the inevitable imprecision of warfare, it is reasonable to err on the side of mercy and life when one's forces are in an overwhelmingly dominant position, even if this means allowing some of the enemy to escape.

Whether the casualties inflicted by the air war on Iraqi ground troops meet the test of proportionality is a matter of some uncertainty. ... Part of the uncertainty arises from the imprecision inherent in the notion of proportionality itself. For this reason, military officers and many moralists prefer to restrict their effective concern to the principle of discrimination. But this invites us to take the lives of soldiers too lightly; for surely it is possible to kill enemy soldiers without necessity or proportionate benefit, and this has to be wrong. But the criterion is extremely hard to apply in the course of war. ...

John Howard Yoder

Just War Tradition: Is It Credible?

Public dialogue in the U.S. about the Persian Gulf war has drawn heavily on the language of the just war tradition – more so than has been the case with any war since at least the 1860s. The tradition has been appealed to by journalists and politicians, as if it were common knowledge, as a basis for making (or denying) the claim that the war in the Persian Gulf should go on.

Most of the time, the just war tradition is used to test a particular war (or a strategy or a weapon) for its moral and legal acceptability. That was done recently in the *Century* by James Turner Johnson and Alan Geyer (February 6–13). The reciprocal approach is also needed: the tradition can be tested by a war. Does the tradition in fact facilitate shared moral and legal decisions by so labeling issues that they can be adjudicated?

Johnson is right that the just war tradition is "deeply rooted in both Christian tradition and international law." He is also right, in the several books he has written on the theme, in reporting that it has never been universally accepted or applied by Christian moralists or statesmen. It has never been promulgated *ex cathedra* by Rome, though it is in the Anglican, Lutheran and Reformed confessions. Deep rootage does not make the tradition morally true; but it does set the stage for giving it a fair test. ...

What I want to do is to view the debate as a test of whether the entire just war mode of moral discourse is adequate to guide the responsible citizenship of people who claim that their first moral obligation is to the God whom Jesus taught them to praise and obey, and their second to the neighbor, *including the enemy*, whom Jesus taught them to love.

Christian Century 108 (March 13, 1991), 295–298. Used by permission of Christian Century Foundation.

The just war tradition does serve, some of the time, as an agenda, a check-list of questions which it is fitting to ask in considering war. ... That being the system's intention, there are three questions we obviously can pursue: a) Does the system as system have integrity in that its concepts are so defined as really to serve as criteria? b) Do the people claiming to use the system have moral integrity in that they will renounce the strategies and actions which the system rejects? c) Is the system compatible with the other elements of Christian moral commitment which it does not expressly include? The first of these questions is our first concern here. My more basic concern as a Christian pacifist would of course be with the third.

Does the just war tradition work? Let's consider some instances.

1) *The facts of the case.* As distinguished from people holding to paci-fism or the "holy war," people holding to the just war tradition claim to make decisions on the empirically knowable facts of the case. It is as-sumed that these facts are knowable in principle and known in fact: Has there been naked aggression? Is the belligerent government legitimate? Has everything else been tried? Moralists have assumed that these facts could be ascertained. In our present experience that is not so easy. The control of information is a science and an art (known in the trade – in the language of billiards – as "spin"). In early February this reached a new level of brazeness. Margaret Tutwiler informed us that when the President had told conservative Protestant broadcasters that the U.S. wanted uncon-ditional surrender and a war crimes trial, he was expressing his emotions, not policy; that when Secretary of State James Baker and his Soviet col-league Alexander Bessmertnykh said that the coalition would accept a cease-fire and would promise a regional peace conference, that was inope-rative because it had not been checked. For "spin" purposes, it helps to have several different statements, each supposed to please somebody or send some message, with none of them binding and no call for consistency among them. From mid-January to mid-February we were told almost daily both that there is no schedule and that the war is proceeding on schedule. ...

2) *Who in fact does decide?* The just war tradition was not originally intended to be used in democracies. It was originally assumed that deci-sions about war belong to sovereigns. The democratic vision which makes the citizenry "sovereign" changes how the system has to work. Disinfor-mation and spin control invalidate the administrators' claim to legitimacy. Civilian and military administrators are not trained to distinguish dissent

from disloyalty, secrecy from security. They thus can refuse to provide "the people" with the wherewithal for evaluating the claimed justifications.

This change makes the availability of usable nonsectarian language like that of the just war tradition all the more necessary, because there must be debate. Yet in the sovereign's eyes the debate seems to be unfair and disloyal. Both George Bush ... would rather that we not all consider ourselves entitled to share in moral decisions about the killing done in our name. ... It is clear that without reliable sources of information there is no basis for evaluating most of the claims on which a just war decision is based. When the head of the Joint Chiefs parries a factual question with "trust me," I don't.

3) *Reality is deep and wide.* The just war paradigm for decision, like much of the rest of ethical casuistry, assumes a punctual conception of legal-moral decision. The decision to go to war, or to use such and such strategy, it is assumed, is made at one time, not before or after that instant. What is either right or wrong is the punctual decision, based upon the facts of the case at just that instant, and the just war tradition delivers the criteria for adjudicating that decision. This procedure undervalues the longitudinal dimensions of the conflict. Here Geyer's reading is truer to the facts than Johnson's, as he takes account of what he calls "the burdens of history." During the first Reagan-Bush decade, other cases of "naked aggression" somehow did not need to be punished so rigorously. Iraq was textually told in July that the U.S. would not intervene; the classical distinction between "moral" just cause and "material" just cause becomes pertinent at this point.

In real life most decisions are not punctual. They have longitude – they were prepared for by a lot that went before. Setting mid-January as a firm deadline, counter to most of the wisdom of ancient diplomacy and the modern social science of conflict resolution, was done weeks before. As the date approached, Bush's definition of its degree of firmness escalated to the point that by the 15th he in fact had no freedom to do otherwise. Yet the just war paradigm had not illuminated the weeks spent painting the U.S. and Iraq into their respective corners in the way it looked on January 15. Even less did it take account of the still longer predisposing factors for which the U.S. is more to blame than Saddam Hussein: the decade spent competing with the U.S.S.R. in building up Hussein's forces, and the explicit statements made in July to the effect that what Hussein might choose to do with border problems was not our concern. The full amplitude of the just war tradition would be capable of considering such components of complicity and even entrapment as part of the definition of just cause, but our public discourse has consistently described the case as if the history of Mesopotamia began in August.

The claim that the UN resolutions suffice to assure "just authority" is belied by destruction in Iraq unrelated to freeing Kuwait (bridges, roads municipal water and sewage systems) and by restatements of war aims (asking Iraqis to replace Saddam Hussein, demanding unconditional surrender and a war crimes trial) which go far beyond the UN objective (note as well the elements of bad faith in the UN appeal ...

Does a vote in which despite enormous pressures 47 senators opposed the resort to military force (and some of the "yea" voters said the president had acted wrongly throughout the fall but now they would rally 'round the flag) constitute a moral mandate? One can grant that this consultation of Congress is better than stonewalling completely the right of Congress to be consulted, and that the UN actions constitute more backing than we ever even thought about requesting for Panama or Grenada. Thus the criterion of "legitimate authority" is more nearly met than at some other times. Yet the scale of the air war has gone far beyond the UN authorization, as did the continuing escalation of the war aims so that by February 15 Pentagon projections were assuming the demand for unconditional surrender rather than withdrawal, and by February 25 flanking actions were undertaken to prevent withdrawal.

4) *Shared definitions?* The public is deceived by the tacit assumption that because the "criteria" can be listed in common-sense language there must be a shared definition of most of the operational terms, as there is in a natural science or even in law. ... In real use, however, most of the just war "criteria" are so subject to bias that they do not serve to adjudicate with any semblance of objectivity. The words like "legitimate authority" and "just cause" provide a common language, but they serve only to talk past each other. ...

5) *What is the alternative?* In most cases we are deceived by the tacit assumption that if and when the criteria are not met, one does not go to war. The doctrine can (theoretically) have teeth at several points: refusal to obey an unjust order, "selective conscientious objection" when called to serve an unjust cause, suing for peace when one cannot win without using unjust means, prosecuting a war crime. Yet no nonpacifist church has prepared its members for such hard choices. No independent information

sources assure the availability of the facts that would demand or enable such resistance.

6) *The rubbery claim of discrimination.* The hopeless debate over the Ash Wednesday bunker attack demonstrates how rubbery is the claim of discrimination. Johnson is right that "smarter" weapons can be discriminating; yet the exponential escalation of the number of sorties throws away much of that gain. More is abandoned when the concept of "military target" is expanded to include the main highway between Baghdad and Amman, so that when Jordanian refugee buses and fuel trucks are destroyed it is the drivers' fault. When antiaircraft artillery is placed on the roof of a home it is the householders' fault. When scores of women and children take overnight refuge in a bunker it is Saddam's fault. Assigning blame is not the same as moral discernment. ... When General H. Norman Schwartzkopf said the next day that "all Saddam Hussein needs to do to stop our killing civilians is to surrender," he replaced a restraint *in bello* with an accusation *ad bellum*.

Discussion is radically distorted by assuming that the only "legitimate means" question is civilian immunity. There are many more treaty commitments, all the way to the October 1980 conventions on "excessive use of conventional weapons" (certainly a fair description of the scale of the air war since mid-January).

7) How does one measure "proportionality"? We must weigh the devastation of Iraq (even if there were no civilian deaths) and the promise of decades of future trouble in the region against the evil of failing to reverse promptly the August 2 annexation. ...

What then is the tradition good for? The current debate, and the Johnson-Geyer exchange as one instance, suffices (other evidences, other hard-to-apply criteria, could be added) to demonstrate the incapacity of the system to yield a clear and commonly accessible adjudication of contested cases. What the just war tradition is really good for is that together with pacifism it can identify and denounce the less restrained views which in fact dominate public discourse and decision-making. These views are in principle three: 1) Many people think that since war consists by definition in the breakdown of civility, it is not only counterfactual but also counterproductive to try to retrieve the notion of moral accountability within the struggle. A maximum effort subject to minimal scruples will best end the anarchy and the suffering. Michael Walzer calls this stance "realism," emphasizing by the quotes that its claims to self-evidence is spurious. ... Against this, the just war tradition maintains that moral accountability and the possibility of restraint do not end when war looms. The a priori presumption against recourse to war needs to be overridden by fact-based warrants (*jus ad bellum*); once hostilities are undertaken the means must be legitimate and proportionate (*jus in bello*).

2) Many people think that what justifies war is a transcendent cause, discerned by a prophetic person. Overlapping with the "just" alternative in early medieval thought, "holy" war or the Crusade differs from the just war (properly so-called) as to cause, last resort, and probable success, and usually with regard to the human dignity of the enemy/infidel. Against this view, the just war tradition maintains that even wrong belief does not deprive humans of their rights, and even a religious rationale does not justify wrong means.

3) Many people think that war frees its actors from moral restraints by offering a unique setting for the proof of the virility of a political elite of military personnel, or of a nation. ... The adversary is not a fellow human with dignity (before God and the law) equal to one's own, but an opportunity to prove one's manly qualities by facing danger and shedding blood.

When held to honestly, the just war tradition agrees with pacifism in rejecting these three views. It is these three views, however, which in fact dominate real politics. The fundamental deception imposed on our public discourse is that despite the use of just war categories by sincere people, the overall shape of the macro decisions is determined by the other three kinds of dynamism.

Sometimes this deception may be intentional and cynical; but that is not my present claim. More prevalent and more insidious is the fact that just war discourse deceives sincere people by the very nature of its claim to base moral discernment upon the facts of the case and on universally accessible rational principles. It lets them think that their morality is somehow less provincial and more accessible to others than if it referred explicitly to the data of Christian faith, including the words and the work of Jesus.

"Has there ever been a just war?" Cynics ask this because they think that their disregard for restraint is thereby validated. Pacifists ask it because they wonder how seriously to take the just war thinkers' claim not to have sold out morally. The question is wrong. The basis of moral obligation is not the record of past success in doing right. Has there ever been a perfectly monogamous spouse? A faithful Christian church? The fitting question is whether *in the current case* those who claim that heritage are *in fact* letting it set the limits of their action. On that question the jury is still out. The claim of my nonpacifist colleagues that the system they are using is more socially responsible, more understandable to ordinary people, more culturally accessible to people of other value communities, more able to manage with discrimination the factual data of political decisions, than is my testimony to Jesus' words and work, still has the burden of proof.

Chapter VIII

Liberation Theology

Background: This chapter begins with a list of definitions and descriptions of liberation theology. The list includes works and speeches by key Latin and South American Catholic and Protestant theologians, reports by the 1968 and 1979 Conferences of Latin American Bishops (CELAM), and liberation passages from the Old and New Testament.

Liberation theologians rely on Christian Scripture to find linkages between biblical and modern liberation. They draw considerable inspiration from the Exodus account of the religious and physical liberation of the Hebrews. The also quote from the prophets because of their brave denunciations of injustices before oppressive or degenerate leaders and their defense of the rights of the poor in the face of their disenfranchisement and alienation. Liberation theologians also find the New Testament rich in descriptions of Christ's identification with the poor. Jesus opened his official ministry with a statement of his purpose: "He has sent me to bring glad tidings to the poor, to proclaim liberty to the captives." (Luke 4:18–19). Like the poor of today, Jesus was an outsider and a victim of the social/political/economic system. According to liberationists as leader of the poor, Jesus called both spiritual and political oppressors to account.

Despite the rich ties between liberation theology and Christ's mission to the poor, there is a debate within the Catholic church over the purpose, methods, ideological heritage, and spiritual depth of the theology of liberation. The debate plays itself out in the dialogue between Pope John Paul II and Cardinal Joseph Ratzinger on the Vatican side and Juan Luis Segundo and Kevin O'Higgins, Jesuit priests stationed in South America, on the other. All express commitment to the poor; they debate the best approach to solving the problems of poverty, exploitation and oppression.

The battle over liberation theology is largely a 1960's Catholic version of

President Lyndon Johnson's war on poverty, the 19th century American Protestant social gospel, and the 20th century third world demand for a New International Order (NIEO.) All addressed the problems of poverty, development, alienation, and social justice. The Catholic church dates its modern commitment to social justice to 1891 with Pope Leo XIII's encyclical on the condition of the worker. The 1984 Vatican "instruction" on liberation theology articulates the continued commitment: "It is not possible for a single instant to forget the situations of dramatic poverty from which the challenge set to theologians springs – the challenge to work out a genuine theology of liberation." The Church hierarchy supports what might be called a moderate or centrist liberation position.

Segundo, O'Higgins, and most of the authors in the introductory section have a more radical (and often Marxist) philosophy in mind. They outline the basic questions of liberation, the action strategy that it requires, and the human rights aspects of the gospel of liberation. For them, liberation theology is not just a Christian "ethic," it is both a call to action (orthopraxis) and to class solidarity with the disinherited classes. They assert that, since God, Jesus, and the Christian church opt for the poor, all Christians ought to see transforming society, so as to alleviate the suffering of the poor, as their first priority. In sum, these theologians tie classic themes of Christianity to the call for a theology of liberation and for greater progress in the establishment of the Kingdom of God on earth.

Authors: Juan Luis Segundo is a Jesuit priest from the Southern Cone of South America who embraces a socialist model of liberation; a model to which Christians must commit absolutely. In the article excerpted below, Segundo writes of two theologies of liberation. The first theology, which was committed to changing the condition of the poor, thrived in the early 1960s under the inspiration of student and intellectual members of the middle class, who saw their whole culture enmeshed in capitalistic oppression. In their view, the victims of this aggression had neither the education nor the means to understand or change the nature of their victimization. Segundo argues that the early formulators of liberation theology sought to redesign theology "to unmask the anti-Christian elements hidden in a so-called Christian society," and to excise passivity and fatalism from the masses. The new "de-ideologized" theology (i.e., one removed from the pervasive oppressive culture) was going to explain the political and spiritual liberation message of the gospel.

The second theology of liberation arrived after conversion of radical, middle class intellectuals and theologians to the "teachings" of the common people about suffering and populism. After bumping their heads against the conservative church hierarchy over the Marxist trappings of their approach, the repressive local governments over the call for revolution, and the poor who maintained passivity with respect to liberation, the theologians felt obliged "to learn how oppressed people lived their faith;" i.e., to learn theology from "grass-root" people. Segundo rejects this grass-roots conversion because it is the role of the theologian to teach (evangelize) the people, largely still trapped by their culture and faith of fatalism, about liberation and "the true meaning of the cross." He wonders "how a passive and fatalistic conception of God [can] evangelize the theologian?"

Kevin P. O'Higgins is an Irish Jesuit who teaches philosophy at the Catholic University in Paraguay. He offers a brief update on the vitality of liberation theology in the aftermath of the massive bankruptcy of communism in East Europe and the Soviet Union in the 1990s. O'Higgins wistfully admires the original fire and insight of the theology of liberation, and reminds the reader that its protest against "a pampered minority" that "condemns the majority to a life sentence of misery and hopelessness" is a profoundly Christian, and still relevant, call to abolish "hell on earth" in the third world.

O'Higgins begins his analysis by noting the decline of the liberation theology movement as it suffered perennial criticism from church leaders, blame for the decline of Catholicism in Latin America, as fundamentalist sects surged in the 1980s, and intellectual stagnation since its heyday in the 1970s. Most tragically, the objectives of alleviating the suffering of the poor and galvanizing resistance to oppression have not been realized. O'Higgins suggests that liberation theology erred in its excitement over the Cuban model of economic salvation and its dismissal of the democratic model. However, he also understands the pull of the "revolution," the skepticism about the elitist American model, and the impatience to overturn poverty and exploitation. O'Higgins blames "the 1960s" for the wrong turn taken by liberationists who saw the U.S. as tainted by neocolonialism and aggression (in Vietnam, for example) and Marxism as a progressive answer to economic and political development.

O'Higgins argues that, as Soviet Marxism failed, mainstream liberation theology began to distance itself from this "counter-productive ideological millstone." It also began, in his view, to accept "representative democracy" as a governing model that included the poor. O'Higgins suggests that the hierarchy of the Catholic church is also changing in the aftermath of atheistic communism's collapse. As a result, he believes that church leaders and moderate liberation theologians will join closer together to protest the exploitation of liberal capitalism in its worst application, as in Latin America. O'Higgins also believes in liberation in the wealthy countries that seem incapable of addressing poverty and marginalization in their own societies. He thus calls for a "world-wide coalition dedicated to the construction of new political, social and economic orders." According to Higgins, this new order can only be realized through a revitalized liberation theology that converts nations and peoples "to the values of the Kingdom of God."

Cardinal Joseph Ratzinger, Prefect of the Congregation for the Doctrine of the Faith, wrote an "instruction" on liberation theology to clarify the Vatican's position on the theology of liberation. He notes the Catholic church's approval of the original economic and social objectives of the liberation movement. But he also expresses skepticism about the naturalistic (the stress on man's reliance on self, knowledge, and science) and collectivistic direction of the movement. Ratzinger also details the dangers of "certain forms of liberation theology" that borrow concepts from atheistic Marxist ideology, which in reality betrays the cause of the poor.

Ratzinger begins by identifying the Catholic church with the aspirations of the poor for liberation from injustice, poverty, oppression, and exploitation. He then explains the biblical origins and the nature of the theme of liberation. Ratzinger's priority here is to distinguish between an exclusively political liberation and a spiritual and redemptive liberation from sin. Both are important, but the latter, in his view, provides the basis of Christian faith in God's new covenant with his people: to liberate them from sin through Jesus' sacrificial death and resurrection and to welcome them to eternal life. In other words, according to Ratzinger, God alone is the liberator of the spiritually and materially poor. He calls us to conversion, repentance, and renewal. Once people follow God, they are "to live and act as new creations in the love of neighbor and in the effective search for justice."

Ratzinger fears that the liberation movement, which demands a radical social revolution, ignores the prerequisite spiritual "search for personal perfection." In his view, putting the problems of poverty first over evangelization and spiritual salvation, reduces the Gospel "to a purely earthly gospel." According to Ratzinger, the Marxist analysis, which undergirds the theology of liberation, not only does precisely this, but also betrays its objective to liberate the poor. In his view, a liberation movement that relies on Marxist analysis and tactics risks merely replacing one form of tyranny with a new tyranny, as seen in the totalitarian prototype, the Marxist Soviet Union. He concludes that many Marxist concepts, the class struggle formulation, for example, are not "compatible with the Christian conception of humanity and society."

Pope John Paul II, while embracing the poor and condemning the exploitation of workers, joins with Ratzinger to warn against the excesses of liberation theologians who let their infatuation with Marxism blind them to its flaws. In his social encyclical of May 1991, John Paul explains the inevitable nature of the collapse of the degrading, repressive, statist, and atheistic communist dictatorship in East Europe and the Soviet Union. He also points out the dangers of capitalist exploitation, materialism, and consumerism in the west. The pope focuses on the plight of the poor in either system and on the responsibilities of people and governments to alleviate this plight. He highlights the right to own private property, to form private associations, to earn a fair wage, to discharge one's religious duties, and to receive due process of law. John Paul also asserts the right to social justice unchecked by state abuse or the dictates of imprisoning self-righteous ideologies. Despite his evenhanded condemnation of the evils of both communism and capitalism, John Paul is most concerned about the falsity, violence, and evils of state socialism.

Key Questions: What are the biblical and Marxist roots of the liberation theology movement's commandment to commit to social justice, the class struggle, and the poor? To what extent may violence be used in this endeavor? In what sense was Christ a "revolutionary" and "liberator"?

On Liberation Theology (excerpts)

Every true theology springs from a spirituality – that is, from a true meeting with God in history. Liberation theology was born when faith confronted the injustice done to the poor. By "poor" we do not really mean the poor individual who knocks on the door asking for alms. We mean a collective poor, the "popular classes," which is a much wider category than the "proletariat" singled out by Karl Marx (it is a mistake to identify the poor of liberation theology with the proletariat, though many of its critics do): the poor are also the workers exploited by the capitalist system; the underemployed, those pushed aside by the production process – a reserve army always at hand to take the place of the employed; they are the laborers of the countryside, and migrant workers with only seasonal work.

All this mass of the socially and historically oppressed makes up the poor as a social phenomenon. In the light of faith, Christians see in them the challenging face of the Suffering Servant, Jesus Christ. At first there is silence, silent and sorrowful contemplation, as if in the presence of a mystery that calls for introspection and prayer. Then this presence speaks. The Crucified in these crucified persons weeps and cries out: "I was hungry ... in prison ... naked" (Matt. 25:31–46).

Here what is needed is not so much contemplation as effective action for liberation. The Crucified needs to be raised to life. We are on the side of the poor only when we struggle alongside them against the poverty that has been unjustly created and forced on them. Service in solidarity with the oppressed also implies an act of love for the suffering Christ, a liturgy pleasing to God.

(Leonardo and Clodouis Boff, *Introducing Liberation Theology*, 1987.)

In fact liberation theology is an interpretation of Christian faith out of the experience of the poor. It is an attempt to read the Bible and key Christian doctrines with the eyes of the poor.

It is at the same time an attempt to help the poor interpret their own faith in a new way. To take a simple but central example, in traditional Latin

America piety Jesus is almost mute, indeed most often represented dead on the cross. Perhaps the fact that their society crucifies them and keeps them mute makes ordinary Latin Americans identify with such a Christ. Liberation theology focuses on Jesus' life and message. For example, in his initial sermon, a kind of manifesto, Jesus quotes Isaiah, "He has sent me to bring glad tidings to the poor, to proclaim liberty to captives …" and says that the passage is fulfilled in him. The poor learn to read the Scripture in a way that affirms their dignity and self-worth and their right to struggle together for a more decent life.

People to not simply happen to be poor; their poverty is largely a product of the way society is organized. Hence, liberation theology is a critique of economic structures that enable some Latin Americans to jet to Miami or London to shop, while most of their fellow citizens do not have safe drinking water. In particular, liberation theologians have critiqued the ideologies that justify such inequality, including their use of religious symbols. Military dictatorships have often practiced torture to defend what they are fond of calling "Western 'Christian' civilization."
(Phillip Berryman, *Liberation Theology*, 1987.)

In the first place, *liberation* expresses the aspirations of oppressed peoples and social classes, emphasizing the conflictual aspect of the economic, social, and political process which puts them at odds with wealthy nations and oppressive classes. In contrast, the world *development,* and above all the policies characterized as developmentalist [*desarrollista*], appear somewhat aseptic, giving a false picture of a tragic and conflictual reality. The issue of development does in fact find its true place in the more universal, profound, and radical perspective of liberation. It is only within this framework that *development* finds its true meaning and possibilities of accomplishing something worthwhile.

At a deeper level, *liberation* can be applied to an understanding of history. Man is seen as assuming conscious responsibility for his own destiny. This understanding provides a dynamic context and broadens the horizons of the desired social changes. In this perspective the unfolding of all man's dimensions is demanded – a man who makes himself throughout his life and throughout history. The gradual conquest of true freedom leads to the creation of a new man and a qualitatively different society. This vision provides, therefore, a better understanding of what in fact is at stake in our times.

Finally, the word *development* to a certain extent limits and obscures the theological problems implied in the process designated by this term. On the contrary the word liberation allows for another approach leading to the Biblical sources which inspire the presence and action of man in history. In the Bible Christ is presented as the one who brings us liberation. Christ the Savior liberates man from sin, which is the ultimate root of all disruption of friendship and of all injustice and oppression. Christ makes man truly free, that is to say, he enables man to live in communion with him; and this is the basis for all human brotherhood.

This is not a matter of three parallel or chronologically successive processes, however. There are three levels of meaning of a single, complex process, which finds its deepest sense and its full realization in the saving work of Christ. These levels of meaning, therefore, are interdependent.
(Gustavo Gutierrez, *A Theology of Liberation*, 1973.)

In its various foms – material deprivation, unjust oppression, physical and psychological illnesses, and finally death – human misery is the obvious sign of the natural condition of weakness in which man finds himself since original sin and the sign of his need for salvation. Hence it drew the compassion of Christ the Savior to take it upon himself and to be identified with the least of his brethren (cf. Mt. 25:40, 45). Hence also those who are oppressed by poverty are the object of a love of preference on the part of the church, which since her origin and in spite of the failings of many of her members, has not ceased to work for their relief, defense and liberation. She has done this through numberless works of charity which remain always and everywhere indispensable. In addition, through her social doctrine which she strives to apply, she has sought to promote structural changes in society so as to secure conditions of life worthy of the human person. ... The special option for the poor, far from being a sign of particularism or sectarianism, manifests the universality of the church's being and mission. This option excludes no one.

This is the reason why the church cannot express this option by means of reductive sociological and ideological categories which would make this preference a partisan choice and a source of conflict.
(Cardinal Joseph Ratzinger, "Instruction on Christian Freedom and Liberation," 1986.)

Just as formerly the first people, Israel, experienced the saving presence of God when he set them free from slavery in Egypt, so we too, the new people of God, cannot fail to feel his saving deliverance for each and every one from less human to more human conditions of life. ...

There are two complementary and inseparable elements. The first is liberation from all the forms of bondage, from personal and social sin, and from everything that tears apart the human individual and society; all this finds its source in egotism, in the mystery of iniquity. The second element is liberation for progressive growth in being through communion with God and other human beings; this reaches its culmination in the perfect communion of heaven, where God is all in all and weeping forever ceases. (Puebla Conference of Latin American Bishops, 1979.)

I should like to stress that the notion of liberation is very concrete. ... The term "liberation" is a very Christian one, deriving from the Hebrew notion in the Old Testament. God told Moses to "liberate" his people from Egypt. The notion of liberation came down through Christianity to such thinkers as Hegel and Marx, and it was then passed along to many of today's liberation fronts. Christians often translate it into such terms as "salvation" and "redemption," but behind all these notions lies the dialectic of oppression and exodus. If we turn liberation into some abstract sort of salvation, then the term loses all meaning. (Spanish Priest stationed in El Salvador, Enrique Dussel, in *A History of the Church in Latin America*.)

The process of colonization, liberation, and organization is best understood in Marxist terms. (Fr. Sergio Torres of Chile, in lecture to fellow liberation theologians in the U.S.)

There is no perfect solution. The only way is for us to choose between two oppressions. And the history of Marxism, even oppressive, offers right now more hope than the history of existing capitalism. ... Marx did not create the class struggle, international capitalism did. (Fr. Juan Luis Segundo to a group of American Jesuits.)

We give the name socialism to a political regime in which the ownership of the means of production is removed from individuals and handed over to higher institutions whose concern is the higher good. (Segundo, *Concilium* 96: *The Mystical and Political Dimension of the Christian Faith*, 1974.)

The theologians are becoming communists and the communists are becoming theologians. (Protestant theologian Jose Miguez Bonino, in *Christians and Marxists,* quoting Fidel Castro.)

Every day, the capitalistic system itself commits aggression in Latin America, aggression far more evil than that committed by the police and the army led by dictators. Millions of children die in the world each year from simple malnutrition. ... Now, it is not as if the resources presently existing in the world were inadequate to produce sufficient nutrition for all. Technologically it is possible. What is happening is that capitalism as a system does not permit existing resources to be directed to the satisfaction of needs. ... Capitalism has seized the resources of humanity. (Mexican priest Jose Miranda, in *Communism in the Bible.*)

[Revolution is] the way to bring about a government that feeds the hungry, clothes the naked, teaches the ignorant, puts into practice the works of charity, and love for neighbor, not just every now and then, and not just for a few, but for the majority of our neighbors. (Columbian priest turned guerilla, Camilo Torres; killed in combat in 1966.)

The first and main question here is a radical one. It is a question of the prevailing social order. Latin American misery and injustice go too deep to be responsive to palliatives. Hence we speak of social revolution, not reform; of liberation, not development; of socialism, not modernization of the prevailing system. ...

"Realists" call these statements romantic and utopian. And they should, for the rationality of these statements is of a kind quite unfamiliar to them. It is the rationality of a concrete, historical undertaking that heralds a different society, one built in function of the poor and the oppressed, and that denounces a society built for the benefit of a few. ...

Only by overcoming a society divided into classes, only by installing a political power at the service of the great popular majorities, only by eliminating the private appropriation of the wealth created by human toil, can we build the foundation of a more just society. This is why the development of the concrete historical march forward of a new society is heading more and more in the direction of socialism in Latin America. But it is a socialism that is well aware of the deficiencies of many of its own concrete forms in the world today. It endeavors to break free of categories and cliches and creatively seek its own paths.

... This effort to create a different society also includes the creation of a new human person. Hence the whole project must start out with their values. For it is among the masses that this radical questioning of the prevailing order, this abolition of the culture of the oppressor, is arising. ...

Those who have made the option for commitment to liberation look upon the political as a dimension that embraces, and demandingly conditions, the entirety of human endeavors. (Peruvian Priest Gustavo Gutierrez, *The Power of the Poor in History*, 1983.)

But perhaps what most shocks Christians who seek to take sides frankly and decisively with the poor and exploited, and to enter into involvement with the struggle of the proletariat, is the conflictual nature of praxis [practice or action] in this context. Politics today involves confrontation – and varying degrees of violence – among human groups, among social classes with opposing interests ... we have to recognize the fact of class struggle and accept the fact that we have class enemies to combat. (Gutierrez, as cited by the Chicago Religious Task Force on Central America, *Statement of Faith*, 1984.)

Poverty, as a lack of the goods of this world necessary to live worthily as men, is in itself evil. The prophets denounce it as contrary to the will of the Lord and most of the time as the fruits of the injustice and sin of men. b) Spiritual poverty is the theme of the poor of Yahweh (Zeph 2:3; Luke 1:46–55). Spiritual poverty is the attitude of opening to God, the ready disposition of one who hopes for everything from the Lord (Matt 5:3). Although he values the goods of this world, he does not become attached to them and he recognizes the higher value of the riches of the

Kingdom. ... c) Poverty as a commitment, through which one assumes voluntarily and lovingly the conditions of the needy of this world in order to bear witness to the evil which it represents and to spiritual liberty in the face of material goods, follows the example of Christ Who took to Himself all the consequences of men's sinful condition and Who "being rich became poor" in order to redeem us. (Medellin Conference of Latin American Bishops, 1968.)

We see the growing gap between rich and poor as a scandal and a contradiction to Christian existence. The luxury of a few becomes an insult to the wretched poverty of the vast masses. ... We affirm the need for a conversion on the part of the whole church to a preferential option for the poor, an option aimed at their integral liberation. ...

The love of God. ... for us today must become first and foremost a labor of justice on behalf of the oppressed, an effort of liberation for those who are most in need of it. (Puebla Conference of Latin American Bishops, 1979.)

The poor are the authentic theological source for understanding Christian truth and practice. (Jesuit Jon Sobrino, stationed in El Salvador, in *Christology at the Crossroads*, 1978.)

A theology of black liberation [theology] ... It is the affirmation of black humanity that emancipates black people from white racism, thus providing authentic freedom for both white and black people. ...

The message of liberation is the revelation of God as revealed in the incarnation of Jesus Christ. Freedom IS the gospel. Jesus is the Liberator! The demand that Christ the Liberator imposes on all men REQUIRES all blacks to affirm their full dignity as persons and all whites to surrender their presumptions of superiority and abuses of power. (James Cone, *Black Theology and Black Power*, 1969.)

Blacks have used Christianity not as it was delivered to them by segregated white churches, but as its truth was authenticated to them in the experience of suffering, to reinforce an ingrained religious temperment and to produce an indigenous religion oriented to freedom and human welfare. (Gayraud S. Wilmore, *Black Religion and Black Radicalism*, 1973.)

But the Lord said, "I have witnessed the affliction of my people in Egypt and have heard their cry of complaint against their slave drivers, so I know well what they are suffering. Therefore I have come down to rescue them from the hands of the Egyptians and lead them out of that land into a good and spacious land, a land flowing with milk and honey. ... So indeed the cry of the Israelites has reached me, and I have truly noted that the Egyptians are oppressing them. (Ex. 3:7–9, *New American Bible*)

Put away your misdeeds from before my eyes; cease doing evil; learn to do good. Make justice your aim: redress the wronged, hear the orphan's plea, defend the widow. ... This rather is the fasting that I wish: releasing those bound unjustly, untying the thongs of the yoke; Setting free the oppressed, breaking every yoke; Sharing your bread with the hungry, sheltering the oppressed and the homeless; clothing the naked when you see them, and not turning your back on your own. (Is. 59: 6–7)

Who keeps faith forever, secures justice for the oppressed, gives food to the hungry. The Lord sets captives free; The Lord gives sight to the blind. The Lord raises up those that were bowed down; the Lord loves the just. The Lord protects strangers; the fatherless and the widow he sustains, but the way of the wicked he thwarts. (Ps. 6–9)

Juan Luis Segundo, SJ

Two Theologies of Liberation

Contrary to the most common assumption, Latin American theology, without any precise title, began to show clearly distinctive features at least ten years before Gustavo Gutiérrez's well known book *A Theology of Liberation.* ...

Let us, therefore, go back to the early sixties. Something was happening, more or less at the same time, all over Latin America, something which established a new context for understanding our Christian faith and, hence, for doing theology. It is, I believe of great importance, to understand precisely the social, political and theological context of this event.

Until 1964, when the military takeover of Brazil began to foreshadow a reversal of privileges afforded to universities within society, the state universities at least were ruled by a students' movement created at the beginning of this century in Argentina. This movement, which was successful in almost every Latin American country, was aimed at giving the university the freedom it needed in the face of political governments and other pressures.

It did not mean a de-politicisation of universities. On the contrary, by making students the principal rulers of university life (together with faculty members and groups of professionals), and by gaining political autonomy, the state university became a sort of parallel power in politics. It was so to speak a state within a state. It became free to support any kind of political ideas, and above all to unmask, through all kinds of intellectual tools, the mystifying ideologies used by our governments to hide and to justify the inhuman situation of the majority of our population.

Etudes (French Jesuit Review) Sept. 1984 and reprinted in *The Month* (Oct. 1984) 321–327. Used by permission.

It was precisely in this context, however one may evaluate it, that a new approach to Christian faith developed among students. It involved a kind of Christian conversion as far as the social consequences of our faith were concerned. Without taking this context into account, one easily falls into the mistaken notion that liberation theology is a specific branch of theology, recently created and somehow inflated, dealing with 'liberation', whatever this term may mean. Another mistake coming from the lack of knowledge of this context consists of believing that liberation theology in Latin America came from a particular understanding of European political theology. Before knowing anything about political theology, if it existed at all at this time, the university student, using above all the option of the social function of *ideologies*, had already discovered that our whole culture, whatever the intention in constructing it may have been, was working for the benefit of the ruling classes. It was not, of course, necessary to be a Marxist to make such a common sense discovery, but it is also true that many Christian students at the university were led by their Marxist fellows to this realization and to be concerned with this fact.

Furthermore, Christian students could do nothing except include *theology* – the understanding of Christian faith – in the ideological mechanisms structuring the whole of our culture. And when I say 'the whole of our culture', I mean by that, that even though ideologies are consciously or unconsciously developed in the ruling classes which benefit from them, they also pervade the whole society since they are injected even into the minds of those who are their victims. Unlearned and so capable of utilizing developed tools of ideological suspicion in a culture considered impartial and the same for all social classes, poor and marginalized people were led by the culture to accept distorted and hidden oppressive elements which 'justified' their situation, and, among all these elements, a distorted and oppressive theology.

From Christian students to theologians working with them, this ideological suspicion thus became a source of a new vision about what theology should become and about how a theologian was supposed to work to unmask the anti-Christian elements hidden in a so-called Christian society. In order to give some concrete flesh to this quite abstract reflection, let me give you an example. ... In an article written two years ago after a month of pastoral experience in one of Brazil's poorest states, the state of Acre on the frontier between Brazil and Bolivia, Leonardo Boff, trying to theologize with the poor and uncultivated members of the Basic Christian Commun-

ities, experienced some difficulties in dialogue and communication between
such different levels of culture. But he tells us in his article that once, at least,
the dialogue was set in motion when he asked: how did Jesus redeem us?
Many people answered: 'through the cross.' Others put the same idea in
slightly different terms: 'through his suffering'.

At this point Boff recalls his reflection on those answers of grass-roots
Christian people. His reflection can be meaningful for us since it shows, in a
particular *theological* case, the global attitude of suspicion which a university student is supposed to have about popular religion and its function in
an oppressive society like ours. Boff writes:

> I asked myself: why do (grass-roots) people immediately associate redemption with
> the cross? Undoubtedly because they have not learned the historical character of
> redemption, that is, of the process of liberation. Perhaps it is so because their own
> life is nothing but suffering and crosses, the cross society has managed to make
> them carry on their shoulders.

And the consequence for theology develops in this article: 'A Jesus who
only suffers is not liberating; he generates the cult of suffering and fatalism.
It is important to *relocate within the mind of (common) people the cross in
its true place*. ...

I think that this example can provide a good indication of both the
method and the aim of this first theology of liberation.

No amount of subtle argument can conceal that the only relevant methodological feature of Latin American theology is, as a matter of fact, to start
thinking not from a systematic listing of theological problems linked by an
inner logic for the sake of orthodox and credible answers to every problem,
but instead in the precise context I am describing, to start both from a
commitment to think for the sake of poor and oppressed people, and from
a consideration of their praxis every time we perceive that this praxis is
linked, through theology, to the oppressive mechanisms of the whole
culture.* This consideration of praxis aims at reformulating a Christian
theology capable of transforming this praxis into a more liberative one, that
is to say, aiming at orthopraxis: in this example, it aims at preventing
passivity and fatalism. ...

---

* Praxis in the context of liberation theology means practice, or action, or application
  as a followup to theory or principle or reflection. Orthopraxis would be "right-
  acting" and orthodoxy would be "right-thinking" or doctrine. [Editor]

That is why the aim of this first theology liberation from the beginning was to re-make, to the extent of what was possible for us, the whole of theology. Being faithful to both, orthodoxy and orthopraxis, we felt the necessity of de-ideologizing our language and our message about God, the Church, the sacraments, grace, sin, the meaning of Jesus Christ, and so on. We were not interested at all in creating a new kind of branch of theology that *spoke of liberation*, or in making liberation the explicit centre of the whole of theology, instead of any other theological theme. In this sense, the title this theological trend received after Gustavo Gutiérrez's famous book *A Theology of Liberation*[2] made us perhaps quite fashionable, but helped also to distort to some extent our aim and to push us toward a useless battle against many European and North American theologians, and finally to create suspicion among Church authorities about our supposed intention of substituting 'supernatural and vertical salvation' with a historical and political liberation.

In any case, de-ideologizing our customary interpretation of Christian faith was, for us, the necessary task in order to get the whole Church to carry to our people an understanding of our faith both more faithful to Jesus' Gospel and more capable of contributing to the humanization of all people and social classes in our continent.

Of course, this theological liberation was supposed through pastoral activities and agents, to reach at a *different pace* different social classes, thus becoming universal with the same kind of universality that can be attributed to the conflict Gospel of Jesus. As I have already said, the context for this new trend in Latin American theology was the university, or, in other words, middle class people. Now, the middle class are usually considered by sociologists as the most mobile and creative part of society, inclined either to provoke rightist upheavals when they feel their interests or social order threatened, or to be involved in restructuring and liberating society when they feel guilty.

Thus it was not the oppressed people, but the middle classes beginning with students, who received the first features of this liberation theology as a joyful conversion and a new commitment. As middle class, they clearly perceived that they themselves belonged to the side of our oppressors and were more or less linked with an ideology fostering their interests. As Christians, they felt increasingly concerned with fighting for the liberation of poor and marginalized people, but also blocked by many oppressive elements which they had always considered constituent parts of their faith.

A new theological vision of faith was thus assumed by a wide range of middle class Christians as a liberating force so that they accepted and fulfilled a new type of Christian commitment to liberation, even against their own material interests and privileges.

As theologians, we believed at that time, and some of us still believe, that this movement among the most active and creative members of the Church could eventually reach, sooner or later, all oppressed people on our continent, through the pastoral activities of a Church following a new line and carrying out a new message. Thus the first theology of liberation was committed to a long-term and far-reaching goal.

But something different happened.

Now as I examine the second line in liberation theology, I believe that it would be useful to recall the elements we have brought forward in the first line, namely: the origin of a theology of conversion among middle class groups, the methodological trend to suspect that the customary way of understanding Christian faith was distorted at all levels of society by ideological bias that concealed and justified the status quo, and finally, the long-term aim of providing the pastoral activities of the Church with a new and de-ideologized theology capable of speaking about the common themes of Christian faith as they were at the beginning, i.e., a revelation of the humanizing and liberating will of God and of God's own being.

Let me briefly look at a new context for theologizing: the common people [and the conversion of intellectuals and theologians to the popular will and viewpoint.]

Conversion means, then, for many intellectuals, a kind of self-negation. Instead of teaching, they should learn. And in order to learn from common people, they should incorporate themselves, even mentally, with these common people, and give up the chronic suspicion among intellectuals that common people are always wrong. Given this background, let us consider, from this example, the crisis of the middle seventies in the Latin American theology of liberation, and the following shift from the first to the second one.

One thing was obvious: the rise of popular or populist movements either outside or inside the Church had shown that common people had neither understood nor welcomed anything from the first theology of liberation, and had actually reacted against its criticism of the supposed oppressive elements of popular religion. They resisted the new pastoral trends trying to correct it. The first theology of liberation had raised hopes, enthusiasm and conversion only among the middle classes which were integrated into a European culture. It is true that their concern for the poor and oppressed had made them dangerous for the status quo, but the persecution of middle class leftists all over Latin America did not close the gap between them and grass-roots people.

It appeared then that if theologians were still to be the 'organic intellectuals' of the common people, that is to say, useful as intellectuals charged with the understanding of popular faith, they were obliged to learn how oppressed people lived their faith. Thus Enrique Dussel coined for theologians and pastoral agents the expression, *the discipleship of the poor. ...* Theologians, wanting to be in religious matters the 'organic intellectuals' of poor and uncultivated people, began then to understand their function as one of unifying and structuring people's understanding of their faith, as well as grounding and defending the practices coming from this faith. ...

Let us recall here as an example the experience of Leonardo Boff trying to dialogue with members of Basic Christian Communities in Acre about Jesus' redemption. He cannot but conclude that theologians must (in his own words) 'relocate within the mind of (common) people the cross in its true place'. In saying that, Leonardo seems to act naturally as a theologian of the first line of Latin American liberation theology. But at the beginning of his article we find a brief introduction containing the methodological principle of the second one. He writes there:

In a Church that has opted for the people, for the poor and for their liberation, the *principal learning of theology* comes from the contact with (grass-root) people. Who evangelizes the theologian? The faith witnessed by faithful people, their capacity to introduce God in all their struggling, their resistance against the oppression they customarily have to suffer.

I do not know if you perceive that there is an undoubtedly involuntary contradiction here between the claim of having been evangelized by the poor and taught by them, and, on the other hand, the pretension of relocating in people's minds the true meaning of the cross and suffering. How can a passive and fatalistic conception of God evangelize the theologian?

I believe that at this point we both grasp the meaning and appreciate the difficulty in the shift in Latin American liberation theology I was alluding to in the title of this paper. No doubt, both share the same global intention of liberating and humanizing those who suffer the most from unjust structures on our continent; but this cannot conceal the fact that we are faced here with two different theologies under the same name: different in scope, different in method, different in presuppositions and different in pastoral consequences. ...

If we look at their scope, both lines seem to have failed, to a considerable extent, to fulfill the expectations raised by them. It is clear by now that the first line of liberation theology failed in providing the Latin American Church with a new and de-ideologized dealing, in a liberating way, with the customary themes of pastoral activities: God, sacraments, grace, and so forth. I think that three principal causes were influential in this failure.

The first was the *title*. Instead of taking over the old theology by slowly giving a new content to every field of theology, the new title sounded as if it were pointing to a new and dangerous kind of theology more concerned with politics than with a serious improvement of theology taught in universities and seminaries. To this inner danger was soon added the pressures and threats of civilian or military authorities against the Church to make it avoid any activities explicitly connected with the theology of liberation.

Secondly, the new theology, identified by its title, to the extent that it reached not only theologians but also large segments of the middle class lay population, raised all over Latin America a wave of doubt and strong criticism about *popular religion* (otherwise and perhaps more aptly called 'popular catholicism') as being oppressive and, all in all, non-Christian. It provoked a growing reaction against liberation theology· among Church officials striving to keep the masses within the Church. The accusation of being more or less influenced by Marxism in this analysis of the relationship between religion and oppression was an easy although unfair reason for preventing the majority of theologians in this line of thought from teaching in institutes, seminaries and faculties destined to prepare pastoral agents for the Church in Latin America. ...

Trying to indicate exactly to what extent the second line of liberation theology has succeeded or not in its own quest, I would say that, considering the context, it can only be said that it has only half achieved its objective and that on two levels.

In the first place, it is true that this second line of thought has had more success in winning over for liberation theology an important part of the ecclesiastical hierarchy. We have already indicated that the resistance to the first line came from a criticism of it vis-à-vis popular religiosity in Latin America. In that regard, the second line dissipated many suspicions when it accepted the religion of ordinary people as a generally liberating element. Where the Church felt itself strongest in protecting ordinary people, even against two governments and their repression, as in the case of Brazil, the second line was widely accepted. From this point of view, the Puebla Conference would have been, if not an acceptance of this line, at least a compromise between it and those who wanted a global condemnation of liberation theology.

Nevertheless, it is impossible to ignore, whatever our opinion about the justification of popular religiosity might be, the political aspect of this second line which is just as or even more accentuated than that of the first. Actually, the first line of liberation theology came in contact with political concerns through a redefinition of faith which paid close attention to the influence of faith on the political activity of Christians. However, the second line accepts, up to a certain point, the control and design of a political posture for liberation from the peoples themselves. When the theologian becomes part of the people, he or she lends even more political support for the political vindication of the people. It is not in vain that a theology linked with Peronism is even more political than an attempt to reformulate theology in general in a de-ideologized way. The same thing could be said about Brazil where the bishops of several dioceses distributed political guidelines for the last election to teach people how to make a political option among different parties. ...

Furthermore, there is another level where the objectives achieved by the second line of liberation theology should be considered, although as very modest achievements. As intense as the theologian's conversion to ordinary people might be, this intellectual cannot totally renounce the exercise of a certain criticism. We have already seen the sort of 'lapse' or contradiction between the pretension of learning theology from common people and the attempt of relocating in people's minds the true meaning of suffering in the example of Leonardo Boff. But generally speaking, this second line of theology has tried to provide more balanced principles despite its seeming lack of criticism toward popular phenomena. It sees the issue as one 'of rescuing and promoting Christian values in popular culture'. To that end, obviously, one has to be immersed in it, but not with closed eyes. Beyond doubt there are negative elements in a culture, while at the same time a theologian discovers magnificent liberating aspects. It is the question, then, of distinguishing one from the other and, to the extent possible, of promoting some while restraining or repressing others.

Cardinal Joseph Ratzinger

Instruction on Certain Aspects of the 'Theology of Liberation'

The Gospel of Jesus Christ is a message of freedom and a force for liberation. In recent years this essential truth has become the object of reflection for theologians, with a new kind of attention which is itself full of promise.

Liberation is first and foremost liberation from the radical slavery of sin. Its end and its goal is the freedom of the children of God, which is the gift of grace. As a logical consequence, it calls for freedom from many different kinds of slavery in the cultural, economic, social and political spheres, all of which derive ultimately from sin and so often prevent people from living in a manner befitting their dignity. ...

Faced with the urgency of certain problems, some are tempted to emphasize, unilaterally, the liberation from servitude of an earthly and temporal kind. They do so in such a way that they seem to put liberation from sin in second place and so fail to give it the primary importance it is due. Thus, their very presentation of the problems is confused and ambiguous. ...

The present instruction has a ... limited and precise purpose: to draw the attention of pastors, theologians and all the faithful to the deviations and risks of deviation, damaging to the faith and to Christian living, that are brought about by certain forms of liberation theology which use, in an insufficiently critical manner, concepts borrowed from various currents of Marxist thought.

This warning should in no way be interpreted as a disavowal of all those who want to respond generously and with an authentic evangelical spirit to

14 *Origins* (Sept. 13, 1984), 195–204. Used by permission.

the "preferential option for the poor." It should not at all serve as an excuse for those who maintain an attitude of neutrality and indifference in the face of the tragic and pressing problems of human misery and injustice. It is, on the contrary, dictated by the certitude that the serious ideological deviations which it points out tend inevitably to betray the cause of the poor. More than ever, it is important that numerous Christians, whose faith is clear and who are committed to live the Christian life in its fullness, become involved in the struggle for justice, freedom and human dignity because of their love for their disinherited, oppressed and persecuted brothers and sisters. More than ever, the church intends to condemn abuses, injustices and attacks against freedom, wherever they occur and whoever commits them. She intends to struggle, by her own means, for the defense and advancement of the rights of mankind, especially of the poor.

An Aspiration

1. The powerful and almost irresistible aspiration that the people have for liberation constitutes one of the principal signs of the times which the church has to examine and interpret in the light of the Gospel. ...

2. The yearning shows the authentic, if obscure, perception of the dignity of the human person, created "in the image and likeness of God" (Gn. 1:26–27), ridiculed and scorned in the midst of a variety of different oppressions: cultural, political, racial, social and economic, often in conjunction with one another. ...

4. Consequently mankind will no longer passively submit to crushing poverty with its effects of death, disease and decline. He resents this misery as an intolerable violation of his native dignity. ...

5. It is widely known even in still illiterate sections of the world that, thanks to the amazing advances in science and technology, mankind, still growing in numbers, is capable of assuring each human being the minimum of goods required by his dignity as a person.

6. The scandal of the shocking inequality between the rich and the poor – whether between rich and poor countries, or between social classes in a single nation – is no longer tolerated. ...

7. The lack of equity and of a sense of solidarity international transactions works to the advantage of the industrialized nations so that the gulf be-

tween the rich and the poor is ever widening. Hence derives the feeling of frustration among Third World countries and the accusation of exploitation and economic colonialism brought against the industrialized nations. ...

Liberation, a Christian Theme

1. Taken by itself, the desire for liberation finds a strong and fraternal echo in the heart and spirit of Christians.

2. Thus, in accord with this aspiration, the theological and pastoral movement known as "liberation theology" was born, first in the countries of Latin America, which are marked by the religious and cultural heritage of Christianity, and then in other countries of the Third World, as well as certain circles in the industrialized countries.

3. The expression "theology of liberation" refers first of all to a special concern for the poor and the victims of oppression, which in turn begets a commitment to justice. Starting with this approach, we can distinguish several often contradictory ways of understanding the Christian meaning of poverty and the type of commitment to justice which it requires. As with all movements of ideas, the "theologies of liberation" present diverse theological positions. Their doctrinal frontiers are badly defined.

4. The aspiration for liberation, as the term itself suggests, repeats a theme which is fundamental to the Old and New Testaments. In itself, the expression "theology of liberation" is a thoroughly valid term: It designates a theological reflection centered on the biblical theme of liberation and freedom, and on the urgency of its practical realization. ...

Biblical Foundations

... 2. The radical experience of Christian liberty is our first point of reference. Christ, our liberator, has freed us from sin and from slavery to the law and to the flesh, which is the mark of the condition of sinful mankind. Thus it is the new life of grace, fruit of justification, which makes us free. This means that the most radical form of slavery is slavery to sin. Other forms of slavery find their deepest root in slavery to sin. That is why freedom in the full Christian sense, characterized by the life in the Spirit, cannot be confused with a license to give in to the desires of the flesh. Freedom is a new life in love.

3. The "theologies of liberation" make wide use of readings from the Book of Exodus. The exodus, in fact, is the fundamental event in the formation of the chosen people. It represents freedom from foreign domination and from slavery. One will note that the specific significance of the event comes from its purpose, for this liberation is ordered to the foundation of the people of God and the covenant cult celebrated on Mt. Sinai. That is why the liberation of exodus cannot be reduced to a liberation which is principally or exclusively political in nature. Moreover, it is significant that the term freedom is often replaced in scripture by the very closely related term *redemption.*

4. The foundational episode of the Exodus will never be effaced from the memory of Israel. Reference is made to it when, after the destruction of Jerusalem and the exile to Babylon, the Jewish people lived in the hope of a new liberation and, beyond that, awaited a definitive liberation. In this experience God is recognized as the liberator. He will enter into a new covenant with his people. It will be marked by the gift of his Spirit and the conversion of hearts.

5. The anxieties and multiple sufferings sustained by those who are faithful to the God of the covenant provide the theme of several Psalms: laments, appeals for help and thanksgivings all make mention of religious salvation and liberation. In this context, suffering is not purely and simply equated with the social condition of poverty or with the condition of the one who is undergoing political oppression. It also includes the hostility of one's enemies, injustice, failure and death. The Psalms call us back to an essential religious experience: It is from God alone that one can expect salvation and healing. God, and not man, has the power to change the situations of suffering. Thus the "poor of the Lord" live in a total and confident reliance upon the loving providence of God. ...

6. In the Old Testament, the prophets after Amos keep affirming with particular vigor the requirements of justice and solidarity and the need to pronounce a very severe judgment on the rich who oppress the poor. They come to the defense of the widow and the orphan. They threaten the powerful: The accumulation of evils can only lead to terrible punishments.

Faithfulness to the covenant cannot be conceived of without the practice of justice. Justice as regards God and justice as regards mankind are inseparable. God is the defender and the liberator of the poor. ...

8. Already proclaimed in the Old Testament, the commandment of fraternal love extended to all mankind thus provides the supreme rule of social life. There are no discriminations or limitations which can counter the recognition of everyone as neighbor. ...

11. It is in light of the Christian vocation to fraternal love and mercy that the rich are severely reminded of their duty. St. Paul, faced with the disorders of the church of Corinth, forcefully emphasizes the bond which exists between participation in the sacrament of love and sharing with the brother in need.

12. New Testament revelation teaches us that sin is the greatest evil, since it strikes man in the heart of his personality. The first liberation, to which all others must make reference, is that from sin.

13. Unquestionably, it is to stress the radical character of the deliverance brought by Christ and offered to all, be they politically free or slaves, that the New Testament does not require some change in the political or social condition as a prerequisite for entrance into this freedom. However, the Letter to Philemon shows that the new freedom procured by the grace of Christ should necessarily have effects on the social level. ...

15. Nor can one localize evil principally or uniquely in bad social, political or economic "structures" as though all other evils came from them so that the creation of the "new men" would depend on the establishment of different economic and socio-political structures. To be sure, there are structures which are evil and which cause evil and which we must have the courage to change. Structures, whether they are good or bad, are the result of man's actions and so are consequences more than causes. The root of evil, then lies in free and responsible persons who have to be converted by the grace of Jesus Christ in order to live and act as new creatures in the love of neighbor and in the effective search for justice, self-control and the exercise of virtue.

To demand first of all a radical revolution in social relations and then to criticize the search for personal perfection is to set out on a road which leads to the denial of the meaning of the person and his transcendence, and to destroy ethics and its foundation, which is the absolute character of the distinction between good and evil. ...

The Voice of the Magisterium

In order to answer the challenge leveled at our times by oppression and hunger, the church's magisterium has frequently expressed her desire to awaken Christian consciences to a sense of justice, social responsibility and solidarity with the poor and the oppressed, and to highlight the present urgency of the doctrine and imperatives contained in Revelation. ...

A New Interpretation of Christianity

1. It is impossible to overlook the immense amount of selfless work done by Christians, pastors, priests, religious or laypersons, who, driven by a love for their brothers and sisters living in inhuman conditions, have endeavored to bring help and comfort to countless people in the distress brought about by poverty. Among these, some have tried to find the most effective means to put a quick end to the intolerable situation.

2. The zeal and the compassion which should dwell in the hearts of all pastors nevertheless run the risk of being led astray and diverted to works which are just as damaging to man and his dignity as is the poverty which is being fought, if one is not sufficiently attentive to certain temptations.

3. The feeling of anguish at the urgency of the problems cannot make us lose sight of what is essential nor forget the reply of Jesus to the Tempter: "It is not on bread alone that man lives, but on every word that comes from the mouth of God" (Mt. 4:4; cf. Dt. 8:3).

Faced with the urgency of sharing bread, some are tempted to put evangelization into parentheses, as it were, and postpone it until tomorrow: first the bread, then the word of the Lord. It is a fatal error to separate these two and even worse to oppose the one to the other. In fact, the Christian perspective naturally shows they have a great deal to do with one another.

4. To some it even seems that the necessary struggle for human justice and freedom in the economic and political sense constitutes the whole essence of salvation. For them the Gospel is reduced to a purely earthly gospel. ...

9. In this present document, we will only be discussing developments of that current of thought which, under the name "theology of liberation," proposes a novel interpretation of both the content of faith and of Christian existence which seriously departs from the faith of the church and, in fact, actually constitutes a practical negation.

10. Concepts uncritically borrowed from Marxist ideology and recourse to theses of a biblical hermeneutic marked by rationalism are at the basis of the new interpretation which is corrupting whatever was authentic in the generous initial commitment on behalf of the poor.

Marxist Analysis

1. Impatience and a desire for results has led certain Christians, despairing of every other method, to turn to what they call "Marxist analysis."

2. Their reasoning is this: An intolerable and explosive situation requires effective action which cannot be put off. Effective action presupposes a scientific analysis of the structural causes of poverty. Marxism now provides us with the means to make such an analysis, they say. Then one simply has to apply the analysis to the Third-World situation, especially in Latin America. ...

7. The warning of Paul VI remains fully valid today: Marxism as it is actually lived out poses many distinct aspects and questions for Christians to reflect upon and act on. However, it would be "illusory and dangerous to ignore the intimate bond which radically unites them, and to accept elements of the Marxist analysis without recognizing its connections with the ideology, or to enter into the practice of class struggle and of its Marxist interpretation while failing to see the kind of totalitarian society to which this process slowly leads."

8. It is true that Marxist thought ever since its origins, and even more so lately, has become divided and has given birth to various currents which diverge significantly from one another. To the extent that they remain fully Marxist, these currents continue to be based on certain fundamental tenets which are not compatible with the Christian conception of humanity and society. In this context certain formulas are not neutral, but keep the meaning they had in the original Marxist doctrine. This is the case with the "class struggle." This expression remains pregnant with the interpretation that Marx gave it, so it cannot be taken as the equivalent of "serve social conflict," in an empirical sense. Those who use similar formulas, while claiming to keep only certain elements of the Marxist analysis and yet to reject this analysis taken as a whole, maintain at the very least serious confusion in the minds of their readers.

9. Let us recall the fact that atheism and the denial of the human person, his liberty and his rights, are at the core of Marxist theory. This theory, then, contains errors which directly threaten the truths of the faith regarding the eternal destiny of individual persons. Moreover, to attempt to integrate into theology an analysis whose criterion of interpretation depends on this atheistic conception is to involve oneself in terrible contradictions. What is more, this misunderstanding of the spiritual nature of the person leads to a total subordination of the person to the collectivity and thus to the denial of the principles of a social and political life which is in keeping with human dignity. ...

11. When modes of interpretation are applied to the economic, social and political reality of today, which are themselves borrowed from Marxist thought, they can give the initial impression of a certain plausibility to the degree that the present-day situation in certain countries is similar to what Marx described and interpreted in the middle of these similarities, certain simplifications are made which, abstracting from specific essential factors, prevent any really rigorous examination of the causes of poverty and prolong the confusion.

12. In certain parts of Latin America the seizure of the vast majority of the wealth by an oligarchy of owners bereft of social consciousness, the practical absence or the shortcomings of a rule of law, military dictators making a mockery of elementary human rights, the corruption of certain powerful officials, the savage practices of some foreign capital interests constitute factors which nourish a passion for revolt among those who thus consider themselves the powerless victims of a new colonialism in the technological, financial, monetary or economic order. The recognition of injustice is accompanied by a pathos which borrows its language from Marxism, wrongly presented as though it were scientific language. ...

Subversion of the Meaning of Truth and Violence

1. This all-embracing conception thus imposes its logic and leads the "theologies of liberation" to accept a series of positions which are incompatible with the Christian vision of humanity. In fact, the ideological core borrowed from Marxism which we are referring to exercises the function of a determining principle. It has this role in virtue of its being described as "scientific," that is to say, true of necessity.

In this core we can distinguish several components.

2. According to the logic of Marxist thought, the "analysis" is inseparable from the praxis and from the conception of history to which this praxis is linked. The analysis for the Marxist is an instrument of criticism, and criticism is only one stage in the revolutionary struggle. This struggle is that of the proletarian class, invested with its mission in history.

3. Consequently, for the Marxist, only those who engage in the struggle can work out the analysis correctly.

4. The only true consciousness, then, is the partisan consciousness.

It is clear that the concept of truth itself is in question here, and it is totally subverted: There is no truth, they pretend, except in and through the partisan praxis.

5. For the Marxist, the praxis and the truth that comes from it are partisan praxis and truth because the fundamental structure of history is characterized by class struggle. There follows, then, the objective necessity to enter into the class struggle, which is the dialectical opposite of the relationship of exploitation, which is being condemned. For the Marxist, the truth is a truth of class: There is no truth but the truth in the struggle of the revolutionary class.

6. The fundamental law of history, which is the law of the class struggle, implies that society is founded on violence. To the violence which constitutes relationship of the domination of the rich over the poor, there corresponds the counterviolence of the revolution, by means of which this domination will be reversed.

7. The class struggle is presented as an objective, necessary law. Upon entering this process on behalf of the oppressed, one "makes" truth, one acts "scientifically." Consequently, the conception of the truth goes hand in hand with the affirmation of necessary violence, and so, of a political amorality. Within this perspective, any reference to ethical requirements calling for courageous and radical institutional and structural reforms makes no sense.

8. The fundamental law of class struggle has a global and universal character. It is reflected in all the spheres of existence: religious, ethical, cultural and institutional. ... In particular, the very nature of ethics is radically called into question because of the borrowing of these theses from Marxism. In fact, it is the transcendent character of the distinction between good and evil, the principle of morality, which is implicitly denied in the perspective of the class struggle.

The Theological Application of This Core

... 2. It is not the fact of social stratification with all its inequity and injustice, but the theory of class struggle as the fundamental law of history which has been accepted by these "theologies of liberation" as a principle. The conclusion is drawn that the class struggle thus understood divides the church herself, and that in light of this struggle even ecclesial realities must be judged.

The claim is even made that it would maintain an illusion with bad faith to propose that love in its universality can conquer what is the primary structural law of capitalism.

3. According to this conception, the class struggle is the driving force of history. History thus becomes a central notion. It will be affirmed that God himself makes history. It will be added that there is only one history, one in which the distinction between the history of salvation and profane history is no longer necessary. To maintain the distinction would be to fall into "dualism". ... There is a tendency to identify the kingdom of God and its growth with the human liberation movement and to make history itself the subject of its own development, as a process of the self-redemption of man by means of the class struggle. ...

Participation in the class struggle is presented as a requirement of charity itself. The desire to love everyone here and now, despite his class, and to go out to meet him with the non-violent means of dialogue and persuasion, is denounced as counterproductive and opposed to love.

If one holds that a person should not be the object of hate, it is claimed nevertheless that if he belongs to the objective class of the rich he is primarily a class enemy to be fought. Thus the universality of love of neighbor and brotherhood become an eschatological principle, which will only have meaning for the "new man" who arises out of the victorious revolution.

8. As far as church is concerned, this system would see her only as a reality interior to history, herself subject to those laws which are supposed to govern the development of history in its immanence. ...

9. In its positive meaning the "church of the poor" signifies the preference given to the poor, without exclusion, whatever the form of their poverty, because they are preferred by God. The expression also refers to the church of our time, as communion and institution and on the part of her members, becoming more fully conscious of the requirement of evangelical poverty.

10. But the "theologies of liberation," which reserve credit for restoring to a place of honor the great texts of the prophets and of the Gospel in defense of the poor, go on to a disastrous confusion between the poor of the scripture and the proletariat of Marx. In this way they pervert the Christian meaning of the poor, and they transform the fight for the rights of the poor into a class fight within the ideological perspective of the class struggle. For them, the "church of the poor" signifies the church of the class which has become aware of the requirements of the revolutionary struggle as a step toward liberation and which celebrates this liberation in its liturgy. ... The "theologies of liberation" of which we are speaking mean by church of the people a church of the class, a church of the oppressed people whom it is necessary to "conscientize" in the light of the organized struggle for freedom. For some, the people, thus understood, even become the object of faith.

13. Building on such a conception of the church of the people, a critique of the very structures of the church is developed. It is not simply the case of fraternal correction of pastors of the church whose behavior does not reflect the evangelical spirit of service and is linked to old-fashioned signs of authority which scandalize the poor. It has to do with a challenge to the sacramental and hierarchical structure of the church, which was willed by the Lord himself. There is a denunciation of members of the hierarchy and the magisterium as objective representatives of the ruling class which has to be opposed. ...

A New Hermeneutic

1. The partisan conception of truth, which can be seen in the revolutionary praxis of the class, corrobates this position. Theologians who do not share the theses of the "theology of liberation," the hierarchy and especially the Roman magisterium are thus discredited in advance as belonging to the class of the oppressors. Their theology is a theology of class. ...

3. Because of this classist presupposition, it becomes very difficult, not to say impossible, to engage in a real dialogue with some "theologians of liberation" in such a way that the other participant is listened to and his arguments are discussed with objectivity and attention. For these theologians start out with the idea, more or less consciously, that the viewpoint of the oppressed and revolutionary class, which is their own, is the single true

point of view. Theological criteria for truth are thus relativized and sub-ordinated to the imperatives of the class struggle. ...

The social doctrine of the church is rejected with disdain. It is said that it comes from the illusion of a possible compromise, typical of the middle class, which has no historic destiny.

5. The new hermeneutic inherent in the "theologies of liberation" leads to an essentially political rereading of the scriptures. Thus a major importance is given to the exodus event inasmuch as it is a liberation from political servitude. ... The mistake here is not in bringing attention to a political dimension of the readings of scripture, but in making of one dimension the principal or exclusive component. This leads to a reductionist reading of the Bible. ...

7. In giving such priority to the political dimension, one is led to deny the radical newness of the New Testament and above all to misunderstand the person of our Lord Jesus Christ, true God and true man, and thus the specific character of the salvation he gave us, that is above all liberation from sin, which is the source of all evils. ...

10. One claims to be reliving an experience similar to that of Jesus. The experience of the poor struggling for their liberation, which was Jesus' experience, would thus reveal, and it alone, the knowledge of the true God and of the kingdom.

11. Faith in the incarnate word, dead and risen for all men, and whom "God made Lord and Christ" is denied. In its place is substituted a figure of Jesus who is a kind of symbol who sums up in himself the requirements of the struggle of the oppressed.

12. An exclusively political interpretation is thus given to the death of Christ. In this way its value for salvation and the whole economy of redemption is denied.

13. This new interpretation thus touches the whole of the Christian mystery.

14. In a general way this brings about what can be called an inversion of symbols. Thus instead of seeing, with St. Paul, a figure of baptism in the exodus, some end up making of it a symbol of the political liberation of the people. ...

Orientations

1. The warning against the serious deviations of some "theologies of liberation" must not at all be taken as some kind of approval, even indirect, of
those who keep the poor in misery, who notice it while doing nothing
about it or who remain indifferent to it. The church, guided by the Gospel
of mercy and by the love for mankind, hears the cry for justice and intends
to respond to it with all her might. ...

That is why the fight for the rights of man, which the church does not
cease to reaffirm, constitutes the authentic fight for justice.

7. The truth of mankind requires that this battle be fought in ways
consistent with human dignity. That is why the systematic and deliberate
recourse to blind violence, no matter from which side it comes, must be
condemned. To put one's trust in violent means in the hope of restoring
more justice is to become the victim of a fatal illusion: Violence begets
violence and degrades man. It mocks the dignity of man in the person of the
victims, and it debases that same dignity among those who practice it.

8. The acute need for radical reforms of the structures which conceal
poverty and which are themselves forms of violence should not let us lose
sight of the fact that the source of injustice is in the hearts of men. Therefore
it is only by making an appeal to the moral potential of the person and to
the constant need for interior conversion that social change will be brought
about which will truly be in the service of man. For it will only be in the
measure that they collaborate freely in these necessary changes through
their own initiative and in solidarity, that people, awakened to a sense of
their responsibility, will grow in humanity. ...

10. By the same token, the overthrow by means of revolutionary violence
of structures which generate violence is not *ipso facto* the beginning of a just
regime. A major fact of our time ought to evoke the reflection of all those
who would sincerely work for the true liberation of their brothers: Millions
of our own contemporaries legitimately yearn to recover those basic freedoms of which they were deprived by totalitarian and atheistic regimes
which came to power by violent and revolutionary means, precisely in the
name of the liberation of the people. This shame of our time cannot be
ignored: While claiming to bring them freedom, these regimes keep whole
nations in conditions of servitude which are unworthy of mankind. Those
who, perhaps inadvertently, make themselves accomplices of similar en-
slavements betray the very poor they mean to help.

11. The class struggle as a road toward a classless society is a myth which slows reform and aggravates poverty and injustice. Those who allow themselves to be caught up in fascination with this myth should reflect on the bitter examples history has to offer about where it leads. They would then understand that we are not talking here about abandoning an effective means of struggle on behalf of the poor for an ideal which has no practical effects. On the contrary, we are talking about freeing oneself from a delusion in order to base oneself squarely on the Gospel and its power of realization. ...

One needs to be on guard against the politicization of existence, which, misunderstanding the entire meaning of the kingdom of God and the transcendence of the person, begins to sacralize politics and betray the religion of the people in favor of the projects of the revolution.

18. The defenders of orthodoxy are sometimes accused of passivity, indulgence or culpable complicity regarding the intolerable situations of injustice and the political regimes which prolong them. Spiritual conversion, the intensity of the love of God and neighbor, zeal for justice and peace, the gospel meaning of the poor and of poverty, are required of everyone and especially of pastors and those in positions of responsibility. The concern for the purity of the faith demands giving the answer of effective witness in the service of one's neighbor, the poor and the oppressed in particular, in an integral theological fashion. By the witness of their dynamic and constructive power to love, Christians will thus lay the foundations of this "civilization of love" of which the conference of Puebla spoke, following Paul VI. Moreover there are already many priests, religious and lay people who are consecrated in a truly evangelical way for the creation of a just society.

John Paul II

Centesimus Annus

Socialism considers the individual person simply as an element, a molecule within the social organism, so that the good of the individual is completely subordinated to the functioning of the socioeconomic mechanism. Socialism likewise maintains that the good of the individual can be realized without reference to his free choice, to the unique and exclusive responsibility which he exercises in the face of good or evil. Man is thus reduced to a series of social relationships, and the concept of the person as the autonomous subject of moral decision disappears, the very subject whose decisions build the social order. From this mistaken conception of the person there arise both a distortion of law, which defines the sphere of the exercise of freedom, and an opposition to private property. ...

14. From the same atheistic source, socialism also derives its choice of the means of action condemned in *Rerum Novarum*, namely, class struggle. The pope does not, of course, intend to condemn every possible form of social conflict. The church is well aware that in the course of history conflicts of interest between different social groups inevitably arise and that in the face of such conflicts Christians must often take a position, honestly and decisively. The encyclical *Laborem Exercens* moreover clearly recognized the positive role of conflict when it takes the form of a "struggle for social justice". ...

21 *Origins* (May 1991) 3–24. Used by permission.
[Editor's note: In this social encyclical on the 100th anniversary of Pope Leo XIII's "Rerum Novarum," (New Things), John Paul criticizes communism and capitalism, especially the former. In his view, while a struggle for social justice that abstains from violence and class hatred is acceptable and even required behavior, the Marxist version of class struggle is not.]

However, what is condemned in class struggle is the idea that conflict is not restrained by ethical or juridical considerations or by respect for the dignity of others (and consequently of oneself); a reasonable compromise is thus excluded, and what is pursued is not the general good of society, but a partisan interest which replaces the common good and sets out to destroy whatever stands in its way. In a word, it is a question of transferring to the sphere of internal conflict between social groups the doctrine of "total war," which the militarism and imperialism of that time brought to bear on international relations. As a result of this doctrine, the search for a proper balance between the interests of the various nations was replaced by attempts to impose the absolute domination of one's own side through the destruction of the other side's capacity to resist, using every possible means, not excluding the use of lies, terror tactics against citizens and weapons of utter destruction (which precisely in those years were beginning to be designed). Therefore class struggle in the Marxist sense and militarism have the same root, namely, atheism and contempt of the human person, which place the principle of force above that of reason and law.

15. Rerum Novarum is opposed to state control of the means of production, which would reduce every citizen to being a "cog" in the state machine.

[Editor's note: John Paul also addresses the problems of the poor in the third world, problems often exacerbated by the insensitivity and greed of outside powers. But he refutes those who offer Marxism as a short cut for building up the nation-state. He uses the example of East Europe to show the treachery of the system that built up totalitarianism, spiritual emptiness, and economic failure instead of justice. John Paul offers the church's social doctrine as a better alternative for true liberation rather than Marxism or unregulated capitalism.]

The crisis of Marxism does not rid the world of the situations of injustice and oppression which Marxism itself exploited and on which it fed. To those who are searching today for a new and authentic theory and praxis of liberation, the church offers not only her social doctrine and, in general, her teaching about the human person redeemed in Christ, but also her concrete commitment and material assistance in the struggle against marginalization and suffering.

In the recent past, the sincere desire to be on the side of the oppressed and not to be cut off from the course of history has led many believers to seek in various ways an impossible compromise between Marxism and Christianity. Moving beyond all that was short-lived in these attempts, present circumstances are leading to a reaffirmation of the positive value of an authentic theology of integral human liberation. Considered from this point of view, the events of 1989 are proving to be important also for the countries of the Third World, which are searching for their own path to development, just as they were important for the countries of Central and Eastern Europe.

[Editor's note: John Paul recounts several positive aspects of the modern capitalist system that persuade him to support it, in its best application only, as a solution to economic development. "Its basis is human freedom ... [and] responsible use of freedom." However, it entails risks as well.]

The fact is that many people, perhaps the majority today, do not have the means which would enable them to take their place in an effective and humanly dignified way within a productive system in which work is truly central. They have no possibility of acquiring the basic knowledge which would enable them to express their creativity and develop their potential. They have no way of entering the network of knowledge and intercommunication which would enable them to see their qualities appreciated and utilized. Thus, if not actually exploited, they are to a great extent marginalized; economic development takes place over their heads, so to speak, when it does not actually reduce the already narrow scope of their old subsistence economies. They are unable to compete against the goods which are produced in ways which are new and which properly respond to needs, needs which they had previously been accustomed to meeting through traditional forms of organization. Allured by the dazzle of an opulence which is beyond their reach and at the same time driven by necessity, these people crowd the cities of the Third World where they are often without cultural roots and where they are exposed to situations of violent uncertainty without the possibility of becoming integrated. Their dignity is not acknowledged in any real way, and sometimes there are even attempts to eliminate them from history through coercive forms of demographic control which are contrary to human dignity.

Many other people, while not completely marginalized, live in situations in which the struggle for a bare minimum is uppermost. These are situations in which the rules of the earliest period of capitalism still flourish in conditions of "ruthlessness" in no way inferior to the darkest moments of the first phase of industrialization. In other cases the land is still the central element in the economic process, but those who cultivate it are excluded from ownership and are reduced to a state of quasi-servitude. In these cases it is still possible today ... to speak of inhuman exploitation. In spite of the great changes which have taken place in the more advanced societies, the human inadequacies of capitalism and the resulting domination of things over people are far from disappearing. In fact, for the poor, to the lack of material goods has been added a lack of knowledge and training which prevents them from escaping their state of humiliating subjection.

Unfortunately, the great majority of people in the Third World still live in such conditions. ...

42. Returning now to the initial question: Can it perhaps be said that after the failure of communism capitalism is the victorious social system and that capitalism should be the goal of the countries now making efforts to rebuild their economy and society? Is this the model which ought to be proposed to the countries of the Third World, which are searching for the path to true economic and civil progress?

The answer is obviously complex. If by *capitalism* is meant an economic system which recognizes the fundamental and positive role of business, the market, private property and the resulting responsibility for the means of production as well as free human creativity in the economic sector, then the answer is certainly in the affirmative even though it would perhaps be more appropriate to speak of a *business economy, market economy* or simply *free economy*. But if by *capitalism* is meant a system in which freedom in the economic sector is not circumscribed within a strong juridical framework which places it at the service of human freedom in its totality and which sees it as a particular aspect of that freedom, the core of which is ethical and religious, then the reply is certainly negative.

The Marxist solution has failed, but the realities of marginalization and exploitation remain in the world, especially the Third World, as does the reality of human alienation, especially in the more advanced countries. Against these phenomena the church strongly raises her voice. Vast multitudes are still living in conditions of great material and moral poverty. The collapse of the communist system in so many countries certainly removes an obstacle to facing these problems in an appropriate and realistic way, but it is not enough to bring about their solution. ...

Kevin P. O'Higgins

Liberation Theology and the 'New World Order'

Germany has been reunited, Communist systems everywhere are rushing to dismantle themselves, and the President of the United States speaks of a "new world order." In the midst of so much euphoria, it is still too soon to predict just what this new order will be like. There are to many imponderables. ... At least one thing is already abundantly clear, however: This is one more banquet to which Lazarus will not be invited. In spite of much talk about "a new era of freedom and democracy," it is the rich and famous, the economically and militarily powerful, who once again bestow upon themselves the right to decree where the world should go from here. The rest – especially the poor majority – have been reassigned their customary role of dumb spectators. ...

Meanwhile, and not just coincidentally, the theology of liberation, no stranger to criticism from the political right, has been coming under a new kind of fire. The Latin American Episcopal Conference (C.E.L.A.M.) is vigorously promoting a "theology of reconciliation" as a more acceptable alternative, and, whatever the true intentions of the bishops, it is becoming increasingly clear that the nuances involved in such a terminological shift are not just semantic.

It is interesting to examine the articles and books, now appearing in Latin America as well as in Europe and North America, that purport to explain "where liberation theology went wrong." Most of the writers evidently assume that liberation theology must stand or fall with Marxism-Leninism, or at least they are intent on convincing their readers that this is so. They usually cite the popular revolts in Eastern Europe, the brutal suppression of

3 *America*, (Nov. 1990), 389–393. Used by permission.

the student revolt in China, the electoral defeat of the Sandinistas in Nicaragua and the increased isolation of Cuba as being among the most significant factors in liberation theology's supposed loss of credibility and influence. Some of them also denounce liberationism as a major cause of Catholicism's decline and the rapid growth of the fundamentalist sects throughout Latin America. Such criticisms are based on assumptions whose validity is never demonstrated, assumptions that do not survive close scrutiny. More disconcerting, however, is the apparent additional assumption that "reconciliation" is somehow a safer proposition than "liberation," and that it does not imply the same demand for fundamental change. Rightly or wrongly, the theology of reconciliation is being widely interpreted as a reaction to, rather than a development of, liberation theology.

... Even before the tumultuous global events of the past 18 months, it was evident that an important crossroads has been reached within liberationist thought. A movement that had begun 20 years ago as a fresh and exciting approach to the challenge of incarnating the Gospel message in situations of extreme poverty and violence was tending to become somewhat stale and repetitive. No major new thinkers were emerging, and the pioneers of the late 1960's and early 1970's seemed to have little to add to what they had already been saying for some years. Recently published works failed to generate the same kind of enthusiasm as the ground-breaking writings of 20 years ago. ...

Most ominously, ... the desperate economic situation of Latin America's poor majority had grown steadily worse during the past two decades, and in many countries they were now finding themselves caught in a deadly crossfire between violent ideologues of both left and right. Wars of words and ideas had quickly turned into wars of bombs and bullets, and the only clear result was a steadily rising death toll.

Sadly, the bitter political divisions were increasingly mirrored within the church. Tension between the so-called "popular" and "hierarchical" churches resulted in a growing polarization that could only serve to weaken the Christian community as a whole and lessen its effectiveness as a force for change.

The language employed by both extremes in this confrontation grew progressively more strident. The "traditionalist" and "radical" camps tended to write each other off as "corrupt puppets of capitalist imperialism" or as "Marxism's useful idiots." In Colombia, a guerilla group led by a Spanish priest proudly accepted responsibility for the assassination of a bishop. In such an atmosphere of intolerance and intransigence, the voice of reason could not hope to make itself heard, since reasonableness was likely to be interpreted by both extremes as a form of sell-out to the other side. The greatest losers in all of this were, as always, the poor.

Liberation theology was also a loser. The demand that one should be unconditionally for or against *any* particular position makes critical debate impossible. All too often, and in spite of the authors' best intentions, the fruits of their reflections became lost in a sea of empty rhetoric and banner-waving. ... The ordinary people were left totally bewildered by the ecclesiastical tug of war. The international press was also duped. There were more and more headlines about theologians "persecuted" by the Vatican, and less and less attention paid to the often unsuccessful struggle of the poor merely to survive. In the case of El Salvador, it took the deaths of six Jesuits to attract the attention of the world's media. Over 70,000 anonymous poor people had not merited even a small fraction of such concern.

Any movement can count on a honeymoon period, during which long-term issues are postponed in the excitement of being part of something new and momentous. For religious and political movements, the transition normally coincides with the passing of the founding generation. Liberation theology's honeymoon has actually been unusually long, but it is now clearly at an end. There has been no "quick fix" solution for the overwhelming problems of the poor; the popular masses have not been galvanized into revolutionary action; the unjust structures, which have been centuries in the making, have successfully resisted attempts to sweep them away overnight. In short, the theologians have not been able to come up with magical answers to all of Latin America's political, social and economic problems. Harsh reality is forcing theories and projects to be revised. The impact of liberation theology can no longer depend upon novelty or stirring rhetoric. The challenge now it to preserve the many positive gains of these past 20 years and to look toward the future.

By the end of the 1980's, there were many indications that universal weariness with empty slogans and futile violence had finally opened up the possibility of a fragile experiment with democracy and dialogue. This experiment is now getting under way in practically all Latin American countries, but if it is to have any chance of success, it is vital that the new democratic structures should be truly representative. The hitherto voiceless majority must be heard. Otherwise, "democracy" and "moderation" will *rightly* be interpreted by the extremists as thinly disguised devices to bolster the position of the privileged minority who oppose fundamental political and economic change. In Latin America, "*we, the people,*" are overwhelmingly poor. Democracy must not become a facade, merely designed to preserve the appearance of respectability. The poor will not be easily fooled, and if the present experiment is allowed to fail, it will be much more difficult to try again.

In the past, *some* liberation theologians were undeniably imprudent and doctrinaire enough to reject the democratic road out of hand, and to propose a revolutionary program as the only hope for Latin America and other third world regions. Whatever may be said about the moral justifiability of revolution in such situations, it is now clear that the proposal simply failed to win sufficiently widespread popular support. A sympathetic analysis of why some theologians should have adopted it in the first place would have to take into accout the backdrop against which this theology first made its appearance. For many Latin American intellectuals of that period, the Cuban revolution seemed to offer the only glimmer of hope in an otherwise hopeless tunnel of poverty and exploitation. Fidel Castro and Ernesto "Che" Guevara quickly became continental folk heroes, soon to be joined by others, like the Colombian priest-guerrillero Camilo Torres.

Of course Latin America as a whole was an unwilling, and largely unwitting, victim of the Cold War. It would be foolish to suggest that the angels were all on one side or the other, but the infamous National Security Doctrine, elaborated and financed by Washington as a central part of its strategy for the containment of Communism, did much to confirm Latin Americans in the belief that the values enshrined in the U.S. Constitution were not for export to the South. If the company we choose to keep says something about who we are, Latin Americans of that period can hardly be blamed for their far from flattering image of the United States. In Guatemala (1954) and Chile (1973), democratically elected Socialist governments were actually overthrown with U.S. connivance. Humanitarian projects did little to soften this negative image, since a large proportion of the much vaunted development aid ended up in the pockets of corrupt and unscrupulous elites.

It is important to remember, also, that Latin America was by no means the only place in which disenchanted intellectuals pinned their utopian colors to the Marxist-Leninist mast. The majority of the first generation of liberation theologians were students, or recent graduates, of progressive

European theology faculties when Paris led the way in the student revolts of 1968. Marxism was in vogue as never before, or since. In the period of postconciliar *aggiornamento*, Christian-Marxist dialogue was being discreetly encouraged, or at least not discouraged, by the highest ecclesiastical authorities. And, of course, there was the Vietnam War, and the strong anti-U.S. sentiments it engendered on both sides of the Atlantic, as well as on both sides of the North-South divide.

In some ways, the first wave of liberationist thought was as much a product of the 1960's as any of the decade's myriad utopian projects for global transformation. Subsequent events may have made utopianism unfashionable, but the fact that something did not turn out to be totally right does not mean that it was totally wrong. The bishops gathered in Medellín in 1968, and a decade later in Puebla, did not have to be Marxists in order to understand that radical and urgent change was called for.

Nevertheless, the neo-Marxist brand of liberation theology was neither the only one, nor the most influential. For the majority of theologians in Latin America, the present turning-point will be welcomed as an opportunity to liberate liberation theology itself from what has proved to be an embarrassing, unnecessary and obviously counter-productive ideological millstone. In the new situation created by the first, still very tentative, moves towards representative democracy, mainstream liberation theology is already defining its social role in terms of the promotion of full political participation by the poor majority.

Liberation theology, part of the response to the popular and official calls for change, was never merely a movement based on the writings of a handful of intellectuals, and this is what most of its critics fail to understand. The charge of an imprudent use of Marxism has proved to be a convenient device for diverting attention from the concrete political and economic issues, but it is totally irrelevant to the real situation of the poor. In far too many instances, the theological battles have assumed greater importance than the human tragedy that gave rise to them in the first place, and the theologians must accept a degree of responsibility for this.

Initially, the role of the professional liberation theologian was defined in terms of articulating and systematizing the hopes and aspirations of the ordinary people, but some writers obviously went far beyond that, adding ideological prescriptions of their own making. To the extent that they did so, their theology became just as theoretical and unconnected as the traditional theologies they criticized. The plight of the poor, and their determination to overcome it, are facts, not abstract theories in search of justification. The central question is not *whether* things should change, but rather *how* the required change can best be achieved. The necessity for an authentic theology of liberation has been acknowledged by, among others, Popes Paul VI and John Paul II, and by practically every episcopal conference in Latin America. Anyone who has had the slightest experience of life in a Latin American slum, or who has seen the appalling poverty to the countryside, knows why this is so and why it will take more than the collapse of the Soviet empire to make this theology disappear. Genuine reconciliation *must* presuppose liberation from such sub-human conditions.

The basic issue is not socialism or capitalism, but rather life or death for millions of human beings. Any particular system will be judged according to its success or failure in ameliorating the situation of the poor. This issue has become more urgent and potentially more explosive in the course of the past 20 years, and it will continue to make the question of liberation absolutely central for serious theological reflection, not only in Latin America, but, increasingly, throughout the whole church.

Ever since its inception with Leo XIII's encyclical *Rerum Novarum* "On the Rights and Duties of Capital and Labor" (1891), modern Catholic social teaching has been highly critical of the philosophical underpinnings and unacceptable consequences of liberal capitalism, but its attention has always been diverted by what was regarded as the more immediate threat of atheistic Communism. It is safe to predict that the latter's collapse can only serve to highlight the conflict between North and South, and the church has already unambiguously declared where it stands. It will no longer be so easy to explain away the righteous anger of the poor majority as part of a Moscow- or Havana-inspired plot to undermine "Western Christian civilization."

Liberation theology is first and foremost, a profoundly Christian protest against a world in which a pampered minority condemns the majority to a life sentence of misery and hopelessness, if not to death. Anyone who fails to realize at this late stage that the world is really like that must be deemed guilty of willful ignorance. ... But those situations have continued to grow worse, and the anger of the poor has been stretched to the limit. Liberation theology has often been accused of vainly trying to build heaven on earth, but it would be more accurate to say that it seeks to contribute to the abolition of the hell-on-earth that is the daily experience of so many millions of human beings. The rhetoric surrounding third world poverty may now seem tired and clichéd, but the presence or absence of rhetoric does not alter the facts.

"Liberation" will inevitably cease to be an exclusively third world theological issue for many reasons. To date, its impact on the church in the wealthy countries has been minimal, largely amounting to token seminars in theology departments. So far there has been little serious reflection on the theological implications of the present unjust world order for those of us who benefit therefrom. It is no exaggeration to speak of a church deeply divided against itself, and the division affects all of us – bishops, priests, religious and laity. Some squander precious resources, while others cannot even survive. The Christian slum-dweller in Lima or São Paulo does not need a Gustavo Gutiérrez or a Leonardo Boff in order to know that something is terribly wrong and has to change, or that the Gospel has plenty to say about the nature of that change. It is the comfortable Christian suburbanite – clerical, religious or lay – in North America or Western Europe who has most difficulty in seeing what is wrong and what is demanded by an authentic faith. Television images of starving babies in Ethiopia, or tortured bodies in El Salvador, are evidently not enough to evoke a concerted and sustained response from Christians in the wealthy countries. Besides, it is not even necessary to depend on the television screen in order to see the problem, since the rich world itself includes millions of marginalized and disenfranchised people, the natural allies of the poor in the third world. ... The church in the wealthy countries also shows many signs of sickness – bitter in-fighting, polarization and widespread demoralization are certainly not monopolized by Latin America.

Only a global church, with a truly global awareness of its common mission and a wholehearted commitment to the sacred task of defending the dignity of *all* human beings, can have the resources and resolve necessary in order to build a worldwide coalition dedicated to the construction of a new political, social and economic orders. This mission is not based on ideological consideration, but on the mandate of the Gospel to teach all nations and convert them to the values of the Kingdom of God. The theology of liberation, or whatever else we choose to call it, is an essential constituent of this global mission, since one of theology's most important tasks is to elucidate the practical exigencies of authentic Christian faith.

Selected Readings

Bellah, Robert N., et al. *Habits of the Heart: Individualism and Commitment American Life*. San Francisco: Harper and Row, 1986.

Borden, Morton. *Jews, Turks, and Infidels*. London: The University of North Carolina Press, 1984.

Colson, Charles. *Kingdom in Conflict*. New York: William Morrow and Co., 1987.

Corbett, Julia M. *Religion in America*. Englewood Cliffs, NJ: Prentice Hall, 1990.

Demerath, N.J. III, and Williams, RHYS H. "Civil Religion in an Uncivil Society." *Annals of the American Academy of Political and Social Science*. July 1985, 154–166.

Dunn, Charles W., ed. *Religion in American Politics*. Washington D.C.: Congressional Quarterly Inc., 1989.

Edel, Wilbur. *Defenders of the Faith: Religion and Politics from Pilgrim Fathers to Ronald Reagan*. New York: Praeger, 1987.

Gehrig, Gail. "American Civil Religion: An Assessment." *Society for the Scientific Study of Religion, Monograph Series, no. 3*. Storrs, CT: Society for the Scientific Study of Religion, 1979.

Greeley, Andrew M. *Religious Change in America*. Cambridge, MA: Harvard University Press, 1989.

Guth, James L., and Green, John C. "Politics in a new key: religiosity and participation among political activists." *Western Political Quarterly*, 43, March 1990, 153–180.

Hertzke, Allen D. *Representing God in Washington: The Role of Religious Lobbies in the American Polity*. Knoxville: University of Tennessee Press, 1988.

Levinson, Sanford. *Constitutional Faith*. Princeton: Princeton University Press, 1988.

Marty, Martin E. *Religion and Republic: The American Circumstance*. Boston: Beacon Press, 1987.

Michaelson, Robert S., and Roof, Wade Clark, eds. *Liberal Protestantism: Realities and Possibilities*. New York: Pilgrim Press, 1987.

Modern Age, A Quarterly Review: A Symposium on Christianity in Sight of the Third Millenium, Vol. 33 No. 2, Summer 1990.

Noll, Mark A., ed. *Religion and American Politics*. New York: Oxford University Press, 1989.

Reichley, A. James. *Religion in American Public Life*. Washington, D.C.: The Brookings Institution, 1985.

Sahliyeh, Emile, ed. *Religious Resurgence and Politics in the Contemporary World*. Albany, NY: State University of New York Press, 1990.

Silk, Mark. *Spiritual Politics: Religion and America Since World War II*. New York: Simon and Schuster, 1989.

Sproul, R.C. *Lifeviews: Understanding the ideas that shape society today*. Old Tappan, New Jersey: Fleming H. Revell Company, 1986.

Wald, Kenneth D., Owen, Dennis E., Hill, Samuel S. Jr. "Political Cohesion in Churches." *The Journal of Politics*, 52 February 1990, 197–216.

Wald, Kenneth D. *Religion and Politics in the United States*. Congressional Quarterly, 1988.

Wood, James. E., ed. *Religion and Politics*. Waco, TX: Baylor University Press, 1983.

First Amendment

Antieau, Chester James; Downey, Arthur L.; Roberts, Edward C. *Freedom from Federal Establishment. Formation and Early History of the First Amendment Religion Clauses*. Milwaukee: Bruce Publishing, 1964.

Berman, Harold J. "Religious Freedom and the Challenge of the Modern State." 39 *Emory Law Journal* (1990).

Berns, Walter. *The First Amendment and the Future of American Democracy*. New York: Basic Books, Inc., 1976.

Chopko, Mark E. "Intentional Values and the Public Interest – A Plea for Consistency in Church/State Relations." 39 *DePaul Law Review* 1143 (1990).

Corwin, Edwin S. "The Supreme Court As National School Board." *Law and Contemporary Problems* 14 (Winter 1949), 10–20.

Kurland, Philip B. "The Irrelevance of the Constitution: The Religion Clauses of the First Amendment and the Supreme Court." 24 *Villanova Law Review* 3 (1978–1979).

– "The Origins of the Religious Clauses of the Constitution." 27 *William and Mary Law Review* 839 (1986).

Laycock, Douglas. "Formal, Substantive, and Disaggregated Neutrality Toward Religion." 39 *DePaul Law Review* 993 (1990).

– "'Nonpreferential' Aid to Religion: A False Claim About Original Intent." 27 *William and Mary Law Review* 875 (1986).

Lupu, Irv. "Where Rights Begin: The Problem of Burdens on the Free Exercise of Religion." 102 *Havard Law Review* 933 (1989).

Maddox, Robert L. *Separation of Church and State: Guarantor of Religious Freedom.* New York: Crossroad, 1987.

Malbin, Michael J. *Religion and Politics: The Intentions of the Authors of the First Amendment.* Washington: American Enterprise Institute, 1978.

Office Of Legal Policy, *Department of Justice, Report To The Attorney General: Religious Liberty Under The Free Exercise Clause.* 1986.

Pfeffer, Leo. *Church, State and Freedom.* Boston: Beacon Press, 1967.

– "The Deity in American Constitutional History." *Journal of Church and State,* 23 (Spring 1981), 215–239.

Podell, Janet, ed. "Religion in American Life." *The Reference Shelf,* Vol. 59, No. 5. New York: H. W. Wilson, 1987.

Smith, Steven D. "Separation and the 'Secular': *Reconstructing the Disestablishment Decision.*" 67 Texas Law Review 955 (1989).

Weber, Paul J., ed. *Equal Separation: Understanding the Religion Clauses of the First Amendment.* Westport, CT: Greenwood Press, 1990.

Fundamentalism

Ammerman, Nancy Tatom. *Baptist Battles: Social Change and Religious Conflict in the Southern Baptist Convention.* Rutgers: Rutgers University Press, 1990.

– *Bible Believers: Fundamentalism in the Modern World.* Rutgers: Rutgers University Press, 1987.

Bromley, David G. and Shupe, Anson D. Jr., eds. *New Christian Politics.* Macon, GA: Mercer University Press, 1984.

Clabaugh Gary C. *Thunder on the Right.* Chicago: Nelson-Hall, 1974.

Falwell, Jerry. *Strength for the Journey: An Autobiography.* Simon and Schuster, 1988.

Ferm, Robert L. *Piety, Purity, Plenty: Images of Protestantism in America.* Minneapolis: Fortress Press, 1991.

Findlay, James F. "Religion and Politics in the Sixties: The Churches and the Civil Rights Act of 1964." *The Journal of American History*, 78:1, June 1991, 66–92.

Harrell, David Edwin Jr. *Pat Robertson: A Personal, Political and Religious Portrait.* Harper and Row, 1988.

Hunter, James Davison. *Evangelicalism: The Coming Generation.* Chicago: University of Chicago Press, 1987.

Jorstad, Erling. *Holding Fast/Pressing On: Religion in America in the 1980's.* Westport, CT: Greenwood Press, 1990.

– *The New Christian Right, 1981–1988.* Lewiston, NY: Edwin Mellen Press, 1988.

Lawrence, Bruce B. *Defenders of God: The Fundamentalist Revolt Against the Modern Age.* San Francisco: Harper and Row, 1991.

Liebman, Robert C. and Wuthnow, Robert, ed. *The New Christian Right.* Hawthorne, NY: Aldine, 1983.

Marsden, George M. *Reforming Fundamentalism: Fuller Seminary and the New Evangelicalism.* William B. Eerdmans, 1988.

– *Understanding Fundamentalism and Evangelicalism.* Grand Rapids: Eerdmans, 1991.

Marty, Martin, ed. *Modern American Protestantism and its World*. Vol. 10, *Fundamentalism and Evangelicalism*. Westport, CT: Meckler, 1991.

May, Henry F. *The Divided Heart: Essays on Protestantism and the Enlightenment in America*. New York: Oxford University Press, 1991.

Neuhaus, Richard John, and Cromartie, Michael, eds. *Piety and Politics: Evangelicals and Fundamentalists Confront the World*. Lanham, MD: Ethics and Public Policy Center, 1987.

Smidt, Corwin. "Evangelicals and the 1984 Election: Continuity or Change?" *American Politics Quarterly*, 15 October 1987, 419–44.

– "Evangelicals Within Contemporary American Politics: Differentiating Between Fundamentalist and Non-Fundamentalist Evangelicals." *Western Political Quarterly*, September 1988, 601–620.

Watt, David. *A Transforming Faith: Explorations of Twentieth-Century American Evangelicalism*. Rutgers: Rutgers University Press, 1991.

Wilcox, Clyde. *God's Warriors: The Christian Right in 20th Century America*. Baltimore: John Hopkins Press, 1991.

Peace, War and Christian Responses

Amstutz, Mark R. *Christian Ethics and U.S. Foreign Policy*. Grand Rapids, MI: Zondervan Books, 1987.

Baker, John C., ed. *The Great Decision*. New York: Holt, Rinehart, Winston, 1968.

Cromartie, Michael, ed. *Peace Betrayed? Essays on Pacifism and Politics*. Washington, D.C.: Ethics and Public Policy Center, 1990.

Finnis, John; Boyle, Joseph M. and Grisez, Germain. *Nuclear Deterrence, Morality and Reality*. Oxford and New York: Oxford University Press, 1987.

Hauerwas, Stanley. *Against the Nations: War and Survival in a Liberal Society*. Minneapolis: Winston Press, 1985.

Johnson, James Turner. *Can Modern War Be Just?* New Haven: Yale University Press, 1984.

Kavka, Gregory S. *Moral Paradoxes of Nuclear Deterrence*. Cambridge and New York: Cambridge University Press, 1987.

Lackey, Douglas P. *Ethics of War and Peace*. Englewood Cliffs, NJ: Prentice-Hall, Inc., 1988

Lewy, Guenter. *Peace and Revolution: The Moral Crisis of American Pacifism*. Grand Rapids, Mich.: Eerdmans, 1988.

MacLean, Douglas, ed. *The Security Gamble*. Totowa, N.J.: Rowman and Allanheld, 1984.

National Council of Catholic Bishops. "The Challenge of Peace." *Origins* (3 May 1983).

Novak, Michael. *Moral Clarity in the Nuclear Age*. Nashville: T. Nelson, 1983.

Nye, Joseph S. *Nuclear Ethics*. New York: The Free Press, 1986.

O'Brien, William V. *The Conduct of Just and Limited War*. New York: Praeger, 1981.

Ramsey, Paul. *War and the Christian Conscience*. Durham, NC: Duke University Press, 1961.

Sider, Ronald. *Nuclear Holocaust and Christian Hope*. Downers Grove, IL: Intervarsity Press, 1982.

Walzer, Michael. *Just and Unjust Wars*. New York: Basic Books, 1977.

Weigel, George and Langan, John, SJ, eds. *The American Search for Peace: Moral Reasoning, Religious Hope, and National Security*. Washington, D.C.: Georgetown University Press, 1991.

Weigel, George. *Tranquilitas Ordinis: The Present Failure and Future Promise of American Catholic Thought on War and Peace*. New York: Oxford University Press, 1987.

Yoder, John Howard. *When War Is Unjust: Being Honest in Just-War Thinking*. Minneapolis: Augsburg, 1984.

Liberation Theology

Berryman, Philip. *Liberation Theology: Essential Facts About the Revolutionary Movement in Latin America and Beyond.* New York: Pantheon Books, 1987.

Boff, Leonardo, and Boff, Clodovis. *Liberation Theology: From Dialogue to Confrontation*, translated by Robert R. Barr. San Francisco: Harper and Row, 1985.

Boff, Leonardo. *When Theology Listens to the Poor.* San Francisco: Harper and Row, 1989.

Ellul, Jacques. *Jesus and Marx: From Gospel to Ideology.* Eerdmans, 1988.

Gutierrez, Gustavo. *A Theology of Liberation*, translated by Caridad Inda and John Eagleson. Maryknoll, NY: Orbis, 1973.

Levine, Daniel H. "Assessing the Impacts of Liberation Theology in Latin America." *The Review of Politics*, 50 Spring 1988, 241–263.

—   "Considering liberation theology as utopia." *Review of Politics*, 52 Fall 1990, 603–621.

Nessan, Craig L. *Orthopraxis or Heresy: The North American Theological Response.* Decatur: Ga Scholars Press, 1989.

Novak, Michael. *Will It Liberate? Questions About Liberation Theology.* New York: Paulist, 1986.

Roelofs, H. Mark. "Liberation theology: the recovery of Biblical radicalism." *American Political Science Review*, 82 June 1988, 549–567.

Segundo, Juan Luis. *Theology and the Church: A Response to Cardinal Ratzinger and a Warning to the Whole Church*, translated by John Diercksmeier. Minneapolis: Winston [Seabury], 1985.

First Amendment Religion Clauses: Cases

Abington School District v. Schempp, 374 U.S. 203 (1963).

Board of Education v. Allen, 392 U.S. 236 (1968).

Bob Jones University v. United States, 461 U.S. 574 (1983).

Bowen v. Roy, 476 U.S. 693 (1986).

Braunfeld v. Brown, 366 U.S. 599 (1961).

Burstyn v. Wilson, 343 U.S. 495 (1952).

Cantwell v. Connecticut, 310 U.S. 296 (1940).

Church of Holy Trinity v. United States, 143 U.S. 457 (1892).

Church of Jesus Christ of Latter-day Saints v. United States, 136 U.S. 1 (1890).

Committee for Pub. Ed. and Rel. Lib. v. Nyquist, 413 U.S. 756 (1973).

Dekalb School District v. DeSpain, 390 U.S. 906 (1968).

Donnelly v. Lynch, 465 U.S. 668 (1984).

Employment Division, Department of Human Resources v. Smith, 110 U.S. 1595 (1990).

Employment Div., Dep't of Human Resources of Or. v. Smith, 480 U.S. 660 (1988).

Engel v. Vitale, 370 U.S. 421 (1962).

Epperson v. Arkansas, 393 U.S. 97 (1968).

Follett v. Town of McCormick, 321 U.S. 573 (1944).

Frazee v. Illinois Department of Employment Security, 109 U.S. 1514 (1989).

Gillette v. United States, 401 U.S. 437 (1971).

Girouard v. United States, 328 U.S. 61 (1946).

Gitlow v. New York, 268 U.S. 652 (1925).

Goldman v. Weinberger, 475 U.S. 503 (1986).

Heffron v. International Soc'y for Krishna Consciousness, Inc., 452 U.S. 640 (1981).

Hobbie v. Unemployment Appeals Commission, 480 U.S. 136 (1987).

Jimmy Swaggart Ministries v. Board of Equalization of Cal., 110 U.S. 688 (1990).

Kunz v. People of the State of New York, 340 U.S. 290 (1951).

Lemon v. Kurtzman, 403 U.S. 602 (1971).

Lyng v. Northwest Indian Cemetry Protective Association, 485 U.S. 439 (1988).

McCollum v. Board of Education, 333 U.S. 203 (1948).

McGowan v. Maryland, 366 U.S. 420 (1961).

Minersville School District v. Gobitis, (1940).

Mozert v. Hawkins County Board of Education, 827 F. 2d 1058 (6th Cir. 1987), cert. denied, 108 U.S. 1029 (1988).

Mueller v. Allen, 463 U.S. 388 (1983).

Murdock v. Pennsylvania, 319 U.S. 105 (1943).

Paty v. McDaniel, 406 U.S. 205 (1972).

Pierce v. Society of Sisters of the Holy Names of Jesus and Mary, 268 U.S. 510 (1925).

Prince v. Massachusetts, 321 U.S. 158 (1944).

Reynolds v. United States, 98 U.S. 145 (1878).

Saia v. New York, 334 U.S. 558 (1948).

Sherbert v. Verner, 374 U.S. 398 (1963).

Texas Monthly, Inc. v. Bullock, 109 U.S. 890 (1989).

Thomas v. Review Board, 450 U.S. 707 (1981).

Tony and Susan Alamo Foundation v. Secretary of Labor, 471 U.S. 290 (1985).

Torcaso v. Watkins, 367 U.S. 488 (1961).

Two Guys from Harrison-Allentown v. McGinley, 366 U.S. 582 (1961).

United States v. Ballard, 322 U.S. 78 (1944).

United States v. Lee, 455 U.S. 252 (1982).

United States v. Macintosh, 283 U.S. 605 (1971).

United States v. Seeger, 380 U.S. 163 (1965).

Wallace v. Jaffree, 105 U.S. 2479 (1985).

Walz v. Tax Commission, 397 U.S. 664 (1970).

Watson v. Jones, 80 U.S. 679 (1871).

West Virginia State Board of Education v. Barnette, 319 U.S. 624 (1943).

Widmar v. Vincent, 454 U.S. 263 (1981).

Wisconsin v. Yoder, 406 U.S. 205 (1972).

Zorach v. Clauson, 343 U.S. 306 (1952).

Robert D. Baird

Category Formation and the History of Religions

1991 (first edition 1971). 15.5 x 23 cm. 178 pages. Paperback
ISBN 3-11-012821-7
(Religion and Reason 1)

This second edition of the first volume in the series RELI-GION AND REASON is concerned with the most basic con-cepts in the discipline of the history of religions, with the definition of "religion", "history" and "understanding".

This work is one of the first attempts to clarify systemati-cally, on the basis of logical analysis, the fundamental cate-gories used in the discipline. The author supports a func-tional-definitional method as opposed to what he terms the essential-intuitional one.

The author analyzes relevant definitions of these basic concepts as they were current up to the 1970s. In this con-nection, the application of these concepts in the work of Bronislaw Malinowski, Mircea Eliade, Wilfred Cantwell Smith, Hendrik Kraemer, Hans Küng and Sarvepalli Rad-hakrishnan is discussed.

As a result of his investigation, the author seeks to differ-entiate the discipline of the history of religions both from other fields of historical study and from other disciplines working in the broader field of the study of religion. This book is suitable as a textbook.

mouton de gruyter
Berlin · New York